THE
RIVAL
QUEENS

By Nancy Goldstone

The Maid and the Queen: The Secret History of Joan of Arc

The Lady Queen: The Notorious Reign of Joanna I, Queen of Naples, Jerusalem, and Sicily

Four Queens: The Provençal Sisters Who Ruled Europe

Trading Up: Surviving Success as a Woman Trader on Wall Street

By Nancy Goldstone and Lawrence Goldstone

The Friar and the Cipher: Roger Bacon and the Unsolved Mystery of the Most Unusual Manuscript in the World

Out of the Flames: The Remarkable Story of a Fearless Scholar, a Fatal Heresy, and One of the Rarest Books in the World

Warmly Inscribed: The New England Forger and Other Book Tales

Slightly Chipped: Footnotes in Booklore

Used and Rare: Travels in the Book World

Deconstructing Penguins: Parents, Kids, and the Bond of Reading

THE
RIVAL
QUEENS

Catherine de' Medici,
Her Daughter Marguerite de Valois,
and the Betrayal That Ignited
a Kingdom

NANCY GOLDSTONE

Little, Brown and Company
New York • Boston • London

Little, Brown and Company
Hachette Book Group
1290 Avenue of the Americas, New York, NY 10104
littlebrown.com

First Edition: June 2015

Little, Brown and Company is a division of Hachette Book Group, Inc. The Little, Brown name and logo are trademarks of Hachette Book Group, Inc.

The publisher is not responsible for websites (or their content) that are not owned by the publisher.

The Hachette Speakers Bureau provides a wide range of authors for speaking events. To find out more, go to hachettespeakersbureau.com or call (866) 376-6591.

Illustration credits begin on page 421.

ISBN 978-0-316-40965-0
LCCN 2014955135

10 9 8 7 6 5 4 3 2 1

RRD–C

Printed in the United States of America

For Larry and Lee, with all my love

Dear native land! And you, proud castles! Say
(Where grandsire, father, and three brothers lay,
Who each, in turn, the crown imperial wore),
Me will you own, your daughter whom you bore?

—From "On Marguerite De Valois,
Queen of Navarre" by
George Buchanan (1506–82)

The lady left alone in power,
The first one in the bed of honor having been extinguished,
For seven years shall be racked with grief,
Then long life in power with great good fortune.

—Prophecy by Nostradamus, reportedly
referring to Catherine de' Medici,
published in 1557, two years before
the death of her husband

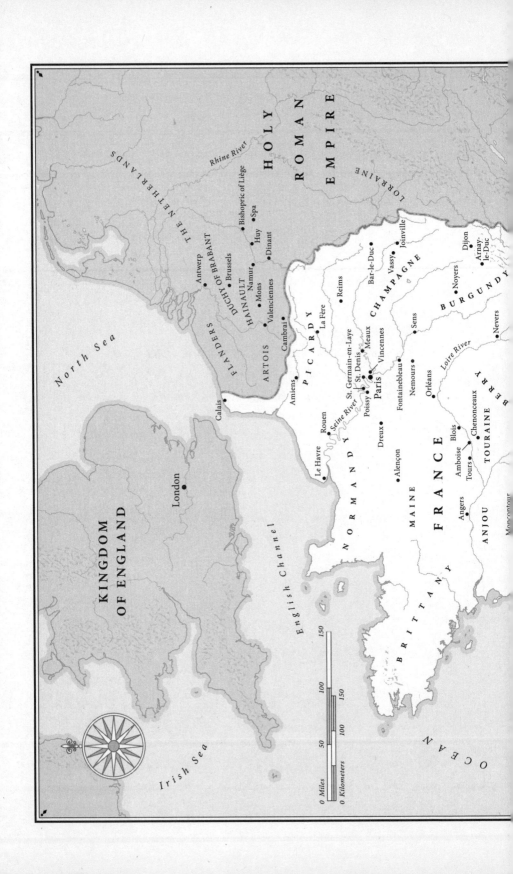

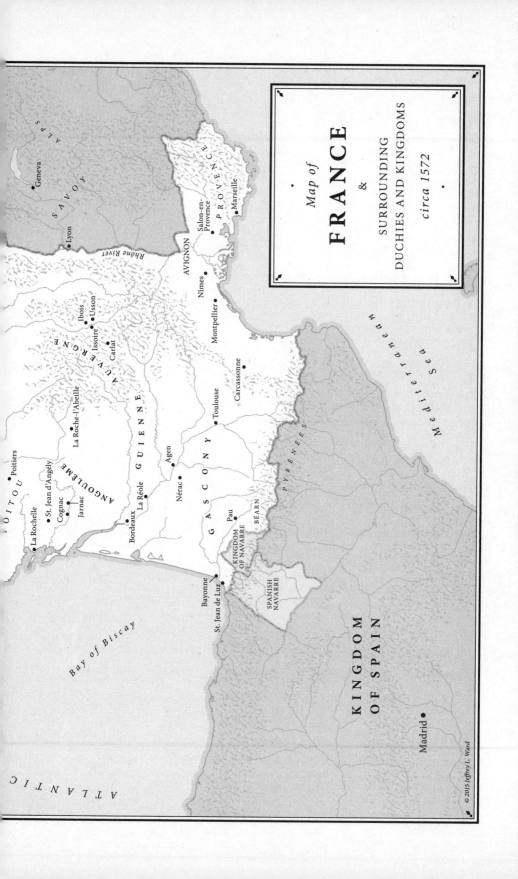

Map of
FRANCE
&
SURROUNDING
DUCHIES AND KINGDOMS
circa 1572

ATLANTIC

ALPS

SAVOY

Geneva •

Lyon •

Rhône River

AVIGNON

PROVENCE

Salon-en-
Provence •
Marseille •

Nîmes •

Montpellier •

AUVERGNE

Ibois •
Issoire •
• Usson
Carlat •

La Roche-l'Abeille •

GUIENNE

Carcassonne •

Toulouse •

POITOU

Poitiers •

Agen •

ANGOULÊME

St. Jean d'Angély •
La Rochelle •
Cognac •
Jarnac •
La Réole •

GASCONY

Nérac •

Bordeaux •

PYRENEES

La Jean de Luz •
Bayonne •

Pau •
BÉARN

KINGDOM
OF NAVARRE

SPANISH
NAVARRE

Bay of Biscay

KINGDOM
OF SPAIN

Madrid •

Mediterranean Sea

© 2015 Jeffrey L. Ward

Contents

Contents

PART III
The Rival Queens

THE
RIVAL
QUEENS

SELECTED GENEALOGY OF THE FRENCH ROYAL FAMILY

Louis XII
King of France
b. 1462
d. 1515

Anne of Brittany
Queen of France
b. 1477
d. 1514

Charles
Count of Angoulême
b. 1459
d. 1496

Louise of Savoy
b. 1476
d. 1531

Henri d'Albert
King of Navarre
b. 1503
d. 1555

Marguerite
Queen of Navarre
b. 1492
d. 1549

Claude of France
Queen of France
b. 1499
d. 1524

François I
King of France
b. 1494
d. 1547

Antoine de Bourbon
King of Navarre
b. 1518
d. 1562

Jeanne d'Albret
Queen of Navarre
b. 1528
d. 1572

Henri II
King of France
b. 1519
d. 1559

Catherine de' Medici
Queen of France
b. 1519
d. 1589

Henry de Bourbon
King of Navarre
(later Henry IV
King of France)
b. 1553
d. 1616

Francis
The Dauphin
b. 1518
d. 1536

Marguerite de Valois
Queen of Navarre
b. 1553
d. 1615

Louise of Lorraine
Queen of France
b. 1553
d. 1601

Henri III
King of France
b. 1551
d. 1589

Elizabeth of Austria
Queen of France
b. 1554
d. 1592

François
Duke of Anjou
b. 1555
d. 1584

Charles IX
King of France
b. 1550
d. 1574

Charles
Duke of Lorraine
b. 1543
d. 1608

Claude de Valois
Duchess of Lorraine
b. 1547
d. 1575

Christine
b. 1565
d. 1637

Philip II
King of Spain
b. 1527
d. 1598

Elizabeth of Valois
Queen of Spain
b. 1545
d. 1568

Isabella
b. 1566
d. 1633

Mary Stuart
Queen of France
(later Mary
Queen of Scots)
b. 1542
d. 1587

Francis
King of France
b. 1544
d. 1560

Introduction

Paris, the Church of Notre-Dame, August 18, 1572

DESPITE THE OPPRESSIVE HEAT, A vast crowd had gathered, pushing and sweating their way into the wide plaza in front of the entrance and spilling over into the boulevards leading to the venerable, centuries-old cathedral. The focal point of the spectators' attention was a long, high platform, recently constructed and ostentatiously hung with cloth of gold, that jutted out incongruously from the western facade of the church. It was on this grand stage that a seminal event would take place, the repercussions of which would be felt all over Europe: the marriage of the French king's sister Marguerite de Valois, Catholic daughter of Catherine de' Medici, to her Protestant cousin, Henry de Bourbon, king of Navarre.

A royal wedding was always a sure source of fascination for the Parisian citizenry. Celebrations of high spectacle, these occasions were deliberately fashioned to confer prestige and authority through magnificence, and the mob of onlookers sweltering under the sun that Monday in August were not disappointed. At three o'clock in the afternoon the doors to the Louvre opened, and the king of Navarre's extensive entourage appeared, beginning the stately procession to the church. The bridegroom wore a doublet and cape of rich yellow satin conspicuously embroidered with diamonds and pearls; he was escorted on either side by the bride's brothers, the dukes of Anjou and Alençon, whose costumes were, if anything, more elaborate. The duke of Anjou, who was particularly conscious of his position and wardrobe, had requisitioned twenty-three thousand *écus* from the royal treasury just for the purchase of his bejeweled cap.

But it was to obtain a glimpse of the bride, nineteen-year-old Marguerite (affectionately known by her childhood nickname Margot), that the populace had turned out in such numbers. The French princess was generally acknowledged to be one of the most exquisite women in Europe. The renowned poet Pierre de Ronsard, a contemporary of Margot's, compared her to Venus; a Neapolitan ambassador rhapsodized that she was "the greatest beauty in the world" and declared that if he had left the kingdom without seeing her, "On my return...if I were asked had I seen France and the Court, [I] could scarcely say I had." Her biographer and sometime correspondent, the abbé de Brantôme, devoted several pages of a manuscript to her ravishing personal charms, observing finally of her décolletage that "never was seen the like in form and whiteness." Less flattering but more telling, perhaps, was the opinion of the Spanish grandee, Don John of Austria, illegitimate son of the emperor Charles V. "The beauty of that queen is more divine than human," he was reported to have remarked after staring at her for some time at an official state reception. "She is made to damn and ruin men rather than to save them."

But it was not just her glamour that drew the inhabitants of Paris out into the streets. The population, overwhelmingly Catholic themselves, adored the princess, who was generous as well as charming, and felt betrayed by this wedding. It was well known even among the common people that Margot was in love, and had been for years, not with her intended but with Henri, the handsome duke of Guise, and that this dashing young nobleman reciprocated her passion. A marriage between these two would have been a cause for wild celebration in Paris, for the duke of Guise, as the head of the powerful Catholic faction at court, was so venerated throughout the capital that he was treated as a hero, and his prestige exceeded that of the king, Charles IX, himself. But the queen mother, Catherine de' Medici, had no intention of encouraging the ambitions of the

Guise family, whose influence and popularity threatened her government, by granting them so great a prize. Henri had been summarily expelled from court and forced to marry another woman. "If he should ever cast his eyes upon her again I will proclaim him renegade and miscreant and make him bite the ground with a dagger in his heart," Marguerite's brother the duke of Anjou had hissed after Henri was safely wedded.

Deplorable enough that Margot had been prevented from marrying the public favorite, but far worse that she was now to be allied to the king of Navarre, leader of the Huguenot party, as the French Protestants were called. The majority of the Parisian populace loathed and feared the Huguenots. Huguenots attacked Catholic churches, destroying precious relics and statues that they claimed were evidence of idolatry; they refused to attend Mass and worked openly to abolish sacred ceremonial processions. Parisians had no doubt that, should the Huguenots succeed in seizing power in France, as it was obvious they were trying to do, the Catholic population would be either forced to convert or suffer annihilation.

But the queen mother had inexplicably insisted upon this marriage, had pushed relentlessly for its consummation for over a year, until at last she had overcome all objections. The king of Navarre and his Huguenot entourage refused to enter the cathedral or partake of the traditional nuptial Mass? Very well; the ceremony would be performed outside the church, on a specially constructed open-air platform. The pope declined to grant a dispensation to allow Margot to marry her heretical cousin? At the last minute, Catherine de' Medici claimed to have received the necessary permission, and as proof she waved a bit of parchment in the air. Although the union was portrayed publicly as an attempt to heal the wounds of religious conflict, the queen mother's urgency hinted at other, less altruistic motives. The eighteen-year-old king of Navarre's principal military adviser and mentor, Gaspard de Coligny, was known to be actively pursuing a marriage between his protégé and Elizabeth I, the Protestant queen of England. Such an alliance was unthinkable for

France; it would have given the English a strong foothold on the Continent from which to launch an assault against the western border of the kingdom. Catherine de' Medici had other plans for Elizabeth I. Coligny was called to court, where he was made the beneficiary of a series of royal favors and privileges, including an outright payment of one hundred thousand *livres*. He dropped his objections to Margot, and the marriage went forward.

In due course the groom's procession arrived at the palace of the archbishop, near the cathedral, from which emerged the bride and her entourage, led by her eldest brother, Charles IX. Magnificently attired—"I blazed in diamonds," Margot remembered—the princess, wearing an ermine-trimmed gown of royal blue silk, complete with a fifteen-foot train carried reverentially by three ladies-in-waiting, joined the wedding party as it made its way to the makeshift stage at Notre-Dame. The bride was very pale. When the cardinal of Bourbon, who officiated that day, asked the princess if she would take Henry of Navarre as her husband, she refused to answer. After a moment's hesitation, Charles IX, who was standing behind her, brusquely pushed his sister's head forward, as though she had nodded. The cardinal took this for an assent and sanctified the union.

The marriage ceremony concluded, the bride and her party went inside the cathedral to hear Mass, as had been stipulated by the nuptial contract. The king of Navarre and his Huguenot entourage remained outside, talking and laughing. An ominous murmur ran through the legion of onlookers, who had heretofore maintained an uncharacteristic silence. Their resentment was palpable.

Five days later Coligny was assassinated, and the streets of Paris ran with blood as the entire Huguenot wedding party was hunted down and slaughtered in one of the most infamous episodes in French history, known today as the Saint Bartholomew's Day Massacre. But this horrific mass murder, which claimed more than five thousand martyrs over the course of a week, was no spontaneous bloodletting. Rather, it was the denouement of a carefully constructed plot that utilized the unsuspecting Margot as both victim and bait to lure Coligny and his faction to their doom, an intrigue planned, instigated, and executed by the one individual in France powerful enough to ensure its success: Marguerite's mother, Catherine de' Medici.

THE SIXTEENTH CENTURY MAY arguably be classified as the Age of the Queen. In no other period in European history did a handful of seemingly indomitable women exercise such extensive sovereign power over so wide a dominion for so many years. The best known of these is of course Elizabeth I, monarch of England, the magnificent Virgin Queen, whose astoundingly long-lived and prosperous reign was threatened any number of times, particularly by her far more beautiful and tempestuous cousin, Mary Stuart, Queen of Scots. Theirs is a famous tale of cat and mouse, of intrigue and struggle, commitment and pathos, which has been told and retold by historians and novelists.

But at the very same time, across the Channel, sat another pair of queens of equal importance and influence whose fascinating history rivals that of their more celebrated neighbors to the west. Like Elizabeth and Mary, the saga of defiant, dazzling Marguerite de Valois and her unscrupulous mother, Catherine de' Medici, is one of passion and power set against a gripping background of espionage and deceit. Catherine, the relentlessly calculating power broker who ruled France almost single-handedly for thirty years; Margot, intelligent and courageous, a free spirit trapped in a loveless marriage, the resilient opponent whom her mother could neither intimidate nor control.

Because they were bound by ties far more profound and intimate than those of Elizabeth and Mary, it is impossible to appreciate the role and character of either woman without the other. Together, their lives spanned one of the most thrilling centuries in history.

Theirs was an age of breathtaking adventure and astonishing events, of vile treachery and valiant swords. It was also an age of extraordinary women—and this is the story of two of them.

PART I

Margot's Mother,
Catherine de' Medici

1

"The Queen, My Mother"

*Fortune is the ruler of half our actions, but she allows the
other half or a little less to be governed by us.*
— Niccolò Machiavelli, *The Prince*

MARGUERITE DE VALOIS WAS BORN on May 14, 1553, at the royal
palace of Saint-Germain-en-Laye, about ten miles northwest of
Paris. She was her parents' sixth surviving child and the youngest of
their three daughters. Her father was Henri II, stern ruler of turbulent, profligate, sublime Renaissance France; her mother, his meek,
plain, afterthought of a wife, Catherine de' Medici. Although the
king was a fond parent who made a point of spending time with his
children, at Margot's birth Henri was distracted by war with his
perennial nemesis, the Holy Roman Emperor Charles V, whose vast
realm, which included Spain, Germany, the Netherlands, and large
portions of Italy, dwarfed and surrounded Henri II's, and so his
youngest daughter's entry into the world was muted. Her mother,
an inveterate and enthusiastic letter writer, did not even bother to
mention the event in her correspondence.

For the first years of her life, the infant princess lived with her
two older sisters, Elizabeth, eight years her senior, and gentle
Claude, six at the time of Marguerite's birth, as well as her exotic
ten-year-old future sister-in-law, Mary Stuart, who had recently
arrived from Scotland, and all their various nurses and governesses

at Saint-Germain-en-Laye. Her brothers—the dauphin, Francis (engaged to Mary); followed by Charles and then Henri (also known as the duke of Anjou)—were schooled elsewhere, although they, like the rest of the royal court, visited frequently. The last of the royal offspring, François, duke of Alençon, Marguerite's younger brother, also spent his infancy and early childhood with the girls at Saint-Germain.*

Life at Saint-Germain-en-Laye was very pleasant for Marguerite and her siblings. The magnificent royal palace was one of her father's preferred residences—he had been raised there himself as a child—and upon his ascension to the throne, Henri II had undertaken substantial renovations, including the addition of two new wings. There were wonderful gardens, a forest for hunting, and even a tennis court. Some two hundred servants, not counting the kitchen staff, were attached to the royal nursery.

From an early age, Marguerite demonstrated a quick intelligence, a light heart, and a spirited temperament. Her jet-black hair was not in fashion—the royal court prized blond curls above all others—but alone among Catherine de' Medici's children, who were known generally for their frail constitutions and unattractive physiques, this youngest princess, with her creamy complexion, joyful good health, and delicate features, stood out.

She certainly seems to have been one of her father's favorites. Her only written recollection from this happy childhood period was about him. "I was then about four or five years of age," Marguerite recounted, "when the King, placing me on his knee, entered familiarly into chat with me." Teasing her, her father asked her which of the two young sons of the nobility playing boisterously in the room with her—one of them, significantly, was the future duke of Guise; the other was the marquis de Beaupréau—she liked best. His small

---

* Actually, Charles was born Charles-Maximilien, Henri was born Édouard-Alexandre, and François was originally christened Hercules (which was especially unfortunate, as he was later deformed through illness), but these names were changed over time, and I have elected to call them by their adult names throughout to avoid confusion.

daughter firmly named the marquis. Her father was amused. "The King said, 'Why so? He is not the handsomest.' 'Because he is the best behaved; while the Prince [the duke of Guise] is always making mischief, and will be master over everybody,'" little Marguerite explained solemnly.

But of her mother there is no fond memory from childhood, no similar episode of affectionate teasing or warm physical contact or even scolding. The queen of France is as absent from Margot's life as though she did not exist. Which, given the reality of Catherine de' Medici's circumstances at court during the years prior to and immediately following her youngest daughter's birth, was not far from the truth.

IT IS AN ASTONISHING irony that the woman whose will would dominate the fortunes and government of the mighty realm of France for more than a quarter century began her residence in the kingdom as an insecure foreigner and social pariah.

Catherine de' Medici arrived on the shores of France in 1533, unloved and disdained, at the age of fourteen. Her mother, a French countess descended from royalty, had died at the heartbreakingly youthful age of seventeen, struck down, it was uncharitably rumored, by the syphilis given to her by her husband, a scion of the powerful Medici family of Florence, who six days later chivalrously followed his wife to the grave with the same ailment.* Luckily for the orphaned Catherine, barely three weeks old, the Medici family held positions of authority elsewhere in Italy. Responsibility for her care and upbringing fell to her uncle the pope, who seems not to have entirely relished his role as adoptive parent. "She comes bearing the calamities of the Greeks!" he is reputed to have moaned when he first saw her.

Poor Catherine's Job-like existence persisted through childhood, where her fortunes rose and fell with those of her father's family.

---

* Actually, Catherine's mother most likely died of puerperal fever, a bacterial infection associated with childbirth. Syphilis doesn't work that fast.

When the Medici were in power and controlled both the Vatican and their hometown of Florence, Catherine lived with relatives in opulent splendor at their sumptuous Florentine palace. But when the family subsequently fell from favor with a breathtaking rapidity, as occurred when Catherine was eight, she was forced into one dreary convent after another. As opposition to Medici rule grew stronger, violence surged around her, the city was besieged, and the defenseless Catherine became an easy target for enemy wrath. She lived in fear of her life; Florentine citizens openly debated whether she should be driven into a bordello, debauched by the army, or merely shackled naked to the city walls. At the height of the crisis, to protect herself, she cut off all her hair and assumed a nun's habit. She was eleven years old.

Thrown back on her own resources and keenly aware, even at this early age, that her survival depended upon the goodwill of others, Catherine strove to accumulate allies, hiding her anger and unhappiness behind a mask of excessive docility. She concentrated first on the unsophisticated women who were her only defense against the malice of the outside world and succeeded in ingratiating herself with the members of the convent. One of the nuns charged with caring for Catherine wrote that she was "so gentle and pleasant that the sisters did all they could to ease her sorrows and difficulties." Catherine was similarly described during these years of girlhood by an Italian courtier as "very obedient." But underneath her servility ran a deep current of resentment. An envoy sent to the cloister to check up on her observed, "I have never seen anyone of her age so quick to feel the good and the ill that are done her."

By the time she was twelve, however, Italian politics being what they were, the Medici were back on top, and she was recalled to Rome by yet another cousin who had succeeded to the papacy, Clement VII, who recognized her value as a means of cementing a military or diplomatic alliance through an advantageous marriage. As her parents' only heir, Catherine had family connections and a claim to Florence that could be exploited by her future husband to yield considerable territory in Italy. It was Clement who arranged for her espousal to Henri, second son of the exuberant if somewhat overweening French king François I.

And now, at last, it seemed that Catherine's luck had finally turned. This marriage, to a member of the French royal family, was considered a significant achievement for a girl of her lineage. For although her mother descended from majesty, her father's ancestors hailed from the plebian merchant class. Two centuries earlier the Medici had been mere shopkeepers and moneylenders. Despite the family's current undeniable wealth and political power, they were still considered parvenus by most of the crowned heads of Europe. Prince Henri was only a second son and his father's least favorite child—there would have been no chance at all of Catherine's marrying the heir to the throne—but still Clement had to throw in all sorts of extra incentives to accomplish this impressive feat. Catherine was dowered (clandestinely, of course, as the pope did not wish to cause unnecessary distress to those of his countrymen who might object to being arbitrarily handed over to the French in this manner) with half a dozen cities in Italy, including the important town of Pisa. Clement further privately agreed to tangibly aid François I in his enduring quest to reconquer affluent Milan, and threw in the duchy of Urbino as a special honeymoon present to the bride and groom. This in addition to a munificent dowry of one hundred thousand gold *écus* and so many jewels and strands of pearls that Catherine would have had trouble standing up straight if she put them all on at once.

Eventually, despite some sharp bargaining on both sides—"This man is the scourge of God," one of the French cardinals complained when Clement tried to wriggle out of the expense of the dowry— negotiations for Catherine's marriage to the French prince were brought to a successful conclusion, and the wedding, a five-day extravaganza, took place in Marseille at the end of October 1533. The brilliance of Catherine's trousseau and retinue, calculated to distract from the disparity in rank between bride and groom, fooled no one, not even the bride, who on her first meeting with her future father-in-law fell to her knees and humbly kissed his feet in recognition of her unworthiness of the honor conferred upon her by an alliance with his family. The marriage contract was signed on October 27; the nuptial Mass, solemnly conducted by Clement, who made a point of attending the wedding, was held on the morning of October 28; and the customary wedding banquet, a raucous masked affair that ended in the small hours of the morning with many ladies uncovering their breasts, if not their faces, followed that evening. The bride and groom missed the more uproarious aspects of the entertainment, having been shunted off to bed at the earliest opportunity. As this match was effectively a declaration of war by the French king against the emperor's holdings in Italy, it was imperative that the marriage be consummated at once to preclude the possibility of a later annulment. To ensure that the two fourteen-year-olds did their duty, François I remained in the bedroom to observe their efforts, so, as a final indignity, Catherine was forced to lose her virginity in front of her father-in-law.

Less than a year later, Clement was dead, the papal alliance with France was repudiated, the promised Italian cities never materialized, and the majority of Catherine's dowry went unpaid. All that was left was an ungainly fifteen-year-old girl who spoke poor French with a heavy Italian accent and whose remaining relatives were of dubious value. François I was not pleased. "The girl has come to my court buff naked," the French king snorted.

AND YET, AS ROILED as Catherine's youth had been, she turned out to be the *less* damaged partner in her marriage. Catherine's childhood experience was positively nurturing compared with what her new young husband, Henri, Marguerite's future father, had endured.

Henri was only two weeks older than his Florentine wife. He had been born at his father's favorite hunting lodge at Amboise at the end of March 1519. Until he was five years old, he had lived a carefree and cosseted existence. He and his brother, the dauphin, only two years older, were close companions; his gentle mother adored and indulged her children; and his father was one of the most important kings in Europe. Henri's personality reflected the warmth and stability of his upbringing. He was outgoing, happy, and charming.

Then, two catastrophes followed in quick succession. His tender, loving mother died, and his father was captured in battle and became a prisoner of the Holy Roman Emperor Charles V. To extricate himself from the unpleasantness of a cramped prison cell in Madrid, François I signed a treaty that contained a number of territorial concessions highly unfavorable to France, then pledged his two young sons as surety that the terms of the peace would be honored. Henri and his brother, the dauphin, ages six and eight respectively and both just over the measles, were immediately summoned to take their father's place in the Spanish jail as hostages to his good intentions. A rendezvous was arranged, the children were ferried across a river, and the affectionate parent was allowed to go free. "I am a king again!" François reportedly exulted as soon as he set foot on French soil and galloped off to spend time with a new mistress.

Unfortunately for the boys, their father never had any intention of abiding by the terms of the treaty, a state of affairs that the emperor was not long in discerning. To induce the French king to honor his commitments, his children were subjected to a series of ever-increasing deprivations and deteriorating prison conditions. Eventually, Henri and his brother were transferred to an austere, isolated stone fortress, where they lived in two small cells with high, barred windows. There was no heat in the winter and no cooling breeze in the summer. They were denied fresh air and exercise; their food was poor; they were often ill. Except for their Spanish guard, they were completely alone.

It took four years and as many tons of gold to secure the young hostages' release. Upon their return to France, their father was surprised to find them much changed, particularly the younger boy, Henri. Henri was no longer the engaging and amiable sprite he had once been. On the contrary, he seemed…angry. He often acted out or turned sullen and morose. His manners were rude, and he had difficulty assimilating into his old life. He had even forgotten how to speak French. This was not François's idea of princely behavior. Nor did the relationship between the king of France and his second son improve when, a mere three years after his return from the Spanish prison, Henri, who, like François himself, warmed only to beauty, was forced to marry a short, homely, socially inferior foreigner in order to further his father's improbable Italian schemes.*

Catherine, conditioned almost from birth to anticipate possible threats to her security, was quick to appreciate the precariousness of her position. Confronted with her new husband's indifference and stripped by Clement's death of the protection of her once-substantial dowry, she faced the very real prospect of repudiation. An annulment would ruin her; the marriage had already been consummated. She knew she could easily be returned to Italy trailing the shame of failure, reduced to scraping by off the grudging hospitality of distant relations or, worse, involuntary confinement to a nunnery.

But Catherine had occupied similar positions of vulnerability in the past and had developed the skills necessary for coping with adversity. As with the Florentine nuns, she assumed a guise of ingratiating amiability and pliancy. No matter how rudely or dismissively she was treated by her new relations or other members of the French nobility, no word of complaint passed her smiling lips. Every slight or insult — and there were many — was overlooked or met with unrelenting goodwill. She was so pathetically eager to please that, although very few among her acquaintances could be said to have actively liked her, she made no real enemies, which itself could be considered something of a victory at the court of François I. After a while, most of the royal circle seems to have simply given up and accepted her presence on the periphery. And since, to her husband,

---

* At twelve, Catherine was bluntly described by the Venetian ambassador as "short and thin; her features are not delicate, and she has protruding eyes, like most of the Medici." Nor did her looks improve with age. "She is a beautiful woman when her face is veiled," observed a courtier of Catherine when she was in her twenties.

she was ever the modest, retiring, adoring wife, happy only when he was happy, touchingly elated by any crumb of affection, even Henri was only lightly inconvenienced by this new, completely undemanding spouse, and simply ignored her.

Not that Henri's opinion really mattered—nothing mattered in Renaissance France but the outlook, attitude, and sentiments of the king. In the little universe that comprised the French court, François I was not simply the sun that shone (or failed to shine) on the anointed royal companions, he was also the moon, the stars, the sky, the clouds. Catherine recognized that whatever protection would be available to her could come only from him. On his benevolence alone did her survival in France as Henri's wife depend.

And so she scrutinized François I as a student at the University of Paris pored over a critical Latin text, as an animal stalked its prey, as a connoisseur studied a particularly valued objet d'art. It would be said later of Catherine that she was a devotee of Machiavelli, but if so she didn't read him very closely. Instead she took instruction in the stratagems of power from her oversized, large-spirited, massively flawed father-in-law.

François I was a big man, especially by sixteenth-century standards. A Welshman who saw him for the first time reported in awe that the king of France stood six feet tall. His chest was strong, his legs long (although somewhat bandy), and the size of his nose singularly impressive. His appetites matched his stature; even as an infant he guzzled so much milk that he needed two wet nurses, and his mother nicknamed him Caesar. His great obsessions in life were gorgeous women, hunting, and Italy, although not necessarily in that order. He kept a corps of peerless aristocratic beauties around him at court, familiarly known as *la petite bande,* whose duty it was to soothe, amuse, and entertain the king. In addition to their many other talents, the women were all expert riders, as François spent most of his time (well, his days, anyway) on his horse, either actively engaged in a hunt or peripatetically moving the court back and forth across the kingdom in search of new, unexplored, more exciting forests in which to hunt.

His preoccupation with Italy dated from 1515, when, only twenty-one and new to the monarchy, he brazenly led his army through Piedmont, crossed the Ticino, and conquered Milan in a ferocious encounter at Marignano described by an eyewitness as a "battle of giants."* Italy was a revelation to the youthful François. The Renaissance was in full blaze. Everywhere artists and craftsmen worked with dazzlingly brilliant pigments of blue and green, or exotic silks from the Orient, or gold filigree and polished marble. New buildings in a splendidly novel style of architecture unknown in France were under noisy construction in all the principal cities. Humanists debated the wisdom of the Greeks while scholars toted around manuscripts recovered from the fall of Constantinople. The king of France took one look and understood that something thrilling was going on in Italy that was wanting in his native realm, and he resolved to rectify the imbalance.

And therein lay Catherine's opportunity. She spoke Italian to the king and amused him with news from her relatives and artistic contacts in Florence, with whom she was in regular communication. She and her father-in-law shared a love of opulence and grand fetes, and she regaled François with descriptions of the papal court at Rome, its many entertainments and pleasures, the delicious dishes served at its multicourse feasts. She encouraged François's dreams of an Italian empire and his determination to bring the region's culture and scholarship to France. She faithfully rooted him on through his many interminable tennis matches. And, of course, she worked on her riding.

The king warmed to her. He began to call her "my daughter." Eventually, he made an exception in her case and she was admitted, despite her relative plainness, into *la petite bande,* an honor that signaled François's approval to the rest of the court and effectively

---

* Ten years later François would try to relive the glory of these days, only to be defeated and captured at the battle of Pavia by the Holy Roman Emperor Charles V, which led to the imprisonment of Catherine's husband, Henri, and his brother, the dauphin.

put her under his protection. This was fortunate, as Catherine was going to need all the help she could get, a state of affairs that became immediately apparent on a hot summer's day in August 1536, less than three years into her marriage, when her husband's older brother, the dauphin, drank a glass of ice water after a particularly strenuous game of tennis, abruptly keeled over, and, to the utter disbelief of the court and the kingdom, went into a coma and died eight days later, leaving Henri as heir to the throne.

As WITH EVERYTHING IN Catherine's life, being suddenly promoted to the position of future queen of France was a decidedly mixed blessing. In a stroke of particularly miserable luck, it turned out that the servant who had brought the dauphin the fateful cup of water was an Italian who had come to court as part of Catherine's retinue. Although an autopsy revealed no evidence of foul play, the hapless cupbearer was nonetheless arrested and his rooms searched. A discourse on toxins being found among his possessions, he was subsequently tortured and executed in appropriately gruesome fashion. Suspicion then naturally fell upon Catherine, who had introduced the reviled assassin to court and who was known to be attracted to astrology and the occult. Her foresight in having so carefully cultivated a relationship with the king was swiftly made manifest when the issue was dropped because François refused to believe the allegations.

Being exonerated from the charge of poisoning, however, while gratifying, did not put an end to Catherine's troubles. On the contrary, her ordeal was just beginning. She faced two formidable, seemingly intractable obstacles to her potential reign and happiness: her inability to conceive and her husband's obvious and impassioned love for another woman.

The court's preoccupation with Catherine's barrenness—she was already seventeen and still childless at the time of the dauphin's death—had been difficult enough to endure while she was only the wife of a younger son, but the pressure to provide an heir became almost unbearable after she was suddenly elevated to the role of future queen of France. In her desperation to conceive, she tried everything—special diets of vegetables and herbs, mysticism and secret prayers, miraculous potions recommended by alchemists and conjurers. She seems to have made a habit of imbibing urine obtained from pregnant livestock. She wore a locket stuffed with a cremated frog. Somehow none of this worked. And just at this time, when she was most vulnerable, it became clear to her—as it was to the rest of the court—that her husband had become involved in an ardent, highly public love affair with a patrician bombshell nineteen years his senior named Diane de Poitiers.

Diane came from a high-ranking French family that had seen its share of political setbacks but had nonetheless managed to recover its influence at court. (Her father had been tried and condemned for treason and was only saved from execution by a last-minute pardon from the king.) She had been married at the age of fifteen to an extremely rich and powerful man of fifty-six, who helpfully instructed his child bride in the ways of the world before (equally helpfully) dying and leaving her an extremely rich and powerful widow of thirty-one. Catherine's husband, Henri, had long admired Diane. He openly carried her colors at jousts and spent as much time as he could with her.* And with good reason—although nearly two decades older than her lover, Diane was dazzling. She should have been: she certainly worked at it hard enough. Her beauty regimen was awe-inspiring. Up with the sun every morning, a cold-water bath, a little light broth, and then onto her horse for a brisk morning gallop of several hours' duration, followed by a little light lunch, an early dinner, and an even earlier bedtime. This was a woman with a purpose.

---

* Diane always wore black and white after the death of her husband, ostensibly as a mark of respect for her widowhood, although less benevolent observers speculated that it was because the stark color combination set off her red-gold hair and flawless skin so strikingly.

And her purpose was to ensnare a king—specifically, France's future king, Henri. Intelligent, mature, disciplined, sexually experienced, and politically adept, Diane was in her prime, and she knew it. Short, stocky, unsophisticated Catherine, whose habits were described by a court observer as slovenly and who ate *"beaucoup"* (although she tried to make up for it by incessant walking and riding), was no match for tall, lithe, condescending Diane.

So began one of the longest-running and bizarre marital farces in history. Catherine was Henri's wife and the future queen of France in name only. Diane was Henri's true spouse and soul mate and was treated as such by the court. To demonstrate this, after his older brother's death and Diane's capitulation to him (two events that would seem related, as Diane had held him off sexually while he was still only a second son), Henri, too, wore only black and white. He designed a special insignia celebrating their love through the interlacing of their initials and had it emblazoned everywhere. It was with Diane, and not Catherine, that Henri spent the majority of his time, his days—and his nights. Diane's bedroom was situated directly under Catherine's at the castle of Saint-Germain. According to Brantôme, a gossipy chronicler who followed court events closely, Catherine had one of her servants bore peepholes into her floor so she could spy on her husband and his mistress. She saw "a beautiful, fair woman, fresh and half undressed... caressing her lover in a hundred ways, who was doing the same to her." Afterward, Catherine whimpered to one of her ladies-in-waiting that Henri had "never used her so well."

But Catherine was powerless to object to the situation—worse than this, she had to pretend to *like* Diane, even to cultivate her. A movement was under way among a cadre of powerful aristocrats close to the king to have the new heir to the throne's barren spouse replaced by a more fertile candidate. Catherine got wind of the intrigue and understood that she had to be proactive if she wished to remain Henri's wife. François she handled by tearfully groveling before him with the offer to retire voluntarily into a nunnery if he willed it, knowing that the king would not have the heart to repudiate her if she confronted him face-to-face. But she could not afford to offend the woman who exerted so much influence over her husband and who, she knew, would have no compunctions about supplanting her either in person or by proxy. So, as she did with all who could harm her, Catherine swallowed her hurt and pride and ingratiated herself with Diane, going to the lengths of spying for her and informing on her enemies at court.

The strategy worked. Diane, who had no wish to see Henri's meek, unattractive, malleable wife deposed for a new, younger, more svelte, and potentially more assertive model, offered her support to Catherine. She assumed an almost maternal role, nursing the younger woman when she became ill, and, most important, advising her on alternative paths to conception. It was Diane who first identified Henri as the probable source of the couple's infertility. Henri had a documented medical condition called hypospadias, which apparently caused his penis, when erect, to point downward. Diane, who was very familiar with Henri's penis, sought to compensate for this by proposing that during coitus Catherine turn around and assume a sexual position known familiarly in France as *la levrette*.*

Because it was so important that Catherine provide an heir, Diane threw herself wholeheartedly into the problem. She knew that Henri found relations with his wife to be less than stimulating, so sex became a team effort. Diane would warm up her lover in her bed at night and at the optimal moment kick him out and send him upstairs to his wife, where Henri would do his manly duty in a few short minutes and then hop out of Catherine's bed to return to Diane's. They went through this charade, off and on, for somewhere between *five and seven years,* until January 19, 1544, when Catherine, age twenty-four, finally secured her position at court by giving birth to a son, whom the couple named Francis in honor of the king. Any

---

* Look it up.

further doubts as to the dauphine's ability to reproduce were effectively silenced the next year when she brought forth a daughter, Elizabeth, followed by another daughter, Claude, in 1547. In the end, the woman who, it was feared, could never conceive proved to be profoundly fertile, bearing ten children over a twelve-year period, of whom seven survived.

And just in time, too, for on March 31, 1547, she lost her mainstay when that virile lover, fine art connoisseur, and redoubtable Renaissance gladiator François I finally succumbed to what was long thought to be a well-earned case of syphilis. (Medical science has since determined that this diagnosis was merely a vicious rumor; the king actually died of gonorrhea.) But either way, Henri inherited the throne in his father's place, and his wife ascended with him. And that was how Catherine de' Medici became queen of France.

IF SHE BELIEVED THAT motherhood and a crown would end her husband's infatuation with Diane and restore her dignity and rightful place at court, Catherine was quickly disabused of the notion. Henri made it abundantly clear both at home and abroad that his mistress took precedence over his wife in every aspect of his reign. Diane was raised to the position of duchesse de Valentinois, a tribute that fixed her rank just below that of the royal family. Both courtiers and commoners knew to address her as Madame, an honorific commonly used to designate a royal princess. Even the pope was aware of the love affair. To honor Henri's succession (and to try to coax him to follow in his father's footsteps and support papal policy in Italy), the pontiff sent Catherine the prestigious Golden Rose — but made sure to include a magnificent pearl necklace for Diane as well.

This was not the only instance in which Diane reaped the rewards of Henri's favoritism. The king showered her with gifts, while Catherine got the leftovers. The pick of the royal jewels went to Diane, as did the exquisite castle of Chenonceaux, one of the most desirable properties in France. Catherine hotly disputed this bequest, claiming that François I had told her that upon his death she was to have it. Her husband overruled her, and she had to be content with the more humble château at Chaumont. Henri's generosity to his beloved consort extended far beyond gifts of homes and expensive trinkets and into the realm of government patronage. Diane had "the right of control over all the offices of the kingdom which are obtained from the new king on payment of a certain sum, and from this she has made 100,000 écus and more," an ambassador observed in an official report. She was given the wherewithal to reward family and friends with titles and high administrative posts. By contrast, Catherine was allowed only to keep the income associated with her much-reduced dowry in addition to the occasional bequest to a cousin.

The peculiar dynamic of Henri II's sex life did not escape the notice of the many foreign dignitaries who visited the royal court. "His Majesty...spends at least eight hours with her [Diane], and if she happens to be in the apartments of the Queen, he sends for her," one diplomat complained. "When the King has told her [Diane] all the business he has transacted in the morning, whether with ambassadors or other people of consequence, he seats himself in her lap, strumming his cither, and often asks the Constable or Aumale [two of the principal noblemen of the kingdom] if she is not beautiful, touching her breasts from time to time and gazing at her raptly like a man in the toils of love," reported another in distaste.

It was not only in her capacity as queen and wife that Catherine was denied her rightful prerogative; even when it came to the children whom she had worked so hard to conceive, Diane completely usurped her role as parent. From the very beginning, with the birth of their first child, Henri put Diane, who had had daughters by her deceased husband and was experienced in child rearing, in charge of the royal nursery. Catherine had no say in her children's upbringing. It was Diane who chose the wet nurses, Diane who managed the household staff and expenses, Diane who monitored and cared for the children when they were ill. This state of affairs persisted as they grew older and approached young adulthood. Diane chose their tutors and governesses, the material and tailors for their clothing, and organized their schedules. The children's doctor, Jean Fernel, commented admiringly on her judgment, acknowledging that Diane appointed "wise and prudent governesses; while she caused [the children] to be instructed by good and learned preceptors, as much in virtue and wise precepts, as in love and fear of God." On the subject of Catherine's maternal guidance, however, the doctor was silent.

The queen of France's undeniable absence from her children's lives when they were young has often been interpreted as a sign of her neglect or indifference, particularly as the majority of the letters she wrote during these years were political rather than maternal in nature. But this does Catherine a disservice. It is true that, after 1552, her correspondence concerning her children dwindles almost to nothing. But before that she regularly inquired anxiously as to their welfare. A letter she wrote on December 21, 1546, soon after the birth of her second child, Elizabeth, to the governor of the royal nursery, Jean II d'Humières (who, with his wife, were openly identified by Diane as "my allies"), reveals the emotions of a mother who was anything but removed—was in fact almost pathetically grateful for any report on her babies' progress: "Monsieur de Humyères," Catherine wrote, "I have received the letter that you wrote me and it has given me very great pleasure to have news of my children. I am pleased that Madame de Humyères has arrived, for the help she will provide you with the care of said children... Monsieur de Humyères, pray continue to keep me apprized of their news often because you could not give Monsieur [Henri] and me any greater pleasure, and for this I will pray to God, Monsieur de Humyères, and recommend you to him."

Far from being voluntarily estranged from her brood, it was probable that the queen of France was simply worn down over time by her husband and his mistress and overwhelmed by her many pregnancies. By the time her seventh child, Marguerite, was delivered in 1553 Catherine seems to have resigned herself to accepting a certain degree of isolation from her children. This accounts for the paucity of her youngest daughter's early memories of her. When her father, the king, played with Margot or teased her affectionately, it was likely Diane and not Catherine who represented the maternal presence in the room.

This perverse and corrupt accommodation, which demanded that Catherine bury her hurt and resentment deep beneath a facade of cheerful approbation so that her husband and his lover would continue to accept her presence at court, ground along year after interminable year. She was not completely snubbed; there were those among her French acquaintance who evidenced sympathy for the new queen's position. Chief among these was François I's sister, Marguerite, one of the most accomplished women of her time.* "God will give a royal line to Madame la Dauphine when she has reached the age at which women of the House of Medici are wont to have children," she had written soothingly to Catherine during those dreadful years of barrenness. "The King and I will rejoice with you then, in spite of these wretched backbiters."

Catherine remembered and reciprocated this support. When François died, Marguerite, an advocate for reform of the Catholic Church, whose court in Navarre formed a haven for persecuted members of the burgeoning Huguenot movement, fell out of favor with the new regime. Despite her age and renown, she was treated disparagingly by Henri and Diane. Catherine stood by her. "I feel for you in your trouble," she wrote, "as I always knew you [felt] for me in mine." Later, after Marguerite's death in 1549, Catherine transferred her affections to Marguerite's daughter, Jeanne d'Albret, queen of Navarre. Jeanne was even more radical in her religious beliefs and committed to the Huguenot cause than her mother had been and was consequently also at odds with the ultra-Catholic

---

* Marguerite was unfortunately a very popular name among the royal family, which can make for some confusion. Margot, Catherine's daughter, was named for this Marguerite, François I's sister.

Henri and Diane. Any enemy of Diane's was a friend of Catherine's, although in this case the two shared more than outsider status. Jeanne, married to the feckless Antoine de Bourbon, a dedicated womanizer and the highest-ranking nobleman in the kingdom after the royal family, had problems with her husband, too.★ Catherine and Jeanne commiserated with each other and on at least one occasion left behind their respective cares to enjoy a bit of fun together. According to the Spanish ambassador, they once went shopping in Paris "disguised as bourgeois ladies in simple headdress. They visited the boutiques around the Palais de Justice and on the Pont St. Michel."

But Catherine's meager circle of supporters was no match for Diane's formidable political machine. Chief among her abettors were the powerful Guise brothers. The eldest, François, duke of Guise, was the kingdom's most successful warrior. The second, Charles, cardinal of Lorraine, highly intelligent, urbane, and ruthless, owed his incumbency to Diane's influence. "I cannot refrain from thanking you again for the special favor you have shown me, and for the great happiness it has given me," he wrote to her on receiving his cardinalship. "I will use every effort to serve you more and more, and I hope from these efforts to reap good fruits for you as well as for myself, since my interests henceforth cannot be separated from yours." A third brother, Claude, married Diane's daughter by her legitimate husband. So entrenched was the Guise family at court that their sons were brought up with the royal princes. And, of course, little Mary Stuart from Scotland, engaged to Catherine's eldest son, the dauphin Francis, was the duke of Guise's niece. Mary and Francis were married in April of 1558, when Mary was just sixteen. The groom was fourteen.

Catherine loathed the Guises. They had been among those of François I's advisers who had pressed most strongly to have her

---

★ When Jeanne first married Antoine, a local bishop congratulated the bride's father: "Sire, it seems to me that in your son-in-law you have acquired a useful helper for what you wish to do." "You do not know him very well," came the short reply.

repudiated when she failed to conceive quickly, arguing that Henri deserved a new, more acceptable wife — the duke of Guise's daughter. Their intimacy with Diane and unquestioned authority only served to heighten her animosity. In their supremacy, the Guises were arrogant and made no secret of their condescension. In a letter of April 21, 1558, the wife of the duke of Guise made plain the family's attitude toward the queen of France. The Medici family (and by extension Catherine herself), she wrote, was "not fit to call themselves our servants." Taking her cue from her powerful relatives, the young bride Mary Stuart also felt comfortable insulting the queen, referring to her as "the daughter of merchants" and making fun of her accent.

There was nothing Catherine could do but endure the endless humiliations, both profound and petty, and pretend to smile. A decade passed, then two, with seemingly no end in sight. Until one summer's day at the end of June 1559, when forty-year-old Henri, approaching middle age, decided to prove his manhood at a tournament by competing three times in a single afternoon. He took a lance in the eye on the third joust, contracted an infection, and died ten days later — and everything changed.

2

The King Is Dead, Long Live the King

However strong your armies may be, you will always need the favor of the inhabitants to take possession of a province.
—Niccolò Machiavelli, *The Prince*

MARGOT WAS ONLY SIX YEARS old when her father died, too young to remember her mother's shocked, almost paralyzing grief or the grim procession that formed within hours of the king's death, signaling the change in succession. Led by her eldest brother, Francis, and his wife, Mary Stuart, Margot and her youngest brother, four-year-old François, were carried out of the castle that held their father's corpse by Mary's uncles the duke of Guise and the cardinal of Lorraine, thereby enhancing the Guises' image as solicitous protectors of the bereaved royal family. Nor did she recall later in her memoirs the long days of official mourning that followed immediately after—fourteen in all—that she spent sitting quietly in a bedroom shrouded in almost complete darkness beside her mother, who from that day forth wore only black.★ So tangible was Catherine's prostration that even the new queen of France was touched.

★ In this way did Catherine signal her allegiance to her native Italy. French women wore white to express bereavement. The Italian tradition of wearing black began during the reign of Joanna I, fourteenth-century queen of Naples, who buried three husbands and so had incentive to invent a new style for mourning.

"She is still so troubled," Mary Stuart observed of her mother-in-law in a letter to Scotland, "and has suffered so much during the illness of the late King that, with all the worry it has caused her, I fear a grave illness."

Catherine was indeed pitiable in her grief. She cried endlessly. Her voice shrank to a whisper. She who rejoiced in ostentation wore no finery save for a band of ermine, symbol of royalty, around her neck. She was obviously devastated by her loss.

But not so devastated that she did not find the energy to utterly vanquish Diane. Even before her husband succumbed to his infection, Catherine made it clear that his mistress was forbidden access to the sickroom. "Up to this hour," wrote one of the Italian ambassadors two days after Henri's injury, "Madame de Valentinois [Diane] has not yet appeared in the chamber of the King lest the Queen put her out." Within twenty-four hours of Henri's passing, Diane was instructed to return the royal jewels and informed that Catherine, who had spent a portion of almost every day of her married life in the courtesan's presence, no longer wished to meet her— effectively banishing her from court. Within a year, Catherine had legally appropriated the beautiful palace of Chenonceaux, forcing Diane to accept the inferior chateau at Chaumont in its place, just as Catherine had once been required to do by Henri.

Nor did the former favorite find comfort or support from her previous allies. The Guises decided to back the docile grieving widow over the grasping, imperious mistress. The duke of Guise took the opportunity of her disgrace to move his belongings at the earliest possible moment into Diane's grand apartments in the Louvre; his brother the cardinal of Lorraine made a point of informing the woman who had secured his papal conferment for him that his family had demeaned itself by a marriage arrangement with her daughter.

Although the new king, Catherine's eldest son, Francis, had been declared legally of age to rule even before his father's death, in reality he was ill equipped to take Henri's place. He was only fifteen, and not a particularly mature fifteen. He had fainted—twice—at his father's bedside and had a fit of hysterics when it was made clear to him that the king was dying. Francis's incapacity was not really his fault. He was seriously ill with an undiagnosed ailment, probably tuberculosis, and had been for most of his life. Although wedded to Mary Stuart the year before, poor Francis was so physically undeveloped that his testicles had not yet descended (his father was apparently not the only one to have trouble in this all-important region), and so could not consummate his marriage. The majority of the court had long since concluded that Catherine's eldest son would not live to see his twenty-first birthday, and certainly they had not expected him to outlive his strong, healthy father. For this reason, Francis was not well-trained in statecraft and knew very little of politics or government.

The obvious solution was to appoint a regent to govern the kingdom until Francis became proficient enough to rule in his own right. But this could not be done—well, not legally—because Francis had already been declared of age. The weakness of the heir to the throne and the absence of a distinct line of command were apparent even before Henri's death. The uncertainty over who would actually rule the kingdom when Francis was declared sovereign created a vacuum of power at the very top of government. That vacuum in turn created an opportunity. And into that opportunity marched the Guises.

They maneuvered so quickly that no one else had a chance to react. Catherine, ever concerned for her own security, seems to have anticipated some move, because Francis's very first proclamation, made on the evening of his father's death, referred the government of the realm to her, "this being the good pleasure of my Lady-Mother and I also approving of every opinion that she holdeth." But this was meant as a defensive measure only. No one expected the grieving widow, who could barely speak, so burdened with sorrow was she, to take on the day-to-day administration of the kingdom. No, this statement was intended merely to prevent whoever did finally assume power—and at this early stage in the proceedings Catherine could not know whether Diane would yet prevail after all—from persecuting her or perhaps even exiling her from court. It was a clever move, and judging by the speed with which the Guises, who needed to cultivate Francis's trust, dropped Diane in favor of Catherine, it worked.

The Guise brothers acted swiftly because they had to. Although they justified their claim to power by emphasizing their family's relationship to the new queen, Mary Stuart, they were in fact usurpers, and they knew it. By right of lineage, Antoine de Bourbon, philandering husband of Catherine's friend Jeanne d'Albret, queen of Navarre, and the person next in line for the throne after Catherine's sons, should have taken command as unofficial regent. But Antoine was more than three hundred miles away in southwest France on the day Henri died. Even after he was informed of the change in succession, and despite the urgent entreaties of his more alert and ambitious younger brother, the prince of Condé, to hurry up and get himself to Paris, the bungling Antoine meandered his way north to the capital city, arriving on August 18, more than a month after Henri's death. By that time the Guises had long consolidated their hold on the government. The English ambassador observed in a letter written less than a week after Francis's ascension that "the house of Guise ruleth and doth all about the French king." Nobody even bothered to meet Antoine the day he arrived at court, and he was eventually ignominiously sent away on the pretext that, as the royal family's nearest relation, it was his job to deliver Catherine's eldest daughter, Elizabeth, who before her father's death had been contracted to marry Philip II, king of Spain, to her impatient fiancé.

The field having been so helpfully cleared of rivals, the two eldest Guise brothers proceeded to split the government of France between them. The duke of Guise, in his capacity as the soldier of the family, took over the management of the kingdom's military affairs, while his brother, the cardinal of Lorraine, who was very good with money and property, having applied himself assiduously throughout his career to the collection of bribes and preferments, shouldered the responsibility for fiscal policy. The late king's ruinous wars against the empire had left the treasury heavily burdened with debt, so the cardinal prudently instituted a strict austerity program, cutting back on military wages and back pay, calling in long-term debts, foreclosing on properties, and eliminating royal subsidies and grants to various recipients. He also significantly stepped up the campaign against heresy, which in this case meant rooting out and exterminating the Protestant Huguenots, building on an ideology initiated by Henri and Diane.

It is a sad political truth that reducing wages and incomes during a period of challenging economic conditions attributable to the lingering effects of a previous war tends to make people grumpy, and grumpy people are more likely to find fault. The cardinal very quickly found himself the most detested man in the kingdom. Most of those affected by the cuts assumed that the monies due them had been diverted not to the accounts of the royal treasury but to the pockets of the avaricious cardinal. They called him Tiger of France and rearranged the letters of his name in clever anagrams such as "Raked up from the gold of Henri" and "A bold thief hides himself." Angry retainers converged on the capital seeking redress. "The court," the Spanish ambassador observed, "will go ten miles from here to Amboise, the King meanwhile hunting for twelve or fifteen days to escape the importunities of captains and others, to whom one owes much and does not pay." Adding to the general dissatisfaction with the cardinal's policies was the unfortunate tendency of the new regime to publicly execute people on a monthly basis. "One is continually burning someone of the lower class," the Florentine envoy complained glumly.

At this stage, by best estimates, only a very small segment—less than 3 percent—of the population of France had been persuaded to accept Protestantism, but that 3 percent included some very high-ranking members of the nobility. In particular, Antoine de Bourbon's wife, Jeanne d'Albret, and his younger brother, the prince of Condé, were known to favor the Huguenot cause. Unlike the Protestants of Germany, who were inspired by the life and work of Martin Luther, Jeanne, the prince, and the other Huguenots were guided by the significantly more severe Church reforms advocated by John Calvin, a Frenchman then living in exile in Geneva, who in addition to rejecting the sacrament of Mass and insisting that the service be conducted in the vernacular preached the doctrine of predestination. Even Antoine seems to have toyed with the idea of converting to Protestantism (although at the first sign of disapproval by the court he hurriedly changed his mind).

Another important recruit to the Calvinist movement was Gaspard de Coligny, who held the title of Admiral of France, which gave him control over the northern coastline and the administration of the French navy. Like the duke of Guise, Coligny was one of the kingdom's most experienced and successful warriors. He embodied the spirit of the professional soldier. During a campaign, Coligny was involved in every aspect of command. He fought harder, and slept less, than any man under his authority. It was Coligny who penned the ordinances governing military behavior, who set the punishment for every infraction from brawling to desertion, and who insisted that the civilian population be protected against the time-honored practice of plunder and violence commonly and enthusiastically perpetrated by the national armed forces. He was related to Antoine de Bourbon's family through marriage; his niece was wedded to the prince of Condé. The admiral had grown up with the duke of Guise and had formerly been one of his closest friends, but the pair had subsequently fallen out over ambition and religion, these two concepts being pretty much indistinguishable at the royal court during this period.

The furor over the government austerity program gave the Huguenot faction the opening they needed to contest the Guises' leadership. With financial help from Elizabeth I—"Now is the time to spend money and it will never have been better spent," declared the

English ambassador, Throckmorton, in a letter to his sovereign—a daring plan to murder the Guises and take over the court was conceived. Bands of armed Huguenots, supported in many cases by formerly loyal French soldiers who had been deprived of wages and back pay by the cardinal of Lorraine, were set to converge on the royal hunting lodge at Amboise, where the king and his court had taken refuge.

Unfortunately for the conspirators, their plan was betrayed almost from the beginning. Espionage was so prevalent in France that it might well have been considered the national pastime. One of the duke of Guise's servants bribed an informant who in turn alerted the family to the plot. The brothers took appropriate precautions, which naturally caught the attention of the spies for the opposing party. The Guises "are in such feare . . . [that they] are in night garded with pistoleers and men in arms," fretted Throckmorton on March 7, 1560, some two weeks before the main attack was launched. Adding to the eventual disaster was the total lack of skill and organization displayed by the Huguenot forces. There appears to have been no active chain of command or communication between regiments. They simply straggled along in groups, some as small as two dozen or so, others numbering in the hundreds, making no effort whatever to disguise their movements.

The first set wandered into Amboise on March 13, were quickly rounded up, and a few of its members selected for interrogation. Francis himself questioned them, offering them coins in exchange for information. Under this happy stimulus, the former malcontents volunteered all sorts of useful intelligence, including how many Huguenot troops were estimated overall and when they might be expected to arrive. As a consequence, most of the rebels were picked off in the forests surrounding the palace before they even had a chance to prepare for action, and the one battle that did take place, on March 20, was a complete rout, owing to the superiority of the royal army. "The Duke [of Guise] himself set out with a Train of Noblemen and other Servants of the Household to reconnoiter the

Enemy, whom he found without a Head, and in such a Consternation, that most of the poor Country Fellows, not knowing what to
do, threw away some old rusty Arms which they had, and begg'd
for Mercy," observed a member of the French court.*

The Guise brothers, who understandably did not appreciate having been singled out for assassination in this way, took their revenge
on those who were implicated in the scheme or who had had the
misfortune of being captured rather than killed in battle. Dozens
were hanged, and as many were sewn into sacks and drowned in the
river. Those of higher rank were subjected to show trials before
being condemned to death. The entire court gathered to watch the
mass execution, by decapitation, of fifty-two men who had been
identified as the principal seditionists. "I know nothing about disputations," the duke of Guise was reported to have observed acidly,
"but I fully understand the cutting off of heads."

Catherine's active relationship with Coligny dates from this period.
Clearly concerned that events were reflecting badly on her son's
regime, the queen mother was as helpless to influence the Guises as
she had been during her husband's reign. In the one instance where
it was recorded that Catherine did lower herself to beg for the life of
a prisoner, she was curtly rebuffed. The admiral, who seems not to
have had advance notice of the Huguenot conspiracy (and it is difficult to believe that he would have countenanced so amateurish a
military operation if he had been in on the plot), was aghast at the
degree of bloodshed. In what would evolve into one of history's
grimmest jests, it was Coligny who, on the lookout for allies, first
put it into Catherine's head that *she* should be running the
government.

---

* According to Michel de Castelnau, a government official and chronicler of the
period, the term *Huguenot* came into general usage at this time. "This Name took its
Rise from the Conspiracy of Amboise," he explained in his memoirs, "for when the
Petitioners fled at that Time for Fear, some of the Country-women said that they were
poor Fellows, not worth a Huguenot, which was a small Piece of Money, of less Value
than a Denier...From whence, by way of Ridicule, they were afterwards called
Huguenots, which Title they likewise gave themselves."

There is apparently no more efficacious tonic for a grief-stricken widow than the prospect of accumulating political power. No sooner had the queen mother absorbed Coligny's advice than she left off crying, reverted to her normal speaking voice, and began inserting herself cautiously—Catherine was nothing if not cautious—into the policy-making process. At first she confined herself merely to the collection of information. What, exactly, did the Huguenots want? Were they advocating treason against her son the king, as the Guises insisted? Or were the Guises alone to blame for the crisis within the kingdom?

She had her answer from, among others, the royal chancellor, Michel de L'Hôspital, who himself leaned toward the Protestant beliefs, albeit in a more moderate form. The vast majority of Hugue-nots supported the king and the royal family and wished to live in peace, he explained. The problem was that the Protestant movement had been more or less hijacked by extremists who desired political power. This radical element was using the general unhappiness with the Guises' governance, and especially with their vicious policy of persecution, to forward their own ambitions. L'Hôspital's solution was to convene a general council charged with reconciling the Catholic and Protestant doctrines—something that could easily be done, he argued—and thereby deprive this opportunistic minority of its principal grievance and, by extension, its support. "Till that is arranged we must try to deal gently with one another," he advised.

The notion that the religious conflict could be resolved simply by calling a general council appealed greatly to Catherine. Despite hav-ing been brought up in a convent, the queen mother was not well educated when it came to religious doctrine, nor was she particu-larly devout. When it came to matters of faith, although she of course conformed outwardly to convention, Catherine held no strong convictions. If convention changed—if, for example, to appease the Protestants, the service was in the future to be con-ducted in French rather than Latin—well, this seemed a small price to pay for peace.

Moreover, L'Hôspital's idea had the advantage of widespread support among moderates on both sides of the issue. Even the cardinal of Lorraine professed himself amenable to referring responsibility for solving the religious controversy to a general council, expressing the sentiment that he "would give his life to bring these poor lost sheep back to the fold" (although not too loudly, lest one of the Huguenots take him up on it). There was also precedent to suggest that such councils could be effective — the German states had recently resolved their disputes over doctrine in this manner. Of course, the German reformists were Lutherans and the Huguenots were Calvinists, but that distinction was not particularly well understood by the Catholic majority at the royal court, who found most of the reformist demands incomprehensible anyway and so tended to lump all Protestants together.

With the unquestioning zeal of the political neophyte, Catherine latched on to the council idea. Working with Coligny and L'Hôspital, she began bustling around between the various factions at court, urging the measure forward and mediating between the hostile parties. Although she had occasionally intervened in government matters while Henri was still alive, it had always been at her husband's behest, and she had in effect been acting as his surrogate. This new lobbying represented Catherine's first independent foray into national politics, and she discovered how much she enjoyed it. She was also remarkably successful, an outcome that she naturally attributed to her diplomatic skills but which in reality had far more to do, once again, with her perceived lack of ambition and reputation for humble docility. The queen mother had been such an unassuming, indeed almost invisible, fixture at court for so long that it was simply taken for granted that she would remain so. There could be no harm in listening to short, round, motherly Catherine, as she could be pushed aside or easily forced to back down if necessary.

And so they did listen to her, and by degrees she won over even the Guises, at least in theory, to this plan. A preliminary assembly that would formally introduce the idea of calling a national conclave to address the religious conflict was scheduled for Fontainebleau in August. In the meantime, to prevent the toxic atmosphere within the kingdom from further deteriorating (until it could be alleviated altogether by the magic pill of the general council), it was decided to call a halt to religious repression, which seemed to be the cause of all the unpleasantness anyway. This expedient would have the additional advantage of separating L'Hôspital's "right" sort of Huguenots — the benign, law-abiding ones — from his "wrong" sort of Huguenots, the radical ones who insisted on noisily practicing their religion in public, proselytizing, and generally challenging the status quo. The troublemakers could then be more easily identified, rounded up, and charged with the sedition of which they were no doubt guilty.

This policy of trying to distinguish between private (acceptable) and public (treasonable) religious dissent made perfect sense to Catherine because it was precisely the way her father-in-law, François I, had dealt with pious divisions during his reign. So long as the Protestants had behaved themselves and did not flaunt their views, François, a pragmatist, had been willing to look the other way. After all, his own sister, Marguerite, had been one of the leading figures in the early days of the Huguenot movement. Far from disowning her, François had attempted to protect Marguerite as much as he could, and she, understanding this, had always taken pains to be discreet. It was only when the dissenters crossed an invisible line of conduct that François took action — as when, in the first year of Catherine's married life, a group of radical Protestants had distributed a militant broadsheet and had even had the gall to attach one of these obnoxious handouts to the door of the king's bedroom at Amboise while François was in residence. Catherine could not have helped but remember this incident, which was instantly labeled treason, because it had unleashed all the king's fury. There had been public burnings of Protestants for months afterward. Then everything quieted down again, and those reformists who had survived the persecution took care to keep their religious opinions to themselves. The fact that the Affair of the Placards, as this episode was called, had occurred a quarter century earlier, when the reform movement was still in its infancy, and that in the interim the Huguenots had become far more organized and committed was perhaps not sufficiently appreciated by the queen mother.

As it was, Catherine, proud of her political accomplishment, blithely issued invitations to all the most important noblemen in the kingdom to come to the assembly in Fontainebleau in August, which, as a signal of her enthusiasm, was to be held in her chamber. The guest list of course included Antoine de Bourbon and his far more assertive younger brother, Louis de Bourbon, the prince of Condé, which was exactly what the Guises had hoped for and why they had so suddenly and inexplicably yielded to Catherine's influence and played along with her plan.

WHILE THE QUEEN MOTHER had been occupied with overcoming objections to a general council, the cardinal of Lorraine and his brother the duke of Guise had been busy furthering their own agenda. Unbeknownst to Catherine, Catholic spies had uncovered evidence strongly linking the prince of Condé, and (less obviously but still damagingly) Antoine de Bourbon himself, to a new Huguenot plan for an outbreak of civil disobedience. Thus, under the policy of limited religious tolerance urged by Catherine and accepted by the cardinal of Lorraine for just this reason, both men could now be charged with treason for breaking the peace and, if convicted, sentenced to death, thereby conveniently ridding the Guises of the greatest threat to their political power. The only question had been how to lure the king of Navarre and the prince out of their home territory in the south of France, where they were safe, to Paris or some other Guise-friendly royal location, where they could be outnumbered and arrested. Catherine's August Fontainebleau assembly provided just the excuse the Guises had been looking for, particularly as the summons to attend issued from her and not from them.

Antoine de Bourbon might have been vain, weak, and untrustworthy, but he was not a complete fool. Upon receiving Catherine's invitation to the assembly at Fontainebleau, Antoine, his wife, Jeanne d'Albret, and his brother the prince of Condé all instantly suspected an ambush. To disobey a royal summons was tantamount to a confession of guilt, so Antoine, responding by letter to both the king and the queen mother, prevaricated. The rumors of civil unrest resulting from religious differences were spurious, Antoine assured the queen mother. He had investigated the matter thoroughly and was satisfied with the obedience and loyalty of the king's subjects. Consequently there was no reason for him to attend the conclave.

Catherine, forced to hold the meeting she had taken such pains to organize without two of the kingdom's key participants, was furious at the snub. "If they see that affairs are going badly, why do they not come and prove it, so that measures may be taken, instead of provoking so many troubles by their absence?" she grumbled.

The Guises did not press the issue but allowed the assembly at Fontainebleau, which began on August 21, 1560, to unfold as the queen mother had planned. When, early in the proceedings, Coligny unexpectedly asked the king to allow the Huguenots to practice their religion in public places, he gave the cardinal of Lorraine the opening he had been looking for. Although he did not go so far as to agree to Coligny's proposal—that would have been tantamount to legitimizing the Protestants and putting the religion on the same footing as Catholicism—the cardinal nonetheless demonstrated a sudden, very surprising degree of conciliation. Experience had taught him that it was pointless to try to bully misguided but peaceful worshippers out of their heresy through extermination and persecution, proclaimed the man who had spent the last few months doing just that. These people should be coaxed back into the fold through reason and enlightenment. Only those of the king's subjects who resorted to violence to try to force the government to accept their religious views should be punished, the cardinal enunciated carefully.

It was a cunning move, for by seeming to compromise with Coligny's (and Catherine's) more tolerant position, the cardinal won agreement on the all-important point that whoever took up arms in the cause of religion must be prosecuted. And no sooner had this rule been established than the Guises sprung their trap. On the final day of the assembly one of the prince of Condé's servants, having been previously suspected and kept under surveillance, was captured and brought to Fontainebleau with documents incriminating both his master and Antoine de Bourbon as leading conspirators in a new revolt planned to take place in Lyon. The duke of Guise laid this evidence before the king and the queen mother like a maître d' presenting a particularly large and unpleasant bill and demanded that both the king of Navarre and his younger brother be summoned to court and arrested for treason.

The stratagem worked. Both Francis and Catherine were shocked and indignant, particularly as a Protestant insurrection *did* materialize in Lyon soon after the Guises made this disclosure. The court again summoned Antoine and the prince of Condé. "If he [Antoine] refuses to obey, I am capable of teaching him that I am King," hissed Francis. To allay suspicions and ensure that this time the wayward conspirators accepted her son's invitation, Catherine dissembled. The queen mother affectionately entreated Antoine and his younger brother to hurry to Orléans for a family visit. "You cannot arrive soon enough to please me," she cajoled.

Antoine, caught, sought frantically for a way out. Remaining at home was no longer an option as word filtered south that the Guises had amassed a large army and had also recruited their Catholic ally, Philip II, king of Spain (who always had his eye on Navarre anyway), to send additional troops to be used against him. Antoine, never much of a fighter, was certainly in no position to wage a two-front war. He was advised by a trusted emissary that the best policy would be for him and his brother to go to Orléans, where the court was then in residence, and for both of them to humbly refute the charges and then throw themselves upon the mercy of the king. It was implied that if this was done quickly they would be forgiven. Antoine seized on this (as it turned out) not particularly good advice, and he and his brother arrived at court on October 30, whereupon the prince of Condé was immediately imprisoned pending trial. Antoine only escaped the same fate because he denied the charges so vehemently that Francis backed down, prompting the cardinal of Lorraine to moan that the young king "is the most cowardly soul there ever was!"

Although Antoine had eluded their snare, the arrest of the prince of Condé, who even as a younger brother outranked them in the all-important sixteenth-century category of lineage, represented an undisputed triumph for the Guises. They were at the very height of their power. Catherine had been present and wept when the prince was arrested, but this was perhaps as much for the deterioration in the kingdom's affairs and her own lost influence as it was for the victim. Certainly when the thirty-year-old Condé was subsequently removed to Amboise for safekeeping, she evinced little sympathy for the prisoner, writing in a letter, "I have [come] back this morning from my journey to Amboise where I have been visiting a little gallant [the prince] who has nothing in his brain but war and tempest. I assure you that whoever finds himself there will not get out again without leave, for the place is already strong and I have been adding to the fortifications. I have also had a good many doors and windows walled up and have had strong iron grating put to others." The prince of Condé was duly tried and condemned to death. The date of execution was set for December 10.

But fortune has a way of upending even the best-laid plans. Francis, as was his wont when visiting Amboise, insisted on hunting despite the foul weather. On November 17 he came down with a bad cold and complained that his ear hurt. He was put to bed. A week later he rallied just long enough to receive a visit from the Spanish ambassador, who was so shocked by the king's appearance that he took it upon himself to lecture the Guises and Catherine on the dangers of prolonged exercise in cold weather, a piece of helpful medical advice that was validated less than two weeks later, when, on December 5, two months short of his seventeenth birthday and a mere five days before the scheduled execution of the prince of Condé, Francis II, king of France, succumbed to a raging bacterial infection and died.

THERE ARE MANY PARENTS who find the death of a child to be an event of unspeakable agony, a grief so profound as to be unsupportable, dwarfing even the decease of a spouse. To have outlived a son or daughter whom it was your duty to protect, soothe, and cherish is a loss from which few recover.

Catherine de' Medici was not one of these. The queen mother displayed no emotional paralysis, no excessive tears, and no whispery little voice at the passing of the eldest son she had worked so hard to conceive and for whose birth she had prayed for nearly a decade—the son whose arrival had solidified her position as queen of France. She was not even with poor sad Francis the night he died but had to be woken up with the news. Unlike her behavior at the time of her husband's death a mere eighteen months earlier—Catherine did not even have to change her clothes, as she was already in black—she did not spend the requisite weeks mourning in darkness beside his body. This humble task was left to his now redundant widow, Mary Stuart. His mother's attitude did not go unnoticed, particularly by those favoring the Huguenot cause. "The Queen was blyeth of the death of King Francis hir sone, because she had no guiding of him," observed an English emissary to the court.

Perhaps. But it was far more likely that Catherine's profound instinct for self-preservation had again asserted itself, as it always did whenever a change in power was about to take place. Only this time, instead of trying to protect herself by fading agreeably and noiselessly into the background, as she had so often done in the past, she seems to have suddenly realized that the best way to ensure her political survival was to take the reins of government into her own hands. This was the direct result of the months she had just spent investigating and then prodding, haggling, and campaigning for a peaceful settlement to the religious question. She had come so close with the assembly at Fontainebleau, only to have it spoiled by the bitter rivalry between the Guises and the Bourbons. But she had learned from the experience. She now knew she could count on the backing of moderates such as L'Hôspital and Coligny. There would never be a more propitious moment to strike. It was only a matter of will.

And so, following the coup d'état blueprint so thoughtfully provided by the Guises at the time of her husband's death, forty-one-year-old Catherine began plotting to take over the government as soon as Francis fell ill, while there was yet hope of his recovery, then put her plan in motion several days in advance of her son's death. Because he had failed during his brief marriage to conceive an heir, with Francis's last breath the succession would pass to her second son, Charles. But Charles was only ten years old — too young to rule. That meant that a regent would have to be named to govern the kingdom until Charles matured and was declared of age.

The Guises, whose influence was linked to the fortunes of their niece, Mary, would have no legitimate claim to the regency unless they could contrive to marry the soon-to-be-widowed queen of France to her dead husband's younger brother Charles, the new king. But this would take time. If Catherine moved quickly she could outmaneuver them and beat the despised Guises at their own game. That left only one other potential challenger to her authority: Antoine de Bourbon.

As the next in line to the throne after Catherine's own family, Antoine was the expected choice to serve as regent. Indeed, by law he was the only legitimate candidate. But the Guises had demonstrated at the time of Henri's death that Antoine's claim could be circumvented by enterprise and simple bravado. Catherine might have previously found herself intimidated by the commanding and contemptuous Guises, but insipid Antoine was quite another matter. She *knew* she could take him.

On December 2, 1560, while her eldest son lay suffering the excruciating agonies of his ear infection, Antoine was summarily called into a meeting with the queen mother in her chamber. The Guises were also present. There, Catherine confronted Antoine with the precariousness of his situation. His brother, she reminded him, was scheduled for execution in little more than a week's time, and he himself was still under suspicion of treason. Without Francis's protection, which would end with his life, Antoine could at any moment find himself again accused of sedition, and this time he would be arrested and face the same fate. She was prepared to help him, but only if he surrendered his legal claim to the regency and stepped aside in her favor. To buttress her position, Catherine presented him with evidence, gathered by her lawyers, of precedent for her action—all the previous cases in French history in which the queen mother had been lawfully installed as regent for an underage son.* If Antoine did as she asked she would see to it that the prince of Condé was released with his head still attached to his body. To help Antoine save face, she promised to raise him to the title of lieutenant-general of the kingdom, and to marry his only son, six-year-old Henry, to her youngest daughter, seven-year-old Marguerite, an alliance that would cement Antoine's family's claims to the succession and inch them ever that much closer to the throne of France. Antoine, who was not a man to stand up under pressure and whose one thought at this point was to put as much distance between his brother and himself and the royal court as possible, agreed almost immediately to her terms. In that instant, Catherine became regent. The formerly all-powerful Guises, who thought they had been invited to this interview to help counsel the queen mother and who were taken aback by Catherine's initiative, suddenly found themselves occupying an unfamiliar and uncomfortable position of subordination. ("She thought of herself before thinking of others,"

---

* One of these was Blanche of Castile, mother of Louis IX, later Saint Louis, one of the most revered kings in France.

the aggrieved cardinal later somewhat hypocritically complained.) Their disconcertedness increased when, faced with the prospect of Condé's unexpected exculpation, they considered that they themselves might be called to account for their role in having had a prince of the blood condemned in the first place. ("No man has ever attacked the royal blood of France without finding himself the worse for it," a member of the duke of Guise's extended family had recently observed with prescience.)

When Catherine subsequently offered them a way out—she knew, she said sweetly, that the Guises had only acted at the king's command (it had been quite the other way around, of course, but poor Francis was luckily dying, so his mother could safely lay the blame on him)—they took it. In so doing they acceded to her regency and sentenced themselves to political exile. The cardinal acknowledged as much the next day to the Spanish ambassador in an interview. "We are lost," he moaned. The queen mother's utter triumph was then underscored when at her urging the vanquished parties, Antoine and the duke of Guise, were forced like two naughty children to bestow upon each other a warm hug and the kiss of peace as a symbol of their reconciliation and restored good feeling. Then they were dismissed.

This masterfully efficient coup, conceived, designed, and orchestrated by Catherine, represented as brilliant a piece of politicking as there was in all Europe. Overnight, the servile woman once scorned for her petty bourgeois lineage was transformed into one of the most powerful monarchs in Europe, on a par with—in fact exceeding, in terms of territory, population, and revenue—her contemporary Elizabeth I of England. When the kingdom of France awoke on the morning of December 6, 1560, its subjects discovered that its young sovereign had died in the night and been replaced by one even younger, and that Mother was now in charge.

3

The Queen and the Colloquy

It must be considered that there is nothing more difficult to carry out, nor more doubtful of success, nor more dangerous to handle, than to initiate a new order of things.

—Niccolò Machiavelli, *The Prince*

THE PERIOD BETWEEN THE DEATH of Henri II, in July of 1559, and that of Francis II, in December 1560, had been one of bewildering loss for seven-year-old Margot. She was bereaved not only of her father and eldest brother but forced also to say good-bye to her sisters. Elizabeth, the eldest, had been wed at fourteen to Philip II, king of Spain, a cold, severe man more than twice her age. Kind-hearted Claude, who had unfortunately inherited her mother's looks in addition to what appeared to be a clubfoot, had exchanged the comfortable safety of the nursery for the regional court at Bar-le-Duc and her new position as the wife of the duke of Lorraine, a member of the extended Guise family. At least Claude's husband, at sixteen, was only four years older than she and not nearly as terrifying as the king of Spain was to poor Elizabeth.

And following hard upon the death of her eldest brother, Francis, was the additional loss of Marguerite's sister-in-law, Mary Stuart, who had been a member of the royal children's circle for as long as she could remember. Although Margot could not know it at the time, Mary's exile to Scotland was the queen mother's work.

Catherine disposed of her former daughter-in-law by following the same unyielding step-by-step pattern she had used against Diane de Poitiers. Within hours of Francis's death, Mary was obliged to return the crown jewels, and as soon as her official period of mourning was over, she was encouraged to leave the court and go to live with her Guise relatives. As Mary was young and beautiful, the names of several potential marriage partners, including (as expected) the new king of France, ten-year-old Charles IX, as well as Don Carlos, the unstable son and heir of Philip II, king of Spain, were put forward. Through clandestine channels Catherine made a point of quashing each of these possible alliances, all the while professing her warm affection for the widowed Mary.*

The effect of Catherine's opposition was to relentlessly winnow down her former daughter-in-law's alternatives until at last only the questionable refuge of her native Scotland remained to her. "Our Queen [Mary], then Dowager of France, retired herself by little and little farther and farther from the Court of France; that it should not seem that she was in any sort compelled thereunto, as of truth she was by the Queen Mother's rigorous and vengeable dealing; who alleged that she was despised by her good daughter, during the short reign of King Francis her husband, by the instigation of the House of Guise," later recalled one of Mary's Scottish subjects. Barely nine months after Francis's death, Mary accepted her fate and sailed from Calais. As her ship crossed the Channel, the eighteen-year-old girl wept uncontrollably, as though her heart were breaking, transfixed by a coastline that became ever more distant with each passing moment and choking on the words, murmured, like a prayer, "Adieu

---

* Catherine even went to the length of referring to Mary in code, calling her "a gentleman" when writing to her daughter Elizabeth, now queen of Spain. She ordered Elizabeth to use her influence with her husband, Philip II, to block a marriage between Mary and his son Don Carlos and to promote one between Margot and Don Carlos instead. "You are not to lose one hour or a single occasion...to bring about [the marriage with Margot]," Catherine lectured Elizabeth sternly in a letter she wrote in March 1561. "Urge these things upon your husband by every persuasion you can think of." This was a mere three months after Catherine had promised to marry Margot to Antoine's son, Henry, if Antoine surrendered the regency in her favor.

France! Adieu France! Farewell dearest France...I think I shall never see you again." The queen mother's response to this poignant retreat was far more prosaic and along the lines of "good riddance." She duly reported Mary's departure in another letter to Elizabeth. "If the winds are favorable, [she] should be in Scotland within the week," Catherine observed with satisfaction.

Nor did Marguerite have the sympathetic intervention of her mother to help her make sense of these changes. Catherine's attention was focused entirely on the regency and consequently on the new king, Charles IX, as the source from which all of her power flowed. "Since it has pleased God to deprive me of my elder son, I...have decided to keep [my second son] beside me and to govern the State, as a devoted mother must do," she informed the royal council on the afternoon following Francis's death. Apparently, being a devoted mother entailed having all letters and other official government documents addressed to her rather than to the king; transacting all business; taking possession of the royal seal (even though Antoine had the clear legal right to it); and even sleeping in her ten-year-old son's bedroom at night in order to ensure that no one had access to the king without her prior knowledge and approval.

Charles, like his recently deceased older brother, Francis, was a sickly child prone to fevers and a persistent cough (although he at least seems to have escaped the dreaded paternal curse, as there was never any mention of irregularity associated with his genitals). One of the Venetian envoys observed worriedly of the young Charles that "he is not very strong; he eats and drinks very little and as regards physical exercise it will be necessary to handle him carefully...he enjoys riding [and] arms, all exercises no doubt worthy of a king but too strenuous; and as soon as he tires himself he needs a long rest for he is weak and very short of breath." As he grew older, Charles became increasingly prone to frenzied, maniacally violent rages that left him exhausted and remorseful, but this behavior did not begin until after his ascension to the throne, when he coincidentally became the victim of his mother's suffocating solicitude. It is worth wondering what the effect of having a mother like Catherine hovering incessantly nearby, never ceding even the semblance of control and cloaking all her actions under the rationale that she was doing this for his own good, would have had on the psychological development of even the most mentally stable adolescent boy.

Adding to the pressure on Charles was the competition from his clever brother Henri, who was only a year younger and next in line for the throne. All the royal siblings, Margot included, understood that Henri was Catherine's favorite child. He alone among her sons was healthy and attractive and precociously intelligent. Catherine was drawn to him—she could not help loving him—and made no secret of her pride and affection for this son over the others. Henri was aware of his mother's partiality and returned and encouraged her affection, as children will, as much as a means of one-upping his older brother the king as for its own sake.

Margot also had a third brother, François, two years her junior and the most tormented member of the family. François had been a relatively happy and good-looking little boy until a bout with small-pox left his face hopelessly scarred and his nose "swollen and deformed"; he was diminutive in stature, even as an adult, and his complexion, in addition to being hideously pockmarked, was unfashionably swarthy. His looks did not improve with age; when he was fully grown a contemporary described him as "one of the ugliest men imaginable." François would labor under this triple-pronged adversity—stunted, disfigured, and consequently despised and dismissed by his more fortunate older brothers—his entire life. Not unreasonably, his physical appearance colored his perceptions about himself and the world. As he grew older he turned sullen, was quick to feel insults, and wholeheartedly returned his male siblings' enmity.

Because the royal children grew up in luxury, many scholars have asserted that they were spoiled and that this accounts for their future narcissism and overtly hedonistic behavior. But this was evidently not the case with Margot, as she would write later of this period that she had been "so strictly brought up under the Queen my mother that I scarcely durst speak before her; and if she chanced to turn her eyes towards me I trembled, for fear that I had done something to displease her." Nor did she participate in her brothers' rivalry as a child. She did not live with her mother and siblings but was instead left at the castle of Amboise or Blois in the care of a governess and a tutor, being deemed too young to live at court.

For solace at this time of sadness and confusion, Marguerite turned to a source that would remain a refuge to her throughout her life: books. Alone among Catherine's children, her youngest daughter demonstrated a passion for reading that would later mature into an impressive aptitude for scholarship. In this Margot was the beneficiary of François I's legacy; her erudition was only made possible by his wholesale importation of Italian Renaissance culture. She was fluent in both Italian and Spanish at an early age. Fueled by her grandfather's extensive additions to the royal library, Margot's education, which included knowledge of history, poetry, art, and philosophy, was supervised by her tutor, Henri Le Meignan, later bishop of Digne. Marguerite was the only member of the royal family able to master Latin, to the point where as an adult she was sufficiently comfortable conversing extemporaneously in the language that she dazzled the ambassador from Poland.

In addition to finding refuge in her books, Margot sought stability and enlightenment through religion. Such scant attention did Catherine have time to pay to her younger offspring that the queen mother did not bother to replace Marguerite's staunchly Catholic governess, Madame de Curton, when she came to power. A holdover from the days of Henri and Diane, Madame de Curton provided Margot with the affection she craved and earned her young charge's love and trust; naturally, she encouraged the girl to adopt her own religious beliefs. From Madame de Curton, strong-willed, passionate Marguerite learned to embrace Catholicism and develop a

spirituality that would prove to be deep, genuine, and unchanging—
and, as such, a problem for her mother.

No sooner had Catherine successfully maneuvered herself into
the regency than she discovered how difficult it was going to be to
hold on to it. To placate Antoine, she had been forced to make good
on her promise to release the prince of Condé from prison, and once
his brother was safely away from the court Antoine suddenly awoke
to the fact that he had voluntarily surrendered his legal right to the
highest office in France to a foreign-born, middle-aged woman
whose only allies were the chancellor, L'Hôspital, and the admiral,
Coligny, two men of significantly lower birth than he. With considerable prompting from his brother, Condé, who had emerged
from his brush with the death penalty more determined than ever
to take power in the cause of the Huguenots, Antoine demanded
the lieutenant-generalship of the kingdom, another of Catherine's
promises. This would give him command of the royal army, a position currently held by the duke of Guise.

The duke of Guise was naturally loath to hand over so critical a
resource as the nation's fighting force to someone whose younger
brother was the acknowledged head of the French Protestants and
who (despite Catherine's insistence on the kiss of peace) might use
the troops against him and Catholics in general. He adamantly
refused to resign the post. Additionally, there was the small problem
that the royal government was completely bankrupt and that when
Catherine tried to solicit funds from the kingdom's representative
assembly, the Estates General, they not only declined to provide the
necessary money but also negated her claim to the regency altogether, throwing their support behind Antoine instead. Even her
son Charles, in whose name she governed, managed to humiliate
the queen mother during those first few critical months in office. As
the great crown of France was lowered onto his brow at his coronation, hastily arranged for May 15, 1561, at the cathedral at Reims,

the eleven-year-old burst into tears, crying out that it was "too heavy."

Not a good omen.

But Catherine still had what she considered to be her trump card—the convocation of the all-important general council, which, she was convinced, would resolve the kingdom's religious differences. The conference was scheduled to begin at the end of July in the town of Poissy, about fifteen miles northwest of Paris. Civil unrest rose precipitously in the months preceding the event, which would be known as the Colloquy of Poissy. The violence was perpetrated by both sides. "In twenty cities, or about that number, the godly [Huguenots] have been slaughtered by raging mobs," Calvin noted grimly to his chief disciple, Théodore Beza, in a letter written in May 1561. In Provence, enraged Protestants ransacked Catholic churches and destroyed relics in retaliation. The court itself was divided just as bitterly between the Catholic faction, represented by the Guises, and the Huguenot party, which looked for leadership to Coligny and the prince of Condé and to a lesser extent Antoine (or at least to Antoine's wife, Jeanne, a much more formidable personality than her husband).

For Catherine, this was an easy choice. Coligny was helpful and respectful, and he wanted her to remain in power. Antoine listened to him and became much more malleable in his demands. The Guises, on the other hand, had soon recovered from the setback she had given them when Francis II died and were rapidly becoming their old arrogant, insufferable, ambitious selves. When they saw their influence ebbing, they gathered their allies against her and went behind her back to complain to the king of Spain and the pope. Catherine was forced to defend herself in a letter to her daughter Elizabeth. Decades of pent-up fury burst forth in this communiqué. "I want to tell you plainly what is the truth, that all this trouble has been for no other cause except for the hate which this entire realm has for the Cardinal of Lorraine and the Duke of Guise," the queen mother fumed. "You know how they treated me during the time of the late King, your brother...if they had been able to do it, they would have appointed themselves to power and would have left me to one side." Antoine got his lieutenant-generalship, and the Guises quit the court in disgust.

With the departure of the acknowledged head of the Catholic party, the Protestants gained a degree of influence over the royal family completely out of proportion to their numbers in the general population. The Huguenot leadership could hardly believe its luck. The reform movement had become fashionable! A number of the queen mother's ladies-in-waiting openly avowed the new religion. Protestant preaching was allowed at court, Coligny was continually at the side of the young Charles IX, and Huguenots were admitted to the royal council. Catherine herself gave every indication that she was actively considering conversion and was sufficiently confident of success at Poissy to bait the duke of Guise in his own castle during an impromptu visit a short time prior to the scheduled colloquy. "What would you do if the King my son were to change his religion?" she inquired coyly of her adversary. "Madame, consider well what you do, you may meet with some surprises," the duke answered coldly in return.

Catherine's flirtation with Protestantism was so pronounced that it penetrated even the children's quarters, where it made a strong impression on eight-year-old Marguerite. "The whole Court was infected with heresy, about the time of the Conference of Poissy," Margot later wrote in her memoirs. "It was with great difficulty that I resisted and preserved myself from a change of religion at that time. Many ladies and lords belonging to the Court strove to convert me to Huguenotism." Her older brother Henri was her chief tormentor. "He often snatched my 'Hours' out of my hand, and flung them into the fire, giving me Psalm Books and books of Huguenot prayers, insisting on my using them," she remembered. "My brother added threats, and said the Queen my mother would give orders that I should be whipped." But Margot stood up to him. "When he used those menaces, I...would reply to him, 'Well, get me whipped if you can; I will suffer whipping, and even death, rather than be damned,'" she wrote.

These words would prove prophetic. In her stubbornness to yield on an issue that touched her core, eight-year-old Marguerite voiced the resistance of the vast majority of the inhabitants of France to Catherine's more cynical attitude that deeply held beliefs could be readily altered by committee. Or, as a Venetian diplomat present at the royal court would later note of the queen mother in a somewhat bemused tone of frustration, "I do not believe that her majesty understands what the word 'dogma' means."

At Catherine's insistence, the colloquy of Poissy began with a private meeting in her chambers to which the chief spokesmen for each side—the cardinal of Lorraine for the Catholics and Théodore Beza, Calvin's trusted lieutenant, for the Huguenots—were summoned. As a result of her initial triumph in the days just prior to Francis II's death, when in her pursuit of the regency she had managed by similar face-to-face diplomacy to steamroll over both Antoine and the unsuspecting Guises, Catherine had developed a great faith in her own powers of persuasion. For the rest of her life she was convinced that she could bend opposing viewpoints to her will if only she could get the people holding them alone in a room with her, a position not always supported by reality.

This was the first time the two men had met, and Beza, who believed himself on the verge of converting the entire French royal family to Protestantism and who consequently had everything to lose if he seemed unreasonable in Catherine's presence, in particular was on his guard. When the cardinal of Lorraine interrogated him on some of the more divisive issues separating the two faiths, he answered so blandly and nonconfrontationally that his adversary was deceived into believing that the differences between them were not substantive after all. The cardinal was pleasantly surprised to find in his opposite number not the doctrinaire fire breather he had expected but a slick politician like himself. Here was a Huguenot he could work with! At the end of the audience, to Catherine's immense satisfaction, the pair even shook hands, and the cardinal became expansive. "You will find that I am not as black as they make me out to be," he confided affably to Beza.

But it turned out that Beza had merely been saving himself for the main event. He was far more of a zealot than the cardinal realized, a disposition that became immediately apparent the next morning, when he stood up before the main body of the assembly and delivered the keynote address outlining the Huguenot agenda. Although he did his best to stress areas of potential agreement between the two religions, he was unable to contain himself when it came to the subject of the observance of Mass and slipped in a direct barb at his Catholic adversaries. "We say that His [Christ's] body is as far removed from the bread and wine as is heaven from earth," Beza explained helpfully.

If he had suddenly turned a blazing scarlet from head to toe and sported pointy ears, horns, a tail, and a pitchfork, Beza could not have shocked his audience more thoroughly. The aged cardinal of Tournon shuddered so violently that he nearly had a stroke on the spot. Even Catherine had a sense that this was perhaps taking the notion of reform a shade too far—the outraged cries of "Blasphemy! Blasphemy!" that greeted this unfortunate pronouncement no doubt alerted her to the problem—and she made haste to distance herself and her son the king from so revolutionary a perspective.

But the damage was done. Although the participants would continue to meet for several weeks, with first Protestants and then Catholics taking turns constructively pointing out the hideous errors inherent in each other's doctrines, the experiment in finding middle ground was in fact over the instant these artless words dropped from Beza's mouth. Only Catherine, who had too much invested in this strategy to abandon it, failed to recognize this.

It is important to understand that the modern concept of tolerance—the idea that people of differing religious beliefs can live side by side in peace within a single kingdom—did not exist in the sixteenth century. It was assumed by all—and this included the queen mother, who was nothing if not conventional—that *one* religion would eventually predominate and the worshippers of the losing sect would be forced more or less into hiding. They would not necessarily be sought out for persecution if they agreed to practice their rites secretly, but by not adapting to the beliefs of the monarchy, followers of the opposing denomination would tacitly accept a form of second-class citizenship. This was already the case in Elizabeth I's England, where that portion of the population who still clung to Catholicism knew to do so in private and comprehended fully that the price of maintaining their faith meant exclusion from power.

But Elizabeth was only able to rule in this fashion because her father, Henry VIII, a *very* strong king, had paved the way for her. When Henry decided to put himself rather than the pope at the head of the Church of England, he shrewdly recognized the need for ruthlessness. He forced both the clergy and all his courtiers to submit to his will and accede to a series of royal acts, and if anyone rebelled—as Sir Thomas More so famously did in 1535—he destroyed them. He further smashed the power of the opposition by looting the monasteries and appropriating their wealth. Then, during his short reign, Henry's young son, Edward VI, fell under the influence of his Cambridge tutor and adopted an even more radical form of Protestantism. Although Elizabeth's older half sister, Mary I, nicknamed Bloody Mary for her habit of burning the reformers, tried to reinstate Roman Catholicism, she died too soon to overturn her father and brother's legacy. By the time Elizabeth ascended to the throne, the population of England had had twenty-five years to get used to the idea of Protestantism, and the English version was an accepted form of worship.

This was most definitely not the case in France. The Huguenots might have made inroads into the aristocracy and the royal court, but they were hugely outnumbered in the ordinary population. The Guises were well aware of this discrepancy. Unbeknownst to

Catherine, they had taken the hiatus offered by Poissy to quietly conduct a house-by-house count of religious preferences and discovered that for every one hundred Catholics living in Paris there were only three Protestants. Fueled by this evidence, and by his conviction that Catherine intended to maintain power by relying on her allies the Huguenots and converting—"What would you do if the King my son changed his religion?"—the duke of Guise answered her by launching a daring two-part plan: first he would kidnap her younger son Henri in order to maintain him in the Catholic faith and set him up against Charles IX as the legitimate sovereign of France; and second he would separate Antoine, who according to tradition and the Estates General was the legitimate regent, from his Huguenot allies and in so doing isolate the queen mother.

THE SCHEME TO ABDUCT Catherine's middle son, Henri, was relatively straightforward. On the day before the conference was set to end, one of the duke of Guise's closest allies took ten-year-old Henri aside and asked him if he was a Huguenot or a Catholic. This turned out to be a difficult question. Henri wasn't sure. To be on the safe side, though, he piped up that he believed he was whatever his mother was. His interrogator admonished him that the Huguenots were about to take over the kingdom, and that once they did Antoine and his brother the prince of Condé were intending to assassinate Henri and his brother Charles IX and set themselves up to rule in their place. The Catholic ally advised the boy that, luckily, the duke of Guise was on his side and was willing to rescue him from this cruel fate by whisking him away to the safety of the duke's castle in Lorraine. He then indicated that further instructions would be forthcoming and warned Henri not to mention the intrigue to anyone. "If they ask you what it is that I have been talking to you about, say that I was talking to you about the comedies," the conspirator recommended.

Having laid the groundwork by frightening the young prince, the duke of Guise followed up by sending in his ace in the hole to close the deal: his eldest son, who (to the despondency of the many future historians attempting to explain these incidents to the general public) was also named Henri. The duke of Guise's Henri was twelve years old.* He had known Catherine's sons almost since infancy and took his lessons with them. Unlike his royal companions, however, the duke of Guise's Henri was tall and healthy, and even at this early age his face and physique gave promise of the devastatingly good looks for which he would be known later in life. Because he was so well made, he was a better athlete than either of Catherine's sons, a fact of which he was also aware. Although he knew to show deference to the king, he was somewhat less successful when it came to masking his superiority in front of the king's younger brother, who was, after all, only ten. "I hear that the Queen means to send you...into Lorraine, to a very beautiful château, to take the air," the duke of Guise's Henri began knowingly after cornering his prey and making sure no one else was listening. (The allusion to the queen mother was a coded reference to the initial conversation with the Catholic ally.) "So make up your mind, if you wish to travel with us, we shall treat you well." Intimidated, Catherine's Henri managed to stammer out, "I do not think the Queen my mother wishes me to leave the King." But the older boy, who was under strict orders from his father to prevail, brooked no dissent. "You will be carried off at midnight and passed out of a window near the gate of the park, and then you will be placed in a coach," he instructed. "You will be in Lorraine before anyone knows that you are gone."

This did not sound like such a great plan to the younger Henri. Although he did not have the courage to confront his schoolmate directly, he was sufficiently alarmed at the prospect of being bundled out the window like a basket of laundry and relayed to a remote

---

* It is very unfortunate that Henri was such a popular name in France at this time. No less than *three* Henris figure prominently in this story—Catherine's son Henri; the duke of Guise's son Henri; and the king of Navarre's son, Henry. I will do my best to always be clear to which Henri (or Henry) I am referring!

location that he took action. Despite the enjoinder for secrecy, he went straight to his mother and tattled.

Catherine was incensed, but as the duke of Guise, who had taken the precaution of using surrogates throughout, categorically denied any involvement, there was not much she could do about it. Nor could she follow him when he left the court soon afterward, as it would have taken an army to pursue so powerful an antagonist to his home duchy of Lorraine, where he would most certainly be well protected. The queen mother had to content herself with having her son repeat his version of events in front of the royal council. Venting her feelings in a letter to the king of Spain under the pretext of asking for political advice in handling the matter, she again railed against the treachery of the duke of Guise.

The revelation of this intrigue against her and her son only deepened the queen mother's already intense hatred of the Guises and confirmed her decision to maintain power by allying herself and her family with the far more deferential Coligny and his loyal band of Huguenots. But her new confederates labored under a significant handicap: although many aristocrats such as the prince of Condé and Antoine's wife, Jeanne d'Albret, had already openly converted, technically Protestantism was illegal in France. Its worshippers could not attend services in public or purchase or build their own churches. It would be difficult to rule in company with—let alone convert to—an outlaw sect. To remedy this predicament, Catherine called for yet another conclave, this one comprised of regional leaders, the royal council, and the highest-born princes. The purpose of this new assembly, which convened on January 3, 1562, was to strengthen the political standing of her new allies— and by extension her own position—by officially legitimizing the Protestant religion in France.

With the Catholic majority again hugely underrepresented and deprived of its most influential and charismatic leadership (the Guise family pointedly refused to participate), the Huguenot faction held sway. As a result, the majority of the delegates favored implementing policies far more radical than the queen mother had anticipated; for example, they voted to wrest a portion of the existing churches away from the Catholics and award them instead to the Protestants. Catherine, who understood that such an extreme measure would only provoke more violence and make it that much more difficult for her to rule, refused to support this action and spoke out against it. The queen mother was much lauded by the Catholics for this response, which is ironic, as it was only through her aggressive promotion of their cause that the Huguenots had been encouraged to even dream of such an ordinance in the first place.

Taking over their rivals' churches would only have been icing on the cake anyway, for on January 17 the Protestants got what they had come for: the assembly issued the Edict of Toleration, by which for the first time the Crown of France granted the Huguenots the legal right to establish public places of worship in the kingdom and to travel to and from religious services without fear of harassment or persecution. And although Catherine insisted that the edict also specify that reparation must be made for any Catholic property stolen or destroyed during the unrest of the previous years and that Protestants should not be allowed to set up new meeting houses inside the walls of predominantly Catholic cities, her subjects were not deceived by these concessions. This was not toleration. This was choosing sides.

It was inevitable that so radical a change would be tested on the ground in towns and villages all over France, and that faced with the reality of hundreds of Huguenots meeting publicly, preaching in French, and singing hymns as loudly as they could, the traditional Catholic majority would mount a challenge to the new policy. It was similarly obvious that the candidate most likely to lead the pushback would be the duke of Guise. And yet the duke initially tried not to interfere. After the bungled kidnapping attempt, he had retired to his estates in eastern France and attempted to play the role of a nonpartisan, immensely wealthy landowner. He rode out and surveyed his estates. He looked over the accounts. He went hunting.

He visited friends. He hosted a small family party in honor of his forty-third birthday. He seemed to have sworn off politics. "My talk is of nothing but dogs and hawks," he reported with resolute if somewhat resigned virtue in a letter to a friend.

Then he went to visit his mother, Antoinette.

The duke of Guise might have been feared throughout France for his warlike demeanor, but he was a rank amateur compared to his mother. An austere widow of sixty-eight, Antoinette ran the ducal finances, raised ten grandchildren, terrorized her various daughters-in-law, and presided over an annual family meeting at which she ordered her grown sons around as though they were still in swaddling clothes. Her eldest son, the duke of Guise, was no exception. Antoinette, a devout Catholic, was having none of this new-fangled reformed religious toleration business. Was her eldest son aware, she demanded, that the Protestants had moved into the neighboring town of Vassy and were brazenly conducting their heretical meetings within earshot of the local church? That they rang the bell to call their worshippers to sermon at unauthorized hours? That the local authorities did nothing to deter them? That if they weren't stopped the Huguenots might spread their vile doctrine to her very doorstep? Must she, who had borne a dozen children and all the commensurate cares of life, be burdened with this filth in her old age? What kind of a son was he, anyway? Go do something about it!

So he did. He rode into Vassy on March 1, 1562, accompanied by an entourage of two hundred armed knights and found the local Huguenot congregation, numbering some five or six hundred people, including many women and children, conducting its Sunday morning meeting not outside the city walls, as was specified in the Edict of Toleration, but right in town—and, worse, *on his property in one of his very own buildings, which they had appropriated without his permission,* an unimaginable insult. An altercation between the duke's people and the Protestants promptly ensued. Being for the most part unarmed, the Huguenots had to improvise. Rocks were thrown.

Members of the lower classes were not supposed to throw stones at their superiors from the upper classes. The duke's soldiers retaliated by shooting and stabbing as many of the dissenters as they could (which was quite a few, as their opponents were trapped inside the building attending a church service), accompanied by rousing shouts of "Kill! Kill! By God's death kill these Huguenots!"

An hour later the Massacre of Vassy, as this infamous incident would later be dubbed, was over. Fifty Huguenots lay dead, another two hundred were wounded, and a flaming torch had been thrust into the tinderbox of religious controversy that would blaze up into the bonfire of the Wars of Religion.

4

A Short War...

A prince should therefore have no other aim or thought, nor take up any other thing for his study, but war and its order and discipline, for that is the only art that is necessary to one who commands.

—Niccolò Machiavelli, *The Prince*

FUELED BY THE PERVASIVE ATMOSPHERE of fear and mistrust, news of the slaughter at Vassy spread quickly through France. In response, the prince of Condé and the other Huguenot noblemen called for their coreligionists, most of whom resided south of the Loire River, to arm themselves and prepare for civil war. The die thus cast, the duke of Guise followed suit, raised an army, and marched on Paris, where the gates of the city were thrown open to him and he was treated as the reincarnation of Charlemagne by the grateful Catholic population. "All the Chief Citizens went out to meet him, and congratulate his Arrival, and upon his Entrance into the City, the People received him with great Acclamations, and some particular Marks of Honour...which pleased the Duke exceedingly, and gave his Family no small Hopes of Increasing their Power," noted a highly placed official of the court. Nor did the inhabitants of the capital confine their appreciation to ceremonial outpourings of affection. City officials informed the duke of Guise that he could count on them to muster twenty thousand Catholic soldiers and two million *livres* in support of a war against the Edict of Toleration and the Protestants.

Unnerved by the swift success of the Guises' revolt, Catherine appealed to her Huguenot allies. She wrote in secret to the prince of Condé, entreating him to "save the [royal] children, the mother [herself] and the realm" (by which she meant that she wanted him to take back Paris from the duke of Guise), adding that "she was not more certain of herself than she was of him and that he could look upon her as if she was his own mother." Since it wouldn't do to have the news get out that the regent had ordered an attack on her own subjects, Catherine thought to add a telling postscript to this document. "Burn this instantly!" she instructed.★

But with the Huguenots so outnumbered in the capital, the prince of Condé "could no more fight Guise in Paris than a fly could attack an elephant," as one of his own military commanders snorted. It was decided instead to fall back on the walled city of Orléans and establish this outpost as the Huguenot base. Coligny wrote at once to Catherine and recommended that she and her son the king drop everything and flee to Orléans for their own protection. Everyone understood that the duke of Guise would march on Fontainebleau, where the court was then in residence, and forcibly remove the young king to Paris so that any subsequent action taken against the Protestants would appear to be by royal command.

But by this time the queen mother had discovered that the duke of Guise had achieved yet another disconcerting victory, this one of a political nature—he had induced the almost comically irresolute Antoine to abandon the cause advanced by his younger brother and Coligny and come over to the Catholics. This was achieved with the aid of the king of Spain, who was at this point openly supporting the Guises and who had been encouraged to bribe Antoine with the possibility of the return of that portion of his home kingdom of

---

★ Alas, he did not. Despite Catherine's protestations of maternal affection, Condé did not trust her, and rather than destroying her letters he ended up publishing them to protect himself when later she denied having appealed to him to attack Paris.

Navarre currently under Spanish control. Without Antoine's active acquiescence, Catherine knew she could not hope to remain regent; the Estates General would without question endorse Antoine should he seek to challenge her position. The king of Navarre's alliance with the Guises was the first step in an overall strategy that the queen mother understood would end with her inevitable disenfranchisement.

And now, seemingly for the first time, the folly inherent in the ambitious program she had championed, and the risks she had incurred as a result, broke upon Catherine. Her alliance with the reform movement, meant to isolate her political enemies and keep her in control of the government, had actually served to empower the Guises and jeopardize her position. For if, as Coligny urged, she and Charles IX openly split with the Catholic majority and abandoned Fontainebleau to seek the protection of the Huguenots in Orléans, the duke of Guise would undoubtedly pursue her there with a substantial army. There would be a great battle or a siege. If the Huguenots emerged victorious, well and good; but given the strength of the Catholic numbers, that was not an outcome Catherine could depend on. If, on the other hand, Antoine and the Guises won (as the queen mother now understood was likely), she would immediately be removed from power and might even have to answer charges of treason.*

Her only hope was to try to convince the Guises and their ally Philip II, king of Spain, that it had all been a terrible misunderstanding, that she had never intended to convert, and that it was in their interest to keep her involved in the government, as only she had enough influence with the Huguenot leadership to avert all-out war. A truce negotiated at her insistence and by her hand was her sole recourse, the one alternative whereby she might yet retain a degree

---

* In France, all legitimate power flowed through the king, even a boy king. The regent only commanded authority through proximity to the sovereign. The duke of Guise would never leave Charles IX in the hands of the Huguenots without a fight. Catherine, on the other hand, was expendable and would have taken all the blame.

of authority and justify her previous actions. "Peace! Peace!" became the queen mother's mantra.

And so she did not flee to Orléans but instead remained with her son and the court. When the duke of Guise and a sizable retinue arrived at Fontainebleau at the end of March and insisted that she and Charles return to Paris, Catherine again relied on her personal nego-tiating skills and attempted to reason with her nemesis. But the duke of Guise was impervious to her diplomacy and, over the objections and tears of both the twelve-year-old king and his mother, forcibly escorted them to the capital, where they remained under house arrest. Catherine, stripped of all power and once again under the thumb of her archenemy, backpedaled furiously, publicly denying any connection to the Huguenots. "I have been anxious that all the Lords should write to the King of Spain in regard to my attitude toward religion, not that I need any testimony before God nor men in regard to my faith nor my good works, but because of the lies which have been told of me. For I have never changed in deed, will, nor habits, the religion which I have held of forty-three years, and in which I have been baptized and brought up," she was reduced to imploring pathetically.

The Huguenots, meanwhile, faced with the prospect of fighting a Guise-led Catholic army augmented by a formidable contingent of Spanish troops and Swiss mercenaries, had turned to Protestant England for aid. Elizabeth I drove a very hard bargain and demanded the port city of Le Havre, in northwest France, in exchange for money and soldiers. This noxious deal, to which the desperate Huguenot ambassadors agreed, devolved into a public relations nightmare, as it forever branded their cause in the minds of French-men with a craven betrayal of sovereignty. By June, bitter fight-ing had broken out all over the kingdom. "It would be impossible," one observer reflected sadly, "to tell you what barbarous cruelties are committed by both sides. Where the Huguenot is master, he ruins the images and demolishes the sepulchers and tombs. On the other hand, the Catholic kills, murders, and drowns all those whom he knows to be of that sect, until the rivers overflow with them."

One of the earliest casualties of the conflict was Antoine, who was mortally wounded in the fall of 1562 while besieging the city of Rouen. The king of Navarre remained consistently inconsistent even in extremity, being unable to make up his mind whether to die as a Catholic or a Protestant; in the end, just to be on the safe side, he both accepted last rites and confessed to a priest *and* had his Huguenot physician read to him from the Gospels, a compromise that admirably covered all the bases. He died on November 10, leaving behind his fervidly Protestant widow, Jeanne d'Albret, queen of Navarre, and an impish, russet-haired eight-year-old son, Henry.

Despite the loss of Antoine, Rouen fell to the Catholics. Catherine, by now avid to prove her worth—the Guises, fully in control of the government, were already openly considering her removal from office, and there were rumors at court that she would be separated from her children and shipped back to Italy—begged again in the wake of the Protestant defeat to be allowed to negotiate a peaceful settlement.* The queen mother promised again to use her leverage with the Huguenot leadership to convince the Protestants to unilaterally lay down their weapons and withdraw. There being nothing to lose, the duke of Guise shrugged and allowed his prisoner to meet the prince of Condé, who seems to have at first accepted the deal but soon thought better of it and, to Catherine's bitter disappointment, reneged.† With his reversal the stage was set for a final decisive encounter between the two armies.

---

* The gossipy royal observer the abbé de Brantôme reported that Catherine had a listening tube surreptitiously installed in one of the council rooms behind a tapestry so she could keep abreast of the intrigues of the Catholic faction (known familiarly as the Triumvirate). On one occasion she overheard "one of the triumvirate give it as his opinion that the queen should be put into a sack and flung into the river." The chronicler made haste to say that the duke of Guise rejected the suggestion, but the incident does give a sense of Catherine's standing at court.

† Through spies, the Huguenots got word that the duke of Guise never intended to honor the queen mother's pledges, and that her negotiation with the prince of Condé was just an attempt to encourage the Protestants to lay down their arms so that they could be more easily slaughtered.

On December 19, 1562, the warring sides met outside the town of Dreux, about fifty miles west of Paris.

The armies that clashed in the woods that bleak winter's day were surprisingly well matched. The Catholic forces held the advantage in cannon and foot soldiers but the Protestant battalion, augmented by German mercenaries paid for with English money, numbered a very respectable twenty thousand and was the superior force in horsemen. Coligny, who despite his official title of admiral was at the head of the cavalry, led charge after charge for the Huguenots with such ferocity that even his opponents' much-admired Spanish troops turned and fled. The main portion of the Catholic army followed suit, and it seemed that victory was assured, so much so that initial reports filtering back to Paris gave the day to the Protestants. This must have provided Catherine no small satisfaction, because the queen mother, although ostensibly on the side of orthodoxy, could not resist a dig at her Guise oppressors when presented with the news. "In that case we shall have to learn to say our prayers in French," she was reported to have observed coolly.

But Coligny's triumph was short-lived. His former companion in arms the duke of Guise, who was every bit the admiral's equal in tactics and valor, had kept his third of the Catholic force hidden behind the trees. When he saw the Huguenot knights turn their horses and break out of formation in an attempt to chase down the retreating Catholic army, leaving their artillery and infantry unprotected, he and his men suddenly appeared at the crest of a hill. "Now, friends, the day is ours!" he cried before thundering down the small slope and into the fray.

The duke's strategy worked. Coligny managed to turn his men around and resume fighting, but by that time he had lost his guns and the main portion of his army to the Catholics. The prince of Condé was surrounded and taken prisoner. The slaughter was terrible: eight thousand Frenchmen died in the course of five hours. Meanwhile the Spanish contingent, after its initial disbursement, had regrouped and was threatening to hem in the Protestant cavalry from the other side. The duke of Guise was in his element. "Courage, my friends; he who rallies last bears off the fruits of victory!" he roared as he led his soldiers forward again. Coligny, thinking to save what was left of his force to fight another day, called a retreat and left the Catholics in command of the field.

Catherine trembled. An unequivocal military conquest led by the duke of Guise was the worst possible outcome for the queen mother; it denoted subjugation or banishment as much for her as for the Huguenot leadership. To prevent this eventuality, she pleaded yet again for a negotiated peace, but this time it was to no avail. The duke of Guise, knowing himself to be on the threshold of triumph, ignored her and pushed on to Orléans, the Huguenot stronghold, to demolish what was left of the enemy. Coligny, understanding that collapse was imminent without additional recruitment, left the city to beg for reinforcements from England. But these were late in coming, and by the beginning of February 1563 the duke of Guise had surrounded Orléans and established a siege. By the middle of February the suburbs immediately adjacent to the city had all fallen to the Catholics. With this, the Huguenot position became untenable. The duke of Guise went in for the kill. On the morning of February 18, confident of victory, he ordered an all-out attack for the following day. And then...

And then, on the evening of February 18, just a few hours before the inevitable surrender of Orléans, a low-level Huguenot nobleman by the name of Jean de Poltrot, sieur de Méré, who had successfully infiltrated the duke's entourage by pretending to be a Catholic, shot the duke of Guise from behind by hiding in the bushes as the commander was returning to camp from inspecting his troops. Four days later, the duke was subjected to an agonizing operation during which his surgeons searched fruitlessly for the bullet. And a mere four days after that, on February 26, 1563, the august duke of Guise, zealous defender of the faith and perhaps the kingdom's greatest warrior, died.

With his death everything changed again. The Catholic army,

deprived of its general, called off the attack. Under torture, Jean de Poltrot implicated Coligny in the murder of Guise, claiming that the admiral had paid him to assassinate his rival. The duke's family screamed their fury and demanded justice. Coligny admitted to paying Poltrot, but only to spy on the Catholics, not to kill their commander; the admiral did, however, feel the need to mention in passing that "this death is the greatest good which could have happened to this kingdom and to God's Church, and particularly to me and my entire house," an unfortunate comment that did nothing to improve his relationship with the dead man's family.*

Coligny's sentiments may have been accurate, but the true benefi- ciary of the effects of Poltrot's well-aimed bullet was Catherine. Overnight, seemingly out of nowhere, the queen mother was deliv- ered from her oldest and most immutable enemy. She must have barely credited the news when she first heard it—the despised, the malevolent, the fiendish duke of Guise, dead! Dead before he had time to force the surrender of Orléans! Dead before the Catholics could claim overwhelming, unconditional victory! But most important, dead before he could usurp her throne and dispatch her to a nunnery in Florence! This was Catherine's first experience of surgical political assassination, and the technique recommended itself to her highly.

With the Catholic leadership in disarray, Antoine already in his grave, and the prince of Condé captured, the queen mother moved quickly to reestablish her authority. She understood now that she and her son must always take care to conform strictly to the trap- pings of Catholicism; the kingdom would never follow her other- wise, and there was too much danger of Spanish intervention or

---

* It is highly unlikely that Coligny hired Poltrot to assassinate the duke of Guise. Honor was everything to the admiral; he would have scorned to take such a low road. Also, who but an innocent man would have made such a compromising statement? Jean de Poltrot had his own grudge against the Guises—he was a cousin of the man who had led the Huguenot attack against them at Amboise in 1560, while Francis II was still alive—and he was known for jests and empty boasts. "He had spoken lightly a long time before he went to Lyons in every place that he would surely kill Guise," a fellow Huguenot later remembered.

even attack, if Philip II believed her personal religious commitment to be wavering. From this moment on, and throughout her long reign, there would never again be even a whisper of the possible conversion of the royal family—no Huguenot tutors for her sons, no reformed ministers in her entourage, no Protestant sermons heard at court. And, of course, everybody went regularly to Mass.

But despite this the deferential, moderate Huguenots remained the queen mother's first choice as political allies. She had a long memory, and she identified the Guise family and their followers as the same people who had demeaned her time and again, who had participated in spreading lies about her (as she saw it), and who would have happily consented to her exile and perhaps even to her death. The Catholic faction had therefore to be kept in check if she hoped to remain in power.

One of the first victims of her revenge was the cardinal of Lorraine, who had been away representing France at a religious council in Trent when his brother the duke of Guise was assassinated. By the time he returned, the cardinal had lost all influence in the royal council and was forced to retire from court. (It is a measure of how far the once all-powerful Guises had fallen when, asked out of the barest civility to deliver the inaugural sermon for Lent the following year, the cardinal arrived at court only to find that the ornate seat set aside for his use during the service had been desecrated by a large pile of human excrement. The cardinal took the hint and beat a hasty retreat.) And, although Catherine wrote tender letters of condolence to various members of the Guise clan, praising the murdered man for his service to the kingdom, and complied with his widow's request to transfer all the dead duke's titles and honors to his eldest son, she did *not* prosecute Coligny for instigating the crime, as the family demanded. The Guises, nursing their resentment, had to be content with having Jean de Poltrot publicly tortured with red-hot pokers and then wrenched apart by four strong horses, the standard punishment for treason and a ghastly episode that unfortunately in no way appeased their thirst for vengeance.

And then, on March 19, 1563, the day after the hapless assassin had been dispatched, to the utter disbelief and rage of the Catholics, who believed they had won the war, Catherine met with the prince of Condé, representing the Huguenots, and his aged uncle the constable representing the Catholics, and negotiated a peace that, with some limitations, restored her signature legislation, the Edict of Toleration. This compromise, predictably, satisfied no one, as the Protestants, too, were dismayed by the new restrictions.* To mollify both sides, the queen mother fell back upon the agreeable tactics favored by her original mentor, François I, whose restless wanderings and lavish entertainments she remembered so fondly. "I have often heard your grandfather say that two things are necessary to live in peace with the French, and to make them love their King: to keep them happy [with feasts and parties] and to occupy them in some athletic exercise," she told her son, and so, following this sage advice, she organized a little holiday.

---

* The new edict scaled back the rights of the Huguenots by granting the nobility freedom of worship only in the privacy of their homes. Commoners were prohibited from public practice except in those towns already considered Protestant before the war. The constable, Anne de Montmorency, was seventy years old. He was very rich and had been a power in France during Henri II's rule. He was a Catholic who fought on the side of the duke of Guise but was more moderate in that he was willing to look the other way so long as aristocratic Huguenots worshipped in private and did not fight the Catholic majority.

5

...And a Long Trip

One who wishes to obtain the reputation for liberality among
men, must not omit every kind of sumptuous display, and
to such an extent that a prince of this character will consume
by such means all his resources and will be compelled . . . to
impose heavy charges on his people, become an extortioner,
and do everything possible to obtain money. This will make
his subjects begin to hate him.

—Niccolò Machiavelli, *The Prince*

THE VOLUMINOUS CAVALCADE THAT LUMBERED slowly out of Paris the
following January 1564, was unique even by the grandiose standards
of its age. Some eight hundred members of the royal court, including
but not limited to family members, high-ranking aristocrats (accompanied, naturally, by their own vassals and servants and advisers), key
administrators, government officials, secretaries, notaries, physicians,
senior household retainers, ladies-in-waiting, cooks, grooms, maidser-
vants, manservants, knights, minstrels, trumpeters, members of the
royal guard, a contingent of dwarves (Catherine loved dwarves), priests
and confessors (all Catholic, of course), and a number of foreign dignitaries had been summoned to accompany the king and his mother
on an extended journey through France.

Snaking behind this venerable company, like the long, sinewy tail
of a lizard, were hundreds of extra horses (eight thousand horses in

all, necessary for the all-important exercise of hunting and jousting, would be called into service on this journey) and an interminable train of carts comprising the luggage: boxes of court dress, formal state attire, receiving gowns, ball gowns, costumes for playacting and tableaux, furs, jewels, gifts, money, food, wine, kitchen utensils, cookware, fine table service, tapestries, bedding, props for grand entrances, painted scenery for backdrops, extra cloth of gold for draping, fireworks, coaches for inclement weather—everything that could possibly be required for the comfort of the travelers or to present an impressively regal facade. The procession stretched so far that those at the front of the line often reached the next day's destination before those at the back had had a chance to pack up and depart from the previous night's resting place. No sultan from the pages of *The Arabian Nights* could claim an entourage more extravagant than the one Catherine de' Medici put together to introduce the widely dispersed citizens of France to her son.

Because the escort was so vast, and because she planned to be away for such a considerable length of time, even the queen mother's youngest children were brought along for the journey. And so ten-year-old Marguerite and eight-year-old François joined the rest of the royal family on what became known as the Grand Tour.

The first stop was Fontainebleau, where the carefully staged brilliance of a series of inaugural fetes was clearly intended to set the tone for the rest of the trip. Despite the financial burden imposed on the royal treasury by the war—according to figures compiled by the Parlement of Paris the previous spring, the kingdom's indebtedness stood at a hair-raising fifty million *écus*—Catherine was determined to bring back the sense of glamour and magnificence she had experienced during the reign of François I.* A glittering

---

* For someone who always claimed to have loved and revered her husband above all else, Catherine lost no time in overturning all Henri II's (and Diane de Poitier's) policies. Both Henri and Diane were zealous Catholics who would never have countenanced the Huguenots. And, although Henri spent money on Diane, he shunned the ostentation of his father's court and was much more inclined (by necessity, because he, too, had accumulated a large national debt) toward austerity.

tournament was held, at which His Majesty (thirteen-year-old Charles) and the duke of Anjou (his twelve-year-old brother, Henri) participated. Later, Catherine hosted an afternoon garden party where everybody had a wonderful time dressing up as charmingly rustic members of the lower classes and listening to the serenades of a series of attractive young women provocatively clothed as sirens. This outdoor excursion was followed by a sumptuous feast and more entertainment in the form of a theatrical offering composed by Pierre de Ronsard, Catherine's favorite poet, at which Margot was allowed to play a role beside her older brother the duke of Anjou and his handsome former schoolmate, fourteen-year-old Henri, now duke of Guise. The evening's program continued with a lavish ball that lasted until the small hours of the morning, at which much of the cloth of gold carted in from Paris was in evidence.

On the last day, to mark the conclusion of this particular round of festivities, Catherine outdid herself with a grand finale: she sent the company, led by Charles and his brother Henri, into the garden, where, according to an eyewitness, "they perceived a large Inchanted [*sic*] Tower, with a great Number of fine Ladies, that were kept Prisoners by the Furies, and guarded by two Porters of Gigantick Size." Charles and Henri immediately determined to rescue the unhappy maidens. Taking the precaution of arming themselves, and with the aid of some of the adult members of the party, the royal siblings overcame the ladies' oversized jailers with ease and went on to commit a few more acts of derring-do on the stairway leading up to the room in which the appealing gentlewomen were confined. Once they managed to "dispel the Magick, and to set the Captive Dames at Liberty" (and everybody moved safely out of the way), the tower dramatically caught fire, the Renaissance equivalent of a cinematic special effect.

And on that thrilling note, the extended court, with its adolescent king and his middle-aged mother in the lead, commenced a journey through France that would take more than two years and would lead them as far south as Provence and as far west as Bayonne, through blizzards, downpours, and blinding heat; over rough roads and rolling hills; into midsize cities, local seats of government, large provincial towns, and picturesque villages. Catherine's objectives in undertaking this monumental itinerary were threefold: to bolster the authority of the Crown and ensure the enforcement of the revised Edict of Toleration through personal contact with regional authorities; to demonstrate in each locale, through conspicuous and highly orthodox religious display, her irreproachable personal piety and steadfast commitment to Catholicism; and, most important, to justify her previous actions and reach an understanding with her powerful son-in-law Philip II, king of Spain, through the medium of a private interview.

It was an ambitious plan, exactly in keeping with the charismatic diplomacy François I had practiced and at which he had excelled. But what Catherine did not understand, or could not see, was that this sort of visceral statesmanship hinged entirely on the magnetic appeal of the sovereign. François I had stood over six feet tall; his personality was expansive, mercurial, imposing. French to his core, he had embodied the kingdom. When François I made a ceremonial entrance into a provincial city or town his subjects looked at him and saw themselves — or, more accurately, the way they *wanted* to see themselves.

But when Catherine and Charles IX entered in procession, many of the townspeople looked right past the cloth of gold and the triumphal arch and the jeweled crowns and saw a very short, corpulent older Italian woman dressed all in black who ate and talked and walked incessantly accompanied by an unhealthy-looking, puerile boy who obediently parroted her commands. They were not a pair who inspired confidence.

IT WAS AN EVENTFUL two years on the road. The pope, frustrated by what he perceived to be a lack of progress on the part of the French government in responding to the threat posed to international Catholicism by the new reformed religion, first excommunicated and then tried to kidnap Antoine's widow, Jeanne d'Albret, queen of Navarre, who had assumed the leadership of the Huguenot party and was becoming more and more militant with each passing day. ("You'll see," Antoine had once dolefully warned the female members of his acquaintance upon hearing of an impending visit to court by his wife. "She'll convert you all.") As an incentive to the faithful, the pope promised the kingdom of Navarre to whoever succeeded in ousting its heretical sovereign. Catherine, who needed Jeanne as a counterpoint to the Catholics and who understood that a papal initiative condemning and dethroning a queen was not a precedent she wanted to encourage, warned her friend and took her under her protection.

But she, too, worried about Jeanne's increasing belligerence. Catherine still divided the reformed party into good, loyal, peaceable Huguenots and bad, violent, troublemaking Huguenots. She was willing to tolerate Jeanne's religious views provided she didn't make a public fuss about them, just as François I had previously indulged his sister's (Jeanne's mother's) unorthodox leanings so long as she kept her activities quiet. But Jeanne was a far more difficult and argumentative person than her mother had been. She passionately believed that Protestantism was the only righteous path and tried to convert not only her own subjects but also anyone else with whom she came into contact. She wrote long, hectoring letters to the court complaining that the revised Edict of Toleration did not go far enough and that Catholic officials discriminated against members of her party. She was even worse in person, combining an unpleasantly prickly temperament with a self-righteous, grating manner. "It is not an unalloyed privilege to have to deal with the Queen of Navarre," a French ambassador to Jeanne's court pointed out glumly in a letter to Catherine.

To keep Jeanne in line, Catherine resorted to a subtle form of blackmail: she kept the queen of Navarre's only son, Henry, with her as a quasi hostage to ensure his mother's good behavior. Henry was seven months younger than Margot. His capricious father,

Antoine, had separated from Henry's proselytizing mother a year before his death, and Henry had stayed with his father in Paris to be raised as a Catholic. Then Antoine had died, and Catherine had kept the boy.

Although well cared for, Henry was not happy at court. He had spent the first years of his life reveling in the rough, backcountry charms of scenic Navarre, with its emphasis on plain outdoor living. His manners lacked polish, and one of his first foods was apparently garlic, of which in later life many people complained he smelled. He adored his difficult mother and had been brought up by her as a Huguenot. He was eight when his parents separated, just old enough to understand that Jeanne had been sent away from him because she refused to attend Mass. He missed her terribly and stubbornly refused to change his religion, enduring the collective disapproval of his father, his cousins, the queen mother, and the rest of the court for a full three months before he finally broke down and attended a Catholic service with Antoine. "He shows himself very firm in the opinions of his mother," the Spanish ambassador informed his master, Philip II, with distaste.*

But then Antoine had died, and Henry had been left rudderless at court. It must have been very difficult for him. An early letter home during this period shows a lonely little boy terrified that he will lose both parents. He had been informed that his mother was ill, and he was writing to a member of her household. "Write me to relieve my anxiety about the Queen, my mother; because I am so afraid that some evil will befall her... that the greatest pleasure anyone could give me is to send me news often," he scrawled in his own hand. His distress must have been so palpable that Catherine took pity on him and, against her own policy, reinstated his Huguenot tutor so that he could have a familiar face about him at court. But

---

* Interestingly, Henry's initial refusal to switch from Protestantism to Catholicism under pressure is highly reminiscent of Margot's resistance to converting from Catholicism to Protestantism at the time of the Colloquy of Poissy. These two exhibited a strong sense of self even as children.

her sympathy did not extend so far as to return the bereaved child to his mother. Instead, explaining to Jeanne that familiarity with the royal court could only benefit the boy—who was, after all, in line to inherit the throne after her own sons—Catherine took Henry with her on the Grand Tour.

So along with Catherine's other children, Margot and Henry were thrown together for the next two years. They could not have helped getting to know each other as they rode or walked in procession in the sunshine or bumped along the uneven roads in the large, nausea-inducing carriage the royal family used to get from town to town during the frequent bouts of inclement weather. They stood in close proximity to each other during the regular ceremonies at which the queen mother introduced her son to the local authorities and took meals together at the many venues in which Catherine stopped to listen to the unending complaints engendered by her revised Edict of Toleration. They were snowed in together, shivered together, sweated together. And they were together on the afternoon of October 17, 1564, when the Grand Tour trundled into the small town of Salon-de-Provence to be met by a delegation of local luminaries—the official consul, another resident magistrate, and an assorted menagerie of awestruck bourgeoisie and lesser nobility. Thrilled to have been singled out for so great an honor—the queen mother's procession included "more princes than Salon had seen in its entire history," an eyewitness noted—the welcoming committee began a series of highly laudatory prepared remarks. But Charles IX, riding forward under his purple-and-white canopy (unpacked from the baggage carts specifically for entrances like this one), unceremoniously cut them off.

"I have only come to see Nostradamus," he announced.

NOSTRADAMUS. EVEN TODAY, NEARLY five centuries later, the name evokes a shiver of mystery and magic. Nostradamus, the Renaissance seer who is credited with predicting, among other calamities, the coming of the French Revolution, the tragic death of Princess

Diana, and the horror of 9/11. Nostradamus, whose strange and lyric quatrains, so tantalizingly suggestive and at the same time so frustratingly obscure, are still in print after all these years. How came he to know so much? How was it possible for one man to see so acutely and (with some 942 prognostications essayed in his magnum opus, *The Prophecies,* alone) so comprehensively into the future?

Although there are still gaps in documentation and areas of scholarly disagreement, over time painstaking research has yielded the outline of his life. He was born Michel de Nostredame in a small municipality in Provence. His grandfather on his father's side was a converted Jew who married a Christian woman. Nostradamus himself was a practicing Catholic who may or may not have been in sympathy with the Huguenot movement. (There is not sufficient evidence on either side to make a firm judgment.) His father, a member of the merchant class, was affluent enough to send his son to the university of Avignon, but Nostradamus never finished his undergraduate work because the school was closed due to plague when he was in his sophomore year. He spent the better part of the next decade as a traveling apothecary, learning the drug trade as he went along. In 1529 he tried to enroll in a doctoral program in medicine at the University of Montpellier but was rejected for lack of a bachelor's degree. The fact that he seems never to have attended, let alone graduated from, an accredited medical school nonetheless did not stop him from setting up shop as a physician who specialized in the plague. Not that a bona fide university degree would have been of much help in Nostradamus's chosen field. Even at the most advanced levels, Renaissance medicine was still pretty much confined to bloodletting, the concoction and imbibing of truly noxious potions, and the study of Aristotle's four humors, none of which, alas, turned out to be of much use against bacterial epidemics. The inadequacies of this line of study were not lost even on those who had taken the time to complete the rigorous years of scholarship demanded by the graduate course. "Get out fast, stay well away, come back late," was the prescription an officially certified sixteenth-century doctor recommended for dealing with the plague.

Nostradamus was no better at curing the Black Death than anybody else—in fact, he lost his first wife and children to the disease. But he was one of the very few practitioners who were willing to brave an outbreak of plague and at least try to help, and his humanitarianism won him a measure of wealth and respect. He remarried and, in 1548, at the age of forty-five, gave up the itinerant life of a medical specialist and settled down for good in the little town of Salon-de-Provence to start a new family.

And it was only in these, his later years, that Nostradamus became known as something more than your average ersatz country plague doctor. Finding himself with time on his hands and having the common middle-aged male complaint of being unable to sleep more than four or five hours a night, he began work on a new project—almanacs.

Almanacs were the horoscopes of the sixteenth century. Inexpensive and hugely popular, aimed at the broadest segment of the market, these short printed pamphlets contained, among other tidbits specific to the author, monthly weather forecasts and astrological predictions for the coming year. It was this latter area of expertise that first attracted Nostradamus to the genre. A longtime devotee of what was known in the Renaissance as judicial astrology—the study of the way the cycles of the stars and planets influenced the course of human affairs—the former medical practitioner put his many hours of insomnia to productive use by carefully charting the movement of heavenly bodies and then just as conscientiously extrapolating the future of mankind from the resulting data. Beginning in 1550, he dashed off a series of almanacs, some eleven in all, published under the erudite moniker Nostradamus (the Latinized version of his own name, Nostredame).

What set Nostradamus's almanacs apart from those of his competitors was the style in which he wrote his prophecies. They were all clever little four-line poems, full of ominous portents but at the same time intentionally ambiguous—each had to be puzzled through to determine the exact nature of the prediction.* This literary wrinkle delighted a reading public that, as a result of the rise of espionage associated with chronic political and religious distrust, was by then more or less conditioned to descry codes, cryptic language, and hidden meanings in even the most mundane communications. So for a nominal fee the purchaser received not only a glimpse into the future but also the fun of deciphering (and no doubt arguing with his or her neighbors about) just what exactly was being revealed. Nostradamus's almanacs sold out, much to the satisfaction of his publisher.

And because Nostradamus's predictions were so enigmatic that they could be interpreted as political foreshadowing—"Near Geneva terror will be great / Through the counsel, that cannot fail: / The new King has his league prepare, / The young one dies, famine, fear will cause failure," read one of the seer's typical almanac riddles—it was perhaps inevitable that he should come to the attention of the queen mother of France, herself a committed follower of the occult arts, albeit more of an amateur enthusiast.

Catherine's first meeting with the prophet apparently occurred in the summer of 1555, while her husband, Henri II, was still alive. Although the summons to appear at court came from the king, it seems likely that his wife put him up to it, as Nostradamus's audience with Henri lasted only a few minutes, while his subsequent interview with Catherine extended over several hours. Catherine's purpose in consulting Nostradamus was twofold: she wished to query him about some of the quatrains that had appeared in his latest almanac, but she was also interested in establishing a personal relationship, perhaps even luring him away from his family in Salon-de-Provence and establishing him as a member of her private

---

* Nostradamus deliberately veiled his prophecies because he was worried about the possible adverse consequences to himself and posterity if he foretold dire events too clearly. "[I composed] in dark and cryptic sentences the causes of the future evolution of human kind... [I was able to do so] without scandalizing and upsetting fragile sentiments by clouding my writing in obscure but, above all, prophetic language," he explained with characteristic incoherence.

mystical circle at court. She already had her own dedicated conjurer, an Italian named Cosimo Ruggieri, who peered into the queen's magic mirror for her, mixed potions (and, it was whispered, poisons) for her, and counseled her on the movements of the stars as they related to the royal family's schedule. But of course when it came to foretelling the future, one couldn't be too careful, and it always helped to have a second opinion.

Nostradamus, however, was wary of allying himself too closely with the eccentric queen of France, who often claimed to be beset by strange and troubling visions herself. Besides that, he considered her cheap. "As a fine reward for having gone to court... His Majesty the King sent me one hundred crowns. The Queen sent me thirty. There you have a fine sum for having come two hundred leagues: having spent a hundred crowns, I made thirty crowns out of it," he groused later to a friend. Nostradamus could be plainspoken when he wanted to be.

It has further been reported that after this meeting, Catherine sent Nostradamus to Blois, almost one hundred miles to the south, and that once there he examined her many children and formulated their individual horoscopes in order to predict their futures. This seems very unlikely, however. There is no evidence at all that the royal princes and princesses were at Blois. Margot, for example, was just two years old, and the baby, François, had only been born the year before; they were definitely at the royal nursery in Saint-Germain-en-Laye, just outside Paris, at the time their mother met with the famous astrologer. Elizabeth and Claude were also at Saint-Germain-en-Laye, as were Charles, who was, after all, only five at the time, and Henri, who was four. Even the dauphin, Francis, who at eleven was old enough to be in Paris at court with his parents, still spent most of his time with the other children in the nursery. Moreover, Diane de Poitiers, a devout Catholic, was at the height of her influence in 1555, and she did not approve of Nostradamus's methods, which were frowned on by the Church. She certainly would never have allowed him to inspect Henri's children.

What probably did happen, though, is that Catherine's evident interest in Nostradamus added to his notoriety and made his prophecies required reading at court, especially after the deaths of Henri II in 1559 and Francis II in 1560, when the queen mother took over the regency. This accounts for a reference to the great seer in a letter written in May 1561 by the Venetian envoy to his home government: "There is another prediction very widely spread in France, emanating from this famous divine astrologer named Nostradamus, and which threatens the three brothers [Catherine's remaining sons, Charles, Henri, and François], saying that the queen mother will see them all kings." Again, there is no evidence that Nostradamus was in personal contact with Catherine at this time. What most likely happened is that the queen mother or one of her courtiers who was hoping to curry favor had seized on one of Nostradamus's quatrains and optimistically construed this much-to-be-desired result from it.

However the rumor came to be in circulation, it is clear from her subsequent actions that this was one prediction Catherine wanted very much to believe. The Grand Tour gave her the opportunity once again to consult personally with Nostradamus to determine what, if anything, could be confirmed from the master's lips; hence the visit to Salon-de-Provence in the fall of 1564. And while Nostradamus was sincere in his belief that his prophecies were genuine and that he was working for the general benefit of humanity, he also understood that his most influential and powerful benefactress, the queen mother and regent of France, would likely want to hear good news. So he had some ready for her.

According to Nostradamus's son, who was present during the course of the interview, the prophet hosted his royal visitors in his own home. They spoke at length, and Catherine left well satisfied with Nostradamus's predictions, some of which she later passed on to the ambassador from Spain. The ambassador in turn passed them along to *his* sovereign, Philip II, although it must be admitted that the tone of his missive was somewhat at odds with the obvious reverence assumed by the queen mother. "Your Majesty should know that everything has gone mad here," the Spanish envoy informed his employer bluntly. "I am told that the Queen [Catherine] when she passed by the place where Nostradamus lives, summoned him to her and awarded him two hundred crowns. . . The Queen said to me today. . . 'Did you know. . . that Nostradamus has assured me that there will be a general peace throughout the world in 1566, and that the realm of France will be very tranquil?' In speaking thus, she talks with [an] air of profundity [as] if she were quoting from St. John or St. Luke," he continued in disbelief.

But world peace was not the only prescription the former physician managed to divine for his royal guests. Nostradamus "promises a fine future to the King, my son, and that he will live as long as you, whom he says will see four score and ten years before dying," Catherine wrote happily to the elderly Constable of France soon after her visit. (Charles was already ill with tuberculosis. It was clearly no great loss to medicine when Nostradamus gave up his day job.) Furthermore, according to the astrologer's calculations, the stars had aligned in such a way as to forecast the marriage of fourteen-year-old Charles IX to thirty-one-year-old Elizabeth I, a fortunate concurrence upon which Catherine immediately acted. The Spanish ambassador, flabbergasted, managed to get wind of this latest development as well. "Tomorrow there leaves secretly a gentleman sent to the Queen of England. The first day that the King and Queen saw Nostradamus he declared to them that the King would marry the previously mentioned Queen," he moaned in yet another damning message home to his sovereign.*

---

* Fittingly, Catherine's ambassador delivered this flattering marriage proposal (along with the appropriate astrological calculations) to Elizabeth on Valentine's Day, 1565. Through a return envoy, the queen of England thanked Catherine for the unlooked-for honor but, sensibly, demurred. Catherine was having none of it. "The first objection you have urged is the age of my son," the queen mother of France replied to the turndown. "But if the Queen Elizabeth will put up with it, I will put up with the age of the Queen." This exchange is especially illuminating because it gives a sense of just how little Charles IX was in control of his life, let alone the realm. "I should be very glad if your mistress would be as well pleased with my age as I am well-pleased with hers," the adolescent king was reported to have trilled in earnest imitation of his mother. "In good sooth I love her," he added, just to be on the safe side.

It is a common misconception that those who lived in the distant past were as a rule superstitious and credulous and that Nostradamus was universally admired, but this was not in fact the case. The magus was a figure of controversy, derided as often as he was applauded. "Ere I forget, or further forage / He writes his verse like stirring porridge / ...Born beneath such a sign and season / As to have neither sense nor reason," ran a typically scathing critique from a contemporary pundit. Catherine's unquestioning acceptance of the prophet and her eagerness—her insistence, really—on acting upon his calculations was an extreme reaction, particularly for a member of the educated class. There was a competing judicial astrologer, John Dee, operating on the fringe of the royal court in England at this time who was sometimes called in for consultation by the English government, but this was mostly because he was an expert on codes and counterintelligence tactics. With regard to Dee's other, more esoteric, interests, Elizabeth's attitude was one of tolerant amusement, and she made a point to keep him at arm's length. But Catherine's gullibility was a different story: the degree to which mysticism influenced the queen mother of France was well known both at home and abroad, and this made her less credible as a ruler. The Spanish ambassador was not the only consul to consider her ridiculous.

Other factors contributed to undermining Catherine's policies. There was the small problem, for example, that as she traveled around the kingdom the queen mother expediently told Catholics one thing and Protestants another. To the faithful, she sighed that the Edict of Toleration was only an interim measure that she was forced to implement because otherwise it was "thought by the King that this might cause the Huguenots to revolt," while to the Huguenots she explained that "the King undertakes this journey in order to make everybody so clearly understand his intention to enforce this Edict that nobody can be able to allege any pretext nor occasion to break it."

This sort of obvious duplicity might have worked in an atmosphere of hermetic secrecy but not in a kingdom plagued by espionage and distrust. It rapidly became apparent to both sides that Catherine had yet to work out a coherent strategy beyond temporizing; further, her fear of a renewed outbreak of religious hostilities was so palpable that she would advance any proposal to maintain the appearance of harmony, no matter how ludicrous. A nuncio for the pope reported that "the Queen Mother. . . greatly desires to reconcile the conflicting opinions and she suggested that I offer [a Protestant minister] money. . . saying that if he would preach the opposite of what he now says. . . all the other Huguenots would follow him." A member of the extended Guise family summed up the frustration of both Catholics and Protestants with the queen mother's government when he complained that all anyone ever got from Catherine were "the most beautiful words in the world of the kind which you know she is accustomed to give."

But Catherine still looked forward to what she considered to be the climax of the Grand Tour, the glittering diplomatic triumph that would justify the endless months of travel, expense, and fatigue: her face-to-face meeting with Philip II, king of Spain. Here, aided by her daughter Elizabeth, Philip's wife, would she and her son-in-law forge common ground and find a practical solution to the religious question. Here would she strengthen this crucial family alliance by arranging to marry her youngest daughter, Marguerite, to Philip's only son and heir (even though Margot was already engaged to her cousin and fellow traveling companion Henry, son of the queen of Navarre), and her second son, Henri, to Philip's sister, the widowed queen of Portugal. Here would she forever separate the Guises and their Catholic supporters from Philip, their most influential and dangerous patron, and appropriate his power for her own use.

And so off she went to the port city of Bayonne, on the extreme southwestern edge of France very near the border with Spain, high hopes and gargantuan entourage in tow, only to run immediately into the inexorable reality of the duke of Alva.

THE DUKE OF ALVA was the king of Spain's trusted lieutenant. Philip himself never had any intention of meeting Catherine. The desire for a deeper, more comprehensive family relationship emanated entirely from her side; as far as Philip was concerned, she could have saved herself the trouble and stayed in Paris. So he delegated the duke of Alva as his surrogate. This was one of the big advantages of being the dominant monarch in Europe—the ability to send an underling to deal with your annoying mother-in-law.

Worse, Philip almost did not let his wife go to see her mother, even though Catherine had traveled hundreds of miles and was only across the river. Through emissaries, the king of Spain made it quite clear to the French court that it was out of the question for his spouse to risk exposure to the heresy currently infecting his neighbor to the north and that therefore Elizabeth would not be allowed to visit her mother unless Catherine could guarantee that the queen of Spain would not come into contact with a Protestant. So all the Huguenots in the area, including Jeanne d'Albret, queen of Navarre (whose home territories surrounded Bayonne, where the meeting was to take place), were instructed to keep away, an unfortunate concession that only reinforced Protestant suspicions that the true purpose of the meeting between Catherine and the duke of Alva was for the pair to find a way to exterminate the Huguenot population altogether.

Having successfully dictated the terms under which the audience could take place, Philip eventually allowed Elizabeth, chaperoned by Alva, to make the journey to Bayonne. The critical nature of the meeting was underscored by the lavishness of the queen mother's preparations. Catherine outdid herself in spectacle and hospitality. Margot had just turned twelve, and the entertainment provided for her older sister made such an impression on her that she still remembered it vividly decades later. It was the summer of 1565 and very hot. Scores of tables, each large enough to seat twelve comfortably, had been set up on a pleasant island in order to catch the breeze: one was raised above the others, and "here their Majesties were seated under a lofty canopy." Every commodity, including the guests, had to be imported and floated down the river by barges; the feast was served by a small army of "shepherdesses dressed in cloth of gold and satin," and the entire company serenaded by "a large troop of musicians, habited like satyrs" and "nymphs...in rich habits." The party was in full swing, guests and actors alike poised to commence an extravagant ball, "when, lo! Fortune no longer favoring this brilliant festival, a sudden storm of rain came on, and all were glad to get off in the boats and make for town as fast as they could. The confusion in consequence of this precipitate retreat afforded as much matter to laugh at the next day as the splendor of the entertainment had excited admiration," Margot revealed.

But the negotiation at Bayonne between Catherine and the duke of Alva was all too serious. The king of Spain, it turned out, was not interested in world peace. Instead, Philip viewed the rise of Protestantism as the greatest threat to his rule and wanted the reformed religion stamped out in France before it had a chance to infiltrate his kingdom. Furthermore, Philip had no problem with the violence in France—in fact, he had every reason to encourage it, as it was obviously in his interest to have the battle over religion fought on somebody else's territory. Already heresy had taken root in England, where the Protestant queen, Elizabeth I, ruled; so, too, in large parts of Germany, where Lutheranism prevailed; and now the reform movement had spread to the Netherlands, which was part of Philip II's own dominion, causing significant unrest. The queen mother's earlier flirtation with the possibility of conversion and her continued reliance upon the Huguenots as political allies had earned her the deep distrust of the pope, the cardinals, and Catholic monarchs across Europe and harmed her even more with the Spanish king than with her domestic opponents, a consequence that Philip II's ambassador now demonstrated by treating her pleas for an alliance with contempt. Spain was perfectly willing to aid Catherine in a war against the Huguenots, the duke of Alva informed the queen mother coldly, but there could be no thought of marriages until heterodoxy was obliterated in France.

That her son-in-law might hold a conflicting position or have interests contrary to her own seems not to have occurred to Catherine prior to this meeting. Certainly she had no backup plan. Faced with Alva's intransigent opposition, the queen mother resorted to the few weapons in her diplomatic arsenal. First she appealed to her daughter to help her. But Elizabeth, whose behavior was no doubt under close scrutiny by the duke of Alva and whose words in any event carried absolutely no weight with her intimidating older husband, could not have influenced Spanish policy in Catherine's favor even if she wanted to. In fact, she had clearly been instructed to use her relationship with her mother to promote Philip's agenda, because she tried to introduce the subject of the state of religion in France in casual conversation. By forcing Elizabeth to choose between France and Spain, Catherine was putting her daughter in a very difficult position, but this had no effect on the queen mother, who was perfectly willing to sacrifice Elizabeth's interests in pursuit of her own. "So your husband suspects me?" Catherine demanded. "What makes you suppose, Madame, that the King suspects Your Majesty?" Elizabeth replied, evidently startled by this response. "My dear daughter, you have become very Spanish," Catherine observed bitterly.

When family ties failed, the queen mother fell back on repetition. Throughout her career, Catherine seems to have believed that simply by reiterating her demands over and over she could either convince her opponents of the correctness of her position or overwhelm them until they conceded to her wishes. The queen mother, the duke of Alva later reported to Philip, was "extremely cold about religion and really attentive to nothing except the matter of the marriages of her children. She kept saying that to help the troubles of religion there is nothing better than to unite the two crowns and the two houses by new bonds." Alva tried to circumvent the queen mother's approach by appealing to Charles IX directly, only to discover that the fifteen-year-old king had no opinions of his own on matters of state. "I perceived that they kept him fettered, and so I passed to other subjects," he concluded in yet another illuminating missive to his sovereign.

The duke of Alva remaining obdurate, Catherine felt she had no choice on the last day of the conference but to fall back on her final negotiating tactic, one she had employed with varying degrees of success in the past—weeping. She wept not only in the presence of the duke of Alva but also, apparently, in front of a goodly number of ambassadors and members of her own court. Naturally, when the queen mother started crying, her son the king cried as well, and when the king cried, his younger brother the duke of Anjou cried, and when her mother and brothers cried, Elizabeth cried also (although this was probably because she was going to have to go back to Madrid and explain all this to her terrifying husband). "At St. Jean de Luz the tears of Her Majesty's mother and brothers began to flow and certainly they were many," one of the Spanish envoys reported as tactfully as possible. "The Constable finally went into the King's room and told him he ought not to cry for it would be much noticed by strangers and his vassals, because tears were very unbecoming to the eyes of a King."

Alas, even the combined sobs of the royal family had no influence on the steely duke of Alva. Faced with the prospect of coming away from so public a negotiation empty-handed, Catherine did what she always did when confronted by strength: she told the duke of Alva what he wanted to hear. In exchange for the marriages she so desperately desired, she agreed at the very last moment to destroy or banish the Huguenot leadership and root out heresy in France. "If the agreement which the Duke of Alva will tell your Majesty was made here is carried out, it is all that can be desired for the service of God and Your Majesty," the Spanish ambassador to the court, who was a witness, assured Philip in his report of these proceedings.

The fiasco of this poorly conceived and amateurishly conducted foreign policy summit would have far-reaching consequences. Because even though it is highly unlikely that Catherine meant what she said even at the moment she said it and probable instead that she was only stalling, as usual, in an attempt to buy time, her craven capitulation to the Spanish at Bayonne immediately negated all the work she had put into enforcing the Edict of Toleration over the course of the previous two and a half years. When the exhausted members of the Grand Tour finally straggled back into Paris in May of 1566, religious tensions in France were, if anything, even more pronounced than they had been before they had left. The Huguenots feared that the queen mother would betray them, and the Catholics suspected that she would renege on her pledge to Spain. The realm was impoverished: the crippling cost of the Grand Tour had only added to the deficit, and Catherine had to borrow even more from Italian bankers and raise taxes, which did nothing to improve her popularity. "I know that many in France blamed this expense as being superfluous," the courtier Brantôme observed delicately. Anger and frustration permeated the capital, the various factions began to arm themselves, and intrigues and plots were surreptitiously organized. The kingdom once again stood poised on the precipice of destruction, with only the slightest provocation necessary to push it over the edge.

And it was precisely at this dangerous juncture that thirteen-year-old Margot was at last deemed old enough to abandon her childhood nursery and was commanded instead to remain with her mother at the court in Paris. The political education of the youngest Valois princess had begun.

PART II

❧

Catherine's Daughter
Marguerite de Valois

6

The Flying Squadron

Experience shows that there have been very many conspira-
cies, but few have turned out well.

        —Niccolò Machiavelli, *The Prince*

OF ALL THE STAGES OF human development, adolescence—the process of becoming an adult—is perhaps the most challenging. In
addition to the obvious physical changes, there is the struggle to
interpret the various and often confusing values associated with
grown-up conventions. Even the most perceptive teenager can have
difficulty appreciating the nuances of interaction, the unspoken
rules and customs, of polite society.

But to be a young princess attached to the curious court of Catherine de' Medici, as Margot was, magnified the pressures of puberty
tenfold. For the queen mother's coterie reflected her own peculiar
moral standards, the product of the twisted circumstances of her
earlier married life. The decades-long nuptial charade imposed on
Catherine by Henri and Diane had taken its toll on her character.
Forced to accept abject public humiliation on a daily basis, it seems
from her subsequent behavior that Catherine coped with the trauma
by mentally separating the concepts of love and sex, of private and
public demeanor. Although Henri had treated her shamefully, in
Catherine's mind it was unacceptable to blame him for the unsatis-
factory nature of her marital relations. Her one protection, the

rampart to which she had clung through the degradation of all those years, had been her status as Henri's legitimate wife. Consequently, her love for him was as vocal and determined as it was pure. It was Diane upon whom Catherine focused all her anger and shame. Diane represented sex—unlawful, profane, indecent sex. Sex wielded as a weapon to secure advantage or information. Sex as a means of control. Sex as a path to wealth and political power. "Never did a woman who loved her husband succeed in loving his whore," Catherine would later write bitterly of Diane. "For one cannot call her otherwise, although the word is a horrid one to us," she amended virtuously.

Compelled to accept Diane's ascendancy while Henri was alive, the queen mother made no secret of her feelings after her husband's death. She deplored licentious behavior. Sex outside the bonds of marriage was sinful. It would not be tolerated. To the end of her days, Catherine was as respectable and irreproachable a matron and grieving widow as could be found in Christendom.

But soon after Henri died and the requisite period of mourning had passed, Catherine did a very strange thing. She reinstituted what had been known in the days of her mentor, François I, as *la petite bande*—the cadre of beautiful women attached to the court.

La petite bande had not survived the death of its original, highly enthusiastic sponsor. Henri II had been indifferent to it, and Diane, who was getting older and did not relish the competition, had actively opposed it. So, on Henri's ascension to the throne, the bevy of lovely young things who had faithfully followed François I from hunting ground to hunting ground, laughed at his jokes, soothed his ego, let him win at games, and slept with him when the occasion demanded had been collectively dismissed and sent home to their respective duchies.

All this changed when Catherine became regent. Suddenly, at the queen mother's invitation, the royal entourage was once again home to the most stunning women in France. "Usually her Court was filled by at least three hundred ladies and damoiselles," the contemporary chronicler the abbé de Brantôme remembered fondly. "Beauty abounded, all majesty, all charm, all grace; happy was he who could touch with love such ladies... Ladies and damoiselles who were beautiful, agreeable, very accomplished, and well sufficient to set fire to the whole world. Indeed, in their best days they burned up a good part of it, as much us gentlemen of the Court as others who approached the flame," Brantôme concluded knowingly.

This was an odd choice for a self-proclaimed inflexibly virtuous widow in her late forties, the mother of young children. It cannot be that Catherine simply craved the company of women, because the ability to physically attract men was a requisite for inclusion, as it had been during the days of François I. But François's motivation had been merely the fulfillment of his own pleasure. He was a healthy heterosexual man who was fortunate enough to have the power to surround himself with beauty. Catherine had a far more complex agenda. She had not forgotten that Diane had once employed her to spy on her enemies and how effective her rival's methods had been as a means of securing and consolidating power. The queen mother now appropriated these techniques for her own use. Her troupe of sirens was in the nature of a lure, a way to glamorize the French court and maintain the kingdom's reputation as an inviting destination in Europe. But the presence of so many femmes fatales also represented a blatantly cynical attempt to undermine her masculine adversaries. So obvious was the women's mission that they were publicly referred to as Catherine's L'Escadron Volant, or her Flying Squadron.

Their instructions were understood rather than explicit. They were there to beguile the queen mother's male political opponents, extract information from them, keep them off balance, and retain them at court, where Catherine could keep an eye on them. Those who succeeded in these tasks were rewarded with royal favor and became intimates of the queen mother. The queen of Navarre, Jeanne d'Albret, was horrified by the overtly seductive nature of Catherine's court. "Although I knew it was bad, I find it even worse than I feared," she admonished after a visit. "Here women make advances to men rather than the other way around." But there was a catch: the outward impression of propriety had to be maintained at all times. This meant that if, in the ordinary course of events, a member of the Flying Squadron found herself pregnant, as inevitably sometimes occurred, she would immediately forfeit all privileges and standing and be exiled from the court in shame. This was how Catherine continued to justify herself as an upright, moral woman and how she separated herself in her own mind from the harlot Diane: by publicly punishing those who reaped the wages of the sin she tacitly encouraged them to commit in the first place.

The result was an ethos that was at once dissolute and sanctimonious, salacious and prudish. Jealousy and competition were rampant, and the behavior of the group as a whole frequently descended into backbiting, spitefulness, and bullying: these were the mean girls of the sixteenth century. And it was at this court that Marguerite spent her formative teenage years. "She is beautiful, discreet, and graceful," Jeanne d'Albret would write later of Margot. "But she has grown up in the most vicious and corrupt atmosphere imaginable. I cannot see that anyone escapes its poison."

Further complicating Marguerite's passage to adulthood was the focus upon, and the conflicting signals emitted in regard to, her future marriage. At least from the time she was eight and was seated beside him at an official banquet, Margot was aware that she was engaged to her cousin Henry, heir to the throne of tiny Navarre. But Catherine's marital ambitions for her younger children, egged on by Nostradamus's predictions, were far more grandiose. As the queen mother was undeterred by mundane considerations of age, religion, and general suitability, this often led to the serious contemplation of almost comically inappropriate matches. After Elizabeth I rejected Charles IX's suit, offering as a further excuse that the king of France was unlikely to spend much time in England, Catherine immediately countered by substituting his younger brother Henri, duke of Anjou, as the prospective bridegroom and later, when that fell through, put forward her youngest son, François, duke of Alençon, twenty-two years Elizabeth's junior, as the most desirable candidate. Catherine proposed Margot repeatedly to Philip II, king of Spain, as an excellent bride for his son, Don Carlos, until Catherine's eldest daughter, Elizabeth, Philip's wife, died unexpectedly in childbirth in 1568, at which point fifteen-year-old Marguerite was immediately offered to the grieving forty-one-year-old widower instead.

So Margot's engagement to Henry was by no means a settled affair, and she understood this. Frankly, as a potential suitor, she found her cousin disappointing. Henry was not Margot's idea of a romantic hero at all. He was not classically handsome, nor was he particularly chivalrous. Uncertain of his position at court, he compensated for his insecurities by clowning and drawing attention to himself. He was only seven months her junior, but he looked younger and was far less sophisticated in demeanor and outlook. Exposure to the values of her mother's court, which was preoccupied with physical perfection and sensuality, had not made Marguerite hard and cynical, as Jeanne d'Albret feared, but it had accelerated her emotional development. Even in her early teens, Margot had very definite ideas about love. She wanted a strong, daring man, a man who risked everything for passion. She wanted a man whose good looks turned heads, a swordsman who laughed at danger, a knight who knew his way around the boudoir as well as the battlefield. She wanted to be swept off her feet, to lose herself completely — spiritually, intellectually, and physically — to the man she loved.

Her cousin Henry fell somewhat short of this ideal. He had been with the royal court six years, since he was eight years old, and probably suffered from too much close exposure. Henry was more like a particularly annoying little brother than a valiant, ardent lover.

Margot also knew that her cousin and his mother, Jeanne d'Albret, along with the rest of the Huguenot leadership, were not in favor at court. In January 1567, a month after Henry turned fourteen, Jeanne had finally succeeded in engineering her son's escape from the royal entourage. Through subterfuge, the pair, along with others of the Huguenot movement, decamped to the safety of Protestant Navarre. To add insult to injury, Jeanne tricked the queen mother into financing this flight. The Spanish ambassador noted that Catherine expressed herself "very much surprised" when notified of Jeanne and Henry's desertion and added that "she was all the angrier because she had just loaned the Duchess [Jeanne] 2,000 écus because she was pleading poverty!"

But the queen of Navarre's departure turned out to be merely the prelude to a confrontation that would result in a bitter rupture between Catherine and the Huguenot leadership, a divide so profound that it would naturally lead her youngest daughter—and, indeed, the preponderance of the court—to reject as ludicrous the notion of a marriage alliance between Margot and her Protestant cousin. For by the fall of 1567, Catherine had become so estranged from her former allies, particularly Admiral Coligny and the prince of Condé, that she not only considered them partisan adversaries, she was actively seeking their destruction.

IT IS IMPOSSIBLE TO overstate the degree of Huguenot paranoia and mistrust that were engendered by Catherine's disastrous meeting with the duke of Alva. Pointedly excluded from the negotiation, the Protestants were reduced to relying on spies and innuendo for intelligence. The information collected by these methods was frustratingly vague, but the complacent attitude of the Spanish in the weeks following the summit indicated that *something* of import had been decided between the queen mother and her son-in-law and, knowing Philip, that this could only be detrimental to their cause. Rumors of an agreement between the French and the Spanish to exterminate those of the reformed religion abounded and spread quickly through the kingdom.

These fears only escalated when, following the Bayonne meeting, Protestant worshippers in the Netherlands, who were supported in their quest for religious freedom by their Huguenot counterparts in France, rebelled against Spain, whereupon Philip announced his intention of sending a huge military force under the leadership of the duke of Alva to put down the revolt. Because it was difficult to get to the Netherlands from either Spain or Italy (where the duke of Alva was busy recruiting troops) without going through France, Philip asked Catherine to authorize a safe passage for his army so they could expedite the march north. This was all the corroboration the Huguenots needed of a conspiracy against them. To them, it was obvious that Philip's request was just a trick to catch them off guard—that the real Spanish military objective was to invade France and wipe out their movement. Although Catherine denied Philip's petition, she unfortunately also hired a contingent of six thousand Swiss mercenaries to supplement the royal guard. Even more disturbingly, she restored the Guises, and in particular the cardinal of Lorraine, the head of the Catholic party, to favor. The Protestants saw this as confirmation of a coordinated scheme against them, and so they, too, began plotting and mobilizing for war as a defensive measure.

Catherine's recall of the cardinal of Lorraine to court is often cited as evidence of the queen mother's sophisticated Machiavellian strategy, the deliberate playing off of one political faction against the other as a way of securing her own position, but in fact it was nothing of the kind. Catherine did not want to restore her old enemy to power, but she had no choice. She was desperate. The duke of Alva's army scared her as much as it did the Huguenots. She couldn't be sure Philip wasn't intending to use it against *her*. While the Spanish soldiers—all sixteen thousand of them—would not be marching through France, they would be passing right along its eastern border, and of course there would be the enormous temptation, so long as they were in the vicinity anyway, to stray over into French territory and take what they could get. That's why she'd hired the pike-wielding Swiss mercenaries, recognized as the fiercest warriors in Europe—not to use them against the Huguenots but as protection against the Spanish.

Problem was, she couldn't pay them. The kingdom was so impoverished as a result of the Grand Tour and the previous war that not even Catherine's Italian bankers would advance her another *écu*. There was only one entity in Europe wealthy enough to finance the military expenses of a kingdom the size of France: the Church. And there was only one individual in the realm with the authority to marshal those funds together quickly: the cardinal of Lorraine. "Her majesty knows that no one is better fitted to find means of raising money and that no one has more credit in the city of Paris," the envoy from Venice wrote of the cardinal of Lorraine. "For this reason he was recalled and entrusted with the burden of affairs."

So Catherine gritted her teeth, put a smile on her face, and invited her old adversary the cardinal, along with his bank balance, back to his former position of power on the royal council. With him came his tall, golden-haired, exceedingly handsome eighteen-year-old nephew Henri, the new duke of Guise.

Marguerite hadn't seen Henri in almost three years, not since she had acted opposite him in the opening ceremonies of the Grand Tour. If he had been impressive at fifteen, he was now downright irresistible. A soldier like his father, he had just returned from fighting the Turks in Vienna. He excelled at combat, and his reputation for athleticism preceded him to court. It was alleged that, to prepare himself for future skirmishes, he had once plunged into a river and swum across to the opposite bank—while wearing his chain mail.

His effect on the women of the court was electric. In an atmosphere that prized beauty and bearing above all, this Adonis—with his dangerous good looks, six-foot frame, and lordly manner—stood out. Nor was he impervious to female attention. On the contrary, he reveled in it. He was aware of his powers of attraction; when it came to romance, he confessed himself a "tyrant." Seduction, like other competitions, was a sport at which he was wildly successful, either "by love or by force."

It was inevitable that he and Marguerite would be drawn to each other. Even at fifteen, Catherine's youngest daughter was rapidly emerging as the acknowledged belle of the court. Her figure was filling out. Her grace on the dance floor was conspicuous. She was beginning to develop the sense of chic that would propel her to the upper echelons of fashionable society and maintain her ascendancy there for decades. And to all these natural attributes was added the incomparable advantage of pedigree: as a member of the royal family Margot offered a potential entrée to the throne. There would have had to be something seriously amiss for these two *not* to fall for each other.

As far as Marguerite could tell, the dashing Henri was a completely appropriate choice as a suitor. After all, her older sister Claude had married into the Guise family. And Henri's uncle, the cardinal of Lorraine, was being very helpful—he had, as requested, underwritten the cost of the imported Swiss troops. More than this, he was also taking an interest in and advising her older brother the duke of Anjou, who had reversed his religious orientation completely in his teens and was now as enthusiastic and intolerant a Catholic as he had once been a Huguenot. This confusing turnaround was no doubt the result of their mother's insistence on at least outwardly adhering to orthodox practices to ward off accusations of lax piety. "To keep up her [Catherine's] Interest among the *Catholicks,* and convince them of her Constancy to their Party, she went frequently with her Children to their publick Assemblies and Processions," the courtier Michel de Castelnau remembered in his memoirs. "This won the Hearts of the Clergy and Nobility as well as the People, and reduced the *Huguenots* almost to a State of Despair, especially when they saw the Cardinal *de Lorrain* gain Ground at court." The prince of Condé issued a statement that "the reason why the King's subjects cannot live in peace and liberty of conscience as he wants them to do, is the friendship between the Duke of Anjou and the Cardinal of Lorraine."

In the fall of 1567, convinced that it was only a matter of time before Spain and the French Catholics struck in concert, the Huguenots took the initiative and launched a surprise raid on the royal family. Their goal was to capture Charles IX and separate him from his counselors, particularly his mother and the cardinal of Lorraine.

The operation was planned for September 28, but the intrigue was betrayed to the court on the twenty-fifth. The royal family was at Meaux, about thirty-four miles east of Paris. At midnight on the twenty-fifth, Catherine sent urgently for the Swiss mercenaries, who arrived early the next morning. It was decided after some discussion to make a run for the capital. The court left in the dead of night, surrounded by the Swiss. The Huguenot army, taken by surprise, was not yet at full strength and numbered only six hundred or so light cavalry. They were equipped with neither heavy armor nor artillery and were unable to penetrate the ranks of the Swiss guard, who outnumbered the Protestants by a factor of ten and who marched in formation around their charges and burnished their pikes in tandem like a gigantic porcupine when challenged.

"I freely confess never to have seen a more disreputable *canaille* [band of hoi polloi]," the Venetian envoy, who made up one of the displaced royal party that memorable evening, reported of these unconventional warriors. "They looked like a lot of porters...but when they ranged in battle, they seemed to me to be other men. Thrice they turned and faced the enemy; and threw at them whatever came to hand, even bottles; and, lowering their pikes, they ran at them like mad dogs at full speed...yet no one outstripped his fellow; and they did it with such a show of readiness and desire for the fight, that the enemy dared not attack." After a few pro forma skirmishes, the Huguenot officers prudently decided that this might not, after all, be the best time to kidnap the king and retired from the field. The weary court reached the safety of Paris later that afternoon.

However, so agitated were the Protestants that even after the failure of this first attempt, they did not give up. Led by Coligny and the prince of Condé, the insurgents simply regrouped their forces and formulated a new plan—to cut off the supply routes to the capital and starve Paris. In a series of written communications addressed to Charles IX, the Huguenots justified their rebellion not only on the grounds that the Crown had made a "promise a long time ago to the King of Spain to seize the leaders of the religion and to exterminate all those who profess it" but also because the king's subjects were suffering from the deplorable effects of excessive debt and taxation "brought about by the greed and avarice of certain strangers, more particularly Italians, because of the credit and influence which they enjoy in this kingdom." In other words, it was all the queen mother's fault.

Catherine was livid. After all she had done for them! Where would they be without her and her Edict of Toleration? There were no good, law-abiding Huguenots: they were all "vermin!" The moderate chancellor L'Hôspital, upon whose advice Catherine had relied since she first seized the regency, was demoted on the spot and eventually forced out of the government altogether. In his place, the queen mother, determined to punish her former allies and dispense with the Protestant faction as a political force once and for all, substituted the cardinal of Lorraine and his extreme Catholic followers, and the kingdom found itself once again at war.

The royal army was mobilized, and a battle in November forced Coligny to retreat, but the Huguenots seized other towns across France. The handsome duke of Guise was sent to defend the eastern border, while at court Catherine, who had lost her commanding general in the November skirmish, used the vacancy as an excuse to promote her favorite son, Henri, duke of Anjou, to lieutenant-general, the highest military position in the realm, a preferment that effectively put a sixteen-year-old in charge of all the kingdom's armed forces.

Even among the most loving and well-adjusted siblings, family dynamics can sometimes be tricky. In the royal household, they were a blood sport. Charles IX was intensely envious of this appointment. As head of the royal army, his younger brother Henri was now in a position to win fame and cover himself with glory. Charles wanted to lead his own troops, but his mother wouldn't let him because of his poor health and because he was king. Having submitted to her will since childhood, he did not yet have the courage, even at seventeen, to override her decision, although he did marshal the presence of mind to object. "Young as I am, Madame, I feel that I am strong enough to bear my own sword, and if it were not so, would my brother, who is younger than I, be any more suitable?" he cried passionately.

His brother Henri, duke of Anjou, was not without his own demons. Two powerful factors shaped Henri's personality as he got older: the certainty that his elder brother was ill—and that if Charles died without issue, he, Henri, would be king—and the growing realization that his own sexual preference was in favor of men, perhaps not the optimal orientation for a devout Catholic living in the 1500s.* The psychological conflict engendered by these realities pushed Henri to emotional extremes that in turn influenced his behavior. He was aware of his mother's partiality and relied upon it; the two were very close. But he was also competitive with his older brother, the king, and jealous of Charles's superior social and political standing. This made him cunning and frequently cruel.

Although Henri reveled in his new title, being lieutenant-general meant frequent absences from the court, as he was now at least nominally responsible for military affairs and had to physically inspect the troops and help to organize sieges, battles, and the like. It worried Henri to be away too long. Not only did he fear what might be said about him, he was also concerned that Charles would get the upper hand while he was gone. Having learned from his early brush with abduction by the Guises to pay attention to court intrigue, the duke of Anjou was already an experienced political tactician at the time of his appointment, and he recognized the need for a highly placed covert agent to provide him with reliable

---

* The question of Henri's homosexuality is a matter of debate among Renaissance scholars. Some have recently suggested that there is not enough data to say definitively that the duke of Anjou engaged in sexual relations with men. I think their evidentiary standards are a little too rigorous. I'm with the late Dr. Louis Crompton, an academic pathfinder in the field of gay studies, who wrote: "Henry's stereotypical lifestyle, his fondness for group orgies with the mignons, his masochistic guilt, and the intensity of his emotional involvements with his handsome young followers, some of whom he addressed by feminine nicknames, all suggest some sexual involvement."

intelligence while he was away in the field. The problem was to find someone he could trust who could penetrate the most confidential circles and still not arouse suspicion. It would take him some time to settle on just the right intermediary. In the interim, he had a war to fight.

THE MILITARY CHALLENGE THAT confronted the novice lieutenant-general was daunting. The Huguenots were better prepared and, initially at least, better funded than the royal troops. This was because, as a result of the legalization of the reformed religion through the Edict of Toleration and the aggressive proselytizing of its ministers, the ranks of the Huguenot faithful had swelled over the years, particularly in western and southern France. Although Paris and the peasantry remained stalwartly orthodox, which ensured that the kingdom as a whole remained overwhelmingly Catholic, the Huguenots could now claim majorities in such important regional cities as La Rochelle and Orléans as well as pockets of control in Gascony, where Jeanne d'Albret ruled, and Provence. Even more significant, the movement now included members of the merchant class as well as skilled laborers, who were already organized into guilds. The guilds gave the Protestants the advantage in terms of money and coordination, and they were able to muster an army much more quickly than the Crown, which was so impoverished that even the financial wizardry of the cardinal of Lorraine was sorely tested. (In the end, Catherine had to fall back on the old-fashioned stratagem of pawning the crown jewels to her Italian bankers.)

The Huguenots also had the upper hand in terms of military leadership. Admiral Coligny was without question the most experienced and respected cavalry commander in the kingdom, and he and the prince of Condé made good use of their contacts abroad among other sympathetic Protestant countries, such as England, Germany, and the Netherlands, to round up additional support. Within three months of sixteen-year-old Henri's ascension to his post, he found himself facing a massive Huguenot army of some thirty thousand soldiers, including a significant contingent of German mercenaries who rivaled their pike-wielding Swiss counterparts in their reputation for fierceness.

Luckily for him, his mother was paying attention. Unnerved by the size and strength of the Protestant battalions and concerned that, for all her fond pride and faith in the abilities of her second son, he might not yet be *quite* up to the job she had so confidently assigned him, in March 1568, Catherine hastily intervened and arranged a peace. The Spanish ambassador threw up his hands and accused the queen mother of duplicity, upbraiding her for "really wanting what she said she didn't want," but in this case he was wrong. Fed up with their demands and ingratitude, Catherine wanted the Huguenots defeated and their leadership annihilated as much as the king of Spain did—probably more, as she took their betrayal as a personal insult. She just wanted better odds. The queen mother remembered how conveniently the duke of Guise had once been dispatched by an assassin's bullet and how much easier it had been for her after his demise. So she attempted to replicate this scenario by appearing to agree to a peace and even acceding to some of the Protestant demands. This in turn induced the Huguenot army to disperse, which was her real goal. Once the enemy troops were scattered and her son no longer had to face the uncertain prospect of a pitched battle, she surreptitiously put out a contract on the lives of the admiral, the prince of Condé, and as many of their supporters and family members as could be gunned down without too much trouble.

The problem with a conspiracy of this nature is that success is more or less predicated on absolute secrecy, and of course absolute secrecy is difficult to achieve when everybody is spying on everybody else. The Huguenots were informed of Catherine's plot so long in advance that they even had time to work out a fancy code phrase to warn the potential targets that the assassination attempts were about to be set in motion. And so, on August 23, 1568, when a messenger delivered a letter to the prince of Condé, who was staying in Noyers, about 150 miles southeast of Paris, that included the obscure but otherwise innocuous sentence "The stag is in the net, the hunt is ready," the prince understood that he did not have a moment to waste. Without another word, he picked up his family and all the other Protestants in the vicinity, and together they began a race across France to the safety of La Rochelle, a securely fortified city already under Huguenot dominion some three hundred miles away on the western coast of the kingdom. At the same time, the warning was delivered to Admiral Coligny and Jeanne d'Albret, and they, too, with all their families, servants, and supporters, dropped what they were doing and made a mad dash for the same stronghold. The Huguenot leadership was followed by the Huguenot rank and file; the Huguenot rank and file were followed by as many of the recently dispersed Huguenot troops as could be mustered at such short notice; and by year's end the Protestant army that had been disbanded by Catherine's sham truce was back at half strength. With some seventeen thousand Huguenot men-at-arms ready for action, the kingdom was once again at war, and a head-on battle between the Protestant and royalist combatants was inevitable.

But by this time Catherine had found an experienced general, Gaspard de Tavannes, to function as her son's military adviser and had so augmented the Crown's forces that Henri now found himself master of some twenty-eight thousand men. Moreover Tavannes, an excellent strategist, was able to anticipate the enemy's movements. In the hours just before dawn on the morning of March 13, 1569, he, the duke of Anjou, and the rest of the royal army caught the admiral and the prince of Condé and their troops by surprise near the town of Jarnac, about a hundred miles southeast of La Rochelle.

Both sides fought bravely. The Apollo–like duke of Guise, recalled from the eastern border, distinguished himself in an early skirmish and cut down an entire squadron of Protestant horsemen before they had a chance to catch up with the main body of cavalry. For their part, the Huguenots, confronted by a marked numerical superiority on the part of the Catholics, still chose to give battle. The prince of Condé led the charge from the center with Coligny anchoring to the left. "For Christ and country!" exhorted the prince, but despite his best efforts the line gave way. The admiral, understanding that defeat was imminent and hoping to fight another day, broke off and escaped with his men, but Condé was not so lucky. Finding himself surrounded, he dismounted and surrendered but, in a treacherous act highly reminiscent of the murder of the duke of Guise, was instead shot in the back by an unknown assailant, rumored to be either an Italian operating under Catherine's instructions or the duke of Anjou's personal captain of the guards. What is not in dispute is Henri's cool response to the assassination of his cousin, whose rank as the first prince of the blood was inferior only to his own: he had Condé's corpse slung over the back of a donkey like the meanest peasant and paraded through the streets of Jarnac, much to the delight of the conquering royalist troops.

The court was overjoyed at the news of the duke of Anjou's triumph. Finally, an outright military victory! The acknowledged head of the Huguenot faction slain, the insurgents in full retreat, and the opposition leadership in chaos and scrambling for mere survival. Understanding that he would never occupy a more estimable position relative to his brother the king, and wishing to milk the moment for all it was worth, Henri sent an envoy back to Paris from his base camp at Tours to summon his mother and the rest of the family to judge the results of his handiwork for themselves. "I leave to your own imagination to suggest to you the impression which such a message from a dearly beloved son made on the mind of a mother who doted on all her children, and was always ready to sacrifice her own repose, nay, even her life, for their happiness," Margot, who was included in this invitation, observed drolly. "She flew on the wings of maternal affection, and reached Tours in three days and a half."★

★ Marguerite's recollections of the timing of this meeting, written decades after the fact, appear to have been faulty. The court was at Metz, more than three hundred miles away, at the time of the battle at Jarnac, and Catherine was bedridden with fever; she remained there for at least a month. So it is likely this rendezvous did not occur until the beginning of June, when Margot had just turned sixteen.

It was during this visit that Marguerite was introduced to her family's delightful, all-consuming pastime of informing on one another. After a ceremonial presentation by the duke of Anjou at which he eloquently outlined the military victories already achieved under his leadership ("It is...impossible for me to describe in words the feelings of my mother on this occasion, who loved him above all her children," his sister noted of this address), Henri unexpectedly invited Margot for a private chat in the garden.

He began with flattery. "Dear sister, the nearness of blood, as well as our having been brought up together, naturally, as they ought, attach us to each other. You must already have discovered the partiality I have had for you above my brothers." This wasn't saying much, but it sounded good.

Having ingratiated himself, Henri then went on to elucidate the incomparable advantages his friendship could confer. "You know the high situation in which, by the favor of God and our good mother the Queen, I am here placed," he reminded his younger sibling. "You may be assured that, as you are the person in the world whom I love and esteem the most, you will always be a partaker of my advancement." Then he went in for the kill. "I know you are not wanting in wit and discretion," Henri continued agreeably, "and I am sensible you have it in your power to do me service with the Queen our mother, and preserve me in my present employments... Whilst I am away, the King my brother is with her, and has it in his power to insinuate himself into her good graces...The King my brother does not want for courage, and, though he now diverts himself with hunting, he may grow ambitious, and choose rather to chase men than beasts; in such a case I must resign to him my commission as his lieutenant. This would prove the greatest mortification that could happen to me." To prevent this calamity from occurring, Henri had determined to place "a confidential person about the Queen my mother, who shall always be ready to espouse and support my cause." There could be no one better suited to this happy employment, he went on, than his beloved sister Marguerite.

Margot was far too green to penetrate the underlying implications of this magnanimous offer. Dazzled by Henri's sudden attention, she saw not intrigue but entrance into the adult world of responsibility and trust. Her brother's rhetoric "was entirely a new kind of language to me," she remembered. "I had hitherto thought of nothing but amusements, of dancing, hunting, and the like diversions; nay, I had never yet discovered any inclination of setting myself off to advantage by dress, and exciting an admiration of my person and figure. I had no ambition of any kind." This is what came of having been shunted off to the nursery for all those years. But the prospect of being useful, of having something of actual importance to do, was irresistible. Her older brother Henri, *the lieutenant-general of the realm,* wanted her, Marguerite. He needed her! There could be no higher compliment. As he had intended, she rose instantly to the challenge. "I shall sacrifice all the pleasures in this world to my watchfulness for your service," she pledged in her enthusiasm. "You may perfectly rely on me, as there is no one that honors or regards you more than I do. Be well assured that I shall act for you with the Queen my mother as zealously as you would for yourself."

And so it was agreed between them that, for the first time in her life, Marguerite would wait upon her mother in her private chambers. "Be the first with her and the last to leave her," Henri, who knew his mother well, instructed his sister. "This will induce her to repose a confidence and open her mind to you." For his part, Henri promised to put in a good word for her to help ensure the success of their little enterprise. This he clearly did quickly, as no sooner had they returned from their tête-à-tête in the garden than Catherine pulled her daughter aside and, in another first in their relationship, offered Marguerite, who had been denied affection since her father's death and who consequently craved it above all else, the prospect of maternal love and intimacy. "Your brother has been relating the conversation you have had together; he considers you no longer as a child, neither shall I," the queen mother observed. "It will be a great comfort to me to converse with you as I would with your brother. For the future you will freely speak your mind, and have no apprehensions of taking too great a liberty, for it is what I wish."

The elation Margot felt at her mother's words was intense; it must have been like being wrapped in the luxurious warmth of a fur blanket after spending years shivering in the cold. "I felt a satisfaction and a joy which nothing before had ever caused me to feel," she related. "I now considered the pastimes of my childhood as vain amusements. I shunned the society of my former companions of the same age. I disliked dancing and hunting, which I thought beneath my attention."

But unbeknownst to the novice informant, she had been seduced into playing a game in which she held no cards. It has been insinuated by novelists and even some historians over the centuries that one or both of Marguerite's older brothers abused her sexually while she was still in her teens. Of this there is absolutely no evidence, and certainly the duke of Anjou's later obvious preference for men would seem to rule out an unconquerable passion for his sister. But from a psychological and—far darker and more damaging—an emotional point of view, the analogy holds. For with this corrosive offer and Margot's guileless concurrence Henri initiated his sister into the corrupt world of the Valois court and arranged, at least figuratively, for her to lose her innocence.

7

Fall from Grace

A prince is . . . esteemed when he is a true friend or a true enemy; when, that is, he declares himself without reserve in favor of someone against another. This policy is always more useful than remaining neutral.

—Niccolò Machiavelli, *The Prince*

FOR THE NEXT FOUR MONTHS, from June to October of 1569, Marguerite scrupulously upheld her end of the bargain she had entered into with her brother. As per his instructions, she was present at Catherine's rising and again at her retiring. She never missed a morning or evening. Why should she? It was the great pleasure of her life to win the approbation of her mother. "She did me the honor, sometimes, to hold me in conversation for two and three hours at a time," Margot remembered proudly. "God was so gracious with me that I gave her satisfaction; and she thought she could not sufficiently praise me to those ladies who were about her." Nor did Marguerite neglect to report the content of these discussions in detail to the absent lieutenant-general and to pursue his advancement at court as though it were her own. "I spoke of my brother's affairs to her, and he was constantly apprised by me of her sentiments and opinion; so that he had every reason to suppose I was firmly attached to his interest." Henri had chosen well: Margot made an admirable intelligence operative.

So when the royal army achieved yet another outstanding victory against the Huguenots on October 3, this time at Moncontour, in southwest France, about halfway between Angers and Poitiers, and the exultant lieutenant-general again summoned his family for a visit to applaud his prowess and bask in the glory of his triumph, Marguerite was only too thrilled to accompany her mother and the rest of the court to Henri's base camp, near Saint Jean d'Angély. She had every reason to believe that she would be greeted warmly by her brother and showered with words of praise and affection. She knew she had done well at the task he had set her, and she was genuinely delighted by his success and excited to share in the joy of it. She was therefore completely unprepared for the reception that awaited her.

She knew something was wrong the instant she saw him. "Upon our arrival... my mother began to open in my praise and express the attachment I had discovered for him," Margot recalled. "This was his reply, which he delivered with the utmost coldness: 'He was well pleased,' he said, 'to have succeeded in the request he had made to me; but that prudence directed us not to continue to make use of the same expedients, for what was profitable at one time might not be so another.'" Catherine was as confused by this statement as her daughter was. "She asked him why he made that observation," Marguerite continued. "This question afforded the opportunity he wished for, of relating a story he had fabricated, purposely to ruin me with her."

And then he hit her with it. "He began by observing... that I was grown very handsome and that M. de Guise wished to marry me; that his uncles, too, were very desirous of such a match; and, if I should entertain a like passion for him, there would be danger of my discovering to him all she [Catherine] said to me; that she well knew the ambition of that house, and how ready they were, on all occasions, to circumvent ours. It would, therefore, be proper that she should not, for the future, communicate any matter of State to me, but, by degrees, withdraw her confidence," Margot reported.

This was a serious accusation. Royal princesses were not supposed to go behind their mothers' backs and arrange marriages for themselves. Moreover, simply by giving voice to this allegation and speculating on the strength of Marguerite's supposed attachment to her suitor, Henri implied that some form of sexual impropriety had already been committed. This, of course, violated Catherine's strict moral code, which expressly forbade physical intimacy outside the bounds of wedlock unless it was done specifically in the queen mother's interests.

In vain did Marguerite protest—indeed insist upon—her innocence. "I did not omit to say everything to convince her [Catherine] of my entire ignorance of what my brother had told her," she remembered passionately. "I said it was a matter I had never heard mentioned before; and that, had I known it, I should certainly have made her immediately acquainted with it." Her words had no effect. Catherine turned on her instantly and "ordered me never to speak to her in my brother's presence. These words were like so many daggers plunged into my breast. In my disgrace, I experienced as much grief as I had before joy on being received into her favor and confidence."

Although for the rest of her life Margot would take Henri's accusations as a personal affront and her reputation would be smeared for centuries by the resulting scandal, in reality her brother's words had very little to do with her and everything to do with the duke of Guise. Because it seems overwhelmingly likely that at the time of this meeting, Marguerite *was* innocent of having conducted a clandestine love affair with the duke of Guise, or of having promised to marry him, for the simple reason that she hadn't seen him in more than a year—and certainly not since the previous interview with her brother, when Henri had placed so much trust in her. The duke of Guise's movements during the war are well documented: he'd been off fighting, first on the eastern front, then later with the royal army, since September of 1568. Even in the bawdy sixteenth century it was very difficult to conduct intimate relations if the two parties involved were separated by hundreds of miles.

The person who *had* seen quite a bit of the duke of Guise, especially over the previous few months, was Henri. Increased proximity had not endeared the lieutenant-general to his former schoolmate. The duke of Guise had not changed much in the decade following the colloquy of Poissy, when he'd tried to bully Henri into being tossed out the window to a waiting carriage and abducted. He was still the better athlete and swordsman, and his prerogative settled on his broad aristocratic shoulders like an exceptionally well-tempered suit of armor. Moreover, Guise's contempt for army discipline had led him to commit an unconscionable blunder that had severely weakened the royal forces: in June, operating independently and without bothering to check with his superiors, the headstrong duke had led a small division of cavalry and infantry across the river at La Roche-l'Abeille, in southern France, only to come face-to-face with four thousand Huguenot horsemen. The Catholics were thoroughly trounced, many of his men were lost, and the duke of Guise himself only just made it back to headquarters without being captured or killed. Henri was livid at his insolence, and even the chief royal military adviser, Gaspard de Tavannes, regarded the insubordinate commander with disgust. "Sir," said Tavannes icily to the shame-faced duke of Guise, "after doing what you have done, you ought never to have come back."

Ironically, if his military career had ended there, Marguerite would likely have been spared the humiliation that awaited her in October, but from July to September the duke of Guise redeemed himself utterly by almost single-handedly holding off Coligny and a much larger force of Huguenots at the siege of Poitiers. It was this action that set up the royalist victory at Moncontour, another battle at which Guise fought with conspicuous bravery and covered himself with glory despite being seriously wounded in the foot.

The only thing worse than an arrogant, insubordinate duke of Guise was an arrogant, victorious duke of Guise whose amazing exploits threatened to dwarf those of the lieutenant-general. Already competitive with his brother the king, Henri did not appreciate having to deal with the superior attitude and growing popularity of somebody who was supposed to be a humble vassal. He was therefore susceptible to giving a robust hearing to any allegation of malfeasance on the part of his rival, and in the wake of the duke of Guise's rise these were not slow in coming.

In her memoirs, Margot identifies the source of the rumor against her as Louis Béranger, seigneur du Guast, whom she contemptuously refers to simply as "Le Guast." Guast would evolve into a particular enemy of Marguerite's; she harbored a bitter (and highly deserved) resentment against him, so anything she writes about him has to be weighed carefully against this bias. But in this instance her instincts were probably correct, as circumstances clearly favor her conclusion.*

Guast was the first in a series of attractive, ambitious young noblemen surrounding the lieutenant-general whom the French court euphemistically referred to as "favorites." Unlike many of Henri's future minions, Guast came from an old and venerable family; his bloodline was unimpeachable, and he, too, knew how to foster an aura of hauteur. He was a captain in the royal guard and just old and sophisticated enough—twenty-five to Henri's nineteen—for his commander-in-chief to look up to him. Guast was eager to make his fortune and advance at court, and one way to do this was to make himself invaluable to the lieutenant-general. This was accomplished through flattery and the regular contribution of choice bits of information obtained through surreptitious channels.

The duke of Guise, who had no reason to dissemble, no doubt made Guast's job easy for him. The prospective suitor believed that

---

* Marguerite's principal French biographer, Eliane Viennot, puts forward the hypothesis that it was not Guast and Henri but Catherine alone, or Catherine in combination with Charles, who first saw what the Guises were up to and simply used Henri to confront Margot. But this gives the queen mother too much credit for subterfuge. Catherine reacted to problems as they appeared, and if she had suspected that her daughter was encouraging the duke of Guise she would have put a stop to it immediately. She certainly would not have spent four months confiding in Margot, as Henri had requested. And the idea that Charles would have noticed something that his mother didn't pick up on first (unless it involved hunting) is also highly unlikely. In fact, neither Catherine nor Charles had much occasion to think about the duke of Guise during the summer and early fall of 1569, but Henri and Guast did.

he boasted a suitably impressive list of nuptial credentials. He came from a historically illustrious family, and his uncle the cardinal of Lorraine was a member of the royal council and the most important churchman in France. The cardinal was intimately involved in the affairs of his nieces and nephews and was in the process of arranging a highly advantageous marriage between the duke of Guise's sister and a member of the extended Bourbon family. If his sister could marry so high, why could his uncle not then arrange for him to wed a member of the royal family?

If this thought had occurred to the duke of Guise it most certainly had already occurred to the politically adept and experienced cardinal as well. After the long dry period following his brother's assassination, the fortunes of the family were finally on their way up again. The cardinal of Lorraine remembered the heady days when his niece Mary Stuart had ascended, however briefly, to the throne of France. This flirtation between his nephew and the royal princess was to be encouraged. Adding to the logic of the alliance was the fortunate coincidence that the duke of Guise seemed genuinely to be in love with Margot, and she appeared not to be indifferent to him. Knowing the royal family to be strapped for cash, he was even willing to contribute two hundred thousand *livres* out of his own pocket as an extra incentive so that the young couple would have something to live on.

Still, however much he favored the plan, the cardinal was far too seasoned a courtier not to proceed with delicacy. He would never have approached Margot directly or allowed his nephew to do so. This was a matter for Catherine and the king. It had to be handled just right.

But young men in love are not always so circumspect. It is possible the duke of Guise was indiscreet. However the rumor came to the attention of the omnipresent Guast, the captain recognized a useful denunciation when he heard it. A love affair with the king's sister made for an effective weapon against the duke. Margot merely represented collateral damage.

But of course it didn't feel that way to her. It felt as though she had been unjustly attacked. And because the insinuation came from the adored Henri, she couldn't make Catherine believe her. There is nothing so hurtful as the realization that a parent loves one child more than another. "My brother's words had made the first impression; they were constantly present in her mind, and outweighed probability and truth," Marguerite reported bitterly of Catherine. "When I discovered this, I told her that I felt less uneasiness at being deprived of my happiness than I did joy when I had acquired it; my brother had taken it from me, as he had given it. He had given it without reason; he had taken it away without cause. He had praised me for discretion and prudence when I did not merit it, and he suspected my fidelity on grounds wholly imaginary and fictitious. I concluded with assuring her that I should never forget my brother's behavior on this occasion." Catherine was not accustomed to being spoken to in this manner, particularly by her daughter. "She flew into a passion and...from that hour she gradually withdrew her favor from me," observed Marguerite sadly.

Soon after the confrontation with her mother, Margot, who had worked herself into a state of exhaustion over these accusations, fell dangerously ill. As often happened during periods of warfare, a virulent strain of pestilence had broken out among the soldiery. The fever was usually fatal. Scores had already died from the infection, including the royal family's own doctors. This dreaded sickness now attacked Marguerite.

The behavior of her mother and brothers, especially Henri, during her prostration and subsequent convalescence is telling. They did everything but admit "We're sorry, we were wrong." Despite the risk of infection, Catherine nursed her daughter herself, and Henri took time away from his many military duties (the lieutenant-general was busy besieging the town of Saint Jean d'Angély) to hang around his sister's sickroom. "He came and sat at the foot of my bed from morning to night, and appeared as anxiously attentive as if we had been the most perfect friends," Margot complained, still stung by his treachery and not understanding that his behavior was indicative of someone who likely felt guilty and was trying to make up. Even her brother Charles, the king, who seems to have had no hand in the intrigue, demonstrated his sympathy by insisting on personally helping to carry her litter when she was moved to more comfortable quarters. (Charles well knew what it was like to have his mother and brother gang up on him. He also reveled in Henri's discomfort and loved to show off his own virtue as a point of contrast whenever his brother was discovered to be in the wrong.) In any event, neither the duke of Guise nor his uncle the cardinal of Lorraine was taken to task in the months following the lieutenant-general's revelation to Catherine. In fact the duke of Guise, laid up with a bad foot, was allowed to convalesce at court (which was moved to Angers as soon as Marguerite was well enough to travel), and the marriage of his sister to Louis de Bourbon was approved by Catherine and celebrated with great pomp on February 4, 1570.★

And this is when Marguerite's troubles began in earnest, because now she *was* in the duke of Guise's presence nearly every day—Henri made sure of it. After his initial efforts at reconciliation with his sister went unappreciated, the lieutenant-general shrugged his shoulders and reverted to his old plan of trying to discredit Guise. Margot's bedridden presence made a highly convenient lure; it was only a matter of setting the trap. Henri "came daily to see me, and as constantly brought M. de Guise into my chamber with him," Marguerite reported. "He pretended the sincerest regard for De Guise, and, to make him believe it, would take frequent opportunities of embracing him, crying out at the same time, 'Would to God you were my brother!' This he often put in practice before me, which M. de Guise seemed not to comprehend."

★ Not to be confused with Louis de Bourbon, the deceased prince of Condé. This Louis de Bourbon was the duke of Montpensier. Louis was, unfortunately, one of those names (like Henri) much favored by the French aristocracy. The Bourbons were members of a large dynasty with many branches and an extremely complicated political history.

Not only the duke of Guise but also the entire court took the bait. By the spring of 1570, the Spanish envoy reported to Philip II that "There is nothing talked of publicly in France but the marriage of Madame Marguerite with the Duke of Guise." The members of the Flying Squadron, always ready to egg on a grand passion, particularly one involving two such celebrated participants, did all they could to encourage the lovers. This worried the cardinal of Lorraine, who knew better than to flaunt a dalliance in the absence of an ironclad marriage contract approved by the queen mother. "The ladies at court are real stirrers and mixers," he complained in a letter to the duke of Guise's mother. "The poor little [Marguerite] and your son are riding luck in such a way that it is very bad." Only Margot seems to have understood (at least in hindsight) that Henri was playing a game. But she'd learned from her previous experience that her mother was unlikely to take her side against her brother, and so she "did not dare to reproach him with his hypocrisy."

More than this, she knew very well that her mother wished to marry her to Don Sebastian, the sixteen-year-old king of Portugal, with whose diplomatic representative Catherine was in active negotiation. This was not an attractive prospect. Reports from the French ambassador at the Spanish court (Philip II would have to approve the alliance) indicated that Don Sebastian was a physically immature religious ascetic who had been taught to disdain and eschew women by his monastic tutors. The Portuguese king's sexual orientation was apparently so ambivalent that no one was certain whether he was "of use to have children," as Catherine's envoy so delicately put it.

That Marguerite was still single at this late date was unusual. Both her sisters had been married as soon as they reached thirteen, the age of consent. The blame for Margot's uncertain matrimonial future rests entirely with her mother. Catherine was unwavering in her desire that all her children marry royalty. In her mind, either Henri or François would certainly wed Elizabeth I and become king of England, and Margot would marry Don Sebastian (Don Carlos,

Philip II's son, being out of the running, having unfortunately expired two years previously). Nothing anyone said dissuaded her; the same French diplomat stationed in Madrid who had described Don Sebastian tried as hard as he could to break through the queen mother's carefully constructed fictions. "I tell you clearly what I think," he wrote to Catherine of Philip II and the Spanish and Portuguese courts. "It is my opinion that there is nothing in these people here except bad will... They reckon that your civil war keeps them at peace and the impoverishment of your kingdom in men and in money is the strengthening of theirs." Margot seconded this opinion about Philip II's open hostility to her mother. "The King of Spain was using his utmost endeavors to break off the match with Portugal," she remembered. Still Catherine persevered and made it a point of honor with Charles that his sister should marry the king of Portugal.

This, then, was the bleak future that Marguerite contemplated as she approached her seventeenth birthday. A passionate spirit, yearning for romance, ripe with emotions and hormones, and just coming into her own as a great beauty, destined at best to be the unloved, unwanted wife of an androgynous monk-king in faraway Portugal. Her desperation was palpable. And there beside her at court, hoodwinked into believing that he had her powerful brother's support and consequently throwing himself at her feet every day, was the tall, strong, definitely heterosexual duke of Guise, the object of her desire, holding out the irresistible prospect of an alternate universe, where she could marry the man she loved and stay in familiar France...*

Matters came to a head in June of 1570, when Guast persuaded a sympathetic lady-in-waiting, who had been helping the princess's romance along by offering her services as a conduit for clandestine

---

* There is no way to know for certain just how intimate the relationship between Margot and the duke of Guise became during the late spring and early summer of 1570. It is assumed that they were lovers. But it should also be noted that after the rumor of this affair was reported at the Portuguese court, Don Sebastian sent a spy into France to check on Marguerite's behavior, and the agent found no evidence at all of indecorous conduct or sexual impropriety.

love letters, to relinquish a private note from Marguerite meant for the duke of Guise. Guast lost no time in presenting this incriminating missive to Henri, who bade him pass it along to Catherine, who in turn shared it with her eldest son, Charles, the king.

Charles was not in a cheerful frame of mind, having had a particularly infelicitous past few months. After the royalist triumph at Moncontour the year before, the veteran general Gaspard de Tavannes had counseled that rather than pursue what was left of the enemy army, peace terms highly favorable to the Catholics should instead be imposed on what remained of the Huguenot leadership. "To engage in battle with these people and risk all is not to combat your true enemies, who, once defeated, will call on the princes of the German league aroused by their loss to have a new army in France tomorrow, while a great part of your principal captains will have been killed," he pointed out. "I will never be of a mind to gamble all of the Kingdom on the fortune of a single battle."

But Charles, who could no longer bear his younger brother's success, had rejected this sound advice and instead ordered that the nearby town of Saint Jean d'Angély, where some of the retreating Huguenot troops had taken shelter, be besieged. He had even defied his mother and stayed to supervise the offensive himself, relegating Henri to a secondary position. Unfortunately for Charles, the siege was spectacularly unsuccessful. The royal army, unable to breach the walls, was forced to camp outside in the cold mud of November. The fever that had attacked Margot spread rapidly under the wretched conditions and carried off a large percentage of Charles's soldiers. Many of those not felled by disease chose to desert instead. By December there were not enough men left to fight off a squadron of cavalry, let alone take a town, and the king was compelled to abandon the endeavor.

Adding to Charles's discomfiture was the fact that his failure at Saint Jean d'Angély had allowed Admiral Coligny, who was not among those who had taken refuge in the town, time to regroup his forces. The admiral then took this small but highly effective squadron (supplemented by an experienced corps of German cavalry, just as Tavannes had predicted) on a rampage through southern France, attacking all the principal Catholic cities, including Toulouse, Carcassonne, Montpellier, and Nîmes. It is astonishing how much damage the admiral achieved with this guerrilla operation; it turned the momentum of the conflict completely back in favor of the Huguenots. Having spent all his money on the fruitless siege, Charles had been unable to mount much of a counterattack, and anyway it was very difficult to catch Coligny, whose horsemen and infantry were so motivated that they could travel "eight or ten good leagues through mountains where artillery can scarce go," as a Catholic commander complained in a letter to Catherine. So in a mere eight months, under his personal supervision, Charles had managed to squander all the political and military advantages of his brother's great victory to the point where it was now likely that he would have to make peace with the Huguenots *on their terms*. This sort of setback would likely put anyone in a bad mood.

And then he discovered that his golden younger brother had been right all along about Marguerite, whose side he had initially taken, and that he was the one who had been duped. According to the Spanish ambassador, who reported on the incident to Philip II in a letter of June 13, 1570, Charles worked himself up into a rage and, still in his pajamas, burst in on his mother at five o'clock in the morning, bellowing for his sister. Margot was awakened and sent for, and when she arrived at Catherine's room a courtier was posted outside the door so the family could have some privacy. Then Charles and Catherine together let off steam and corrected Marguerite's behavior by beating her so severely that it took nearly an hour after they had finished for the queen mother to calm her daughter down and fix her appearance, as Margot's clothes had been shredded where they pummeled and scratched at her.

Violence against women was, unfortunately, extremely common in the Middle Ages and the Renaissance. A woman was considered the property of her husband, her father, or her brother, and they could do what they liked with her.* What was unusual was to have one's mother participate in a free-for-all of this nature. Charles is frequently indicted, both by contemporaries and historians, as being subject to uncontrollable fits of rage, giving rise to speculation that the king was unstable. But Margot's experience indicates that it is possible that Charles's tantrums were evidence not of mental illness but rather of accepted behavior, as Catherine conducted herself, at least in this instance, with a similar lack of restraint.

Again, poor Marguerite represented merely an easy stand-in for her mother's real frustration, which was her inability to control events to her satisfaction. Even if she believed that the duke of Guise had deflowered her daughter, Catherine did not dare openly break with the Guises at this time. The Crown was in the process of putting a new army into the field to combat Coligny, and of course the cardinal of Lorraine's financial acumen, not to mention his and the duke's many Catholic supporters, were integral to this effort. Hence the assault on the helpless Marguerite rather than on her presumed seducer.

Accordingly, the Guises remained unmolested, and the royal army duly took the field. The Catholic force, which outnumbered the opposing Huguenot militia by a factor of two to one, met Coligny in the small town of Arnay-le-Duc, in Burgundy, just southwest of Dijon, on June 26 and was beaten back by the admiral's superior tactics. Catherine had no choice but to sue for peace. On August 8, 1570, Charles signed the Peace of Saint-Germain, which not only reaffirmed the old Edict of Toleration but also granted the Protestants new rights of worship as well as outright possession of a number of important French cities, one of which was La Rochelle. "We defeat them again and again...but the edicts are always to their advantage," a highly placed Catholic nobleman complained bitterly after the terms were made public. "We win by arms and they by these devilish writings."

---

* It is part of the secret of Elizabeth I's astonishingly long and successful reign that she was unburdened by male relatives. Marguerite was not so lucky.

This armistice marked not only the cessation of open hostilities but the fall of the Guises as well. Within a week of the signing of the peace agreement, Catherine accosted the cardinal of Lorraine, whose money and support she no longer needed, in his bedroom in Paris, where he was recovering from a fever, and gave the venerable churchman a lacerating tongue-lashing for promoting a marriage between his nephew and her daughter behind her back. That was the end of the cardinal's influence at court. And very soon after this, the duke of Guise, who for all his good looks and undeniable courage seems not to have been particularly bright, was discredited and banished from Paris after making the mistake of approaching the king in a friendly way at an evening reception. "I no longer have need of your service," snarled Charles, thereby unwittingly fulfilling his detested younger brother Henri's original objective.

As for Marguerite, the brutality her mother and older brothers displayed in this affair stripped her of any remaining illusions she might have entertained about her standing within the family. She was sufficiently intimidated that she seemed almost in fear for her life. In the weeks before the duke of Guise's ultimate banishment, she swore to her mother, "Not a single person of the Guises ever mentioned a word to me on the subject [of marriage]" and begged her to "forward this match with the King of Portugal, and I would convince her of my obedience to her commands." But these measures failed to appease Catherine. "Every day some new matter was reported to incense her against me," Margot despaired. "In short, I was constantly receiving some fresh mortification, so that I hardly passed a day in quiet."

Eventually, pushed to extremity, she understood that she would never be safe as long as the duke of Guise remained unattached and appealed to her sister Claude, who had married into the Guise family, to compel the duke to wed one of his old girlfriends. "I resolved to write to my sister, Madame de Lorraine, who had a great influence in the House of Porcian, begging her to use her endeavors to withdraw M. de Guise from Court, and make him conclude his match with the Princess [of Porcian, a minor independent duchy], laying open to her the plot which had been concerted to ruin the Guises and me," Margot reported. Appalled by her younger sister's letter, kindhearted Claude came hurriedly to the rescue. "She [Claude] readily saw through it, came immediately to Court, and concluded the match, which delivered me from the aspersions cast on my character, and convinced the Queen my mother that what I had told her was the real truth," Marguerite pronounced with some relief.

Although the duke of Guise was apparently none too pleased with this outcome — he sneered to his family that they were making him marry a "negress," most likely a reference to his fiancée's Protestantism — he nonetheless bowed to pressure, and the wedding was hurriedly arranged for the end of September. (Just to make sure the duke didn't wriggle out of it, Charles provided the bride's dowry of one hundred thousand *livres* out of the royal treasury.) It is a measure of just how far the Guise family fortunes had fallen that less than six weeks after the August signing of the Peace of Saint-Germain the cardinal of Lorraine, the recognized head of the Catholic party in France, was forced to stand witness at the elaborate Parisian nuptial ceremony that united his nephew to a gentlewoman of the reformed religion.

The royal family was naturally in attendance at the wedding. It must have been wrenching for Marguerite to stand and observe impassively as her poignant first love was pledged to another and to hear her brother Henri, who had so callously used her for his own purposes, threaten to have the duke of Guise stabbed through the heart if after his marriage he ever dared look at his sister again. But for all the bitterness, the lessons of this experience were extremely useful. They drilled into Margot the urgency of being on her guard at an early age, and they honed the skills she would need to exist in a family as duplicitous and dangerous as hers.

And this was fortunate indeed, because after this events spiraled out of control with such ferocity that it was going to take everything she had simply to survive.

8

The Marriage Trap

*One ought never to allow a disorder to take place in order
to avoid war, for war is not thereby avoided, but only deferred
to your disadvantage.*

—Niccolò Machiavelli, *The Prince*

WHATEVER RELIEF FROM FAMILY PRESSURE Margot experienced as a
result of the wedding of the duke of Guise was short-lived, as there
still remained the question of her own continuing eligibility. It
wasn't just Marguerite: all Catherine's children were growing older,
and arranging prestigious matches for her offspring was uppermost
in the queen mother's mind. In November, she finally managed to
marry Charles to the Holy Roman Emperor's second daughter, an
event that was marred only slightly by the fact that Philip II once
again bested her by wedding the emperor's much more desirable
eldest daughter, who had been originally pledged to the king of
France. By deliberately stealing Charles's intended, Philip II doubly
managed to insult the French: he both very publicly rejected the
idea of uniting himself to Marguerite or allowing the king of Portugal to espouse her while also demonstrating his superior appeal
and political clout.

Catherine had no better luck furthering her designs to see her
adored Henri wed to the queen of England. To her great dismay,
the lieutenant-general brusquely rejected the proffered bride on the

grounds that Elizabeth I was a Protestant. The queen mother was eventually forced to substitute his younger brother, François, duke of Alençon, as a candidate. (Sixteen-year-old François "will not show himself so scrupulous in the matter of religion," Catherine wrote soothingly to thirty-eight-year-old Elizabeth.) But Sir Francis Walsingham, the English ambassador to France, did not hold out much hope for the success of this latest stratagem. "To be plain," Walsingham observed in a report to his government, "the only thing that I fear in this match is the consideration of the delicacy of her majesty's eye and of the hard favor [ugliness] of the gentleman besides his disfigurement with the small pox: which if she should see with her eye, I misdoubt much would withdraw her liking to proceed."

Catherine was not the only marriage broker to cast an appraising glance on the throne of England. From his home base in La Rochelle (by that time officially recognized as the property of the Huguenots, thanks to the Peace of Saint-Germain), Admiral Coligny was making discreet inquiries through Protestant ambassadors at the English court as to whether Elizabeth might consider *his* candidate for the future king of England: Jeanne d'Albret's son, seventeen-year-old Henry of Navarre.

A tenuous peace had followed the signing of the Peace of Saint-Germain, and Coligny had used this respite to formulate a course of action designed to promote stability within the realm and allow the kingdom of France time to recover from the destruction wreaked upon the civilian population by the continuing Wars of Religion. For all his militarism, at heart the admiral was a patriot who did not relish his role as an antagonist within his own country. Coligny *wanted* to serve the king, he just didn't think he should have to give up his faith to do so.

After some consideration, based upon his long years of experience in government and the army, the admiral concluded that the problem was not with the fight but with the battlefield. France had been materially weakened by the internal religious conflict. Good men were lost on both sides, crops were destroyed, and the kingdom was seriously in debt. Coligny's idea was to turn the focus of hostilities outward and make it a war, not of Frenchman against Frenchman but of France against Spain. He proposed moving the field of operation out of the kingdom altogether. The Protestants of the Netherlands were already rebelling against their Catholic overlord, Philip II. Why not intervene on the side of his coreligionists to the north and fight this out in the Spanish empire? If the Protestants won with French help, then the Netherlands would become part of France, and its people would become subjects of the French king. This would give everyone in France a real boost in morale when they needed it most and might just unite the religions sufficiently for them to learn to live in peace. After all, even French Catholics would enjoy taking territory away from the condescending Spanish. And if the Protestants in the Netherlands lost, well, at least it would be Philip II who would be materially weakened for a change and who would have to deal with the surly population, the destruction, the lost crops, and the drain on the royal treasury. Not that Coligny was intending to lose.

Spain being the richest and most powerful kingdom in Europe, the admiral conceded that it wouldn't hurt to go into the fight with the support of a couple of Protestant allies — such as England and Germany, for example — as a means of improving the chances for success. Elizabeth I didn't commonly like to send cavalry, but she could usually be talked into providing money. And Coligny knew that the queen of England would be less suspicious of France's motives and more likely to support the French effort if her future husband were helping to lead the charge. Hence the inclusion of Henry of Navarre's name in the roster of suitors vying for Elizabeth's hand.

The discovery that the admiral was negotiating independently with the English government (and promoting policies contrary to her own!) was highly unpleasant to Catherine. Henry of Navarre, while not classically handsome, was good-looking enough in his own way and certainly more attractive than poor stunted, pock-marked François. Moreover, he boasted the distinct advantage of championing the same religion as the queen of England and the majority of her subjects and was already earning a name for himself as a soldier. Coligny had taken both Henry and his cousin the new prince of Condé (son of the deceased prince of Condé) on his recent offensive through southern France, and both young men were advancing in the military arts under his tutelage. When his mother died, Henry would be a king in his own right—true, it was only of tiny Navarre, a vassal state to France, but Elizabeth might look with favor on this, as it meant that if she married him he could retain his rank and still have no problem taking up residence in England.★

The idea that fickle Antoine's son might become king of England in preference to one of her own brood was anathema to Catherine. Even worse, she could not forcibly prevent Coligny from treating separately with the English. The Huguenots were so impregnable at La Rochelle that they could operate virtually as a shadow government. The port city was one of the most well fortified in France. It was protected by water on three sides—the harbor from the sea to the south, which assured diplomatic access to England and the Netherlands as well as a valuable supply route in case of siege, and marshland to the east and west. La Rochelle's northern aspect, the only direction by which it could be accessed by land, was guarded by a series of strong walls and towers upon which the Huguenots had thought to install state-of-the-art artillery. So safeguarded were Coligny and his supporters that it was doubtful that even an army could dislodge them—not that Catherine had any money left to raise one. There was only one way for the queen mother to stop the admiral, and that was to co-opt him.

And so Catherine gritted her teeth once again and initiated a policy of conciliation toward Coligny and his abettor, the coleader

---

★ It is fascinating to think of how history would have been changed if Elizabeth I had agreed to this marriage.

La Rochelle During the Period of Huguenot Possession

of the Huguenot movement, Jeanne d'Albret. As early as January 1571, she sent warm family greetings to Jeanne, explaining that "the King, my son, [intends] to embrace the affairs of the Prince of Navarre [Henry], whom the King and I infinitely desire to see here, with you." But Jeanne, who had experience with the queen mother's hospitality, which in the past had tended to turn into house arrest, demurred. Catherine's next move was to invite Coligny to visit the court at Blois to discuss areas of mutual interest. To ensure that her advances were taken seriously, the queen mother dangled the prize of an alliance between the Huguenots and the royal family by reviving the idea of marrying Marguerite to Henry of Navarre, thereby conveniently removing this potentially damaging suitor from the list of those pursuing Elizabeth. She also hinted that Coligny, whose estates had been confiscated as a result of his opposition to the Crown, might have his property returned to him, in addition to other lucrative forms of compensation, if he would agree to become reconciled to the royal family.

The admiral was perfectly happy to wed Henry of Navarre to Marguerite in order to make way for a marital alliance between Catherine's son and the queen of England. What he really wanted was to move the war of religion out of France and into the Netherlands with English support, and this would have been achieved by either betrothal, as Elizabeth would be equally reassured of the good faith of the French if she married a member of the royal family. He knew he chanced arrest, or even possibly assassination, if he accepted the invitation to court, but he was so convinced that his plan would work that he decided to take the risk. "Better to die by a bold stroke than to live a hundred years in fear," he affirmed to those of his supporters who warned him against trusting the queen mother's benevolence.

And he had another reason for going: despite all Catherine's power, Coligny understood that ultimately he held the advantage over her. Not because of his military successes or the number of his cavalry or the unshakable resolve of the Huguenot party—these factors were mutable and subject to outside forces. But the admiral recognized that there was one point on which Catherine was vulnerable, although, after so many years as head of state, she did not yet know it. Her son Charles IX had finally reached manhood.

It was, after all, Charles, not his mother, who was king.

CHARLES IX WAS TWENTY-ONE years old when Admiral Coligny accepted the invitation to court and rode into Blois on September 12, 1571. The king was by this time a married man who also kept a Protestant mistress by whom he would soon father an illegitimate son. Despite his poor health, he was a tireless hunter and sportsman whose one overriding desire was to distinguish himself in battle.

Charles was not a scholar but nor was he intellectually impaired; he was certainly capable of governing. The problem was, his mother wouldn't let him. He wasn't even permitted to fire his own servants. "His chief attendant, the Count de Retz (given to him much earlier by his mother), is an Italian," the Spanish ambassador observed.* "And I know that he has said, 'If I could once see myself free from that dog I would never allow another Italian in my house.'" Charles was also tortured by jealousy of his brother Henri and Catherine's obvious preference for him. "My mother loves him [Henri] so much that she steals the honor due to me for him," he sniffed. "I wish that we might take it in turn to reign, or at least that I might have his place for a half-year."

Then Coligny and his exciting Netherlands idea turned up at court.

The admiral could not have dreamed up a project more enticing to his young sovereign than the plan he laid out before him in all its vivid detail over the course of the next five months. Here was a chance for Charles to prove himself a true king, to take charge, to demonstrate his prowess and bravery, and under Coligny's tutelage to win a great battle and achieve the glory for which his ancestors were renowned. The admiral "is to be found each day at the rising of the King, as well as when he dines and sups," an eyewitness reported. "At all hours he is close to his chair, and with the same freedom as those who never left the court." For his part, Coligny, who had experience mentoring fatherless young men, including, just recently, Henry of Navarre and the prince of Condé, understood exactly what Charles needed: a strong male presence to instill in the fledgling monarch the values and courage necessary to rebel against his mother's will. It was Dad against Mom. Charles even began to call the admiral *mon père.*

It took some time, however, for Catherine, who was intent on persuading a reluctant Jeanne d'Albret to approve the engagement

---

* Actually, he was the duke of Retz by his marriage to the duchess of Retz in 1565, but these titles were often used interchangeably.

of her son to Marguerite (and so prevent him from pursuing Elizabeth I), to understand this. At first Catherine considered Coligny an ally. She believed that she had bought his support for her plan by bribing him, especially as he had not come cheaply. The admiral walked away from his visit to court with an outright cash bequest of one hundred thousand *livres* in his pocket. His forfeited estates were returned to him, and he also resumed his old place on the royal council. Under the circumstances, Catherine felt she could ask him to use his friendship with Henry's mother to reassure her of the Crown's good intentions. "We are too old, you and I, to deceive each other," the queen mother told the admiral. "Can she [Jeanne d'Albret] believe that the King would seek an alliance with her son in order to do away with her?"

To keep the pressure on Jeanne, Catherine wrote repeatedly requesting the queen of Navarre's presence, and that of her son, at court, making sure to stress that her motives were benign. Jeanne raised an eyebrow at this approach. "I cannot imagine why you should find it necessary to say that you want to see me and my children, but not in order to do us harm," the queen of Navarre shot back with withering sarcasm. "Forgive me if I laugh when I read these letters, for you are allaying a fear I have never had. I have never thought that you fed on little children, as they say."

Eighteen-year-old Marguerite, the prospective bride, followed the course of these negotiations with a sinking heart. To the outside world, the union with her cousin was portrayed as a healing event, a way to bring the two religions together amicably after the horrors inflicted by the prolonged civil war. The alliance "is a resolution I have taken with such careful consideration that I expect from it not only the peace and welfare of my kingdom...but also of Christendom in general," Charles boasted to the papacy. "The Prince [Henry] is so young and so favored by inheritance that it should not be too hard to lead him in the path His Holiness desires, as was the case with his late father [the ever-wavering Antoine]." Through Coligny, the Huguenots were made to understand that the marriage of

Henry of Navarre and the king's sister was a symbol of Charles's military commitment to the Protestants of the Netherlands. "Upon the success of the Navarre marriage depends the enterprise of Flanders," the English ambassador Walsingham reported flatly to his government.

But Marguerite, once again the pawn of her family's schemes, knew better. The marriage would not bring happiness and prosperity to the kingdom; it would only bring misery to her. Henry would never convert to Catholicism; it was she who would be expected to practice her beliefs in secret or, worse, give way altogether and become a Huguenot. This she refused to do. Her religion was very important to her. "A marriage was projected betwixt the Prince of Navarre...and me," Marguerite remembered. "The Queen sent for me to attend her...she was desirous to learn my sentiments upon it." For a faithful daughter of the Church such as Marguerite this was the equivalent of being asked how she felt about being consigned for eternity to the fires of hell. But having so recently endured the consequences of her mother's displeasure, Margot had no wish to repeat the experience. The princess knew better than to express a preference. "I answered that my choice was governed by her pleasure," she replied, tight-lipped, "and that I only begged her not to forget that I was a good Catholic."

This was precisely the excuse that her brother Henri had used to shun a union with Elizabeth I, a rejection that had caused Catherine no little embarrassment in addition to potentially costing the royal family of France the kingship of England. The lieutenant-general had informed his mother loftily that "he would be damned unless he could have his mass, and that he would not be content with the permission to have it privately in a chapel, for he was very devout and fasted...much in Lent." Catherine had relented and let him have his way, but in Marguerite's case the queen mother paid no attention. Margot was not Henri.

Catherine was of course aware that Coligny wished Charles to intervene in the Netherlands against Spain. By late fall everyone at court knew it. Even the Spanish ambassador was in on the secret. "It is perfectly well understood that the Admiral sleeps not, and that in the end every design will be turned against the states of the Catholic King [Philip II]," he warned in a letter of November 16, 1571, to his sovereign. But the queen mother underestimated Coligny's influence over the king; she thought she could control Charles as she always had. She had no idea how far the plan had progressed until the Spanish envoy pointed out to her that her son was withholding information from her about the Netherlands expedition because "the Admiral told him very politely that they were not questions to be discussed with women and clerks. When the Queen Mother heard of this, she was on very bad terms with the said Admiral, as was also Anjou [Henri]." The ambassador from Venice agreed with this assessment. "The war would maintain his [Coligny's] authority, power, and supremacy, because none could lead it better than he and the war would let him assure the fortune of all of his party," he reported shrewdly. "On the other hand, if the war were not waged, he must leave the court considering that he would not be able to hold his head up against his enemies and above all against the Queen and Monseigneur [Henri] who hated him to the death."

Catherine opposed Coligny's Netherlands offensive on two counts: she feared Spanish retaliation and she dreaded losing power, and these were the two most likely outcomes of the admiral's initiative. For if the French won, Charles would become even closer to his Huguenot mentor, and his mother's role in government would be severely curtailed, if not extinguished altogether. And if Charles and Coligny lost, the Catholics would blame her as well as her son and band together with Philip II to seek her removal. Already the duke of Guise, who nurtured a profound grudge against the admiral (who, he was convinced, had murdered his father and gotten away with it) and was consequently appalled at his renewed influence at court, was stirring up trouble. "In Paris there are a growing number of gentlemen friends of the lords of Guise, and they have rented rooms in various quarters, plotting nightly something between them…and that among the plans they have one will go and kill the admiral in his house," reported the governor of the city toward the end of December.

A few weeks later, in January of 1572, the duke of Guise, intent on seeking justice either in the form of a private duel with Coligny or, failing that satisfaction, a court of law, entered the capital accompanied by an entourage of five hundred soldiers. Although he eventually backed down, this show of force delighted the city's Catholic majority, with whom the handsome duke (in contrast to Charles and Catherine) was immensely popular. Emboldened, a celebrated priest gave a rousing sermon at Notre-Dame that Easter, during which he proclaimed that "if the king ordered the Admiral killed, it would be wicked not to kill him."

But Catherine could not afford to have the admiral killed—at least not yet—because if she did so she knew she would forfeit her much-desired goal of wedding Henry of Navarre to Marguerite. Jeanne d'Albret would never agree to the alliance if Coligny was assassinated or even removed from power. The Huguenots would have gone right back to Elizabeth I, and that would have been the end of poor little François's chances. As it was, it had taken the queen mother nearly a year to coax Jeanne to court to discuss the matter. The queen of Navarre finally gave in and came to Blois in February 1572. She brought her thirteen-year-old daughter with her, but, significantly, left her son behind; she was still highly suspicious of Catherine's motives and wished to interview her prospective daughter-in-law before approving the final terms of the marriage.

If Jeanne was hoping to convince Marguerite to convert, or even have a genuine conversation with her, she was destined to be disappointed. Margot was rigidly correct throughout the course of her visit, having no doubt been threatened if her behavior or attitude was found to be lacking. The queen of Navarre wrote a series of letters home to her son chronicling the negotiations for the marriage that evidence her ever-increasing frustration with the royal family's obvious dissembling. "Madame [Marguerite] has paid me great honor...assuring me that she favors your suit," Jeanne wrote at first. "Given her influence with the King and her mother...if she embraces the Religion, we can count ourselves the luckiest [persons] in the world, and not only our family but the whole kingdom of France. But if, with her caution and judgment, she is determined to stick stubbornly to her religion—as I am told—I fear this marriage will be the ruin...of our friends and domains, and such an aid to the Papists...that we and all the churches of France will be destroyed."

Within a few short weeks this less-than-optimistic attitude had descended into outright gloom: "I am being obliged to negotiate quite contrary to my hopes—and to their promises," Jeanne wrote grimly. "I am not free to talk with either the King or Madame, only with the Queen Mother, who goads me...Monsieur [Henri] tries to get around me in private with a mixture of mockery and deceit; you know how he is. As for Madame [Marguerite], I only see her in the Queen's quarters, whence she never stirs except at hours impossible for me to visit her."

Then a little later: "My son, since writing this letter, I have told Madame the contents of yours to her...she replied that when these negotiations began we well knew that she was devout in her religion. I told her that those who made the first overtures to us represented the matter very differently, giving the impression that religion would be no problem as she had already shown some inclination toward ours, and that, had this not been so, I would not have proceeded thus far...I think she says what she is told to say. I also believe that what we were told—about her alleged inclination to our religion—was a trap for us...Last evening I asked whether she had a message for you. At first she said nothing, then, when I pressed her, admitted, 'I can send nothing without permission.'" Her prospective mother-in-law was correct in assuming that Marguerite had been rigorously coached; months before Jeanne's visit, a Florentine envoy reported that "the Queen of Navarre wishes to examine and tempt Madame...but Her Highness [Margot], already warned of the very words that will be used, will answer in a certain way."

But Catherine would brook no dissent; she steamrolled over every difficulty and objection and was perfectly willing to use threats to get her way. The queen of Navarre was made to understand that if she did not approve the marriage of her son, Catherine would have Henry declared illegitimate by the pope and written out of the French succession. At the end of March 1572, Jeanne finally bowed to pressure and agreed to the alliance.

The Florentine ambassador recounted the final encounter between Jeanne and Marguerite. The strain on the princess was obvious. There was no going back. Catherine and Jeanne had come to terms. The marriage would take place. Margot knew she had to yield to her family's will, but she also refused to dissemble. She had to find an honorable way to serve as queen to a Huguenot husband and kingdom and yet save her soul. Her future mother-in-law continued to thrust the knife in deeper by her unrelenting insistence that her son's fiancée convert. "Two days ago," the Italian envoy reported, "*Navarra* [Jeanne] said to [Marguerite] that, since the marriage could from now on be considered a *fait accompli,* she wished to know whether she would be content to follow the religion of the Prince."

This was the question Margot most dreaded.* She was conscious that she risked the wrath of both sides by remaining true to herself and that the punishment for failing to give satisfaction to either party would be great. And yet this was a point on which she could not compromise. She had evidently turned the matter over in her mind and come up with, if not a solution to her problem, at least a moral imperative by which to navigate the treacherous road that lay ahead. "Madame replied with great wisdom that if it pleased God she would not fail in obedience to her and the Prince in all reasonable

---

* It is a commonplace in history that physical love, or rather the lack thereof, was at the root of Marguerite's objection to the marriage with her cousin. While it is true that she neither loved nor was attracted to Henry, a close examination of the evidence reveals that the difference in their religions far outweighed any other consideration. Although there were people in the sixteenth century, such as Catherine, who were cynical about Catholicism, Margot was not one of them.

ways, but that even if he were King of the whole world she would never change her religion."

If Jeanne had been able to see into the future she might perhaps have been grateful for the younger woman's resolute commitment, despite her deep religious misgivings, to her sovereign duty. But the queen of Navarre was not a fortune-teller. She found Margot's response unbearable and, according to the diplomat, flew into a passion. "Thereupon [Jeanne] said, 'The marriage shall not take place.' Then Madame said she would do as the King wished...So they parted with little satisfaction on either side." Marguerite clearly loathed her prospective mother-in-law. "Since then, Madame has pretended to be indisposed," the Italian observed pointedly.

But Jeanne knew when she was beaten and wrote soon after this to both her son and Elizabeth I, announcing that she had resolved to go through with the alliance. Her final words of advice to Henry reflected her understanding of the values of the court to which she was consigning him: "Every enticement will be offered to debauch you, in everything from your appearance to your religion...I know it is their object because they do not conceal it," she wrote. "This is all I have to say...except this: try to train your hair to stand up and be sure there are no lice in it."

PLANS FOR THE WEDDING then proceeded in earnest. But for the fact that the groom fell severely ill in April and was unable to travel for two months Marguerite would have been a bride before her nineteenth birthday. Although unintended, the delay worked significantly to the Catholic advantage, for on June 4, while shopping in the unseasonably oppressive heat of an early summer's day in Paris for her son's ceremonial apparel and other gifts appropriate for the bridal party, Jeanne d'Albret suddenly collapsed, complaining of an intense pain under her right shoulder. Less than a week later, the queen of Navarre was dead.

An autopsy was conducted, and Jeanne's Huguenot physicians concluded that she had died a natural death caused by the rupture of an ulcer aggravated by an underlying case of tuberculosis. Later, in the light of subsequent events, Catherine would be accused of murdering the queen of Navarre through the medium of a pair of poisoned gloves provided by an Italian merchant operating in Paris, but this seems unlikely, as an abscess would not have had time to form that quickly. Still, Jeanne's death was an unqualified boon to the queen mother, as she had promised the Catholic faction that if they supported the alliance she would see to it that Henry converted, and this he would never have done while his mother was still alive. And certainly once she had agreed to the marriage, the queen of Navarre had outlived her usefulness to the royal family and could only cause trouble in the future. There is also the disturbing evidence that Catherine exhibited absolutely no grief at the demise of her former friend. "The Queen of Navarre lies without hope of life... whom the Queen-Mother, the King and all his brothers and sisters have visited and departed without any hope of seeing her again," reported an English envoy in Paris, so perhaps Catherine had managed to find a subtle way to help this death along after all.

Jeanne's passing brought only relief to Marguerite, who even decades later behaved as though she had been delivered of a mortal enemy. In her frustration at the royal family's tactics during the negotiations, the queen of Navarre had lashed out not only at her future daughter-in-law but also at many members of the Catholic constituency at court, including those *très chic* ladies of the Flying Squadron allied to the Guises. In a letter to Brantôme, Marguerite described the scene at which the royal court paid its last regards to Jeanne's corpse. "Whilst the Queen of Navarre lay on her deathbed, a circumstance happened of so whimsical a nature that, though not of consequence to merit a place in history, may very well deserve to be related by me to you," she wrote. "Madame de Nevers [widow of the murdered duke of Guise, remarried to duke of Nevers]... attended by the Cardinal de Bourbon, Madame de Guise, the Princesse de Condé, her sisters and myself to the late Queen of Navarre's apartments, whither we all went to pay those last duties which her rank and our nearness of blood demanded of us. We found the Queen in bed with her curtains undrawn...after the simple manner of the Huguenots; that is to say, there were no priests, no cross, nor any holy water. We kept ourselves at some distance from the bed, but Madame de Nevers, whom you know the Queen hated more than any woman...approached the bedside, and, to the great astonishment of all present, who well knew the enmity subsisting betwixt them, took the Queen's hand, with many low curtseys, and kissed it; after which, making another curtsey to the very ground, she retired and rejoined us."

The profound enmity illustrated by this story between the religions at the very top of French society was magnified a thousand times in the general population, particularly among the overwhelmingly Catholic citizens of Paris. To them, the Crown and Coligny's single-minded pursuit of the Navarre marriage could only mean that the royal family, in combination with the Huguenots, intended to force a theological solution on the kingdom that in all likelihood would entail the renunciation of their most cherished rites and symbols. Already the king had insisted that a huge cross, which had been erected to commemorate the notorious execution of a Protestant for heresy, be torn down because it was considered offensive by those of the reformed religion. When city officials, responding to an impassioned public outcry against the proposed demolition, refused to comply with the royal command, they were threatened with removal. "You must decide whether to obey me and whether to tear down this pyramid [the cross]," Charles had written summarily to the provost of Paris. "I forbid you to come before me until such time as it has been torn down."

But the open hostility of the capital city to the marriage had no effect whatever upon either Catherine or the admiral, who, each for separate, conflicting reasons, continued to press for its accomplishment. As the day of the ceremony drew closer, the competition between these two for the king's soul intensified, until at last it boiled over into a public confrontation. The queen mother had taken advantage of one of Coligny's brief absences from court to hold a tearful interview with her son (unlike the duke of Alva, Charles was susceptible to Catherine's tears) in which she had accused him of conspiring with the admiral to wage war in the Netherlands behind her back. The scene was choreographed to elicit maximum guilt: "After all the pains that I had to bring you up, and to preserve your Crown…after having sacrificed myself for you and run a thousand dangers, how could I ever have dreamed that you would reward me thus miserably?" Catherine had wailed, according to a courtier familiar with the episode. "You hide yourself from me, from me who am your mother, in order to take counsel of your enemies; you wrench yourself from my arms, which have guarded you, to lean on the arms of those who once desired to kill you. I know that you hold secret counsels with the Admiral—that you wish to plunge us rashly into war with Spain…and send away also your brother [Henri], who may call himself unhappy in that he hath spent his life to preserve yours."

Unable to resist his mother, Charles had sworn never to keep anything from her and to obey her unconditionally in the future, a promise he kept until Coligny returned to the court in July. The admiral then promptly returned the favor by taking advantage of one of Catherine's brief absences from court—the queen mother had been called to the bedside of her daughter Claude, who was seriously ill—to hold a military council to approve French intervention in the Netherlands. Informed by spies that the king was wavering in the admiral's favor, Catherine was forced to abandon her daughter's sickroom; she just made it back in time to squelch Coligny's initiative. Her last-minute intervention infuriated him, and he vowed to accomplish his military objectives with or without approval. Then he lashed out at her in front of Charles and the council. "His Majesty refuses to adventure the war," he pronounced, staring at her with cold contempt. "God grant that he be not overtaken by another from the which he will have no power to retreat."

If Catherine had been undecided prior to this outburst whether to dispense with the admiral altogether or simply banish him from court, this brief speech sealed his fate. She understood that he had rejected the council's recommendation as the last word on the Netherlands intervention and would continue to work privately on Charles until he had his way, and that his influence over her son was very strong. For the first time she recognized that his political authority might overtake hers. If it did, she would be cast aside, and with her would go her adored Henri, whom she knew Charles hated and feared and would like nothing better than to be rid of. For these reasons, then, Coligny had to be eliminated.

But not just yet. First she had a gala wedding reception to host.

9

Queen Margot

It cannot be called a virtue to kill one's fellow-citizens,
betray one's friends, be without faith, without pity, and
without religion, by which methods one may indeed gain
an empire, but not glory.

—Niccolò Machiavelli, *The Prince*

THE FINAL WEEKS LEADING UP to her marriage must have comprised
a particularly exquisite brand of torture for Marguerite. She was
forced to smile and pretend to participate as her mother bustled
around, organizing the last-minute details of the ceremony. In honor
of Margot's exalted rank as a princess of France, Catherine behaved
as though her daughter was about to be united in nuptial bliss to the
Holy Roman Emperor rather than to the neophyte overlord of a
petty vassal state. Marguerite's dowry was set at 550,000 *livres* (which,
unfortunately, the Crown did not have readily available, being still
pretty much bankrupt from the recent civil wars), and she was to
receive from her future husband additional income from his estates
in Navarre. To prime the bride's enthusiasm for the match, which
was obviously somewhat lacking, Margot was further showered
with jewelry valued at approximately thirty thousand *livres,* including a magnificent diamond engagement ring. "The Comte de Retz
and I are attending to it in such a way that you will see her as
honorably provided for as her sisters," the queen mother clucked

complacently of Marguerite's trousseau. "And with less expense," she added virtuously, mindful of the drain on the royal treasury.

The arrival of her intended on July 8, 1572, only added to the bride's desolation. The king of Navarre entered Paris accompanied by an entourage consisting of eight hundred Huguenot followers, all dressed in mourning for Henry's mother, Jeanne d'Albret; they must have resembled an ominous parade of black beetles infesting the city. In such a polarized environment, reports of the bridegroom's appearance were naturally skewed depending upon the religious affinity of the observer. To the Protestants, Henry "had the graces of a courtier...women lost their heads over him" (although even his mother admitted he was short, about the size of Marguerite's younger brother, François, who was routinely described as stunted), while Catholic commentators sounded a slightly different note. The king of Navarre was "crude beyond the pale," a high-ranking government official involved in the nuptial negotiations despaired flatly.

It is highly probable that, like Marguerite, Henry dreaded the impending ordeal of his marriage. He had not been at court since he was thirteen. He'd spent the previous five years out in the provinces, tramping around in the outdoors and relishing the sort of traditional rural lifestyle that repudiated ornate manners, clothing, and etiquette (to say nothing of hygiene). To add to his discomfort, his mother, who had guided him from the time he was small and whom he had trusted implicitly, had just died, and he was forced to rely upon other advisers, such as Coligny, to reassure him of the usefulness of this alliance.

And although Henry loved pretty girls, Marguerite was no more to his taste than he was to hers. Her beauty, education, and rank were intimidating. Although passionate, she required a more complex wooing. The groom's taste ran to more easily available conquests. (Or, as a future scholar would tactfully put it, "Henry needed much affection, openly expressed.") Having grown up under the highly discriminating influence of the Flying Squadron, Margot had developed into a rarefied species, a hothouse orchid that bloomed only under specific romantic conditions that Henry couldn't be bothered with. Henry was a quick-roll-in-the-clover kind of guy.

But whatever misgivings the king of Navarre may have had were overruled by Coligny. The admiral was convinced that he would be in a much stronger negotiating position once the marriage took place and the royal family was irrevocably allied to the Huguenot movement. The arrival of Henry and his extensive black-clad entourage buoyed his spirits and served to renew his confidence. He wrote exultantly to Elizabeth I that he believed that, in the aftermath of the ceremony, for which more guests were pouring into the capital every day, he would "be able to get the king [Charles] to agree to anything."

The only potential stumbling block that remained was the procurement of a papal dispensation, for the bride and groom were related within the prohibited bands of consanguinity. But any hopes Margot may have nurtured of being rescued by Rome were dashed when her brother Charles announced that he intended to go through with the marriage with or without the approval of the pope and set a date of August 18 for the ceremony.

And now it broke upon Marguerite that she was trapped, that she was going to be forced to unite herself permanently to the leader of the Huguenot party, whose members she viewed as heretics and traitors to France, and to take vows she found abhorrent and that could only be broken at the risk of eternal damnation. In her desperation, she made one final bid for deliverance. This beautiful princess, one of the loveliest women in Europe, spent the long sweltering night before her wedding on her knees at the feet of the king and the queen mother begging through anguished tears to be released from so impious a commitment.

Despite her own preference for just such an approach, Catherine remained impervious to her daughter's sobs. The queen mother's chambermaid, who witnessed this scene, later testified that Catherine vindictively threatened "to make her [Marguerite] the most wretched lady in the kingdom" if she did not go through with the marriage. Margot's brother Charles was equally obdurate. The king was very publicly tied to the Navarre alliance. It represented his signature initiative; there was too much at stake to repudiate it. Besides, he wanted it — it enabled the tempting Netherlands campaign, in which Charles still hoped to participate.

And so at last the clock ran out, and it was the afternoon of August 18. In the stifling heat, Marguerite, pale and wan, put on her many glittering diamonds, an impressively jeweled crown, and her appropriately sweeping, ermine-trimmed robe, symbol of royalty, and proceeded woodenly to her fate. There were no more tears. Her pride demanded that she publicly conquer her demeanor, and she succeeded in holding herself rigidly correct throughout the ceremony. Nonetheless she made no secret of her aversion to this alliance. Even the sweating crowds observing the rites at a distance were aware that the princess was being coerced into this union. But the officiating cardinal, who was the bridegroom's uncle and an enthusiastic supporter of the match, overlooked the bride's evident distress. Margot and Henry became man and wife.

There followed four full days of brilliant merrymaking celebrating the joyous occasion. Charles loved court amusements and threw himself wholeheartedly into the party planning. This might have been a backhanded attempt to placate Marguerite, who also delighted in balls and fetes, or a way to further legitimize the marriage, as many important Catholics and foreign ambassadors had boycotted the ceremony. But more likely the king just wanted to use the occasion of Margot's wedding as an excuse to carouse to his heart's content. His mother encouraged him to give full vent to his creativity, and he so consumed himself with aesthetic details that he had no time for anything else. "So great was the magnificence of the banquets and shows, and the king so earnestly bent to those matters, that he had no leisure…to take his natural sleep," a Protestant eyewitness later reported.

In honor of the admiral, the wedding feast and formal ball immediately following the awkward services at Notre-Dame had a seafaring theme, with a company of mermaids and dolphins and other decorative ocean life presided over by Neptune; this affair went on so long that the entire court overslept until the late hours of the afternoon and nearly missed the opening banquet preceding the next day's soiree.

On the third evening, the king hosted an elaborate ballet staged in the great hall of the Louvre, which had been decorated as "a garden, filled with greens and all sorts of flowers, arched over with an azure heaven where shone a huge wheel of zodiac, seven planets, and a multitude of tiny stars, all gleaming with artificial brilliance." This was intended to represent heaven. A little farther down was a man-made river offering passage to another chamber that had been designated as hell. This room was not nearly so nicely adorned and was moreover populated by annoying fiends costumed with horns and tails, who chattered constantly. As good Catholics, Charles and . his brothers, Henri and François, dressed in armor, rigorously guarded the entrance to heaven. Henry of Navarre and his party were initially consigned to hell, a none-too-subtle reminder of the court's aversion to their religious affiliation, and barred passage to the garden, although Charles eventually relented and the groom and his men were allowed to join the rest of the party. This elaborate morality play was succeeded the next day by a grand tournament followed by yet another raucous ball that lasted into the early hours of the morning.

The whirling nights of dancing and feasting and frolicking did not bring the newly married couple closer together. Rather, the bride and groom seem to have used the extended revelry as an excuse to stay away from each other. The sometimes overly harsh judgments children form in adolescence frequently have an obstinate way of persisting into adulthood, and these two evidently took one look at each other and decided that neither had improved much since they had last met at thirteen. They shared common rooms and even the same bed, but according to Marguerite's later testimony they did not at this time consummate the marriage. And anyway,

when they did retire to their quarters, they were rarely alone—
Henry generally had his closest advisers with him. His bedroom was
one of the few places at court where the Huguenots could huddle
in private and discuss their plans, and even then they spoke in whispers for fear of Catholic spies. Nor was the king of Navarre reliant
upon his queen for sex; Catherine's court was full of sex. "So great
is the familiarity of men and the women of the queen mother's train,
as...may seem incredible and be thought of all honest persons a
matter not very convenient for preservation of noble young ladies'
chastity," the same Protestant witness observed drily.

But all the hilarity and the drinking and the riotous late hours and
the indiscriminate flirting and lovemaking that followed the ceremony distracted the court, and particularly the king, from another,
much darker purpose. For Catherine, along with her favorite son,
Henri, had come up with a bold scheme to dispose of their common
enemy Coligny once and for all, and the commotion surrounding
the nuptial festivities served this pair well. The queen mother had
only been waiting for the marriage to be solemnized before launching the attack. On the morning of Friday, August 22, just four days
after Margot's wedding, she struck.

THE PLAN WAS REASONABLY straightforward. Hire a sniper to kill the
admiral. Have the assassin hide somewhere close to where the target
was sure to pass, and then, when the Huguenots least expected it,
have him shoot Coligny from this strategic position. The great
advantage of this method was that it exactly replicated the manner
in which the previous duke of Guise had been murdered all those
years ago. The motive for the crime would therefore appear to be
personal rather than political. As a result, suspicion would fall
immediately upon the present duke of Guise, who had already very
publicly vowed to punish the admiral for his father's death and who
was conveniently in town for the wedding, and not on Catherine
and Henri, the true perpetrators.

The queen mother was aware that Charles was likely to be enraged by Coligny's death and might be intent on bringing *all* the culprits, including the aristocratic masterminds behind the attack, not just the lowly paid killer himself, to justice. Consequently it was very, very important to have a highly placed fall guy to take the blame. Catherine was no longer regent; Charles had been declared of age long before. To so openly flout his wishes and authority in this manner constituted treason, and the punishment for treason was death by all sorts of profoundly uncomfortable methods. Obviously, it wouldn't do at all for the king to find out that his mother and younger brother, working in concert, had deliberately gone behind his back and basically staged a coup d'état by butchering the man he called father. If that happened, he might just find the strength within himself to punish *them*.

No, it had to look like the Guises had done it. Fortunately for mother and son, the duke of Guise had already badly compromised himself with the king by falling in love with Marguerite, so Charles was already prone to think the worst of him. And neither Catherine nor Henri had any problem giving up the duke; he was as much a nuisance to both of them as was the admiral. In fact, it was part of the beautiful symmetry of their plan that, if they were lucky, they might get rid of both their political rivals—Catholic *and* Huguenot—with the same well-placed shot.

Of course, the difficulty lay in the logistics of this daring operation, in particular ferreting out an appropriately talented subordinate to execute the project. But as luck would have it, both Catherine and Henri were already personally acquainted with a hit man who met all their requirements. Just after Henri's signal victory at Moncontour three years earlier, a minor Catholic nobleman, the seigneur de Maurevert, who had been assigned to infiltrate the Huguenot camp as an undercover agent, had suddenly appeared before the queen mother at court claiming to have assassinated Coligny's second in command. He had meant to kill the admiral, but the opportunity had not presented itself, so he had settled instead for Coligny's first officer.

Upon confirmation of this intelligence, Catherine had shared the happy news with Charles, who had written specifically to Henri to recognize Maurevert's achievement. Henri, in his capacity as lieutenant-general, had called Maurevert in, praised him for his service to king and country, and dubbed him an honorary member of the Order of Saint-Michel. Even better, the Guises had been so impressed by Maurevert's initiative that they had demonstrated their gratitude by further rewarding the helpful assassin with the gift of a priory located in their home duchy of Lorraine, so Maurevert was now very publicly associated with the family. Catherine and Henri could not have hoped to secure the services of a candidate better fitted to the task at hand; even if he were caught, everyone would naturally assume that he had been employed by the Guises!

The prospective killer having been sounded out in advance and found willing, it became only a matter of finding an appropriate venue for the stakeout. There being very few bushes in Paris to hide behind, it was decided instead to install the gunslinger in an official court residence used frequently by the Guises (a nice touch) located on the main thoroughfare near the Louvre. Coligny, who was ensconced in apartments a short distance from the palace, was almost certain to use this route on his way to and from court.

And that is exactly what happened. On the morning of Friday, August 22, with the wedding festivities for the most part over, Coligny attended a meeting of the royal council. The conclave adjourned around noon, and the admiral, accompanied by a large number of his Huguenot compatriots, decided to go home for lunch. The whole group walked out of the Louvre and took the main boulevard, the admiral continuing to work by reading letters as he strolled along. The sharpshooter could see them approaching from his hiding place in the adjacent building. He went to the window, took aim with his long-barreled harquebus (the Renaissance equivalent of a shotgun), and fired.

Just at the moment he squeezed the trigger, one of those peculiar accidents of history occurred. The admiral, who was used to tromping around in his riding boots, had had to wear his fancy official court shoes to the council meeting. He'd been in them all morning: they pinched, they were difficult to walk in, and he'd had enough of them. He suddenly put down his letter and bent over to take them off. As a result, the assassin's bullet, intended to be a full-body, point-blank frontal assault, instead winged Coligny in the left hand and the right elbow. "If he had simply walked straight ahead," confirmed the Venetian ambassador, who was in Paris for the wedding and wrote a detailed report of the shooting and subsequent events to his government, "it would have hit him in the chest and killed him."

Old soldier that he was, Coligny concentrated less on his injuries and more on securing the immediate territory by pinpointing the source of the attack. "The shot came from the window where the smoke is," he observed and instructed his entourage to investigate.

A Huguenot messenger ran to tell Charles what had happened. The king happened to be playing tennis at the time with, of all people, the duke of Guise. For once both Protestant and Catholic accounts of Charles's reaction agree in describing the king as being absolutely outraged by the news. "'Sdeath!" the king swore. "Shall I never have a moment's quiet? Must I have fresh troubles every day?" a Huguenot official recounted. "His face [the king's] turned pale and he appeared to be shocked in the extreme. Without another word he retired to his rooms," the Venetian envoy concurred. Although he would later be the subject of venomous attacks charging him with conspiracy, there is nothing at all in his history to indicate that Charles was the sort of person who was adept at dissembling. It is clear that he had no idea that this was coming.

Initially, as Catherine had anticipated, suspicion fell fully upon the Guises. "Everyone supposed it had been done by order of the duke of Guise to avenge his family, because the window from which the shot was fired belonged to his mother's house, which had purposely been left empty after she had gone to stay in another," the official Venetian report confirmed. But the ambassador was an experienced politician, and he knew to dig deeper. After consulting various high-ranking officials of his acquaintance, he discovered "that from start to finish the whole thing was the work of the queen [mother]. She conceived it, plotted it, and put it into execution, with no help from anyone but her son the duke of Anjou [Henri]." The ambassador further revealed darkly, "But in a whisper (and it would be best if we kept it to ourselves)...there was no Frenchman they trusted for the job, so they had it done by a Florentine officer named Piero Paolo Tosinghi." Publicly, however, the court continued to maintain that Maurevert had committed the crime. "But nothing was seen of him and he never turned up as one would have expected."*

This was exactly what Catherine most feared. If a Venetian diplomat could discover her secret so easily, others would as well. Already Charles had called for a full investigation into the ambush and that very afternoon had taken the unprecedented step of visiting the injured man in his own chambers. Catherine and Henri had hastened to accompany him; they could not take the chance of leaving Coligny alone with the king. They were therefore present when Charles, after first reassuring himself that the patient was in stable condition and that his wounds were being cared for appropriately, declared his firm intention of getting to the bottom of the conspiracy. "You bear the wound, but I the smart [insult]," Charles asserted fiercely. "I swear that I will take such terrible revenge, that it shall never be forgotten."

Catherine and Henri's first reaction was to try to cover up by pretending to be as shocked and upset as the king. After all, the admiral had sustained two reasonably serious injuries, including losing a finger. He was not young; there was always the risk of infection. He might yet die from his wounds, in which case the Huguenot leadership would be in turmoil and they could reevaluate the

---

* Most modern historians still credit Maurevert with having fired the shots. But I lean to the savvy Venetian ambassador's account. Using an Italian, and particularly a Florentine, would definitely have been Catherine's first choice.

situation. Accordingly, Henri curried favor with Charles by immediately ordering that members of the king's own guard be assigned to Coligny's bedside to protect him in the event of a second attempt by the vile traitors. He even suggested that those Huguenots lodged at a distance (Paris had been so packed for the marriage celebrations that some of the Protestant wedding guests had been forced to rent rooms in the suburbs) be called in to help assure the wounded man's safety and peace of mind.

But by the next day, a change of the admiral's bandages revealed that his wounds were healing and his prognosis optimistic. The royal investigation was only just getting started, and the Guises were still considered the chief suspects. The duke, fearing that the Huguenots might attempt to ambush him in retaliation, drew his many supporters together and took the precaution of stockpiling weapons as a defense against a possible assault.

It is likely that at this point it became clear to Catherine that she had botched the operation and that she had better fix it or she and Henri were going to be found out. Every hour that passed worked against her influence with the king and in favor of Coligny's. She was going to have to convince Charles that what she and Henri had done was in his service, and she was going to have to do it fast.

She began by breaking the news to him that the duke of Guise, whom Charles, like everyone else, believed to be the culprit and wanted to arrest, might not have been the principal perpetrator after all. So volatile was this piece of information that Catherine did not have the courage to impart it herself but instead sent in her trusted Italian surrogate, the duke of Retz, Charles's chief attendant. According to Marguerite, who knew nothing about the intrigue at the time but made it her business to find out afterward, the duke of Retz "went to the King in his closet, between the hours of nine and ten [Saturday night], and told him he was come as a faithful servant to discharge his duty, and lay before him the danger in which he stood, if he persisted in his resolution of punishing M. de Guise, as he ought now to be informed that the attempt made upon the Admiral's life was not set on foot by him alone, but that his (the King's) brother...and the Queen his mother, had their shares in it." (Even this was only a partial truth, as the duke of Guise likely had nothing at all to do with the assassination attempt. It defies reason that either Catherine or Henri, who both detested the duke, would have chosen to take him into their confidence.*) This intervention, the duke of Retz continued, had been initiated only with the king's best interests in mind, as "the Admiral must be ever considered as dangerous to the State, and whatever show he might make of affection for his Majesty's person, and zeal for his service in Flanders, they must be considered as mere pretences, which he used to cover his real design of reducing the kingdom to a state of confusion."

While Charles was no doubt listening open-mouthed to this surreal confession, the duke of Retz smoothly transitioned to the real objective of the meeting: securing Catherine and Henri's safety by transforming them from the treasonous plotters they were into unselfish guardians of the king's person. The duke of Retz, said Marguerite (and she was in a position to know by the time she wrote this), "concluded with observing that the original intention to make away with the Admiral...having been so unfortunate as to fail... and the Huguenots becoming desperate enough to resolve to take up arms, with design to attack, not only M. de Guise, but the Queen his mother and his brother [Henri], supposing them, *as well as his Majesty,* to have commanded Maurevert to make his attempt, he saw nothing but cause of alarm for his Majesty's safety." In other words, the wicked, ungrateful Huguenots were turning on him, just as his mother and brother had predicted they would, and Charles's life and throne were now at stake.

But of course the duke of Retz was only the warm-up act. While Charles was still struggling to comprehend the enormity of this

---

* The Venetian ambassador reported, "As for the harquebus shot...the duke of Guise knew nothing about it. He would never have dared to do such a thing against the king's will, because His Majesty...could later have done Guise and his family harm."

betrayal, his mother appeared to make her own impassioned plea for survival.

There are no records of this conversation, but it appears that Catherine followed the same guilt-inducing script that she had utilized with such success in the past. She reminded her son how she alone had preserved his throne for him against enormous odds when his older brother Francis had died and he was but a child of ten. How she had for more than a decade sacrificed herself completely to his honor and welfare, working tirelessly to promote his interests. She spoke of the many dangers she had faced for him and how she had never for a moment considered her own gratification, being only consumed with anxiety for his safety and security.

Then she went to work on the Huguenots. Charles thought he understood Coligny, but she, Catherine, knew better. The admiral, she said, was not the heroic character her son took him for. For example, he had cravenly assassinated one of her own household, an extremely loyal and honest attendant, years earlier, while she was still regent. At the time "she had vowed to avenge his death"; the recent assassination attempt was retribution for that crime, "which rendered him [Coligny] deserving of the like treatment." And now she had it on good authority that the Huguenots meant to rise up and kill the king and all his family in their quest to take over the realm. He *must* listen to her and follow her counsel or they were all doomed.

Now, Charles was not an imbecile, and he knew that this last bit in particular was ludicrous. Coligny was not part of a grand conspiracy to overthrow and kill the royal family. On the contrary, Coligny was patently the most honorable and trustworthy man among Charles's acquaintance. "The King had so great a regard for the Admiral... and Teligny [another Huguenot commander], on account of their bravery, being himself a prince of a gallant and noble spirit, and esteeming others in whom he found a similar disposition," Marguerite explained. But the parameters of the predicament in which the king now found himself precluded compromise. To his horror he realized that in order to behave honorably, stand by his word and his principles, and uphold truth by defending Coligny, he would have to condemn his mother and forever cut himself off from her.

It is testament to just how clearly he saw this choice and how repugnant the implications of his decision were that it took her several hours to break him down. In the past she had only to confront him and he would immediately beg her pardon and promise to follow her advice from then on. In the aftermath of what seems to be a string of inexplicable events, Charles has often been portrayed as psychologically disordered, prone to irrationally violent fits of temper, and this label has stuck with him through the centuries. But it is worth noting that mental illness is not something that can be turned on and off at will and that the king *never* demonstrated disturbed or destructive behavior when he was in the presence of Coligny.

Far from being insane, it was Charles's acuity that caused him to react with such hysteria. Otherwise he would not have struggled so with the moral burden—he would have just given in. In the whole of Shakespeare's brilliant oeuvre no character demonstrated a more heartbreaking tragic flaw than did Charles IX on that wretched night, or one that yielded more shattering repercussions. It was his body as much as his nerve that seems to have betrayed him; never strong physically, the king had been further weakened by a parade of late nights and frivolity. He was exhausted mentally as well as physically, as Catherine well knew. She and Henri and a small coterie of advisers kept hammering at him until the small hours of the morning. Poor Charles was like a political prisoner being relentlessly interrogated in a cell. Catherine had in her hand a list of the principal Huguenots surrounding Coligny. She insisted that the Crown act preemptively against this group.

In the end her son was no match for her. The king could not find the mental or emotional strength to reign without his mother's approval. In fairness to Charles, even the great Saint Louis, thirteenth-century king of France, had been in his thirties before he dared defy his indomitable mother, Blanche of Castile; Catherine's son had only just turned twenty-two.* It might have been a different story if Coligny had been in the room, but Coligny was asleep in bed a few blocks away, recuperating from his wounds.

Suddenly, like a man under the wheel, the king broke. "Kill them!" Charles shrieked at his mother and her list. "Kill them all!"

BY HER OWN ADMISSION, Marguerite was kept far away from these nefarious deliberations. The new queen of Navarre was of course aware of the atmosphere of heightened tension at court, but she had no notion of the coming holocaust taking shape in the king's study. She, like everyone else, believed the assassination attempt on Coligny to have been revenge on the part of the duke of Guise for his father's death. "I was perfectly ignorant of what was going forward," Margot affirmed. "I observed every one to be in motion: the Huguenots, driven to despair by the attack upon the Admiral's life, and the Guises, fearing they should not have justice done them, whispering all they met in the ear." The bride was, however, only too aware of the untenable position she inhabited by virtue of her marriage. "The Huguenots were suspicious of me because I was a Catholic, and the Catholics because I was married to the King of Navarre, who was a Huguenot. This being the case, no one spoke a syllable of the matter to me," Margot stated flatly.

But by midnight or soon thereafter, nearly every high-ranking member of the Catholic faction at court, including Marguerite's sister Claude (in town for the wedding), was fully cognizant that the king had secretly ordered a mass slaughter of Coligny and his adherents to be carried out at dawn. Because so many Huguenots had accompanied Henry of Navarre to Paris for the ceremony, the

---

* Catherine had read about Saint Louis's reign and was reported to have justified her actions by comparing herself to Blanche of Castile. Again, the queen mother seems not to have understood the material fully, as it was inconceivable that Blanche would ever have conspired with one of her younger sons to commit treason against her elder son the king, as Catherine did.

royal guard was considered insufficient on its own to conduct the assault, and so Catherine had been forced after all to throw in with the duke of Guise, whose extensive entourage was already armed and primed for a fight. "They [the queen mother and the duke of Retz] called in the duke of Guise and gave him...and the king's natural brother [Henri] the assignment of murdering the admiral, his son-in-law Teligny, and any followers who were with him," the Venetian ambassador reported. "You can imagine how delighted the duke of Guise was to be given this task, and how enthusiastically he carried it out," the envoy added mordantly. In addition, other important Huguenots, including those staying at court, were to be cut down by royal troops under the direction of Gaspard de Tavannes, Henri's chief military adviser. Significantly, Charles, who had yearned for the glory of battle all his life, did not participate in the combat, another indication that this decision was forced on him by his mother.

The French court regularly kept very late hours. That same Saturday evening (or, rather, as it was past midnight, early Sunday morning), Marguerite wandered into her mother's bedroom to visit with her sister. It was at this point that she first understood that something very grave indeed was brewing. "I placed myself on a coffer, next my sister Lorraine [Claude], who, I could not but remark appeared greatly cast down," Margot remembered. "The Queen my mother was in conversation with some one, but, as soon as she espied me, she bade me go to bed. As I was taking leave, my sister seized me by the hand and stopped me, at the same time shedding a flood of tears: 'For the love of God,' cried she, 'do not stir out of this chamber!' I was greatly alarmed at this exclamation; perceiving which, the Queen my mother called my sister to her, and chid her very severely. My sister replied it was sending me away to be sacrificed; for, if any discovery should be made, I should be the first victim of their revenge. The Queen my mother made answer that, if it pleased God, I should receive no hurt, but it was necessary I should go to prevent the suspicion that might arise from my staying."

There was no refusing Catherine's command. Claude continued to sob but could do nothing further to try to save her sister. Marguerite, by this time thoroughly frightened, retired to her own rooms, "more dead than alive," as she put it, to ponder the meaning of this cryptic threat. What did Claude know that she did not? Clearly the danger was real—and potentially deadly—or her sister would not have wailed so. "As soon as I reached my own closet, I threw myself upon my knees and prayed to God to take me into his protection and save me; but from whom or what, I was ignorant," she related. "Hereupon the King my husband, who was already in bed, sent for me. I went to him, and found the bed surrounded by thirty or forty Huguenots, who were entirely unknown to me; for I had been then but a very short time married. Their whole discourse, during the night, was upon what had happened to the Admiral, and they all came to a resolution of the next day demanding justice of the King against M. de Guise; and, if it was refused, to take it themselves."

Impossible from the distance of so many centuries to fully appreciate the dread that gripped Marguerite during those long, terrible hours while she waited for she knew not what to make its appearance. "For my part I was unable to sleep a wink the whole night, for thinking of my sister's tears and distress, which had greatly alarmed me," she confessed. And yet, despite her vigilance, she was unable to penetrate the mystery of the peril facing her. No crisis materialized; no alarm sounded. The room in which she lay, surrounded by her husband and his compatriots, remained quiet, and certainly Henry, also unable to sleep, perceived no special menace, as Marguerite testified that "as soon as day broke, the King my husband said he would rise and play at tennis until King Charles was risen, when he would go to him immediately and demand justice. He left the bedchamber, and all his gentlemen followed."

But the danger was only too real. By the time Henry of Navarre and his men left the safety of the bedroom and headed for the tennis court, as the first faint light of dawn approached, the duke of Guise and his men had already overrun the gates of the residence where Coligny was quartered. From his second-floor bedroom, the admiral could hear the clanging of swords and the shrill screams of pain on the stairs as the gentlemen of his entourage tried desperately to hold off the Catholic attack and knew that his execution was imminent. He was helped to his feet by a servant so as not to die helplessly in bed, but he was too weak to wield a weapon. The first of Guise's men (including a captain of the royal guard who, in a cruel irony, had just two days before been assigned by Henri to protect the wounded man) burst through the door. "Are you not the Admiral?" demanded the soldier. "I am; but, young man, you should respect my grey hairs and not attack a wounded man," Coligny was reported to have appealed.

But his plea was ignored. The defenseless warrior, a veteran of more than thirty years of combat and service to the Crown of France, was bludgeoned repeatedly by swords and axes, his body ultimately thrown from the window to land at the foot of the duke of Guise, who had remained in the courtyard to supervise the raid. The admiral's visage had been so mutilated by blows that the duke reportedly had to mop the blood away to confirm the identity of the victim. Having established that the grisly mound of flesh at his feet was, in fact, the remains of the man he sought, he viciously kicked at the corpse of his nemesis to emphasize his family's superiority and give vent to the nobility of his feelings.

With the confirmation of Coligny's murder, broadcast by the ringing of the bell at the Palais de Justice, horrific, uncontrollable violence suddenly erupted all over the city. The Parisian civilian militias, whose twenty thousand or so Catholic members had been surreptitiously forewarned of the coming attack and mobilized within hours by the provost of Paris under direct orders from the king, sprang into action. "Well done, my men, we have made a good beginning!" the duke of Guise cried out to his troops. "Forward—by the king's command!" "Kill, kill!" Gaspard de Tavannes bellowed as he rode. A house-by-house search was conducted, and wherever a Huguenot was suspected to be hiding a mob would break in, "cruelly butchering those they encountered, without regard to sex or age," an eyewitness account confirmed. "Carts filled with the dead bodies of aristocratic damoiselles, of women, girls, men, and children were conducted to and discharged into the river, which was covered with corpses and all red with blood, which also ran in diverse places in the city, like the courtyard of the Louvre." The Venetian ambassador reported that every Huguenot nobleman of significance who lived near the court was assassinated at daybreak before the common people were even aware of what was occurring. "But then...the king gave the order that all the other Huguenots in Paris should also be murdered and robbed," he continued, "and things began to happen with fury."

Marguerite had only just fallen asleep after her long night of wakefulness when the brutality suddenly burst upon her. "As soon as I beheld it was broad day, I apprehended all the danger my sister had spoken of was over; and being inclined to sleep, I bade my nurse make the door fast," she recalled. But "in about an hour I was awakened by a violent noise at the door, made with both hands and feet, and a voice calling out, 'Navarre! Navarre!' My nurse, supposing the King my husband to be at the door, hastened to open it."

Instead of Henry, however, an unknown stranger, bleeding profusely, staggered in. To Margot's utter bewilderment, the man "threw himself immediately upon my bed. He had received a wound in his arm from a sword, and another by a pike, and was then pursued by four archers, who followed him into the bedchamber. Perceiving these last, I jumped out of bed, and the poor gentleman after me, holding me fast by the waist. I did not then know him; neither was I sure that he came to do me no harm, or whether the archers were in pursuit of him or me. In this situation I screamed aloud, and he cried out likewise, for our fright was mutual," she recalled. "At length, by God's providence, M. de Nançay, captain of the guard, came into the bedchamber, and seeing me thus surrounded, though he could not help pitying me, he was scarcely able to refrain from laughter. However, he reprimanded the archers very severely for their indiscretion, and drove them out of the chamber. At my request he granted the poor gentleman his life, and I had him put to bed in my closet, caused his wounds to be dressed, and did not suffer him to quit my apartment until he was perfectly cured." This was the first of her husband's Huguenot subjects that Marguerite would save that day.

And then, at last, she was made acquainted with the ghastly events of the previous few hours and understood the extreme danger in which her mother had placed her. Her sister Claude had been correct; if the Huguenots had discovered the Catholic intrigue in time, her husband's entourage would have assumed she was a spy and would have in all likelihood taken their revenge on her.* "I changed my shift, because it was stained with the blood of this man, and whilst I was doing so, De Nançay gave me an account of the transactions of the foregoing night, assuring me that the King my husband was safe, and actually at that moment in the King's bedchamber. He made me muffle myself up in a cloak, and conducted me to the apartment of my sister," Margot said. But even here, in the guarded hallways of the Louvre, the terror caught up with her. "As we passed through the antechamber, all the doors of which were wide open, a gentleman of the name of Bourse, pursued by archers, was run through the body with a pike and fell dead at my feet. As if I had been killed by the same stroke, I fell, and was caught by M. de Nançay before I reached the ground. As soon as I recovered from this fainting-fit, I went into my sister's bedchamber, and was immediately followed by M. de Mioflano, first gentleman to the King my husband, and Armagnac, his first *valet de chambre,* who both came to beg me to save their lives. I went and threw

---

* There are those scholars who claim that Marguerite was never really at risk, that her rank would have precluded her being harmed. Easy to say from a quiet perch in a modern library. No one was safe that day, least of all the Catholic princess who was perceived as having been the bait that lured the Huguenots to their doom in Paris. In fact, many women of high aristocratic birth were deliberately marked for death that terrible morning.

myself on my knees before the King and the Queen my mother, and obtained the lives of both of them." This from Margot, who only the week before had wept and pleaded with Charles and Catherine to be extricated from marriage to the Huguenot king of Navarre.

But it was not only her husband's servants who needed Marguerite's intervention. Henry himself was in grave danger. There had been no tennis match that morning; the king of Navarre never reached the court. No sooner had he left his wife's bedroom than he had been summoned to Charles's chambers. His entourage accompanied him but was refused admittance to the king of France; this was Henry's first inkling of Charles's reversal, and he understood immediately what it meant. Just before the door slammed shut behind him, he turned to address his friends. "God knows if I will ever see you again," he said presciently.

Once inside, Henry had been confronted with a choice. To justify the murderous rampage he'd ordered, Charles — or, rather, his mother — had invented a fictitious plot on the part of Henry, Coligny, and the other Huguenot leaders against the Crown. Henry had to sit there and listen as he and his coreligionists were accused of conspiring to murder Charles and all his family. There was nothing to be done about Coligny and the majority of his followers, Charles informed Henry. They had been condemned to death, and the sentence was at that moment being carried out. But as his new brother-in-law, Charles was willing to overlook Henry's treason and allow him to live — *if* he would give up Protestantism and return to the Catholic faith. This, coincidentally, was exactly what Catherine and Charles had promised the pope would happen if Henry married Marguerite.

Henry was eighteen years old and alone in the world, king of a minor principality whose most prominent subjects were in the process of being massacred. Both his parents were dead, he was married to a woman he didn't know or trust, and he was at the mercy of a royal family whose ruthlessness was matched only by its mendacity. He had no choice but to acquiesce. (His cousin the prince of Condé was offered the same deal and originally put up a small fight, refusing to convert, but soon thought better of it.) The Venetian ambassador, again demonstrating an uncommon degree of candor, reported that "in birth and rank the chief [Huguenot] leaders are Condé and the king of Navarre, but they are boys who have no followers. What's more, they are in the king's power and might as well be in prison." Two days after his interview with Charles, Henry very publicly accompanied him and the rest of the royal family to Mass. They had to wind their way through decaying corpses to get to the church. The queen mother made a point of rising from her pew in order to have an unobstructed view of the king of Navarre piously receiving the sacrament and guffawed outright at the tableau.

Although the genocide that occurred that Sunday would forever be remembered as the Saint Bartholomew's Day Massacre (for having commenced on August 24, 1572, the official Church holiday associated with the apostle), the killings in fact continued unabated for days afterward, and the violence spread through France to other major cities, such as Orléans. It is estimated that some five to six thousand people perished in Paris alone. Not all the victims were Huguenots. Many ordinary residents took advantage of the carnage and atmosphere of general lawlessness to settle old scores or simply butcher wealthy citizens for profit. (Catherine's favorite goldsmith, for example, was among those slain, and his shop was ransacked.) Nor did the Crown succeed in exterminating the Huguenot movement. Some of the Protestant wedding guests, including the count of Montgomery, a high-ranking member of Coligny's inner circle, escaped death by having had the foresight to lodge on the far side of the river. The head start allowed him and his party to outride the duke of Guise and his men, who nonetheless pursued them relentlessly far into the countryside.

The most obvious beneficiary of the debacle was Philip II, who, without having to lift a finger or spend a single Spanish *real,* succeeded in ridding himself of both the threat of Huguenot intervention in the Netherlands and any possible future competition by France for international dominance. "As I write, they are killing them all, they are stripping them naked, dragging them through the streets, plundering the houses, and sparing not even children. Blessed be God who has converted the French princes to His cause! May he inspire their hearts to continue as they have begun!" the Spanish ambassador wrote joyfully to his sovereign that Sunday. A few days later, the same envoy had a chance to congratulate the queen mother personally on her triumph. The slaughter was in its last stages; the Seine was choked with dead bodies; the gory remains of disembodied limbs, trunks, and even heads lay strewn in the gutters or piled high in carts. "She has grown ten years younger!" the Spaniard chortled after the audience. In Rome, the pope echoed the Spanish exuberance and ordered a Te Deum sung.

But in fact, France's standing in Europe was severely weakened by this episode. Elizabeth I did not break off relations, but neither did she ever accept Catherine's explanation that the massacre had been necessary to ward off a Huguenot insurrection, and from this time on she never seriously considered working with her French counterparts. The same was true of Germany. And for all his satisfaction with the outcome, Philip II viewed Catherine with even more derision than before, especially when it came out later that her action had not been planned but had instead been the impromptu result of a failed assassination attempt. The mighty kingdom of France, which had dominated the continent in the glory years of her mentor and father-in-law, François I, only a few decades earlier, dwindled at Catherine's hands that Sunday in August and would not return to its former prominence until well into the next century.

But the queen mother was unconcerned with anything but the security of her own position and that of her son Henri. To this end she was unresolved about her initial decision to allow the king of Navarre to survive. Catherine knew it was a risk to keep Henry alive, especially after the count of Montgomery resurfaced in Protestant England and the Huguenot stronghold of La Rochelle refused to submit to the king's authority. Even with his conversion (which everyone knew was forced anyway), so long as the king of Navarre drew breath, the Huguenot movement would have a royal figurehead around whom they could coalesce. She had succeeded in underscoring her political victory and bolstering her own Catholic credentials by forcing Henry to publicly attend Mass. Now he was superfluous, and a danger besides. Caution dictated that he be eliminated.

And so a new intrigue was hatched in the immediate aftermath of the violence. Marguerite was again to be the innocent mechanism by which this latest treachery was sprung. "Five or six days afterwards," she recalled, "those who were engaged in this plot, considering that it was incomplete whilst the King my husband and the Prince de Condé remained alive, as their design was not only to dispose of the Huguenots, but of the Princes of the blood likewise; and knowing that no attempt could be made on my husband whilst I continued to be his wife, devised a scheme which they suggested to the Queen my mother for divorcing me from him. Accordingly, one holiday, when I waited upon her to chapel, she charged me to declare to her, upon my oath, whether I believed my husband to be like other men. 'Because,' said she, 'if he is not, I can easily procure you a divorce from him.'"

Catherine was asking if the marriage had been consummated. If it had not—and she likely suspected this was the case, as Margot and Henry had made no secret of their emotional indifference to each other—then she would help her daughter obtain an annulment. This was the bait, and a stronger lure could not have been proffered to Marguerite. To be done with this marriage, the marriage she had fought against from the very beginning. To be free from a man she did not love and so perhaps have the opportunity to find real passion with one whom she did.

But Margot was a very intelligent woman, and she understood that her emancipation would come at the price of Henry's life. Now that the king of Navarre had agreed to return to Catholicism and her own soul was no longer in jeopardy, she recoiled at the thought of being the cause of further villainy. Although Marguerite had been ignorant of the conspiracy surrounding her marriage and had been as much a dupe as her husband and his followers, she felt keenly the moral burden of the atrocities committed in its wake. The Huguenots who had been murdered had been guests at *her* wedding. She had spent the evening before the massacre listening to them debate the assassination attempt on the admiral, and she *knew* that they were innocent of the charges against them, that there never was a Huguenot plot to harm the king, that on the contrary, they had believed in the king. They had come in good faith to partake of her hospitality, to celebrate her investiture as their queen, and they had been hideously, treacherously betrayed by her family.

Every now and then there comes a moment in history when an individual not previously credited with any particular integrity is elevated to a position of authority and unexpectedly assumes the character of the office and rises to a higher purpose. Although it meant sacrificing her personal happiness, Marguerite, appalled by all she had witnessed and understanding that, as queen of Navarre, she was all that stood between her husband and annihilation, refused to participate in the bloodshed and elected to save Henry.

" 'Madame,' she answered her mother, 'since you have put the question to me, I can only declare I am content to remain as I am;' and this I said because I suspected the design of separating me from my husband was in order to work some mischief against him."

At that moment, by her courage and compassion, Margot truly became a queen. The question was, queen of what?

10

Queen of Paris

Whoever thinks that in high personages new benefits cause
old offences to be forgotten, makes a great mistake.
—Niccolò Machiavelli, *The Prince*

WHEN MARGUERITE DECLINED HER MOTHER'S offer of an annulment,
she understood that she was not simply saving Henry's life but tacitly
guaranteeing his continued submission to the Crown. No semblance
of independence at Catherine's court came without a price tag, and
this was Margot's. The queen of Navarre had thrown a net of protection around her husband, and from this point on she was responsible
to her family for his good behavior. Although he had chosen to recant
and been officially pardoned by Charles, Henry was still considered a
threat and was treated with contempt and suspicion, especially by her
mother and older brother Henri, duke of Anjou. Marguerite knew
that if Henry disobeyed a ruling, relapsed into Protestantism, or
attempted in any way to assert his prerogative against her family's
wishes, she as well as he would be punished.

And so she did her best to help him. It was important, for example,
that Henry's adoption of orthodoxy be at least outwardly convincing
in order to reassure Spain and the papacy, the two world powers
Catherine was trying most to impress, that the Huguenots were no
longer a factor in French politics. Of course, as a devout Catholic
herself, Marguerite was hopeful that her husband's conversion would

be genuine. She tried to encourage him to listen to the teachings of his uncle the cardinal of Bourbon (who had officiated at their wedding), and she introduced him to a particularly persuasive Jesuit confessor. Henry, who was still feeling his way through this new and treacherous environment, docilely accepted the proffered religious instruction and went to Mass regularly. In October, he and his cousin the prince of Condé, who also found it expedient to feign devotion, even sent a toadying letter to the pope expressing remorse for their previous transgressions and begging to be reinstated as good Catholics. To demonstrate his pleasure at the return of two such important princes to the Church, the pontiff finally issued an official dispensation legitimizing Henry and Marguerite's marriage.

But despite the outward appearance of harmony, marital relations between the king and queen of Navarre were no more intimate than they had been on their wedding night. Henry simply did not trust Marguerite. He did not know she had saved him by rejecting an annulment, and her devotion to Catholicism prejudiced him against her.* His position at court was miserable; he was under constant watch and was humiliated as a matter of sport. The dashing duke of Guise, in high favor with the royal family as a result of his enthusiastic participation in the Saint Bartholomew's Day Massacre, made a point of persecuting the unhappy husband of his former love. "On All Hallows' Eve," a courtier observed, "the King of Navarre was playing tennis with the Duc de Guise, when the scant consideration which was shown this little prisoner of a kinglet, at whom he threw all kinds of jests and taunts, as though he were a simple page or lackey of the Court, deeply pained a number of honest people who were watching them play." (The duke of Guise had been extremely disappointed by Marguerite's unwillingness to abandon her husband.

---

* Marguerite's conversation with Catherine remained private until her memoirs were published the following century. Nor could Henry have anticipated that Catherine would keep her own daughter in ignorance of the Saint Bartholomew's Day plot. As far as he was concerned, Margot had spent the night before the massacre in the bedroom with him and his fellow Huguenots listening to their plans without ever bothering to warn them.

Displeased with his own wife, he had evidently been hoping for a double annulment. Certainly he was the catnip behind Catherine's plan to rid herself of Henry: one of Margot's handmaidens later revealed that "many a time I have heard Queen Marguerite say that after she had given her affections to the King of Navarre, the Queen Mother spoke to her of loving the Duke of Guise, and that she invariably replied that she had not a heart of wax.") There were also rumors swirling about that, should Marguerite be delivered of a son, Henry would be considered superfluous and could then be eliminated. Understandably, this intelligence did not have a rousing effect on Henry's desire to have sex with his wife. For all these reasons, then, the king of Navarre regarded Marguerite as just one more serpent in a court packed with deadly predators and did not pursue an amorous relationship with her.

Which is too bad, because at least in the beginning, once the religious issue was settled in her favor, Margot seems to have been open to establishing normal conjugal relations and even demonstrated a degree of tenderness toward her husband. After all, she was only nineteen and very romantic by nature, and she *wanted* to be swept up by the passion that other young brides reputedly experienced during the first few months of wedded bliss. And Henry was in a tough spot, which made him appealingly vulnerable; she probably couldn't help but feel sorry for him. But she was also extremely proud, and his rejection of her overtures, however subtle, hurt. She drew away from him, and the emotional distance between them grew and hardened over time.

It must therefore have come as something of a relief when in November, less than three months into her marriage, the Huguenot stronghold of La Rochelle refused to pay taxes to the Crown or accept the Catholic magistrate appointed by the king to govern the city, and Charles sent the royal army, led by his brother Henri, the lieutenant-general—along with the duke of Guise, the king of Navarre, the prince of Condé, and Marguerite's younger brother, François, duke of Alençon—to bring the rebels to compliance.

Freed momentarily from the responsibility of guiding her indifferent husband and from the no-longer-desired attentions of the duke of Guise (not to mention the malicious schemes of her older brother Henri), the lovely queen of Navarre was left in Paris with the rest of Catherine's Flying Squadron to entertain herself.

AND THEN, AT LAST, for the first time since she was sixteen, Marguerite perceived the intrinsic advantage of being a married woman, particularly one whose husband promised to be away for an extended period. Suddenly there were no restrictions on her movements. No one was telling her what to say or pressuring her to change her mind or go against her instincts or making odious plans for her future. She had always possessed rank and beauty, and to this was now added a measure of independence. When it came to her own amusement, provided she remained discreet, she could do as she liked.

To be young and alluring and royal in Paris is fabulous in any era, and the sixteenth century was no exception. Marguerite immediately fell in with the most glamorous crowd in town. Her two closest friends were Henriette de Clèves, duchess of Nevers, and Claude-Catherine de Clermont-Dampierre, duchess of Retz, the acknowledged chieftains of haute society.* Both women were in their thirties, highly educated, very sophisticated, and filthy rich. The duchess of Retz, who was fluent in Latin and Greek (languages she had acquired as a result of her first husband's frustrating lack of sociability, which had obliged her to live like a hermit out in the countryside for years, with only her books for company), was especially interested in the literary arts. She was a great patron of poets and hosted fascinating soirees in her rooms at the elegant, exclusive, centuries-old Hôtel de Dampierre, another vestige of her challenging but ultimately rewarding first marriage. In the duchess's Green

---

* Claude-Catherine was married to the duke of Retz, Charles's detested chief gentleman of the bedroom, the man whom the queen mother used to spy on her son. It was the duchess of Retz's second marriage. Arranging for favored courtiers to wed titled widowed heiresses was a fairly standard reward for services rendered at Catherine's court.

Salon—a witty reference to both a line in a sonnet by the fourteenth-century Italian scholar Francesco Petrarch and Claude-Catherine's taste in interior decoration—graceful courtiers mixed with artists, writers, and dramatists. The most famous bards of the period, Pierre de Ronsard and Philippe Desportes among them, were to be found at the duchess of Retz's parties, alongside wags like the wickedly entertaining court gossip Brantôme and other suave gentlemen and charming ladies of Claude-Catherine's acquaintance. Marguerite was an adored member of the duchess's inner circle, which numbered nine women collectively known as the Muses or the Nymphs of Paris. Philippe Desportes was so smitten by Margot that she became the inspiration for his masterwork, *Les Amours d'Hippolyte,* in which he described the queen of Navarre as the world's "unique pearl and everlasting flower."

It was at the duchess's Green Salon that Margot met Joseph de Boniface, seigneur de La Môle. She'd known him before, of course; he was a member of her younger brother François's household. La Môle was in his forties, polished, elegant, and urbane. He was a peculiar mix of devout Catholic and equally devoted ladies' man—Charles IX used to laugh that he could always tell how successful La Môle had been the night before by the number of times he attended Mass the next day. So practiced was La Môle in the art of seduction that it was he who had been delegated as François's nuptial ambassador to England, charged with sweet-talking Elizabeth I into marrying his homely master.

La Môle would never have dared to approach Marguerite while she was still single—the penalties associated with deflowering a maiden princess were severe, as this compromised her value as a potential negotiating chip for international alliances—but now that she was a married woman, well, that was a different story. Infidelity was not simply prevalent at court, it was expected. *Everyone* had a mistress, starting with Charles IX. Before her death, Jeanne d'Albret had reported to her son, Henry, "The king spends much of his time making love, but he thinks nobody knows it. At nine in the evening he goes to his study, pretending to work on a book he is writing. His mistress's room adjoins the study." Marguerite's closest friend, Henriette, duchess of Nevers, was having a torrid affair with Annibal de Coconnas, another of François's noblemen. Even Margot's brother Henri adhered to standard court practice and made surreptitious love to the prince of Condé's wife.*

La Môle was everything Henry of Navarre wasn't. He knew exactly what to say to a woman like Marguerite and, more important, how to look and sound while he was saying it. The duke of Guise had been her first crush. La Môle was a seasoned man of the world. She was two decades his junior, her husband was away for an extended period, and anyway he didn't want her, and all around her were the coquettes of the Flying Squadron urging her to just let go and experience the intoxicating pleasures of love. She never had a chance.†

WHILE MARGOT SPARKLED IN Paris, her husband was suffering miserably along with the rest of the royal army outside the walls of La Rochelle.

Despite the potency of the Crown's forces—Charles had allocated his brother more than thirty thousand soldiers with whom to besiege the city, supplemented by a battery of heavy artillery, consisting of twenty mounted guns—the Huguenot stronghold proved difficult to conquer. Dissension arose almost immediately among the French commanding officers. Henri, as lieutenant-general, was nominally in charge, but he was continually challenged by his younger brother, François, duke of Alençon (whom he loathed), as well as by the arrogant duke of Guise (of whom he was also none

---

* Although Henri was capable of having sex with women, as he grew older he demonstrated a marked preference for men.

† There seems to have been so much illicit *l'amour* in Paris at this time that there was some confusion over exactly who was sleeping with whom. A Parisian chronicler of the period, Pierre de L'Estoile, recounted the story that Charles IX, the duke of Guise, and a number of the duke of Nevers's friends, suspecting that La Môle was the duchess of Nevers's lover, once waited at the stairway of the Louvre to ambush him on his way out of her apartments. But he never showed up, because he had actually spent the night with Marguerite.

too fond). The king of Navarre and his cousin the prince of Condé, while wielding no real authority, were also annoying to the lieutenant-general because they had to be watched carefully lest they defect to the Huguenot side.

It's never fun to slog out the frigid winter months in an exposed military camp plagued by hunger and disease and surrounded by legions of sullen, shivering, unwashed companions at arms, but it is even less appealing to have to endure these conditions while obviously losing. The Huguenot militias entrenched behind the stout walls of the city were well armed and used to defending themselves; when the royal cannons were fired, they shot back to devastating effect. The siege persisted dispiritingly and without prospect of ending through the winter and into the spring. Thousands died, and thousands more deserted. The discontent evidenced among the rank and file was echoed by a number of the aristocracy who found the entire exercise pointless and self-defeating. Increasingly, the Crown—which included not only the king but also the queen mother and the lieutenant-general—was viewed as incompetent by this group of moderate Catholics, disgruntled knights, and opportunistic noblemen, and they looked about them for a candidate around whom to rally their support, one who could force a change in policy. It had to be someone of royal birth or almost-royal birth, as no sixteenth-century political opposition movement could succeed without the participation of a leader of exalted rank. There being very few aspirants available who met this all-important qualification, by process of elimination they eventually settled on the lieutenant-general's ambitious younger brother, François, duke of Alençon, and the equally disaffected first prince of the blood Henry, king of Navarre. This was the beginning of what would become known as the Politique movement.

Not that Henry and François particularly liked or trusted one another. Nor did they have the same goals. François was motivated by wounded pride and an overriding competitiveness with his older brothers. He felt he was routinely overlooked and slighted, and he seethed over these perceived insults. Just eighteen, François yearned for wealth and honors in accordance with his rank but was unable to persuade either his mother or the king to grant him additional favors. The lieutenant-general thought so little of his younger brother's opinion that he didn't even bother to include him in the military planning sessions, where the battle preparations were discussed.

Henry's sole aim, on the other hand, was to escape to the safety of his own lands and subjects in Navarre and put as much distance as possible between himself and the hell of the royal court, his Catholic wife, and her murderous family. About the only thing these two young men did agree upon was that the lieutenant-general was overbearing and obnoxious, they didn't like taking orders from him, and they wanted to be rid of him. On this somewhat tenuous basis was their relationship—and, later, the Politique movement—founded.

As it turned out there was no need to revolt against the lieutenant-general, at least in the short term: fate—or, rather, the queen mother—intervened. For in the late spring of 1573 came word that Henri had received the rather dubious honor of being elected king of Poland.

To fulfill Nostradamus's prophecy and see all her sons crowned kings was Catherine's most cherished objective. Over the years she had devoted countless hours and much deliberation to its accomplishment. It was this goal (along with her survival as head of state), not the welfare of France, that lay at the root of all her foreign policy and fueled her diplomatic efforts. She cared not which realm she secured for her progeny—Catholic or Protestant, wealthy or impoverished, ally or enemy—so long as the land in question boasted a throne. She had sacrificed her daughter to Henry of Navarre in order to keep the crown of England safe for François, but this still left her favorite son, Henri, without a monarchy to call his own. When the last of a long line of hereditary rulers in Poland died without a male heir, Catherine saw her chance. She immediately dispatched Jean de Monluc, the bishop of Valence, the only court official of her acquaintance who had ever visited that faraway Slavic kingdom, along with one of her favorite dwarves who happened to be Polish, and instructed the pair to do whatever it took to procure the crown for Henri. What it took was a bribe of four hundred thousand *livres* outright, along with the promise of hundreds of thousands more in the future, in order to underwrite an army, wipe out the Slavic national debt, and provide scholarships to Paris to educate a hundred sons of the Polish aristocracy, all to be paid out of the already bankrupt French royal treasury. But in the end Henri got his title. The first time one of the members of the Flying Squadron curtsied low before her and murmured with cunning flattery, "I salute you as the mother of the King of Poland," Catherine was so overcome with emotion that she sobbed in ecstasy.

The election of the lieutenant-general of France to the throne of Poland was a source of unmitigated joy to many besides his mother. In an instant François, Henry of Navarre, and the prince of Condé were relieved of their most reviled tormentor. Margot, too, had the satisfaction of knowing that the older brother who had persecuted her before her marriage and then taken a leading hand in ensuring that her wedding would go down in history as one of the most despicable betrayals of hospitality of all time would be leaving the kingdom to take up a post in a land so remote that it was unlikely she would ever be called upon to visit it. Even Charles, who had finally been diagnosed with consumption (tuberculosis) and was visibly failing, was comforted by the fact that his mother's favorite, the detested Henri, who had conspired treasonably against him and gotten off scot-free, would not be around to gloat at his death. As for the Huguenots, they could hardly believe their luck: Henri's ascension to the Polish crown was so expensive that the siege of La Rochelle had to be immediately abandoned and peace terms drawn up in their favor so that funds could be diverted to purchase the lieutenant-general's kingdom for him. So, again to the Catholics' incredulity, less than a year after the catastrophe on Saint Bartholomew's Day, the Protestants had gained back almost all the political ground they had lost in the immediate aftermath of the massacre.

About the only person in France who was not completely thrilled by this unlooked-for honor was the prospective king himself. Being monarch of Poland might not have been too bad if it meant only an appreciation in rank, but it seemed that everyone expected him to actually take up residence in his newly acquired realm. Poland! What did Catherine's son know of Poland? He'd never been out of France. He didn't speak the language. He didn't know the customs. He could barely find it on a map. It is entirely likely that at this point Henri deeply regretted his decision to reject Elizabeth I. If he'd played along with his mother from the beginning, marriage negotiations with England would probably still be dragging on and that little toad François would have been the one exiled to the Slavs instead of the other way around.

But there was nothing he could do about it. Step by step the formalities associated with his coronation, set in motion by Catherine, moved relentlessly forward, propelling him toward his fate, just as the preparations for the Navarre wedding, also instigated by the queen mother, had previously overtaken and conquered Marguerite. On August 19, 1573, an embassy from Poland consisting of a dozen or so of the most important noblemen in the kingdom, accompanied by their servants and retainers, trundled into Paris in a line of fifty coaches. They were welcomed officially into the city by the royal family and treated to a magnificent dinner and entertainment at the Tuileries Palace in celebration of the exalted occasion. Brantôme was a guest at this affair and described it in detail. Marguerite dazzled the Polish delegation at the reception and ball; she must have taken distinct pleasure in doing all she could to recommend her brother to his new subjects and in so doing hurry his departure. "For my part," Brantôme recalled, "the most becoming array in which I ever saw her was, as I think, and so did others, on the day when the queen-mother made a fête at the Tuileries for the Poles. She [Marguerite] was robed in a velvet gown of Spanish rose, covered with spangles, with a cap of the same velvet, adorned with plumes and jewels of such splendor as never was. She looked so beautiful in this attire, as many told her, that she wore it often and was painted in it."

The Polish envoys, out of their element in the ornate surroundings, were apparently struck dumb by the sight of their new king's sister: "She seemed to them so beautiful and so superbly and richly accoutred and adorned, and with such great majesty and grace that they were speechless at such beauty," Brantôme reported. "Among others, there was Lasqui, the chief of the embassy, whom I heard say, as he retired, overcome by the sight: 'No, never do I wish to see such beauty again. Willingly would I do as do the pilgrims to Mecca...where they stand speechless, ravished, and so transfixed at the sight of that superb mosque that they...burn their eyes out with hot irons till they lose their sight...saying that nothing more could be seen as fine, and therefore would they see nothing.'"★ So taken with Marguerite were the Polish envoys that they turned up at the Louvre the next day to pay their respects to the king and queen of Navarre. As befit a formal audience, the bishop of Kraków, another of the Polish ambassadors, made a pretty speech to Henry in Latin. To the bishop's open-mouthed astonishment, it was Margot who stepped forward afterward and, having obviously understood what was said, graciously answered for her husband in kind with a degree of fluency no other member of her family had managed to acquire. When she finished, the members of the Polish embassy unanimously applauded Marguerite as "a second Minerva, goddess of eloquence," and later referred to her simply as "that divine woman."

Margot's unqualified diplomatic triumph and easy mastery of the Polish delegation underscored her rapidly growing influence at court. As a queen and member of the royal family, she embodied authority—people looked to her for leadership. Nothing bespoke the strength of her political position more than Henri's desperate attempts to regain her friendship before his banishment to Poland.

★ A trifle melodramatic for modern tastes, but he was probably sincere in his admiration. This is just the way they talked in the sixteenth century.

"For some months before he quitted France, he had used every endeavor to efface from my mind the ill offices he had so ungratefully done me," Marguerite reported later in her memoirs. "He solicited to obtain the same place in my esteem which he held during our infancy; and, on taking leave of me, made me confirm it by oaths and promises." But Margot was no longer the naive girl of sixteen who had fallen so readily under the charm of her older, more calculating brother. She was a married woman of twenty with a wealth of firsthand experience of court intrigue. She swore the oaths Henri demanded, but she knew better than to trust him.

The pressure Henri felt to secure allies who would remain loyal to him in his absence was rooted in a glaring political reality: his older brother, the king, was visibly dying. Too weak to hunt, Charles was frequently incapacitated with high fevers and had even begun vomiting blood. By right of succession, since the king had failed to produce a legitimate male heir, when he died the crown would fall to Henri. But if Charles expired while Henri was away in Poland, the resulting confusion and uncertainty that inevitably accompanied a change in rule would encourage plots against him. His brother François might challenge his right to the throne and take over France before Henri had a chance to return. Henri knew that Catherine would do her best to save the kingdom for him, but even she might not be able to withstand a concerted effort to unseat him. Henri tarried in France as long as he could, hoping the king would die quickly so that he would not have to leave at all, but Charles saw through this stratagem. Too ill to stand, the king called his mother into his sickroom and from his bed issued an executive order that Henri be forced to depart for Poland immediately. Catherine bowed to his authority and accompanied her favorite son as far as the duchy of Lorraine before seeing him off on his journey. "Go! Go!" she whispered to the unwilling Henri at their parting. "You will not stay long." And so the new king of Poland took final leave of his family and rode despondently out of Lorraine in quest of his distant, alien domain during the last week of November 1573.

Henri had been correct to worry. He wasn't gone five days before the first of what would prove to be a series of attempted coups designed to take advantage of his absence broke out at court. And Marguerite was right in the middle of them.

IT ALL BEGAN OVER the coveted title of lieutenant-general. Obviously Henri could not simultaneously serve as a foreign potentate *and* head of the French armed forces, so just prior to his departure for Poland he had reluctantly resigned his commission. François, as next in line, naturally assumed that he would be named his brother's successor. After all, Catherine had elevated Henri to the title when he was only sixteen and had no practical experience of battle, and François was eighteen and had already participated in the siege of La Rochelle.

It had therefore come as a highly unpleasant shock to discover that the king had no intention of naming him to this prestigious post. Neither Catherine nor Charles trusted François. They knew he was ambitious and that both the Politiques (the moderate Catholics who resented both Henri and the Guises) and the Huguenots (empowered once again by having withstood the siege of La Rochelle and forcing the queen mother to come to terms) saw him as a counterpoint to the Crown. Under the circumstances, it did not seem like a good idea to either Catherine or Charles to give François, whom the opposition parties were obviously cultivating for leadership, command of the royal army. He might just turn around one day and use it against *them*.

Piqued by this slight to his honor, François had surreptitiously complained to his supporters through trusted members of his household, and they had come up with an impulsive plan. Both the duke of Alençon and Henry of Navarre had accompanied Catherine to Lorraine to bid adieu to Henri. On the return journey the two teenagers plotted to escape from the court (where they were both under close surveillance) and rendezvous with a band of opposition cavalry and soldiers. "The Huguenots, on the death of the Admiral, had obtained from the King my Husband, and my brother Alençon, a written obligation to avenge it," Marguerite explained. "Before St. Bartholomew's Day, they had gained my brother over to their party, by the hope of securing Flanders for him [i.e., they bribed him]. They now persuaded my husband and him to leave the King and Queen on their return, and pass into Champagne, there to join some troops which were in waiting to receive them."

Unfortunately, the conspirators were not terribly discreet, with the result that the king of Navarre's chancellor, Monsieur de Miossans,* soon got wind of the intrigue. Appalled, he tried to put a stop to it.

This was not a case of a fanatical Catholic, a Guise disciple, or one of Catherine's own spies working against the Huguenots. Miossans was one of the two men in Henry's household whom Marguerite had personally saved from death after the Saint Bartholomew's Day massacre by going down on her knees in front of her mother and the king. He had been a Huguenot before being obliged, like his master, to convert to Catholicism in order to save his life. He was one of the men who had stayed up the night before the massacre with the king of Navarre in his bedroom discussing what to do about the assassination attempt on Coligny. There is no reason whatever to doubt his loyalty to Henry. If Miossans was against Henry and François's rushing off half-cocked to start what amounted to a rebellion, then most likely the two teenagers were out of their depth and there was something seriously amiss with the plan.†

As further proof that Miossans was trying to protect his lord and was not motivated by ideology or personal gain, he did *not* take his information directly to either Catherine or the king, both of whom would have rewarded him handsomely for his service but most likely

---

* Margot spells this man's name variously as "M. de Miossans" and "M. de Mioflano," but it is the same counselor.

† Subsequent events would prove him right. The Politiques and the Huguenots were very adept at devising plots but not nearly so skillful at implementing them. Either Miossans suspected that Henry and François were being set up (since their secret escape plans were obviously not nearly so secret as they assumed) or he doubted that there would be an armed force of any significance awaiting them should they manage to escape after all. In either case, they would have been captured and Henry likely executed for treason.

would have dealt harshly with Henry. Instead he turned to the woman to whom he owed fealty, who had previously shown him such mercy: Marguerite. "M. de Miossans, a Catholic gentleman, having received an intimation of this design, considered it so prejudicial to the interests of the King his master, that he communicated it to me with the intention of frustrating a plot of so much danger to themselves and to the State," Margot reported. The queen of Navarre immediately saw his point. The last thing she needed was for Henry to be caught and tried for treason. She couldn't approach her husband directly; he already didn't trust her. He'd never believe that she was acting as much in his interest as in her own. So she handled it as deftly as she could. "I went immediately to the King and the Queen my mother, and informed them that I had a matter of the utmost importance to lay before them; but that I could not declare it unless they would be pleased to promise me that no harm should ensue from it," she declared. Catherine and Charles agreed, and she told them of her brother and husband's plans to escape the court and join forces with the Huguenots. "I begged they might be excused, and that they might be prevented from going away without any discovery being made that their designs had been found out. All this was granted me, and measures were so prudently taken to stay them, that they had not the least suspicion that their intended evasion was known," Margot concluded.

Perhaps; but it seems that someone alerted at least François, if not Henry, to the possibility that the queen of Navarre had interfered with their plans, because very soon after this incident the duke of Alençon made a concerted effort to gain his sister's affections—and, coincidentally, her support for his cause. "Soon after [the thwarted escape attempt], we arrived at St. Germain, where we stayed some time, on account of the King's indisposition," Marguerite recalled. "All this while my brother Alençon used every means he could devise to ingratiate himself with me, until at last I promised him my friendship, as I had before done to my brother the King of Poland. As he had been brought up at a distance from Court, we had hitherto known very little of each other, and kept ourselves at a distance. Now that he had made the first advances, in so respectful and affectionate a manner, I resolved to receive him into firm friendship, and to interest myself in whatever concerned him, without prejudice, however, to the interests of my good brother King Charles, whom I loved more than any one besides, and who continued to entertain a great regard for me, of which he gave me proofs as long as he lived."

Despite his having once beaten her and forced her into a marriage she didn't want, Marguerite's fondness for Charles seems to have been genuine. Certainly these two drew closer together after the horror of Saint Bartholomew's Day, as the realization set in that both of them had been deliberately set up and duped by Catherine and Henri. The guilt Charles experienced over the massacre consumed him every bit as relentlessly as his tuberculosis. He blamed his mother for having forced his hand: "Madame, you are the cause of all!" he once spat at her. Shunning Catherine but needing warmth, he turned to Marguerite, who understood and shared his pain and who was also starved for affection. Their attachment was not sexual, as has often been implied; this was not about passion but rather a shared exclusion from maternal love. They had been used and rejected and had bonded together in self-protection as a result.

François, too, was an outsider in the family, scorned by both Charles and Henri and slighted by Catherine. Perhaps it was this quality that awakened Marguerite's sympathies and persuaded her to join forces with her youngest sibling. Or it may have been her knowledge that Charles was dying and that when he did, Henri would come back. It was better to take a chance on the devil she didn't know than to leave herself completely unprotected against the man who (despite his recent assurances of devotion) had made it his business to torment her in the past. Certainly it didn't hurt that her lover, the seigneur de La Môle, was a trusted member of François's household.

To be true to both Charles *and* François, however, represented something of a challenge, as Margot soon discovered. For no sooner had she pledged her friendship to the duke of Alençon than another intrigue involving his and Henry's flight from court surfaced. Inexplicably stymied in their previous attempt to liberate the princes, the Politiques, in alliance with the Huguenots, tried again to free their two leaders, but this time in a far more menacing manner. Instead of having François and Henry run away from court to join forces with an army, they decided to bring the army to them.

So bold a stroke might have represented a serious threat to the Crown—if the plan could be carried off with precision and discipline. Luckily for Charles and Catherine, these qualities were not much in evidence among the members of the opposition party. For example, it is helpful when organizing the overthrow of an established government if everybody involved in the cabal pays attention to minor details such as the date on which the various troops comprising the rebel force are supposed to rendezvous and storm the castle. Obviously it is better to show up all at once and surprise and overwhelm your adversaries rather than trickle in piecemeal and hang around waiting to be discovered. In any event, one of the cavalry commanders failed to take this bit of acknowledged wisdom sufficiently into account and showed up ten days early with just enough men to arouse the queen mother's suspicions but not enough to mount an attack on the palace.

The court was still in residence at Saint-Germain. At the sighting of the small Huguenot force, panic ensued. Catherine called for reinforcements, including the fearsome Swiss Guard. "The excitement was very great, baggage was trussed up, the Cardinals of Lorraine and Guise leapt to horse to escape from Paris and many others followed their example," an eyewitness reported. Petrified at the consequences of being found out and accused of treason, François broke down immediately, rushed to his mother (who, he rightly concluded, was more likely to be lenient with him than his brother the king), and gave away the entire conspiracy, implicating not simply Henry of Navarre but also everyone he knew, including the seigneur de La Môle and Annibal de Coconnas (lover of Marguerite's best friend, Henriette), who had acted as liaisons between him and the

Politiques. That same night, the entire court fled to Vincennes, with the duke of Alençon and the king of Navarre under heavy guard. "We set off...two hours after midnight, putting King Charles in a litter, and the Queen my mother taking my brother and the King my husband with her in her own carriage," Marguerite reported.

The queen of Navarre has sometimes been accused by historians of having gained advance knowledge of this plot through her relationship with La Môle and of betraying him to her mother. This is because Margot observes in her memoirs that, with Charles "daily growing worse...the Huguenots [were] constantly forming new plots. They were very desirous to get my brother the Duc d'Alençon away from Court. I got intelligence, from time to time, of their designs." But there is no indication that Catherine had any hint of this particular intrigue until the rebel band arrived prematurely and François blabbed to save his own skin, so it seems unlikely that Marguerite informed on her lover. Also, the queen of Navarre was not one of those implicated by her brother in the scheme, and her subsequent actions would indicate that her sympathies lay rather with the insurgents than their opponents.

It was well known that François had thrown himself upon the mercy of his mother. It probably saved his life, for Charles was as angered by this blatant repudiation of his rule as he had been at any time during his reign. "They could at least have waited for my death," he was heard to fume as they carried him hurriedly in his litter from Saint-Germain. The duke of Alençon and the king of Navarre were both arrested and thrown in prison pending trial. Marguerite tried to get them out: "I had resolved to save them at the hazard of my own ruin with the King, whose favor I entirely enjoyed at that time," she stated. As a result of her high rank at court, the queen of Navarre had unique access to the prisoners. "I was suffered to pass to and from them in my coach, with my women, who were not even required by the guard to unmask, nor was my coach ever searched," Margot remembered. "This being the case, I had intended to convey away one of them disguised in a female habit. But the difficulty lay in settling betwixt themselves which should remain behind in prison, they being closely watched by their guards, and the escape of one bringing the other's life into hazard. Thus they could never agree upon the point, each of them wishing to be the person I should deliver from confinement," she reported.

La Môle and Coconnas fared far worse than their master; they were repeatedly tortured. La Môle was singled out especially because his rooms had been searched and a small, crude wax image discovered with a skewer stuck in its chest. Catherine, of course, was immediately interested and claimed that the figure represented the king and that this sorcery was responsible for Charles's diseased lungs. La Môle was shackled and subjected to the boot—a hideous device consisting of two iron plates, studded with spikes, which were attached to the lower leg—a sort of steel vise—then slowly compressed, crushing the bone inside. "God! May I die if I've ever made any image of wax against the King…Put me to death if poor La Mole ever thought of such a thing," he moaned and begged.*

While her lover endured the agony of this interrogation, Marguerite's husband and brother were hauled before a special commission of judges and required to defend themselves against the charge of treason. François addressed this body in a long, rambling, seat-of-the-pants explanation in which he justified himself on the grounds that Coligny had promised him the governorship of Flanders and that his sole intention in escaping the court was to use the Huguenot troops to this end. In his recitation, he managed to incriminate nearly all his closest friends and most loyal supporters.

Henry's rejoinder to the court, which he read aloud from a prepared statement, was far more sophisticated and persuasive. That was because it had been written by his wife. "My husband, having no counselor to assist him, desired me to draw up his defense in such a manner that he might not implicate any person, and, at the same

---

* In fact, the image was intended as part of a love spell. The figure was that of a girl. The needle stuck in her heart had been placed there to promote her admirer's suit.

time, clear my brother and himself from any criminality of conduct," Margot confirmed. This she managed to do by masterfully turning the tables on the prosecution. In substance, her argument was that because the king of Navarre was treated so badly by the court, with so little respect for his undeniable rank and position and at constant risk of his life, he had little choice but to try to escape from these unnatural conditions. If, on the other hand, the king and the queen mother would grant him the respect and honor he deserved as a sovereign in his own right and the first prince of the blood, then he would prove "to them both, a very humble, faithful, and obedient servant." Marguerite's argument proved unassailable. "With God's help I accomplished this task to his great satisfaction, and to the surprise of the commissioners, who did not expect to find them [Henry and François] so well prepared to justify themselves." This was the second time since her marriage that Marguerite had saved Henry of Navarre's life.

But alas, in saving her husband she destroyed her lover. Denied the opportunity to execute the principals in the scheme, Catherine and Charles chose instead to take their vengeance on La Môle and Coconnas. It was decided that both servants would be put to death and that as a further insult they would be treated as common criminals and publicly decapitated. Coconnas was quick to see the hypocrisy of the sentence. "You see, my lords, the humble are punished and the mighty, who are responsible, abide in safety," he cried on hearing himself condemned. Guilt-ridden, François begged Catherine and Charles for his loyal friends' lives, weeping and going down on his knees. Eventually, he succeeded in convincing Catherine to spare the two men the humiliation of a public execution and dispatch them quietly in private, but the order arrived too late. It was said later that La Môle's last words were, "May God and the Blessed Virgin have mercy on my soul! Commend me to the good graces of the Queen of Navarre and the ladies!"

In her memoirs, Margot says only that La Môle was executed. But the memoirs of the duke of Nevers, written later, are more suggestive.

According to that document, on the night following the execution, the queen of Navarre and her friend the duchess of Nevers slipped silently out of the Louvre and, shrouded in grief and veils, took a carriage to the Place de Grève, site of La Môle's and Coconnas's martyrdom. There they claimed their lovers' heads, carrying them to a private chapel in Montmartre, where they had them interred, perfumed, and embalmed as a mark of honor and respect.★

On May 30, 1574, exactly one month after the slaying of La Môle and Coconnas for treason, Charles IX died of tuberculosis. He was twenty-four. Cut down so early in life, he was unable to redeem his name after the Saint Bartholomew's Day Massacre. The young man who had craved honor and dreamed of courage and constancy as a child would go down in history as a depraved madman. This is not quite fair, as even in death he was dominated by a greater power. In her letter to the king of Poland advising him of the demise of his elder brother, Catherine claimed that Charles "begged that I should take the administration of the kingdom" and that his last words were "my mother."

Margot took Charles's death very hard, particularly as it came so close on the heels of La Môle's execution. She called him "the only stay and support of my life, — a brother from whose hands I never received anything but good... In a word, when I lost King Charles, I lost everything," she grieved.

Her sorrow was not only over the demise of a beloved brother. Charles's end meant the ascension of the duke of Anjou to the throne. "He [Charles] begged me that I should send in all haste to get you," Catherine wrote to the new king of France. "You know how much I love you and when I think that you will never more leave us that makes me take everything with patience," the queen mother added with satisfaction.

Henri was coming home.

★ Because the duke of Nevers's memoirs, like Marguerite's own, were published in the following century, there is no way to prove or disprove this story. Certainly, though, it was in keeping with Margot's romantic temperament and at the very least is reflective of how she was viewed at court.

11

Of *Mignons* and Mistresses

[A prince] is rendered despicable by being thought change-
able, frivolous, effeminate, timid, and irresolute; which a
prince must guard against as a rock of danger, and manage
so that his actions show grandeur, high courage, seriousness,
and strength.

—Niccolò Machiavelli, *The Prince*

CATHERINE WAS SO EAGER FOR Henri's return that she sent not one but two messengers, each instructed to travel by separate roads so as to minimize the chance of delay or interception, to inform the king of Poland that his older brother had passed away and that consequently he was now monarch of France. The first of these arrived in Kraków on June 13, 1574, just two weeks after Charles's death.

The news could not have been more welcome to Henri and the coterie of nine young gallants who had elected to remain with him during his exile. Henri had not been at all happy in his adopted realm. He had arrived with an impressive retinue of French aristocrats, but the majority of these had been only too pleased to return to France after the opulent coronation festivities had concluded, leaving Henri and his companions, among whom were Guast (Marguerite's bitter enemy, who had taken a leading role in persecuting her for her romantic attachment to the duke of Guise before her marriage) and two very attractive rakes, René de Villequier and

Jacques Lévy de Quélus, also called Caylus, to face the bleak isolation of a winter in Poland.

The fact was, there wasn't anything to *do* in Poland. There wasn't much in the way of nightlife, nobody knew how to flirt or throw a good party, and Henri didn't care for cold weather or outdoor sports like hunting. He sulked in his castle away from everyone but his small French entourage. He did no official or administrative work but instead wrote letters home to his mother every day and penned passionate love notes to the prince of Condé's wife, even pricking his finger and scribbling to her in his own blood. After a while, his subjects, displeased by their new sovereign's ill humor and general unavailability, complained about his behavior and Henri roused himself enough to throw a few banquets, but his heart clearly wasn't in it. He was lonely and miserable, and in his misery the homosexuality that he had kept hidden in France, perhaps even from himself, came out. For according to the ambassador to Poland from Savoy, who seems to have been in a position to know, while Henri was pouring out his heart in blood letters to the princess of Condé he was also engaged in a sexual relationship with at least the handsome Villequier and possibly others of his circle. "He has been imbued by him [Villequier] with the vice which nature detests which he could not unlearn," the Savoyard reported. "I will say only that his cabinet has been a real harem of all lubricity and lewdness, a school of sodomy, where filthy revels have occurred which all the world has known about."

Henri's Polish subjects did not view the tidings of his brother's death with the same enthusiasm as did their sovereign. For all Henri's faults as a king, they wanted to keep him (and his promised future income stream) in Poland. They naturally felt that their realm was every bit the equal of France in terms of prestige and importance and insisted that Henri stay with them. Consequently, he and his little band of devoted acolytes had to pretend to agree to remain and then make a mad dash for freedom by first feigning sleep and then hiding in the kitchen in a very unkinglike manner before fleeing through the servants' entrance at midnight. Even so, their ruse was discovered, and they were pursued by the Polish baronage all the way to the border with Moravia, which, luckily, was under imperial rule, enabling them to cross over the river and into safety.

For a man who had voiced such anxiety about possible challenges to his succession should he stay too long away from France, Henri certainly took his time getting back. He had made his somewhat inglorious escape from Kraków on the evening of June 18, just five days after learning of Charles's death, and within a week was in Vienna. There, the whopping sum of fifty thousand crowns awaited him, sent by a doting Catherine to pay for his journey home.* But instead of going straight to France, he lingered for two weeks in Vienna, where he and his followers were lavishly entertained by the emperor, before proceeding on to a leisurely two-month tour of Venice, Padua, Ferrara, Mantua, and Turin. His behavior was that of a man who had lost years in prison (he had been in Poland approximately seven months) and was finally back in civilization, where he intended to enjoy himself. He did not write his mother once during his travels and ignored her many pressing appeals to return. Like any good tourist, he admired the sights, shopped extensively, and reciprocated his hosts' profuse hospitality. He particularly adored Venice, where he was in his element and could meander from merchant to merchant or simply float for hours on a golden barge provided by the doge. He spent 1,125 *écus* on perfume alone and bought gold, diamonds, and a pearl necklace from the most expensive jeweler in Italy. By the time he finally crossed over into French territory he had spent all the money his mother had sent him.

He made his official entry into Lyon, where the royal court was waiting for him, on September 6, 1574. The entire family was present, and there was a great show of unity and bonhomie. The queen mother cried in happiness at her son's homecoming, and both

---

* A crown was the colloquial name for a gold coin of the period. Exchange rates fluctuated widely, but one gold crown could be worth anywhere from ten to thirty *livres*. Catherine was only able to send Henri this much money by diverting funds that were supposed to have been used as wages for the royal army.

François and Henry of Navarre pledged their undying loyalty to the new king. Only Marguerite, who had anticipated this moment with dread for months, struggled to keep her composure. "Amidst the embraces and compliments of welcome in that warm season, crowded as we were together and stifling with the heat, I found a universal shivering come over me, which was plainly perceived by those near me," she later recalled. "It was with difficulty I could conceal what I felt when the King, having saluted the Queen my mother, came forward to salute me."

Her fears for her safety and position at court would prove only too true. Henri was not in Lyon three days before he went right for her.

ALTHOUGH HENRI HAD NOT bothered to communicate with his mother while he was on holiday in Italy, this had not prevented her from writing to him, and so the new king of France was aware that Catherine was keeping both his younger brother and the king of Navarre under such close surveillance that they were virtual prisoners. "I have forbidden any subject of my lord and son the king to quit the realm without my permission," the queen mother had informed him coolly. Henri was further cognizant that Marguerite had stepped in and saved her husband from execution by coordinating the defense at his trial and that since this time a tenuous trust had developed between the king and queen of Navarre. The establishment of amicable relations between these two, in combination with Margot's friendship and protection of François, made the possibility of a revolt against him that much more likely. Encouraged by his principal adviser, Guast, he rode into Lyon determined to do what he could to dissolve this alliance by setting husband against wife and cousin against cousin. This being the court of France, he naturally chose sex as his weapon of choice.

It was the queen of Navarre's first visit to Lyon, so soon after she arrived she and some of the members of the Flying Squadron decided to do a little sightseeing. "Mademoiselle de Montigny...observing to us that the Abbey of St. Pierre was a beautiful convent, we all resolved to visit it," Marguerite reported. The entire party piled into Margot's coach and drove to the church, which was located in a part of town where many courtiers had rented rooms. "My carriage was easily to be distinguished, as it was gilt and lined with yellow velvet trimmed in silver," Margot observed. The coachman was commanded to wait in the square while Marguerite and her friends visited the convent. While they were inside, "the King passed through the square on his way to see Quélus, who was then sick," said Margot. "He had with him the King my husband, D'O [another courtier, unnamed]—and the fat fellow Ruffé.

"The King, observing no one in my carriage, turned to my husband and said: 'There is your wife's coach, and that is the house where Bidé lodges. Bidé is sick, and I will engage my word she is gone upon a visit to him. Go,' said he to Ruffé, 'and see whether she is not there.'" Ruffé, understanding the implication—that Margot was not tending to a sick man but meeting a lover—did all he could to ingratiate himself with the king. "I need not tell you he did not find me there; however, knowing the King's intention, he, to favor it, said loud enough for the King my husband to hear: 'The birds have been there, but they are now flown.' This," Margot concluded grimly, "furnished sufficient matter for conversation until they reached home."

To be caught in open daylight in a compromising situation violated Catherine's unspoken rules of decorum, so Henri made haste, as soon as he had returned to court, to inform her of her daughter's supposed indiscretion. Marguerite finished her tour of the abbey and came back to discover herself the centerpiece of a laughably contrived but nonetheless odious scandal. Luckily Henry, who had evidently warmed to his wife after she had saved his life a second time, warned her of the plot: "Upon this occasion, the King my husband displayed all the good sense and generosity of temper for which he is remarkable," Margot recalled gratefully. "He saw through the design, and he despised the maliciousness of it." Her husband laughed and sent her to her mother to find out the details of her sin but made it a point to reassure her. "I do not give the least credit to the story," said Henry, "which I plainly perceive to be fabricated in order to stir up a difference betwixt us two, and break off the friendly intercourse between your brother [François] and me."

Bewildered, Margot sought out her mother, who received her in high dudgeon. "She would not hear a word I had to offer, but continued to rate me in a furious manner; whether it was through fear, or affection for her son, or whether she believed the story in earnest, I know not. When I observed to her that I understood the King had done me this ill office in her opinion, her anger was redoubled, and she endeavored to make me believe that she had been informed of the circumstance by one of her own *valets de chambre,* who had himself seen me at the place."

But of course the presence of so many witnesses who could vouch for Marguerite's innocent visit to the chapel made it very difficult for Catherine to persist in believing Henri's story, and within a day or two both were obliged to retract their accusations. The queen mother took the usual way out—she punished an underling. "She had discovered, she said, that there was not the least foundation for the report her *valet de chambre* had made, and should dismiss him from her service as a bad man," Margot related wryly. But this was not enough for her daughter. "As she perceived by my looks that I saw through this disguise, she said everything she could think of to persuade me to a belief that the King had not mentioned it to her. She continued her arguments, and I still appeared incredulous. At length the King entered the closet, and made many apologies, declaring he had been imposed on, and assuring me of his most cordial friendship and esteem; and thus matters were set to rights again." Score: Margot, Henry, and François 1; Henri and Catherine 0.

Sadly, this episode, seemingly so trivial, represented the high point of cooperation between Marguerite and her husband. Henri had assumed that Margot was the weak link in the alliance, but he had underestimated her. The next time he struck, which was very soon, he would not take his sister on directly but take aim at her through Henry and François. And this time, his blade would thrust home.

AFTER LYON, THE COURT set off on an extended journey through Provence before eventually turning north in preparation for an elaborate coronation ceremony in Reims. Along the way, Henri's subjects began to get glimmers of their new king's character and notions of government.

Henri faced a number of serious, but not insurmountable, problems upon his ascension. The most pressing concern was the bleak condition of the royal treasury. Put simply, the kingdom was bankrupt. In addition to the money Henri had squandered on his way home from Poland, Catherine had spent a truly staggering sum — estimated at 150,000 crowns — on Charles's funeral. The debts incurred during the siege of La Rochelle were still unpaid, the royal army was owed back wages, and even Catherine's ever-present Italian bankers refused to lend to her. They had good reason: every year, the French royal government incurred expenses of approximately twenty million *livres,* to which had to be added current and past-due debt of some additional twelve million *livres.* But as a result of the damage to the agricultural economy from the continuing civil wars, the treasury was only taking in about 4.5 million *livres* a year in revenues, leaving a deficit of some 27.5 million *livres.* "The bad administration of money, and the bad policing of the country which has prevailed with the civil wars, have brought the kingdom of France . . . to such a pass that at present it is deformed in practically every part," reported the Venetian ambassador. "Everywhere one sees ruin: the livestock for the most part destroyed, and great stretches of good land uncultivated, and many peasants forced to leave their homes to become vagabonds. Everything has risen to exorbitant prices, principally victuals, [for] which I have paid six times their former value," he complained. There is no question that Henri was aware of the problem, as one of his most senior military advisers sent him a letter immediately upon his return from Poland urging him to address this woeful state of affairs. "The most important and chief point is finances, because without these, everything is stayed and nothing can be executed," the counselor wrote forcefully.

A dire lack of funds was not the only obstacle plaguing the kingdom upon Henri's return in the fall of 1574. The Huguenots were threatening to renew open hostilities. The prince of Condé, who *had* managed to escape the court, was in Germany negotiating for troops. Elizabeth I was covertly supplying the French Protestants with money. And the Politiques had even come to an arrangement in Languedoc whereby Catholics and Huguenots had put aside their differences to work together for freedom of religion and to expel Catherine's Italian advisers, who were perceived as being particularly greedy and influential, from France.

And yet despite these admittedly adverse economic and political realities, Henri's position was not nearly as precarious as it seemed. The king had a number of advantages working in his favor. The Catholic majority, for example, was firmly behind him and against the Huguenots. To them he was the lieutenant-general, a seasoned, victorious commander and keeper of the faith who had distinguished himself on Saint Bartholomew's Day. The Guises and all their vassals and supporters were with him. If he had behaved with energy and decisiveness; if he had lived up to his reputation as a warrior or, better yet, co-opted the Politiques by naming François lieutenant-general, as was his due as next in line to the throne; if he had made even the faintest show of reining in spending, the likelihood is that the opposition movement would have collapsed and the kingdom would have been brought back to stability.

But Henri did none of this. He had come back from Poland a changed man. Far from demonstrating the drive and ambition of his teenage years as lieutenant-general, Henri indulged in an extravagant, almost epic laziness. He spent most of his time in his room under his silken covers, comfortably propped up by the royal pillows. Occasionally he roused himself enough to lie around on a golden barge floating on the Rhône, as he had in Venice. Guast, Villequier, and Quélus were always with him. A papal envoy attending the court in Lyon was taken aback by Henri's behavior. "The king is a young man as juvenile in mind as can well be imagined," he chided in a report to Rome. "He is a poor creature, most indolent and voluptuous, passing half his life groveling in bed."

Henri's chief concern, the issue that clearly kept him up at night, revolved around etiquette. He spent hours debating fashion, interior design, and the rules by which he as king might be properly approached by those of his subjects whom he deemed worthy of the honor. After extended consultations it was decided that no one could come near the king unless he or she followed a rigorous dress code, which eventually evolved into a list of some twenty or thirty separate outfits—including specifications for the number of ruffles on each shirt—deemed necessary for admission to court. According to one eyewitness, for example, Henri allowed no male visitor into his rooms unless he had on "white pumps, high slippers of black velvet, with stockings with garters and other garments, which had to be worn with the utmost care." The king was also never to be approached while eating; a boundary was erected around his dining table and guards strategically placed to ensure his privacy. This represented a significant change from the past, when the monarch had made himself accessible to society by taking his meals in the presence of a large company. Similarly, as soon as he became king, the former lieutenant-general suddenly broke with established custom by refusing to go about on horseback, as every other French sovereign before him had done for centuries. Instead he chose to travel in a shuttered coach so no member of the hoi polloi could peek in at him. Finally, tradition dictated that any citizen of France could petition the sovereign at any time, but because Henri disliked being accosted by crowds he instituted a new, highly unpopular procedure whereby he would hear such appeals only at certain hours. In fact, every revision Henri made was designed to isolate him from his subjects and keep him from public view.

Which was odd because no one loved spectacle more than Henri. His taste in clothing was so flamboyant that it bordered on the fantastic.

A Spanish diplomat who was in Lyon when Henri arrived described one of his costumes. "For four whole days he was dressed in mulberry satin with stockings, doublet and cloak of the same color. The cloak was very much slashed in the body and had all its folds set with buttons and adorned with ribbons, white and scarlet and mulberry, and he wore bracelets of coral on his arm," he observed. In addition to bracelets, Henri favored diamond earrings and makeup. Prematurely bald, he often wore tall turbans that, with the jewelry, gave him an especially exotic look. His favorite ensemble for costume balls was to dress up as a woman. "The king made jousts, tournaments, ballets, and a great many masquerades, where he was found ordinarily dressed as a woman, working his doublet and exposing his throat, there wearing a collar of pearls and three collars of linen, two ruffled and one turned upside down, in the same way as was then worn by the ladies of the court," a Parisian lawyer confirmed.

But without question the most controversial aspect of Henri's court was the introduction of a new class of favorites. In yet another and perhaps the most bizarre incarnation of *la petite bande,* Henri surrounded himself not with beautiful young women, as had his mother and François I, but with beautiful young men. They were known familiarly in France as Henri's *mignons.* The *mignons* caused sufficient stir among the populace that there is no shortage of eye-witness accounts describing them. They "wear their hair long, curled and recurled by artifice, with little bonnets of velvet on top of it like whores in the brothels, and the ruffles on their linen shirts are of starched finery and one half foot long so that their heads look like St. John's on a platter," observed a Protestant nobleman caustically. "The King arrived...with his troop of young *mignons,* frilled and curled with their crests lifted, the crinkles in their hair, a disguised carriage, with the same ostentation, measured, diapered and covered with violet powders and odiferous scents, which smell up the streets, squares and houses they frequent," seconded the ambassador from Venice. Henri lavished money and titles on his *mignons,* especially the core group of those who had accompanied him to Poland and who remained his closest companions after his return to France.

Even Catherine disliked the *mignons,* mostly because their influence over her son limited her own ability to control the government. When Henri first arrived in Lyon, his mother tried to get him to take the duke of Retz, who had served his brother Charles before him, into his household as a senior official. The same canny Venetian envoy reported that "this strong desire of the Queen Mother was not so much on de Retz's account, as to assure herself more firmly in government; because it is the duty of the first gentleman of the chamber to stay always in the room of the King and to be always near him and so she was sure to know not only what her son did, but, as it were, what her son thought. It was her custom, as I am informed, during the life of the last King, to have reported to her every morning everything the King had said and all that had been said to him, in order to take measures against anything that was being arranged against her power in the government." (Poor Charles.) But Henri was not his brother, and he had his own ideas about what to do with his evenings in the privacy of his own rooms. It was Villequier, Henri's particular intimate from Poland, not the duke of Retz, who attended the king at night.

Unfortunately, Henri's sexual preferences were at odds with acknowledged Catholic dogma, which regarded sodomy and other homosexual acts as mortal sins. The dichotomy between his erotic conduct and his strong Christian beliefs created a fierce moral struggle within the king that triggered extreme swings in behavior. Periods of licentious activity were followed first by long, listless days in bed and then by public penance. He must have been particularly conflicted when he got to Avignon, because he joined an especially masochistic order of penitents known as the Flagellant monks, who walked the streets of the city barefoot and in sackcloth, moaning and chanting while continually scourging themselves. The entire court was obliged to participate one evening in December 1574, when Henri, decked out in a coarse shift attractively embellished with little black death's head ornaments, led a wailing procession through a cold rain, flagellating himself as he went.* This night in the frigid air suffering alongside his howling sovereign was too much for the forty-nine-year-old cardinal of Lorraine, once the greatest power in France. The cardinal, in his open-toed sandals, caught a bad cold and fever and died three weeks later, on the day after Christmas.

The gulf between what his subjects expected of him and what Henri turned out to be was so vast, the comparisons between his gratuitously frivolous lifestyle and their cruel poverty and suffering so stark, that it created its own momentum. The opposition saw its opportunity and pounced, fanning the flames of public disapproval to their advantage. Again, none of his eccentric behavior would have mattered—or mattered as much—if Henri had made even a vague attempt to project the image of an engaged sovereign, a vigorous leader who intended to address the kingdom's many woes. But the only battlefield in which Henri applied himself with any energy at all was in the arena of court intrigue, where he strove to destroy his siblings. And there, it must be admitted, he showed himself indefatigable.

THE KING'S NEXT PLOT, like his previous attempt, again revolved around sex. (Henri and his *mignons* were consistent, if not particularly imaginative.) "After staying some time at Lyons, we went to Avignon," Margot related. "Le Guast, not daring to hazard any fresh imposture, and finding that my conduct afforded no ground for jealousy on the part of my husband, plainly perceived that he could not, by that means, bring about a misunderstanding betwixt my brother and the King my husband. He therefore resolved to try what he could effect through Madame de Sauves."

Charlotte de Sauve was in her early twenties, very pretty, and a valued member of Catherine's Flying Squadron.† Married to a non-

---

* The princess of Condé, to whom Henri had written his blood letters while in Poland, had recently died from complications of childbirth, causing the king great distress. The death's head motif was in her honor.

† Although Marguerite refers to her as "de Sauves," today the generally recognized spelling of Charlotte's name is "de Sauve."

descript midlevel functionary, Charlotte sought advancement by securing the intimate friendship of gentlemen of high rank and then reporting on them to the king and queen mother. Her great value was that she seemed to require no physical attraction at all in order to have sex, which meant that she was willing to sleep with both Marguerite's brother François *and* her husband, Henry. "This occasioned such jealousy between them," Marguerite observed drolly, "that though her favors were divided with M. de Guise, Le Guast, De Souvray, and others, any one of whom she preferred to the brothers-in-law [François and Henry], such was the infatuation of these last, that each considered the other as his only rival."

A practiced coquette, Madame de Sauve was expert at leading one young swain to the brink of rapture, thereby plunging the other into despair, and then with exquisite timing abruptly reversing the process. By this technique did she keep both François and Henry at each other's throats and in a perpetual state of ecstatic anticipation. So smitten were the rival lovers that they availed themselves of any stratagem that could be used to gain advantage over the other in their mistress's affections. Since Charlotte made it plain that the confiding of privileged information yielded her sweetest smiles, the two outdid each other at volunteering secrets. There was no surer line of communication in the kingdom than the love whispers that emanated from Charlotte de Sauve's bedroom directly to Catherine and Henri. Marguerite knew it, but she was helpless. "I now turned my mind to an endeavor to wean my brother's affection from Madame de Sauves," she recalled. "I used every means with my brother to divert his passion; but the fascination was too strong, and my pains proved ineffectual. In anything else, my brother would have suffered himself to be ruled by me; but the charms of this Circe, aided by that sorcerer, Le Guast, were too powerful to be dissolved by my advice. So far was he from profiting by my counsel that he was weak enough to communicate it to her!" Margot exclaimed.

But the competition over Charlotte de Sauve was not the only cause for division between the duke of Alençon and the king of Navarre.

They were also contending for political supremacy within the Huguenot party. And here François, by virtue of his higher rank as a member of the royal family and as next in line to the throne should Henri die without siring sons (which, in light of his preference for male company, was certainly a possibility), held the distinct advantage.

Henry was very bitter about this. After all, his family had been associated with the leadership of the reformed religion almost since its inception; he was clearly the heir apparent to the cause. Yet even the prince of Condé, negotiating for men and support with the Protestant princes of Germany, recognized François as the head of the opposition party in France, and when Elizabeth I sent funds to shore up the Huguenot defenses, she sent them to the duke of Alençon. A Protestant broadside appeared referring to François as "that puissant Hercules commissioned by Heaven to exterminate the monsters who devour and oppress France."★ Henry was unable to contain his resentment. François, he predicted tartly, would "start by being the master of the Huguenots and end by being their valet."

Naturally this information went straight from Charlotte to Catherine and Henri, who leaped on it. The king of France, who seems to have detested François with a passion that exceeded every other emotion, much preferred his brother-in-law to his brother. There were other effective inducements (besides sex) by which the king of Navarre might be coaxed to abandon the Huguenots to his rival and instead join forces with the Crown, and Henri dangled some of these provocatively in front of Margot's husband. According to a chronicler who knew Henry of Navarre, sometime after leaving Avignon for Reims the king of France called his brother-in-law to him, made him captain of the guard, then held out the prospect not only of the lieutenant-generalship of France but also, eventually, of the throne itself. "I would rather that you reigned than that *malotru* [lout] of a traitor, my brother," Henri snarled. "What! Shall I leave my crown to this vile profligate? *Mon frère,* take my advice; [after

---

★ François had been christened Hercules but had subsequently changed his name.

my death] find means to rid yourself of him and gather your friends, so as to be ready at the first moment to seize my crown!"

Henry of Navarre understood in that moment that the king of France was offering to cut his own brother out of the succession and name Henry as his direct heir if he would break off his friendship with François (and by extension with Marguerite, who supported François's advancement) and come over to the monarchy's side. It was a bribe of immense proportion, in recognition of the degree of dishonor that accompanied it, for Henry would have to turn his back on everything he as king of Navarre had stood for: the teachings of his beloved mother, Jeanne d'Albret; the still-searing memory of Coligny and all his friends and vassals who had been betrayed and brutally slaughtered attending his wedding; the profound loyalty of those of his Huguenot subjects who continued to believe in him. Mephistopheles himself could not have fashioned a more corrupt lure. And it cost the king of France nothing to proffer it.

Henry took it. From that time on, the tenuous alliance between the duke of Alençon and the king of Navarre vanished, supplanted by open hostility. To replace his old friends, Henry assiduously courted the Guises, despite the fact that he knew the family had taken the lead in gleefully putting to death all his closest confidants and childhood companions on Saint Bartholomew's Day. The king of Navarre and his former nemesis, the duke of Guise, who must have been in on the scheme, were suddenly to be found constantly in each other's company. They "slept, ate and played their masquerades, ballets and carousels together," reported the chronicler. The English ambassador reported that the Guises intended to support Henry's claim to the throne over François's should the king die without a male heir.

Marguerite, unaware of the significant incentives tendered to Henry by her brother the king, was grieved by her husband's sudden reversal of loyalties and attributed the deterioration in their marital relations, which she had made such efforts to cultivate, to Madame de Sauve's pernicious influence. Charlotte, she said, "persuaded the King my husband that I was jealous of her, and on that account it was that I joined with my brother. As we are ready to give ear and credit to those we love, he believed all she said. From this time he became distant and reserved towards me, shunning my presence as much as possible; whereas, before, he was open and communicative to me as to his sister...What I had dreaded, I now perceived had come to pass. This was the loss of his favor and good opinion; to preserve which I had studied to gain his confidence by a ready compliance with his wishes."

Although she did not perhaps grasp the depth of Henry's defection, Margot was correct in her assessment that Charlotte de Sauve's increasing influence over her husband was somehow connected to his rejection of their marriage. Madame de Sauve's favors had evidently been thrown in as a reward for Henry's acceptance of the king's Faustian bargain, for, to her lover's acute joy (and François's abject wretchedness), Charlotte suddenly began to spend much more time with the king of Navarre. The price of her affections was his complete estrangement from his wife, a condition that no doubt originated with Henri—or, as Margot was convinced, with Guast acting for Henri. Madame de Sauve "now entered more fully into the designs of Le Guast," the queen of Navarre despaired. "In consequence, she used all her art to make the King my husband conceive an aversion for me; insomuch that he scarcely ever spoke with me. He left her late at night, and, to prevent our meeting in the morning, she directed him to come to her at the Queen's levée, which she duly attended; after which he passed the rest of the day with her." Nor could Margot run to François for companionship, for, unwilling to cede the prize to his rival, "my brother likewise followed her with the greatest assiduity, and she had the artifice to make each of them think that he alone had any place in her esteem. Thus was a jealousy kept up betwixt them, and, in consequence, disunion and mutual ruin!" recounted an exasperated Marguerite.

And so the stage was set for a new round of scheming and conspiracy, treason and treachery. And in the middle of it all, for the first time in her life, Margot fell truly in love.

Three in a Marriage

Henri II and Catherine
de' Medici as a young
wedded couple...

...the bewitching Diane
de Poitiers at her toilette.

Catherine de' Medici's outsized father-in-law, François I, king of France.

Antoine de Bourbon, indecisive king of Navarre, father of Henry IV.

Jeanne d'Albret, leader, with Admiral Coligny, of the Huguenot movement and mother of Henry IV.

Catholic Versus Huguenot

The Massacre of Vassy, March 1, 1562, the beginning of the French Wars of Religion.

François, duke of Guise, murdered outside Orléans by a Huguenot spy, February 1563.

Gaspard de Coligny, Admiral of France, target of a botched assassination attempt by Catherine de' Medici that resulted in the Saint Bartholomew's Day massacre, August 1572.

Catherine de' Medici, queen mother of France, in her omnipresent black widow's weeds.

Catherine de' Medici's eldest son, François II, briefly married to Mary Stuart before his premature death at the age of sixteen on December 5, 1560.

Catherine's second son, Charles IX, king of France at the time of the Saint Bartholomew's Day massacre. Charles subsequently died of tuberculosis on May 30, 1574, at the age of twenty-four.

Marguerite de Valois, Catherine de' Medici's youngest daughter, as a child.

Catherine's third and favorite son, Henri III, king of France and Poland.

François, duke of Alençon, Catherine's youngest son and Marguerite's political ally, before his face was ravaged by smallpox.

Marguerite de Valois after her marriage, as queen of Navarre.

Marguerite's husband, Henry of Navarre, later Henry IV, king of France.

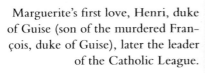

Marguerite's first love, Henri, duke of Guise (son of the murdered François, duke of Guise), later the leader of the Catholic League.

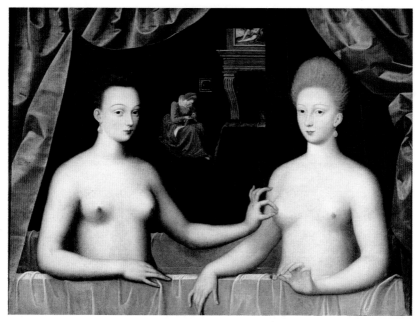

Gabrielle d'Estrées (on the right), Henry of Navarre's mistress, with her sister—a portrait that reflects the mores of the court and perhaps explains why Marguerite's marriage was in difficulties from the beginning.

Ball given by Henri III in honor of his brother François, one of a series of inducements intended to separate François from his Huguenot and Politique allies. Catherine and Henri are pictured standing to the left.

Henri III on his deathbed, bestowing his kingdom on Marguerite's husband, Henry, king of Navarre, later Henry IV.

12

The Great Escape

The character of people varies, and it is easy to persuade
them of a thing, but difficult to keep them in that persua-
sion. And so it is necessary to order things so that when
they no longer believe, they can be made to believe by force.
—Niccolò Machiavelli, *The Prince*

HIS NAME WAS LOUIS DE Clermont d'Amboise, seigneur de Bussy,
better known simply as Bussy. Twenty-five to Marguerite's twenty-
one, the most dangerous swordsman at court, Bussy embodied the
reckless audacity and devastatingly good looks of a professional
swashbuckler. Brantôme praised him as "without equal in our time."
Bussy radiated "an invincible courage...as valiant as his sword, and
as worthy to command an army as any captain in France," another
contemporary concurred admiringly. Even in her memoirs, written
long after the fact, when she was striving for objectivity, Marguerite
could not quite disguise the adoration she felt for this particularly
bold and talented cavalier. Bussy, she noted, was "received with all
the favor which his bravery merited."

Like his predecessor La Môle, Margot's new passion was a member of her brother François's entourage and one of his closest friends.
But this was a relatively recent development. The fearless Bussy had
originally been in service to Henri and had even accompanied his
sovereign to exile in Poland. But Bussy had not found the king's

mode of living in Kraków to be to his taste and had decamped early. Worse, he had switched his allegiance to the duke of Alençon and his beautiful sister upon his return to France, "an acquisition which, on account of the celebrity of Bussy's fame for parts and valor, redounded greatly to my brother's honor, whilst it increased the malice and envy of his enemies," Margot reported. Henri hated Bussy for this betrayal almost as much as he abhorred François himself, and Henri's *mignons* were none too fond of their former compatriot, either.

But he was everything that the queen of Navarre—and many other women at court—dreamed of in a lover. He laughed at danger. He wooed with intensity but also humor. He was an avid reader, accomplished in both Greek and Latin, and manifested a deep appreciation for poetry, even dashing off verses in his spare time. With his gloriously heedless chivalric temperament, Bussy "had no peer for courage, fame, grace, or wit," Marguerite avowed.

She caught up with him in Paris, where the court finally settled in the spring of 1575. It had been an eventful few months. Henri's coronation had been held in Reims in February. In an eerie reenactment of the previous king's investiture, when the heavy crown was placed on his head, Henri had cried out that it hurt him, just as his brother Charles had. (Of course Charles had been a child of ten.) The coronation ceremony had been followed almost immediately by the king's marriage to a younger daughter of a branch of the house of Guise.* She was apparently chosen for her physical resemblance to the deceased princess of Condé. Henri—by then officially Henri III, king of France—had not bothered to consult his mother before making his decision. Catherine's feelings may well be imagined when she discovered that her future daughter-in-law, a mousy, unremarkable girl, came not from royalty but from the Guises. "It

---

* It was necessary for the king to marry in order to attempt to provide France with a male heir, although a papal envoy observed in a letter to the Vatican that "it is only with difficulty that we can imagine that there will be offspring...He is so feeble that if he sleeps *en compagnie* for two or three nights he is unable to get up from his bed for two or three days."

is much discoursed what the Queen Mother may think of it, for although she may like the person well enough because she is not like to take over much upon her, yet she may well doubt what may become of the greatness of the Guises by this affinity," mused the ambassador from England. Marguerite, too, could not have helped but register the irony of her brother's choice, after he had worked so assiduously to prevent her from marrying into the same family. But Henri was king, and he insisted on having his way. The royal nuptials were concluded so quickly that there was not even time for the guests to procure appropriately lavish gifts, although the ceremony itself, originally planned for the morning after the coronation, had to be delayed for hours while the groom painstakingly styled the bride's hair.

The estrangement between the king and queen of Navarre (and, more significant, between the king of Navarre and the duke of Alençon) had persisted throughout the journey north. By the time the court reached Paris, any semblance of amity between Margot's husband and her younger brother had completely disintegrated, threatening Huguenot and Politique prospects for a successful challenge to Catholic dominance. "The quarrel between the King of Navarre and the Duke is greater than ever it was, so that one of these days they will cut the throats one of the other," an English envoy observed glumly. Henry himself seconded the ambassador's assessment in a memorable letter to one of his cousins. "The court is the strangest place you ever saw," Margot's husband wrote. "We are nearly always ready to cut each other's throats. We carry daggers, mail coats and often cuirasses under our clothes...The king is just as much threatened as I am. He loves me more than ever. Monsieur de Guise and Monsieur du Maine never leave me...You never saw how strong I am in friends in this court," he boasted. "I brave all the world. All the cliques which you know about hate me to the death for the love of Alençon and have the third time forbidden my mistress to speak to me and watch her so closely that she wouldn't dare to look at me. I am only waiting the hour to give them battle, because they say they will kill me and I want to get ahead of them."

Under the circumstances, the introduction of so remarkable a swordsman as the revered Bussy on the side of Marguerite and François represented a coup that instantly boosted the legitimacy of the opposition movement and changed the political equation. "At Paris my brother was joined by Bussy," Marguerite explained. "He was inseparable from my brother, in consequence of which I frequently saw him, for my brother and I were always together, his household being equally at my devotion as if it were my own." Henri and Guast, sensitive to the damage to the Crown's image caused by Bussy's defection, moved quickly to counteract the threat. They began by informing Henry of Marguerite's indiscretion, hoping that he would intervene against their target. But for all his bravado ("I am only waiting the hour to give them battle") the king of Navarre, noting the size and martial abilities of his wife's lover and demonstrating that instinct for self-preservation that would serve him so well in the years ahead, prudently demurred. He would take on the world, yes, but Bussy—no.

Frustrated in his first attempt, Henri tried to slander Margot and Bussy again, this time with Catherine. "The King...mentioned it to the Queen my mother, thinking it would have the same effect on her as the tale which was trumped up at Lyons," Marguerite related. But Catherine, who considered the arrangement of her children's marriages to be hers by divine right and who was still furious with Henri for failing to consult her and impetuously marrying the Guise girl—rather than, say, the princess of Sweden, who had been his mother's choice—was having none of it. "But she, seeing through the whole design, showed him the improbability of the story, adding that he must have some wicked people about him, who could put such notions in his head... 'Bussy is a person of quality, and holds the first place in your brother's family,'" Catherine was reported to have continued. "'What grounds are there for such a calumny? At Lyons you caused me to offer her [Margot] an affront, which I fear she will never forget.' The King was astonished to hear his mother talk in this manner," Marguerite observed.

Having failed to dispose of Bussy by intrigue, Henri and Guast determined to rid themselves of him by force. "They entered into a design of assassinating Bussy as he left my brother to go to his own lodgings, which was generally late at night," Margot explained. "They knew that he was always accompanied home by fifteen or sixteen gentlemen, belonging to my brother, and that, notwithstanding he wore no sword, having been lately wounded in the right arm, his presence was sufficient to inspire the rest with courage. In order, therefore, to make sure of the work, they resolved on attacking him with two or three hundred men," she added.

To add the element of surprise to the ambush—three hundred to sixteen evidently not being considered enough of an advantage on its own where Bussy was concerned—Guast ordered his men to extinguish their torches, wait until Bussy and his party came into range, and then fire their harquebuses into the group. Any survivors of the first onslaught were to be cut down with swords. Ordinarily it would be difficult to tell who was who in the dead of night, but Bussy was using a scarf as a makeshift sling for his wounded arm. Guast instructed his men to look for the scarf and take particular care to butcher the man wearing it.

The trap was set. Sometime after midnight on a late summer evening, Bussy and his companions, as predicted, left François's apartments in the Louvre. They were on their way home by the usual route when they turned a dark corner and shots rang out. Instantly on their guard, they drew their swords and, despite the swarm of attackers, confirmed their reputation for ferocity by brawling their way through the onslaught to the safety of Bussy's nearby rooming house. Only one of their party fell: a gentleman in Bussy's service who had had the misfortune of also hurting his arm and binding it with a scarf. Because of this, it was reported back to the Louvre that Bussy had been murdered. Marguerite, who had not yet undressed for bed, heard the messenger cry, "Bussy is assassinated!"

and ran frantically to her brother's rooms to discover the truth. François, incensed, demanded to go out and investigate, but Catherine, concerned for his safety, ordered the doors of the Louvre locked.

They needn't have worried. Three hundred men, it turned out, were not enough to massacre a man like Bussy.* The assassination attempt had not only failed, it backfired completely by adding to the warrior's renown. "The next day Bussy showed himself at the Louvre without the least dread of enemies, as if what had happened had been merely the attack of a tournament," Marguerite marveled. "My brother exhibited much pleasure at the sight of Bussy, but expressed great resentment at such a daring attempt to deprive him of so brave and valuable a servant, a man whom Le Guast durst not attack in any other way than by a base assassination." If the queen of Navarre had not already given herself to this man before the attempt on his life, then certainly his debonair response to the threat broke down any of her remaining reserve.

But she also feared that he would be targeted again, and to protect him she agreed with Catherine that he should leave Paris. "The Queen my mother, apprehensive of evil consequences from this affair, and fearing a dissension betwixt her two sons, advised my brother to fall upon some pretence for sending Bussy away from Court," Marguerite observed. "In this advice I joined her, and, through our united counsel and request, my brother was prevailed upon to give his consent...Bussy, who implicitly followed my brother's directions in everything, departed with a company of the bravest noblemen that were about the latter's person." It must have been very difficult for her to see him go, but she consoled herself with the thought that at least he would be out of immediate

---

* This number is not an exaggeration. Guast, Marguerite observed, "commanded a regiment of guards [and] furnished the requisite number of men, whom he disposed of in five or six divisions." The King's Guard consisted of a total of eleven companies of soldiers with approximately two hundred men serving in each company. Marguerite's husband was also a captain in the King's Guard, and some of his men participated as well (although not Henry himself).

danger. "Bussy was now removed from the machinations of Le Guast," Margot proclaimed with relief.

Bussy may have been safe. But she was not.

SOON AFTER THESE EVENTS, in the heat of that long, fraught summer, Henry fell ill. He had some sort of seizure, which the court physicians diagnosed as epilepsy. However, this seems unlikely, as he had no history of the condition and his symptoms did not persist. More probably it was stress-related; the presence of so much conflict and so many volatile, armed young men at court might certainly induce the occasional panic attack in even the most seasoned warrior. Marguerite, on the other hand, put it down firmly to an overactive libido. "One night my husband was attacked with a fit, and continued insensible for the space of an hour—occasioned, I supposed, by his excesses with women, for I never knew anything of the kind to happen to him before," she reported. Despite his ill treatment of her and general indifference, she nursed him back to health so gently and faithfully that he credited her with saving his life. If so, this represented the third time in the space of as many years that Henry of Navarre had been rescued from death by his wife. "From this time he treated me with more kindness, and the cordiality betwixt my brother and him was again revived, as if I had been the point of union at which they were to meet, or the cement that joined them together," Margot observed.

Certainly the tenderness his wife displayed when he was laid low helped, but other factors contributed to the couple's reconciliation as well. The most conspicuous of these was the absence of any tangible profit from Henry's covert alliance with his brother-in-law the king. Henri III's lofty promises and flattering blandishments had turned out to be just empty words. Henry had not been named lieutenant-general. He had received no special favors or promotion. Worse, Henri III had recently levied a large and highly controversial tax, none of which had found its way into the purse of the king of Navarre, although a significant portion of it *had* gone to augmenting the estate of the royal favorite, Guast.

Henry also could not help but notice how unpopular the new king of France was becoming with his subjects. According to a chronicler, they called him "Henri, by the grace of his mother dubious king of France and imaginary king of Poland, concierge of the Louvre... [and] official hairdresser to his wife." Public opinion was shifting away from the king and toward François and the opposition. Margot's generosity during his illness presented the king of Navarre with a path back to his Huguenot supporters, where his natural sympathies lay.

A renewed coalition between Marguerite, François, and Henry was the last thing the king and his *mignons* wanted, and they moved quickly to break it up. Again Henri identified his sister as the chief threat and concentrated on separating her from her husband. Knowing Margot's character and instinctively perceiving that nothing in the world was more likely to induce an outsize, rip-roaring quarrel between Henry and his wife than for Henry to imperiously countermand her orders when it came to the management of her personal household, the king called Henry to his chambers and summarily instructed him to force Marguerite to dismiss Gillonne de Goyan, demoiselle de Thorigny, her intimate friend and most trusted lady-in-waiting, from her service.

Gillonne, or Torigni, as Marguerite called her, had been brought up with Margot and her sisters as a childhood playmate at the royal nursery. She was the daughter of a high-ranking official, Monsieur de Matignon, governor of Normandy, one of Catherine's closest advisers. Torigni was the queen of Navarre's oldest and dearest companion. The ambassador from Florence claimed that it was Torigni whom Marguerite used to communicate confidentially with Bussy, which was probably why she was singled out by the king for banishment. Even Henry understood how incensed his wife would be by this commandment. Besides, Torigni had worked side by side with Marguerite to nurse him through his recent crisis, and he naturally felt gratitude toward her. He tried to talk Henri out of it, but the king, suspicious of Henry's newly established rapport with Margot, made it a test of his allegiance. "The King...told my husband that he should have no more love for him if he did not remove Torigni from about me the very next morning," Marguerite testified indignantly. "Accordingly, Torigni left me that very day, and went to the house of a relation, M. Chastelas."

As he had correctly predicted, if he had put her on the rack, Henri could not have devised a more effective torment for his sister. Margot was utterly unable to control her fury. "I was so greatly offended with this fresh indignity, after so many of the kind formerly received, that I could not help yielding to resentment; and my grief and concern getting the upper hand of my prudence, I exhibited a great coolness and indifference towards my husband," she admitted. "Le Guast and Madame de Sauves were successful in creating a like indifference on his part, which, coinciding with mine, separated us altogether, and we neither spoke to each other nor slept in the same bed."

But although he had succeeded in dividing his sister from her husband, by this maneuver did Henri, paradoxically, reconcile the duke of Alençon and the king of Navarre. Marguerite might not have been speaking to her husband, but his counselors were, and they were quick to point out that Henry's being forced to prove his loyalty by stooping to the level of dismissing his wife's household staff did not bode well for his future prospects at court. "A few days after this, some faithful servants about the person of the King my husband...observed to him that already matters were brought to such a pass that the King showed little regard for him, and even appeared to despise him. They afterwards addressed themselves to my brother...representing to him that the King my husband and he were both circumstanced alike, and equally in disgrace." In other words, neither prince was getting anywhere by remaining at court; the king clearly had no intention of promoting either of them.

And so Henry and François once again decided to flee—not together, as their previous plans for joint action had been betrayed and failed so spectacularly in the past—but separately, and soon. "It was concerted betwixt them that my brother should depart first, making off in a carriage in the best manner he could; that... afterwards, the King my husband should follow, under pretense of going on a hunting party. They both expressed their concern that they could not take me with them, assuring me that I had no occasion to have any apprehensions, as it would soon appear that they had no design to disturb the peace of the kingdom, but merely to ensure the safety of their own persons, and to settle their establishments," Margot noted.

The matter-of-fact tone of Marguerite's recollection belies the dismay she must have felt at her prospective abandonment. For she knew as well as Henry and François that, despite their blithe assurances, the king would interpret any unauthorized departure from court as a threat to his rule and would lash out in fury at the betrayal. But by that time they would be gone, out of reach of the king's vengeance. She alone would be left to bear the punishment.

In spite of this she said nothing; she let them go. In fact she helped. Late in the afternoon of September 15, 1575, François, disguising himself under a large cloak, slipped quietly out of the Louvre and walked unobserved to the Saint-Honoré Gate. There a lady's carriage stood waiting, rumored to have been lent to him for his escape by Marguerite's close friend the duchess of Nevers. François jumped in, and the coach drove quickly out of the city. A short distance away, the loyal Bussy had gathered a band of fifty armed soldiers to guard the duke of Alençon on his journey. François reached the point of rendezvous without incident, leaped out of the carriage and onto a horse that Bussy had thoughtfully provided, and the group galloped safely away.

It had begun.

HE WASN'T MISSED UNTIL nine o'clock at night, when he didn't show up for dinner. Instantly suspicious, Catherine and Henri confronted Marguerite. "The King and the Queen my mother asked me the reason he did not come to sup with them as usual, and if I knew of his being indisposed. I told them I had not seen him since noon," Margot returned. An inquiry into the duke's whereabouts was then conducted. His rooms were searched—no François. They knocked on the doors of his various mistresses—he was similarly absent. "There was now a general alarm," reported Marguerite. "The King flew into a great passion, and began to threaten me. He then sent for all the Princes and the great officers of the Court; and giving orders for a pursuit to be made, and to bring him back, dead or alive, cried out: 'He is gone to make war against me; but I will show him what it is to contend with a king of my power.'"

But the great knights of the court dragged their feet. No one, it turned out, wanted to get involved in what was well known to be an ugly family disagreement. "They observed that...as their duty directed, they were willing to venture their lives in the King's service; but to act against his brother they were certain would not be pleasing to the King himself [here Henri undoubtedly would have disagreed]; that they were well convinced his brother would undertake nothing that should give his Majesty displeasure, or be productive of danger to the realm; that perhaps his leaving the Court was owing to some disgust, which it would be more advisable to send and inquire into," Marguerite recalled.

A later report from the Venetian envoy confirmed her account. "The major part of the nobility of the realm cannot decide what course to take," he wrote home to the doge. "Those who take up arms against Monsieur [François], to be sure, will be worse off than those who support him after a settlement is reached, for His Highness will always hold it against them. By contrast, His Majesty will be forced to pardon all those who have demonstrated against him," he concluded knowingly. A prolonged discussion about the best course to take ensued, and although eventually an armed party was sent out with instructions to bring the truant back by force (led, hilariously, by the duke of Nevers, whose wife's coach had been used as the getaway vehicle in the first place), they got such a late start that the trail was cold and the reluctant pursuers were obliged to return to the castle empty-handed.

But this was no laughing matter for Marguerite, who had witnessed Henri's rage firsthand and understood that she was likely to be the object upon which he took his revenge. She literally made herself sick with worry. "I was in tears the whole night of my brother's departure and the next day was seized with a violent cold, which was succeeded by a fever that confined me to my bed," she confessed. She who had so diligently cared for her husband during his recent illness received no comparable kindness from Henry in her time of need; on the contrary, to keep himself above suspicion he deliberately shunned her. "Meanwhile my husband was preparing for his departure, which took up all the time he could spare from his visits to Madame de Sauves; so that he did not think of me," she reported hollowly. "He returned as usual at two or three in the morning, and, as we had separate beds, I seldom heard him; and in the morning, before I was awake, he went to my mother's levée, where he met Madame de Sauves, as usual."

It was fortunate that Marguerite was confined to her bedchamber, for the king was incensed at François's escape, in which he suspected his sister was complicit. Having no real proof, Henri was unable to avenge himself openly on the queen of Navarre, so he sought instead to wound her through a surrogate. Specifically, he decided to assassinate her former lady-in-waiting Torigni, now living quietly outside Paris under the protection of a relative. It is difficult to believe that the sovereign of a kingdom as large and important as France, responsible for the welfare of millions of subjects, in the middle of an economic disaster, faced with mounting problems of poverty and ruin, and facing an opposition movement manifestly growing stronger every day, would devote time and energy to planning the abduction and murder of a defenseless young woman. But this was nonetheless what Henri focused on when he was not lying in bed or driving around the countryside with the queen, all the while wearing a basket containing the small lapdogs he loved around his neck.

Guast was again at the forefront of the plot. "He prevailed on the King to adopt a design for seizing Torigni, at the house of her cousin Chastelas, and, under pretence of bringing her before the King, to drown her in a river which they were to cross," Marguerite revealed. "The party sent upon this errand was admitted by Chastelas, not suspecting any evil design, without the least difficulty, into his house. As soon as they had gained admission they proceeded to execute the cruel business they were sent upon, by fastening Torigni with cords and locking her up in a chamber...Meantime, according to the French custom, they crammed themselves, like gluttons, with the best eatables the house afforded."

This native fondness for fine dining would be their undoing. For while the brave officers sent to drown the dangerous lady-in-waiting were gorging themselves on Chastelas's larder, they failed to notice their host's domestics escaping through the back door. By coincidence, the frightened servants ran into a company of soldiers on their way to join François, who had established a base of operations in the city of Dreux, about fifty miles west of Paris. Leading the group were two members of François's household who knew and admired the queen of Navarre. Upon hearing the servants' stories, they instantly decided to rescue the unhappy damsel. "Accordingly, they proceeded to the house with all expedition, and arrived just at the moment these soldiers were setting Torigni on horseback, for the purpose of conveying her to the river wherein they had orders to plunge her," Margot recounted. "Galloping into the courtyard, sword in hand, they cried out: 'Assassins, if you dare to offer that lady the least injury you are dead men!' So saying, they attacked them and drove them to flight, leaving their prisoner behind, nearly as dead with joy as she was before with fear and apprehension." To prevent a future attempt on her life, Torigni was courteously escorted to Dreux, where she remained "under my brother's protection and was treated with as much respect as if she had been with me," the queen of Navarre concluded gratefully.

Marguerite maintained that her mother had no knowledge of the conspiracy against Torigni, and this seems likely. Henri was far more adept at keeping information away from Catherine than his brother Charles had been. And the queen mother certainly would not have approved of the scheme, since she was doing all she could to broker a peace between the king and his younger brother. Upon reaching Dreux, François had issued a proclamation in which he cloaked his resentment at being passed over for promotion under the general banner of his desire to serve the public good. He pointed particularly to the financial burden placed on the population by the imposition of crippling taxes, much of which went "to enrich only a very few persons, nearly all foreigners, who have monopolized the king and the principal offices and governments of the kingdom...Seeing this wound grow worse day by day and our own person treated more unworthily than ever, and with so many princes, nobles, clergymen, citizens, and bourgeoisie with their eyes fixed upon us, imploring us to join hands and help them...we have resolved, without any concern for our own safety, to try to escape from our captivity and to take the public cause in hand," he announced virtuously.

But no one at court had any doubt that what François really wanted were the honors and riches that he felt were due him as the brother of the king and next in line to the throne. If Henri had been named lieutenant-general when he was only sixteen, François reasoned, why should this appointment not now come naturally to him, who was already twenty? Similarly, Henri, as crown prince, had been made duke of Anjou, the realm's most significant (and lucrative) appanage while Charles was still alive, so why was François, who now occupied this coveted position, still only the lowly duke of Alençon? François was not a Huguenot himself, but he was willing to espouse the principle of freedom of religion if it meant that he could use Protestant money and forces to compel his older brother into giving him his birthright. And those forces were significant. The prince of Condé had spent more than a year recruiting soldiers in Germany. Rumors were that by spring he would have assembled an army of over thirty thousand men—enormous for its day—with which to invade France.

Under the circumstances, even Henri, who did not have the funds to raise a competing force of anywhere near that size, understood that he was going to have to make some concessions to his despised brother or risk losing the throne altogether. Despite her age and corpulence—she was by this time fifty-six and so obese that the Huguenots christened their largest cannon the *Queen Mother* after her—Catherine volunteered to act as mediator, traveling back and forth repeatedly between the duke of Alençon's headquarters and the court. To protect Henri, the queen mother conceded almost everything François wanted. Mindful of the bond that existed between her youngest children, Catherine planned to bring Marguerite along with her to these negotiations in order to ensure a successful result. This, however, was not to be. Fate (or, more accurately, vengeance) intervened when, on the evening of November 1, 1575, All Saints' Day, Guast was discovered murdered in his town house in Paris.

By daylight, the details of the crime were well known. According to the Parisian chronicler Pierre de L'Estoile, who recorded the event in his diary, Guast had been lying in bed reading when a small band of intruders led by a masked man burst into his rooms. Taken by surprise, the victim reached for the weapon he routinely kept hidden by the side of the bed but in his haste mistakenly came up with only a pillow. This instrument, alas, proved of limited worth against the swords and daggers of his assailants. Demonstrating that presence of mind that had made him so successful in life, with his last breath, just before he expired, Guast identified his murderer as the baron of Vitteaux, who had borne the king's favorite a long-standing mortal grudge.*

The problem was, however, there were so many people who had

---

* According to L'Estoile, two of Guast's servants, including his *valet de chambre,* were killed with their master; presumably one of the other servants survived to witness the dying man's last words.

also borne Guast a mortal grudge that it was difficult to believe that Vitteaux had acted alone. The Parisian chronicler maintained that the assassin had performed the execution on behalf of François as retribution for the open scorn Guast had displayed for the duke of Alençon while he was still at court. Similarly, Marguerite's hatred of the king's favorite was well known, and it was rumored that she and her usual accomplice, the duchess of Nevers, had arranged for Vitteaux to dispose of the odious Guast. Still others whispered that the assassination had been a crime of passion, not politics — that Vitteaux had been hired by the jealous husband of Guast's most recent mistress, who did not believe that his patriotic duty extended to sharing his wife with one of Henri III's *mignons*.

Of all these tantalizing conspiracy theories, the one involving Marguerite is the least likely. The queen of Navarre was seriously ill in September and was still weak and confined to her room at the time of Guast's murder in November. Moreover, she knew she was unprotected and under constant surveillance; this would not have been the time to risk so bold a strike against her brother Henri, who had already threatened her life. Nor did she dissemble at the news of the crime. Brantôme reported that "when he was killed, and they came to announce it to her, she...said, 'I am very vexed that I am not quite cured, in order to have the joy of celebrating his death.' "*

Whatever pleasure she took from the slaying of Guast was short lived. For early the next year again came the threat of serious punishment from the king when Marguerite's husband, following her younger brother's example, slipped away from the court and escaped to his home territory of Navarre, far to the southwest. During the months since François's flight, Henry had managed to prove his loyalty to the Crown by shunning his wife and leaving her to take all the blame for her brother's defection. The king of Navarre had continued to profess great friendship for the duke of Guise and had even sent his own men to fight alongside the Catholic duke in a

---

* Never in her life was Margot involved in an assassination attempt.

skirmish against the Huguenots. He cultivated a carefree, comic demeanor that amused the king, and Henri III had evidently been lulled into believing that his brother-in-law was firmly on his side— so much so that he allowed Henry the freedom to hunt. This proved to be a mistake when, on February 3, 1576, Henry took off on one of these sporting expeditions and never came back. As soon as he returned to Navarre, he converted back to Protestantism. One of his traveling companions noted that, when he knew he was safely away, Henry quipped "that he regretted only two things he had to leave behind in Paris—the Mass and his wife."

In accordance with this cavalier attitude toward Marguerite, to whom he owed his life several times over, Henry did not bother to forewarn her of his plans, although he must have known that she would be blamed for his escape and possibly severely punished as a result. "He quite forgot his promise to my brother of speaking to me, and when he went away, it was without taking leave of me," Margot reported sadly.

And now there was no escaping Henri III's wrath, the full force of which was directed at his sister. "The King, supposing that I was a principal instrument in aiding the Princes in their desertion, was greatly incensed against me, and his rage became at length so violent that, had not the Queen my Mother moderated it, I am inclined to think my life had been in danger," said Marguerite. "Giving way to her counsel, he became more calm, but insisted upon a guard being placed over me, that I might not follow the King my husband, neither have communication with anyone, so as to give the Princes intelligence of what was going on at Court. The Queen my mother gave her consent to this measure," she added.

In fact Catherine broke the news to the queen of Navarre herself. She came to Margot's room while her daughter, still weak from her long illness, was struggling to change into an appropriately magnificent costume so as to be presentable at court. "My child [said the queen mother], you are giving yourself unnecessary trouble in dressing. Do not be alarmed at what I am going to tell you. Your own good sense will dictate to you that you ought not to be surprised if the King resents the conduct of your brother and husband, and as he knows the love and friendship that exist between you three, should suppose that you were privy to their design of leaving the Court. He has, for this reason, resolved to detain you in it, as a hostage for them...On this account it is that the King has ordered his guards to be placed, with directions not to suffer you to leave your apartments...I beg you will not be offended with these measures, which, if it so please God, may not be of long continuance. I beg, moreover, you will not be displeased with me if I do not pay you frequent visits, as I should be unwilling to create any suspicions in the King's mind," Catherine concluded.

So saying, she left her beautiful, vivacious daughter, who had just been humiliatingly discarded by her husband, to her punishment. In an unusual and particularly vindictive feature of her sentence, twenty-two-year-old Marguerite was not only imprisoned in her room under house arrest, she was denied all intercourse with the court. She was forbidden news of the outside world and was given no indication of the expected duration of her captivity or whether it would end with her freedom or her trial and eventual death. She knew only that she faced the long bleak days and nights entirely alone but for the menials who tended to her physical requirements. Deprived of all visitors, friends, and social companionship, the young queen who loved balls and dancing, whose undeniable charm and grace had won the court of France international renown, who had never spent a solitary moment in her life, sat alone day after day in the silence of her cushioned prison with no hope of deliverance.

13

A Royal Hostage

Men commit injuries either through fear or through hate.
—Niccolò Machiavelli, *The Prince*

THE FIRST WEEKS WERE THE most difficult, as Margot soon realized that Henri and Catherine had succeeded in turning the entire palace against her. "I remained a close prisoner, without a visit from a single person, none of my most intimate friends daring to come near me, through the apprehension that such a step might prove injurious to their interests. Thus it is ever in Courts," she observed bitterly. "Adversity is solitary, while prosperity dwells in a crowd." Only one of her former familiars, a lord named Grillon, defied the king's order and, at risk to his own safety, insisted on attempting to comfort her in her solitude. "Brave Grillon...came five or six times to see me, and my guards were so much astonished at his resolution, and awed by his presence, that not a single Cerberus of them all would venture to refuse him entrance to my apartments," Marguerite recounted fiercely in gratitude.

However, like her former sister-in-law Mary Stuart, who was similarly constrained under house arrest by Elizabeth I, the queen of Navarre seems to have managed to circumvent at least some of the restrictions of her captivity. She contrived, for example, to smuggle letters in and out of court by bribing the servants, a stratagem that brought her news of the outside world. In this way she learned that she was not quite so bereft of allies as Henri would have her believe: her brother François had learned of her imprisonment and was threatening retaliatory measures if his sister were not released. "Some few days after I had been put under arrest, my brother had intelligence of it, which chagrined him so much that... [he wrote] to the Queen my mother, informing her that, if I was thus treated, he should be driven upon some desperate measure," Marguerite reported triumphantly.

But certainly the most unexpected—and encouraging—message she received while a prisoner came from her husband. Henry might have sneered at her while in Paris, but he was induced to change his mind upon his return to Navarre. "Meanwhile, the King my husband reached the States under his government. Being joined there by his friends and dependents, they all represented to him the indignity offered to me by his quitting the Court without taking leave of me," Margot wrote. "They observed to him...that it would be for his interest to regain my esteem; that...he might derive to himself great advantage from my presence at Court. Now that he was at a distance from his Circe, Madame de Sauves, he could listen to good advice...Accordingly, he wrote me a very affectionate letter, wherein he entreated me to forget all that had passed betwixt us, assuring me that from thenceforth he would ever love me, and would give me every demonstration that he did so, desiring me to inform him of what was going on at Court, and how it fared with me and my brother."

What Henry's love was worth at this point is questionable—and certainly this communication, for all its professed sentiment, was a far cry from François's threats and indignant demand for her release—but it did represent an olive branch and an apology of sorts, and Margot accepted it. "I received this letter during my imprisonment, and it gave me great comfort under that situation," she admitted. "Although my guards had strict orders not to permit me to set pen to paper...I found means to write many letters to him." Margot understood that when he requested information about the court,

Henry was actually asking for her analysis of the political climate and, if possible, intelligence relating to Henri III's plans against the Huguenots, and this, in her outrage at being kept a prisoner, she was happy to provide to the best of her ability, given her constrained circumstances. Thus the king and queen of Navarre, separated by hundreds of miles, began cautiously to repair their relationship.

In addition to her smuggled letters, Marguerite had another important solace in her captivity: books. Her quarantine apparently did not extend to the royal library. She had always loved poetry and literature, but for the first time in her life she had leisure to devote herself to more serious scholarship. "I had found a secret pleasure, during my confinement, from the perusal of good books, to which I had given myself up with a delight I never before experienced," she explained. "I consider this as an obligation I owe to fortune... to prepare me, by such efficacious means, to bear up against the misfortunes and calamities that awaited me... My captivity and its consequent solitude afforded me the double advantage of exciting a passion for study, and an inclination for devotion, advantages I had never experienced during the vanities and splendor of my prosperity."

She put on a brave face, but underneath the queen of Navarre must have entertained many doubts and suffered sleepless nights while locked away in her room. She could not help but apprehend that there was a strong possibility this situation might not end well. Arrest and imprisonment had in the past presaged execution for many political prisoners, even those of the highest rank. Certainly this would prove to be the case for Mary Stuart, whose royal status did nothing to save her from Elizabeth I's enmity—or the ax.

But Marguerite's luck held where Mary's did not. For during her months of captivity, while she lost herself in a world of books, Henri III, faced with the escalating threat of an invasion led by his brother François, lost the confidence of the majority of the aristocracy and had to beg his mother to arrange a peace. Catherine, armed with a new array of bribes and concessions with which to coax her youngest son to call off his military campaign, trundled off again in her jolting, cumbersome carriage to meet François but was forced to turn around empty-handed almost as soon as she arrived, having been made aware, "of his [François's] firm resolution not to listen to any terms of peace until I was restored to my liberty, and reparation made me for the indignity I had sustained," Margot rejoiced.

In consequence there occurred a scene that must have been highly satisfying for the formerly helpless prisoner. Hard upon Catherine's return from this aborted negotiation, Marguerite suddenly found herself released from her cell and ushered solicitously into her mother's chamber. Catherine, having already "acquainted the King with my brother's determination," and "the King...on a sudden, as eager to reconcile matters betwixt us as she was herself," explained that she needed her daughter's aid to mediate a peace and "expressed her hopes that I would forget the injuries I had received." The queen mother further "assured me that the King was sorry for what had happened; that he had even expressed his regret to her with tears in his eyes, and had declared that he was ready to give me every satisfaction," Marguerite noted wryly.

Restored to freedom, Margot graciously agreed to accompany Catherine to a rendezvous outside Sens with the leaders of the opposing party for the purpose of negotiating a treaty. In a show of strength, François greeted his mother and sister in the company of his numerous aristocratic allies, including the prince of Condé. Henry wasn't in attendance, but his presence was effectively represented by a contingent of some six thousand German cavalry "raised by the Huguenots, they having joined my brother, as the King my husband and he [again] acted in conjunction," the queen of Navarre explained.

To ensure her youngest son's cooperation, Catherine brought François the happy news that Henri III had had a sudden change of heart and was anxious to name his younger brother duke of Anjou. He was throwing in the duchies of Berry and Touraine for good measure, an investiture that increased François's annual income from rents and property by approximately three hundred thousand *livres* a year. To sweeten the pot still further, the queen mother also announced that the king had ordered that his younger brother be awarded an outright annual pension of three hundred thousand *livres,* to be scraped together somehow by the already impoverished royal treasury. Nor were the Huguenots forgotten: their demand for a new, more comprehensive Edict of Toleration was accepted. French Protestants were for the first time to be guaranteed "a free, public, and general exercise of religion" throughout the kingdom with the exception of Paris and its immediate environs. "With respect to these [the articles of the Edict of Toleration], when at length agreed upon, they were too much to the advantage of the Huguenots, as it appeared afterwards, to be kept," Margot noted, "but the Queen my mother gave in to them, in order to have a peace, and that the German cavalry before mentioned might be disbanded. She was, moreover, desirous to get my brother out of the hands of the Huguenots; and he was himself as willing to leave them, being always a very good Catholic, and joining the Huguenots only through necessity."*

With the queen mother conceding almost every point, negotiations were concluded quickly, and on May 6, 1576, what became known as the Peace of Monsieur—"Monsieur" being a reference to François's elevated status as the new duke of Anjou—was signed. It represented an unqualified victory for François and also for Marguerite, whose influence, advice, and intermediary services had been critical to the success of the strategy. It was the queen of Navarre's first exposure to a winning political coalition, and she loved it. To have succeeded was exhilarating, but even more gratifying was the feeling of being useful and valued. And in François she believed she had found a brother to replace Charles. She never forgot that he had stood up for her and gotten her out of captivity. He had even tried,

---

* This observation would prove only too true. Later, François would scoff that "in order to hate the Huguenots he had to get to know them better."

during the negotiations, to ensure that she receive the dowry monies and property due her that had never been paid by making this a condition of the treaty. "My mother, however, opposed it, and persuaded me to join her in it, assuring me that I should obtain from the King all I could require," she observed. Her gratitude toward her younger brother for his support and protection during her time of need was profound. She would remain intensely loyal to him for the rest of her life.

At this moment of triumph, to add to her felicity, came a message from Henry. "The peace being thus concluded and ratified on both sides, the Queen my mother prepared to return. At this instant I received letters from the King my husband, in which he expressed a great desire to see me, begging me, as soon as peace was agreed on to ask leave to go to him," recounted Marguerite. "I communicated my husband's wishes to the Queen my mother, and added my own entreaties."

Margot was sincere in wishing to go to Navarre. Despite Henry's ignominious treatment of her while at court, she was still his wife and a queen in her own right. She wanted to establish her own court, where she could express her aesthetic and rule beside her husband. She and Henry might never love each other, but they could learn to respect each other. More important, it was time to start a family—not simply to establish a line of succession in tiny Navarre but also because Marguerite's sons would be in line for the throne of France.

It was with dismay, then, that she once again encountered her mother's opposition. "The Queen my mother expressed herself greatly averse to such a measure and used every argument to set me against it," Margot reported. "She observed that, when I refused her proposal of a divorce after St. Bartholomew's Day, she gave way to my refusal, and commended me for it, because my husband was then converted to the Catholic religion; but now that he had abjured Catholicism, and was turned Huguenot again, she could not give her consent that I should go to him." (This argument is particularly amusing, as Catherine was the one who had insisted that Marguerite marry the Huguenot Henry in the first place.)

The truth was that a united king and queen of Navarre represented a strong political alternative to Henri III and to Catherine herself, particularly given Marguerite's close relationship with François. The queen mother feared her daughter's influence would eclipse her own and, when reasoning failed, was forced to resort to her usual negotiating tactic in order to get her way. "When I still insisted upon going, she burst into a flood of tears, and said, if I did not return with her, it would prove her ruin; that the King would believe it was her doing; that she had promised to bring me back with her; and that, when my brother returned to Court, which would be soon, she would give her consent," said Marguerite.

If their positions had been reversed—if Catherine had wanted her to go and Marguerite had wept and begged that she would be ruined if she went—there is no question that Catherine would have sent her anyway. But Margot was not her mother. She returned reluctantly to Paris.

THE TERMS OF THE Peace of Monsieur, when they became known, stunned the Catholic majority. The Parisian populace in particular, who not without reason had been under the impression that the Saint Bartholomew's Day Massacre had more or less permanently settled the religious question in their favor, openly revolted against the treaty. The Parlement of Paris declined to register the edict granting the Huguenots freedom of worship throughout the realm; the priests of Notre-Dame retaliated against the Crown by refusing to allow Henri III to enter the cathedral; and there were placards in the streets railing against the royal family's capitulation to the heretical Protestants. The Guises were, as always, at the vanguard of the protest. "There is much heartburning touching the execution of this peace," worried an English diplomat. "The churchmen and the Guises show themselves open enemies to it, and solicit the towns to make resistance, namely, touching the exercise of religion."

The Catholic faction did more than just protest against its defeat; it adapted. Their leaders could not help but notice how well organized the Huguenots were—how much better organized, in fact, than the Catholics themselves. It was the Protestants' ability to call up men and resources quickly that made them so dangerous. To neutralize this advantage, the Catholics, under Guise management, decided to put into place a similarly structured political organization that would link their coreligionists town by town and so present a united front against the enemy. "A league was formed in the provinces and great cities, which was joined by numbers of Catholics," Marguerite explained. "M. de Guise was named as the head of all." This was the beginning of what would evolve into the Catholic League, a confederation of orthodox believers operating within France as a quasi-independent regime outside the law, not unlike a shadow government.

As it turned out, the Guises and their allies needn't have bothered to get so upset about the Crown's concessions to the Huguenots. Once the threat was over and the German horsemen paid off by the royal treasury, with funds accumulated through yet another highly unpopular tax on the royal subjects, it rapidly became apparent that neither the king nor his mother had any intention of keeping their side of the bargain and enforcing the edict. Catherine went out of her way to point this out to the majority of the Catholic aristocracy (who had remained out of the Politique movement). The duke of Nevers recorded in his diary that the queen mother had informed him to his face that she "had made the peace in order to get back Monsieur, and not to reestablish the Huguenots, as everybody now realizes."

Unfortunately, this cavalier attitude toward official commitments extended to promises made to Marguerite as well. Her dowry went unpaid, and even after François returned to the court in November the king did not allow his sister to join her husband in Navarre, although Henry asked repeatedly for his wife and even sent an ambassador, Monsieur de Duras, to fetch her. "After some time,

M. de Duras arrived at Court, sent by the King my husband to hasten my departure," Marguerite recalled. "Hereupon, I pressed the King greatly to think well of it, and give me his leave. He, to color his refusal, told me he could not part with me at present, as I was the chief ornament of his Court; that he must keep me a little longer, after which he would accompany me himself on my way as far as Poitiers... These excuses were purposely framed in order to gain time until everything was prepared for declaring war against the Huguenots, and, in consequence, against the King my husband, as he fully designed to do," she concluded.

As difficult as it is to believe from his treatment of her when they were together, the king of Navarre was sincere in his desire to have his wife returned to him. Allied with François, she had proved herself a significant political asset. Marguerite may not have had her dowry, but she brought legitimacy and powerful allies to the marriage. If she turned against him, or encouraged the new duke of Anjou to support Catholic policies over those of the Huguenots, Henry's position in the kingdom could be severely weakened. He was stronger with his wife, the king of Navarre realized belatedly, than without her.

The problem for Henry was that his brother-in-law the king realized this as well and was intent upon breaking the three-way alliance between his younger siblings and the king of Navarre. When the duke of Anjou returned to court, Margot remembered, "The King received him very graciously, and showed, by his reception of him, how much he was pleased with his return. Bussy, who returned with my brother, met likewise with a gracious reception." (Henri III must indeed have felt the need to placate his younger brother and sister to have swallowed his anger at the redoubtable Bussy.) "The King," Marguerite continued, "turned his thoughts entirely upon the destruction of the Huguenots. To effect this, he strove to engage my brother against them, and thereby make them his enemies; and that I might be considered as another enemy, he used every means to prevent me from going to the King my husband.

Accordingly, he showed every mark of attention to both of us, and manifested an inclination to gratify all of our wishes."

One of these wishes had to do with the revival of the old plan for a military campaign in the Netherlands, originally sponsored by Coligny. The Dutch Protestants, brutally repressed by their Spanish overlord, Philip II, were extremely impressed by François's successful rebellion and the religious freedom promised by the Peace of Monsieur. It was decided that the French king's younger brother was just the sort of man they needed to help them throw off the yoke of oppression imposed by tyrannical Spain. Accordingly, one of their leading barons, William of Nassau, prince of Orange, made overtures to François, promising him a million florins and the rule of Holland if he would lead an army into the Netherlands to fight against Philip II.

To conciliate his brother, Henri III pretended to consider this offer but in reality he had other plans for François. Marguerite was correct: the king was plotting to renew hostilities against the Protestants. Henri used the occasion of the meeting of the main representative body, the Estates-General, in November 1576 to formally rescind the edict to which he had so recently agreed and declare war on the Huguenots. To induce the duke of Anjou to join in repudiating the treaty that he himself had negotiated, François was finally appointed as commander of an army—but only if he agreed to lead it against his former allies, the Huguenots. "The King called my brother to his closet, where were present the Queen my mother and some of the King's counselors," Marguerite reported. "He represented the great consequence [threat] the Catholic league was to his State and authority...that the Catholics had very just reason to be dissatisfied with the peace, and that it behooved him [François], rather to join the Catholics than the Huguenots, and this from conscience as well as interest."

Henri III's bribe proved efficacious. Six months after leading an insurgency against the king in the name of the Huguenots, François, perhaps not the brightest of Catherine's children, committed himself to leading another army, this time against the Huguenots in the name of the king.

François's defection put Marguerite in the extremely awkward position of having her favorite brother, to whom she was still intensely loyal, commanding a military operation whose aim was to annihilate her husband and his subjects, whom, as queen of Navarre, she was honor-bound to protect. No matter which side won in this conflict, she would lose, which was just what Henri III had intended. She wasted no time confronting him. "I went directly to the closet of the Queen my mother, where I found the King. I expressed my resentment at being deceived by him, and at being cajoled by his promise to accompany me from Paris to Poitiers, which, as it now appeared, was mere pretence," she fumed. "I represented that I did not marry by my own choice, but entirely agreeable to the advice of King Charles, the Queen my mother, and himself; that, since they had given him to me for a husband, they ought not to hinder me from partaking of his fortunes; that I was resolved to go to him, and that if I had not their leave, I would get away how I could, even at the hazard of my life." (This after having been so recently confined under house arrest. Marguerite was nothing if not brave.)

"Sister...what the Queen my mother and I are doing is for your own good," Henri lectured her fatuously in reply. "I am determined to carry on a war of extermination until this wretched religion of the Huguenots, which is of so mischievous a nature, is no more. Consider, my sister, if you, who are a Catholic, were once in their hands, you would become a hostage for me, and prevent my design! And who knows but they might seek their revenge upon me by taking away your life? No, you shall not go amongst them; and if you leave us in the manner you have now mentioned," he concluded ominously, "rely upon it that you will make the Queen your mother and me your bitterest enemies, and that we shall use every means to make you feel the effects of our resentment; and moreover, you will make your husband's situation worse instead of better."

Infuriated by Henri's feigned solicitude for her welfare and undaunted by his threats, Marguerite retired from this interview and sought the counsel of her friends and especially her brother François. Fleeing the court for Navarre against the king's express command was considered too risky to undertake, but Margot refused to stay and play the role of helpless pawn in which she had been cast by her mother and older brother. Her friends agreed. "I found them all of the opinion that it would be exceedingly improper for me to remain in a Court now at open variance with the King my husband," the queen of Navarre affirmed. But if she could not escape to Henry, then where to go?

Various options were floated for a neutral locality. It was suggested, for example, that Marguerite might go on a pilgrimage somewhere. Or perhaps visit friends or family who lived outside of France—there were her cousins in Savoy. While she was weighing these alternatives, the princess of Roche-sur-Yon, who had been ailing, piped up that she was intending to journey to a town in Belgium known for its healing waters and would be only too thrilled to have Margot come along.* At the mention of this locale, a new member of François's household, a gentleman by the name of Mondoucet, who was also among those present, was gripped by sudden inspiration. Mondoucet had very recently returned from a posting in Flanders, where he had had an opportunity to acquaint himself with the political situation in the Netherlands. He had seen firsthand the discontent with Spanish rule and had made a number of important contacts. "He stated that he was commissioned by several nobles, and the municipalities of several towns, to declare how much they were inclined in their hearts towards France, and how ready they were to come under a French government," recalled Marguerite. "My brother readily lent an ear to Mondoucet's proposition, and promised to engage in it...Mondoucet was to return to Flanders under a pretence of accompanying the Princesse de Roche-sur-Yon in her journey to Spa...and he suggested to my

---

* The town in Belgium was called Spa. And you thought history was irrelevant.

brother that I might be of great use to him in Flanders, if, under the color of any complaint, I should be recommended to drink the Spa waters and go with the Princesse."

Here at last was a proposal that appealed to Marguerite — appealed greatly. To be François's covert agent in the Netherlands, to be useful, to win him allies and pave the way for French sovereignty — that was an endeavor worthy of a queen. François also leaped at the opportunity. "My brother acquiesced in this opinion, and came up to me, saying: 'Oh, Queen! You need be no longer at a loss for a place to go to. I have observed that you have frequently an erysipelas [a skin infection, also known as cellulitis] on your arm, and you must accompany the Princess to Spa. You must say your physicians had ordered those waters for the complaint; but when they did so, it was not the season to take them. That season is now approaching, and you hope to have the King's leave to go there.' My brother did not deliver all he wished to say at that time," Margot confided, "because the Cardinal de Bourbon was present, whom he knew to be a friend to the Guises and to Spain. However, I saw through his real design, and that he wished me to promote his views in Flanders."

The very next day Marguerite went to Catherine and, holding out her arm, showed her mother her rash and informed her that her doctors had recommended that she take the cure at Spa as the best means of healing the inflammation. As it happened, the princess of Roche-sur-Yon was also intending to go — might Margot be allowed to accompany her? Strangely, Catherine agreed instantly to this plan and without further inquiry promised to use her influence with Henri to obtain the necessary permission. "She was as good as her word," reported Marguerite, "and the King discoursed with me on the subject without exhibiting the smallest resentment," an accommodation that Margot put down to Henri's exultancy at having bested his sister by keeping her away from Navarre. "Indeed, he was well pleased by now that he had prevented me from going to the King my husband, for whom he had conceived the greatest animosity," she commented.

The speed with which her request was granted in fact hinted at other, less altruistic motives than concern for her skin, but in the excitement of packing—this would be the queen of Navarre's first trip outside France—and her triumph at what she believed to be the successful dissembling of her true objectives, Margot failed to notice. She saw only that Henri went out of his way to be helpful, ensuring that the proper authorities were informed of her impending visit. He even "ordered a courier to be immediately dispatched to Don John of Austria—who commanded for the King of Spain in Flanders—to obtain from him the necessary passports for a free passage in the countries under his command, as I should be obliged to cross a part of Flanders to reach Spa, which is in the bishopric of Liège," relayed Marguerite happily, not perhaps fully appreciating the dubious worth to an aspiring French agent provocateur of having Don John, the brutal governor of the Spanish forces in the Netherlands and one of the most feared men in Europe, forewarned of her impending arrival.

14

Queen of Spies

A prince need trouble little about conspiracies when the people are well disposed, but when they are hostile and hold him in hatred, then he must fear everything and everybody.
—Niccolò Machiavelli, *The Prince*

THE COURT SPLIT UP AT the end of May 1577. François went off with the royal army to besiege the Huguenot town of Issoire, in southern France; Catherine and the king traveled to Poitiers in preparation for a future attack on Henry of Navarre in Gascony; and Marguerite embarked for Flanders, in the company of the princess of Roche-sur-Yon and a large party of some twenty-five or thirty companions, including a dozen or so ladies-in-waiting, one cardinal, a bishop, a count, her chief steward, and other members of her household deemed necessary to the queen of Navarre's comfort and well-being, to take up her new role as secret agent.

In keeping with her cover story of elegant female sovereign en route to a fashionable watering hole, she journeyed in high style. "I travelled in a litter raised with pillars," Marguerite remembered fondly. "The lining of it was Spanish velvet, of a crimson color, embroidered in various devices with gold and different colored silk thread. The windows were of glass, painted in devices. The lining and windows had, in the whole, forty devices, all different and alluding to the sun and its effects. Each device had its motto, either in the Spanish or Italian language. My litter was followed by two others; in the one was the Princesse de Roche-sur-Yon, and in the other Madame de Tournon, my lady of the bedchamber. After them followed ten maids of honor, on horseback, with their governess; and last of all, six coaches and chariots, with the rest of the ladies and all our female attendants." Margot acknowledged that this procession "excited great curiosity as it passed through the several towns in the course of my journey."

Her first stop outside France was Cambrai, at that time an ecclesiastical state under Spanish dominion. Cambrai boasted a large fortress, extremely useful for military purposes, commanded by an officer by the name of Monsieur d'Ainsi, "a polite and well-accomplished man, having the carriage and behavior of one of our most perfect courtiers, very different from the rude incivility which appears to be the characteristic of a Fleming," Marguerite observed. (Like many first-time travelers, the queen of Navarre brought her native prejudices with her on this trip.) The spy saw at once that procuring the allegiance of Monsieur d'Ainsi and his stronghold for François would provide her brother with a secure foothold from which to conquer the rest of Flanders. That evening, a grand ball was given in her honor, and it naturally fell to Monsieur d'Ainsi, as the highest authority in the town after the bishop (who, luckily, retired early that evening), to escort the guest of honor to the dance floor. "I employed all the talents God had given me to make M. d'Ainsi a friend to France, and attach him to my brother's interest," Marguerite reported. Monsieur d'Ainsi was unused to being the object of the attentions of beautiful highborn women. "Through God's assistance I succeeded with him," Margot advised modestly.★

Next stop on the goodwill ambassador's tour was Valenciennes, about twenty-five miles to the northeast. By the time she left

---

★ Some of Marguerite's biographers have cited this passage as evidence that she slept with Monsieur d'Ainsi. This shows a want of knowledge of the period. Ainsi was not of sufficient rank to approach a queen. Marguerite might have flattered him in conversation and by dancing with him, but she would not have considered Ainsi suitable as a lover.

Cambrai, Monsieur d'Ainsi was so smitten that he obtained leave to accompany Marguerite all the way to Namur, deep in Spanish-held Belgium, where Don John had arranged to meet the visiting French dignitaries. This afforded plenty of time for plotting. Monsieur d'Ainsi "took every opportunity of discoursing with me... and declaring that he heartily despised being under the command of his Bishop, who, though his sovereign, was not his superior by birth, being born a private gentleman like himself, and, in every other respect, greatly his inferior," the queen of Navarre confided. The Flemings, it seemed, were not without their own native prejudices.

At Valenciennes they were met by the governor of the city, the comte de Lalain, a dignitary of much higher rank and authority than provincial Monsieur d'Ainsi, as witnessed by the impressive train of three hundred noblemen who accompanied him to his rendezvous with Marguerite and her entourage. Like the queen of Navarre's first conquest, the comte de Lalain detested Spanish rule, but he was more circumspect than Monsieur d'Ainsi, as befit his higher rank. "Although he had hitherto abstained from entering into a league with the Prince of Orange and the Huguenots, being himself a steady Catholic, yet he had not admitted of an interview with Don John, neither would he suffer him, nor any one in the interest of Spain, to enter upon his territories," said Marguerite. Another plum ripe for picking! "With this disposition of mind, the Comte de Lalain thought he could not give me sufficient demonstrations of the joy he felt by my presence," observed the undercover agent.

This time, however, Marguerite prudently elected not to approach her target, a married man, directly but instead appealed to him through the good offices of his wife. "On our arrival at Mons [outside Valenciennes, about halfway to Namur], I was lodged in his house, and found there the Countess his wife, and a Court consisting of eighty to a hundred ladies of the city and country... The Flemish ladies are naturally lively, affable, and engaging. The Comtesse de Lalain is remarkably so, and is, moreover, a woman of great sense and elevation of mind... We became immediately intimate, and commenced a firm friendship at our first meeting," Marguerite declared. So pleasant did she find her hostess's company that what the queen of Navarre had intended to be only an overnight stay lengthened into a week's visit. By the end of this period, "the Countess and I were on so familiar a footing that she stayed in my bedchamber till a late hour, and would not have left me then had she not imposed upon herself a task very rarely performed by persons of her rank, which, however, placed the goodness of her disposition in the most amiable light. In fact, she gave suck to her infant son; and one day at table, sitting next me...she, dressed out in the richest manner and blazing with diamonds, gave the breast to her child without rising from her seat, the infant being brought to the table as superbly habited as its nurse, the mother," Marguerite marveled. "She performed this maternal duty with so much good humor, and with a gracefulness peculiar to herself, that this charitable office— which would have appeared disgusting and been considered as an affront if done by some others of equal rank—gave pleasure to all who sat at table, and, accordingly, they signified their approbation by their applause." It seems that even a queen's perspective could be broadened by travel.

But of course the main order of business was not an introduction to quaint local customs but the substitution of François's rule for that of Don John's and Spain's. Luckily, Marguerite's hostess made the broaching of this sensitive subject very easy by openly deprecating the Spanish. "We entertain the utmost dislike for the Spanish government, and wish for nothing so much as to throw off the yoke of their tyranny," the countess complained. "But as the country is divided betwixt different religions, we are at a loss how to effect it. If we could unite, we should soon drive out the Spaniards; but this division amongst ourselves renders us weak. Would to God the King your brother would come to a resolution of reconquering this country, to which he has an ancient claim! We should all receive him with open arms."

Margot made haste to disabuse the countess of the notion that

Henri III might ever be induced to take up arms in Flanders's defense. "I told her that the King of France my brother was averse to engaging in foreign war, and more so as the Huguenots in his kingdom were too strong to admit of his sending any large force out of it," she stressed. Then she made her pitch. "My brother Alençon has sufficient means, and might be induced to undertake it," Margot continued, as though, in her natural desire to aid her new friend, the idea had just occurred to her. "He has the command of the King's army against the Huguenots, and has lately taken a well-fortified town, called Issoire, and some other places that were in their possession." Then, warming to her task: "You could not invite to your assistance a prince who has it so much in his power to give it; being not only a neighbor, but having a kingdom like France at his devotion, whence he may expect to derive the necessary aid and succor. The Count your husband may be assured that if he does my brother this good office he will not find him ungrateful, but may set what price he pleases upon his meritorious service," she added helpfully. Marguerite was getting the hang of the espionage business.

The upshot of this confidential talk was the appearance in Marguerite's rooms the next morning of the count himself. "He explained to me the means whereby my brother might establish himself in Flanders," said Margot, "having possession of Hainault, which extended as far as Brussels . . . we agreed upon an interview betwixt my brother and M. de Montigny, the brother of the Count, which was to take place at La Fère [in northern France, where Marguerite owned a château] upon my return, when this business should be arranged."* Cambrai, Valenciennes, and Hainaut all to go to

---

* The business to be arranged was for François to be invited to rule what amounted to present-day Belgium and the Netherlands (which in the sixteenth century was ruled by various local lords, such as the count, who owed allegiance to an overlord). As the count already had an overlord—Spain, in the person of Don John, who was acting as governor for Philip II—it was understood that François would need to raise an army in order to wrest these lands and castles from Spanish control. The count was volunteering to send his brother, who was familiar with the terrain, to formalize this arrangement and help plan the invasion at a later meeting at La Fère.

François, and she had been in Flanders barely more than a week! In her exhilaration at having succeeded so thoroughly at her assignment, upon her departure Margot presented her hosts with diamond jewelry of "considerable value," which no doubt added convincingly to their impression of French generosity.

Flushed with triumph, armed with the knowledge that she had immeasurably aided François's ambitions, the queen of Navarre left Mons for Namur. The comte de Lalain and his men accompanied her part of the way but turned around as soon as Don John and his entourage appeared on the horizon, leaving the covert French operative in the company of only the faithful Monsieur d'Ainsi to face the Spanish governor.

DON JOHN WAS THE king of Spain's illegitimate half brother. He had recently replaced the unpopular duke of Alva, whose repressive government had been disturbingly effective, as Philip II's ranking commander in the Netherlands. Don John was thirty years old and highly experienced in the art of warfare, having spent the previous dozen or so years in the Spanish navy, the most successful fighting force in Europe. He was universally admired—and feared—for having destroyed the seemingly invincible Turkish fleet at Lepanto six years earlier.

He was also well informed about the political situation in France. In fact, Don John had passed through the kingdom on his way to his Netherlands assignment just the year before, where he had caught a glimpse of Marguerite at a court ball. More to the point, perhaps, he had also had an opportunity to engage in secret negotiations with the duke of Guise at his château in Joinville. There, a daring Catholic plot had been devised between the two men for the overthrow of Elizabeth I. As soon as he dealt with the annoying problem of Protestant unrest in the Netherlands, Don John volunteered to lead an armed raid across the Channel to rescue Mary Stuart from her English prison. As a reward for his bravery and initiative, the duke of Guise promised that the hero of Lepanto could then wed Mary and rule England with her in her cousin's place. In return, Don John would aid the Guises and the Catholic League in France. The duke of Guise had explained all about the enmity between Henri III and his brother François and the political alliance between François, Marguerite, and Henry of Navarre that had resulted in the odious Peace of Monsieur. Accordingly, when Henri III wrote to Don John to advise him that his sister would be coming to Belgium, the Spanish governor was already fully aware of Marguerite's political sympathies and knew to keep a close eye on her activities, surmising that she might be intriguing for her brother François.

Being far more adept at espionage than his royal guest, Don John of course hid his suspicions from Marguerite. Just as she played the part of fashionable queen on a sightseeing holiday to Spa, so he took on the corresponding role of charming, infatuated host. He met her outside Namur and "alighted from his horse to salute me in my litter, which was opened for the purpose," Margot remembered. "After an exchange of compliments, he mounted his horse, but continued in discourse with me until we reached the city." Darkness having already descended, Don John had thoughtfully ordered all the lamps in the city to be lit in honor of the queen and her entourage. "Namur appeared with particular advantage, for the streets were well lighted, every house being illuminated, so that the blaze exceeded that of daylight," Marguerite admitted.

Nor could she complain about her accommodations. Don John had gone out of his way to impress her, and Marguerite was suitably dazzled. "The house in which I was lodged had been newly furnished for the purpose of receiving me," she remembered. "It consisted of a magnificent large *salon,* with a private apartment, consisting of lodging rooms and closets, furnished in the most costly manner, with furniture of every kind, and hung with the richest tapestry of velvet and satin, divided into compartments by columns of silver embroidery, with knobs of gold, all wrought in the most superb manner." When one of her party questioned the furnishings, observing that they "seemed more proper for a great king than a young unmarried prince like Don John," he was informed that they were a gift from an exalted Turkish lord whose sons had been captured at Lepanto. "Don John having sent the...sons back without ransom, the father, in return, made him a present of a large quantity of gold, silver, and silk stuffs, which he caused to be wrought into tapestry at Milan, where there are curious workmen in this way; and he had the Queen's bedchamber hung with tapestry representing the battle in which he had so gloriously defeated the Turks."

There was a short delay involving her transportation to Liège, the next stop on her journey before arriving at Spa, so she was obliged to stay over an extra day. Don John again exerted himself to the very best of his abilities to entertain her in grand manner. There were two balls, with dancing late into the evening, and a wonderful boat ride on the river. "In short, Don Juan manifested, by every mark of attention and politeness, as well to me as to my attendants, the very great pleasure he had in receiving me," Marguerite recalled.

The next day the barges necessary to transport her party were ready, and the queen of Navarre made preparations to leave. Don John personally escorted her to her vessel "and there took a most polite and courteous leave." As Marguerite and her entourage floated away to begin the last leg of their trip, Don John offered a final adoring salute from the bank of the river.

No sooner was she out of sight than he rode out at the head of a well-armed company, attacked the region surrounding Namur, arrested a number of high-ranking people, forcibly took possession of the strongest castle in the region, and, in the parlance of Cold War espionage, rolled up her networks.

HAVING NO INKLING THAT anything was amiss, Marguerite arrived at Spa and stayed six weeks, the customary length of the water cure. Although her sojourn was marred by tragedy—the teenage daughter of Madame de Tournon, Margot's first lady of the bedchamber, was stricken with terrible chest pains en route to Liège and died two days later of an unknown ailment★—on the whole the queen of Navarre enjoyed herself greatly at the resort. "I was every morning attended by a numerous company to the garden, in which I drank the water, the exercise of walking being recommended to be used with them," she noted. "From this garden we usually proceeded to the place where we were invited to dinner. After dinner we were amused with a ball; from the ball we went to some convent, where we heard vespers; from vespers to supper, and that over, we had another ball, or music on the river." Vacation destinations devoted to health being invariably self-contained and remote, their purpose being to promote wellness in body and soul through the avoidance of terrestrial cares, very little news of the outside world reached the queen of Navarre and her companions while she was preoccupied with her cure.

It therefore came as something of a shock, as she prepared to return to France, to learn of Don John's duplicity. She got her information firsthand from a thoroughly frightened noblewoman from Mons who had only just escaped the Spanish governor's clutches herself.† And coming hard on this unsettling information was an equally disturbing letter from François, specially delivered by messenger. It seemed that in her absence her favorite brother's fortunes had taken a turn for the worse. In his missive, François complained that, despite having successfully routed the Huguenots, as he had been requested to do by the king, upon his return to the court "he had found it entirely changed, so that he had been no more considered than if he had done the King no service whatever." Reading further, Margot found that the real purpose of her brother's letter

---

★ Attributed by Marguerite to unrequited love but more likely involving a physiological heart defect.

† By seizing the fortress of Namur on July 24, 1577, and arresting a number of high-ranking local noblemen (and their wives), Don John had violated the Pacification of Ghent, a 1576 treaty between Spain and the States General of the Netherlands (that region's representative body), which among other articles of agreement prohibited the Spanish army from launching this sort of military offensive.

was to warn her that "the King had repented of giving me leave to go to Flanders, and that, to counteract my brother, a plan was laid to intercept me on my return, either by the Spaniards, for which purpose they had been told that I had treated for delivering up the country to him, or by the Huguenots, in revenge of the war my brother had carried on against them, after having formerly assisted them." So Henri III had betrayed her yet again, and now, of the three opposing factions in Flanders openly at war—Catholics, Protestants, and Spaniards—two were after her. "I found I was in great danger of falling into the hands of one or other of these parties," Marguerite conceded soberly.

There then settled upon the queen of Navarre the anxious uncertainty universal to spies left out in the cold. What to do? Should she make a run for it or stay put and chance arrest or capture? If she chose to flee she would require aid in the form of safe houses, guides, and protection. But whom to trust and whom to fear?

She began with Mondoucet, whose bright idea it had been to undertake this dangerous mission in the first place. Seeking to neutralize at least one of the enemies allied against her, she sent him to the prince of Orange, the head of the Protestant party, to request a safe passage through Flanders, "as he [Mondoucet] was acquainted with the Prince and was known to favor his religion." The result of this endeavor was not encouraging. "Mondoucet did not return, and I believe I might have waited for him until this time to no purpose," she stated flatly.

Having failed with the Protestants, she turned to the Catholics. She was extremely fortunate that her host, the bishop of Liège, within whose jurisdiction the town of Spa fell, and "who most certainly acted towards me like a father," offered tangible aid in the form of horses and his own grand master, the ranking member of his household, to accompany her on the homeward journey. But of the allegiance of some of the members of her own entourage she was less certain. She was particularly wary of her chief steward and her treasurer, both cohorts of the unfaithful Mondoucet. The two men strenuously opposed any plan to escape and insisted instead that she stay where she was. When she overruled their objections, they tried to keep her at Spa by pretending that there was not enough money to pay the bill she had amassed during her visit and that consequently the management intended to keep her horses. "I suspected a plan was laid to entrap me," Margot noted grimly.

But the princess of Roche-sur-Yon, in whom Marguerite had also confided, came to the rescue. Being an extremely wealthy woman and having no desire to see either the queen of Navarre or herself fall into enemy hands, the princess loaned Marguerite the money necessary to settle her accounts. Margot retrieved her elaborate coaches and livestock and set off with her company at once, attended by the bishop's men.

It was immediately apparent that she was in fact in grave danger. The mood of the countryside, unsettled by the prospect of war, was ugly. In Huy, the very first town where she stopped to rest for the night, the citizenry, despite owing allegiance to the bishop of Liège, were terrifyingly hostile and threatening. "They paid no respect to the grand master of the Bishop's household, who accompanied us, but knowing Don John had taken the castle of Namur in order, as they supposed, to intercept me on my return, these brutal people, as soon as I had got into my quarters, rang the alarm-bell, drew up their artillery, placed chains across the streets, and kept us confined and separated the whole night," Margot recalled. Still, to detain a member of the French royal family against her will was a significant offense and might invite repercussions. By daybreak, when Don John did not appear to relieve them of their prisoner, the townspeople obviously reconsidered. "In the morning we were suffered to leave the town without further molestation, and the streets we passed through were lined with armed men," she concluded tensely.

The next stop, Dinant, despite being only about twenty miles south of Namur, was staunchly allied with the Catholic party and opposed to both Don John and the prince of Orange. The municipality ought to have been a safe haven, but even there the inhabitants armed themselves at her approach and shut the gates of the city against her. Nor could she establish communication with the local government, as it turned out that she had arrived on election day. "In consequence...it was a day of tumult, riot, and debauchery; everyone in the town was drunk, no magistrate was acknowledged," Marguerite despaired. With darkness coming on quickly and nowhere else to go, she sent in an advance squad of servants to entreat the local officials to allow her to stay for just one night, but the men were immediately arrested. "They bawled out to us from within, to tell us their situation, but could not make themselves heard," Margot observed in frustration. "At length I raised myself up in my litter, and, taking off my mask, made a sign to a townsman nearest me, of the best appearance, that I was desirous to speak with him...I represented that it was far from my intention to do them harm...I only begged to be admitted to go into their city."

It was agreed that Marguerite and her women, and some of the elderly men, including the grand master, who was eighty, could stay the night. But no sooner had the queen of Navarre and her attenuated entourage passed through the main gate than the bishop's representative was recognized. Unbeknownst to Marguerite, the entire town had a grudge against the old man, and they moved to attack him. The queen of Navarre, the princess of Roche-sur-Yon, Madame de Tournon, and the other women of her party had to surround the venerable grand master to protect him. "At length I got him into my lodgings," recounted Margot, "but the mob fired at the house, the walls of which were only plaster."

At her wits' end, Marguerite went to the window and, braving the threatening rabble, begged to speak to someone—*anyone*—in authority. "At length, after much bawling from the window, the burghermasters came to speak to me, but were so drunk that they scarcely knew what they said. I explained to them that I was entirely ignorant that the grand master of the Bishop's household was a person to whom they had a dislike, and I begged them to consider the consequences of giving offence to a person like me, who was a friend of the principal lords of the States." In her desperation, Marguerite began naming the Flemish lords of her acquaintance, which naturally included the comte de Lalain.

This turned out to be an inspired move. "The principal person amongst them asked me, with some hesitation and stammering, if I was really a particular friend of the Count's," Margot reported. "Perceiving that to claim kindred with the Count would do me more service than being related to all the Powers in Christendom, I answered that I was both a friend *and* a relation." (Under the circumstances she may perhaps be forgiven this small falsehood.) "They then made me many apologies, stretching forth their hands in token of friendship; in short, they now behaved with as much civility as before with rudeness."

She had won over the town, but the relief from peril was only momentary. For in the morning appeared an envoy named Du Bois, representing Don John. Henri III had expressed his concern for his sister's safety to the Spanish governor, Du Bois revealed. Don Juan had thoughtfully sent Du Bois and a troop of armed horsemen, led by one captain Barlemont, to escort Marguerite and her party to the castle of Namur, where they would again become guests of Don John's hospitality. All that was necessary, said the smiling Du Bois, was for the queen of Navarre to explain the situation to her hosts and prevail upon them to let the soldiers into the city so that they could adequately protect her and her small company and begin their journey to safety.

It seems that Don John, as a result of his initial encounter with Margot, had formed a rather indifferent opinion of the queen's abilities. In this he seriously underestimated her. Marguerite was not fooled by the ambassador's solicitude. "Thus had they concerted a double plot; the one to get possession of the town, the other of my person," she observed grimly.

Returning Du Bois's smile, she excused herself for a moment and went to find the cardinal of Lenoncourt, one of her original companions from France. In a few hushed words, she outlined the situation.

The cardinal was no more desirous of becoming Don John's prisoner than was she. They worked out a plan of action together. He would keep Du Bois occupied while she sought out the principal magistrates of the town and asked for their help. "Accordingly, I assembled as many as I could, to whom I represented that if they admitted Barlemont and his troop within the town, he would most certainly take possession of it for Don John," reported Marguerite. "I gave it as my advice to make a show of defense, to declare they would not be taken by surprise, and to offer to admit Barlemont, and no one else, within their gates." Margot then quickly explained how she intended to circumvent Don John's men without risk to the city. The magistrates "resolved to act according to my counsel, and offered to serve me at the hazard of their lives," she remembered appreciatively.

The inhabitants of Dinant did as she suggested, and there then occurred an elaborate bit of theater by the city gates. Barlemont was ushered cordially into the town, but as soon as he had entered the great doors were slammed shut and bolted behind him, leaving the rest of his force waiting impotently outside the thick walls. "Hereupon, the citizens flew into a violent rage, and were near putting him [Barlemont] to death. They told him that if he did not order his men out of sight of the town, they would fire upon them with their great guns. This was done with design to give me time to leave the town before they could follow in pursuit of me," Marguerite explained. Completely outnumbered and in fear for his life, Barlemont had no choice but to order his men to draw back a substantial distance from the city.

Meanwhile, the queen of Navarre had once again assumed the role of innocent royal princess on holiday. She graciously allowed Du Bois and Barlemont to convince her of the necessity of allowing Don John's soldiers to escort her and her helpless companions to the safety of Namur. Of course, being a devout great lady, she had to hear Mass first, which was then followed by a short repast to prepare her for the hardships of the road. This gave the townspeople a chance to organize, so that when she was finally packed and ready to go, the Spanish envoys found the queen of Navarre "escorted by two or three hundred armed citizens, some of them engaging Barlemont and Du Bois in conversation. We all took the way to the gate which opens to the river, and directly opposite to that leading to Namur. Du Bois and his colleague told me I was not going the right way, but I continued talking, as if I did not hear them," she observed sweetly.

In this manner they reached the gate in question, Du Bois and Barlemont still protesting that they were not taking the correct route. A quick look confirmed that the Spanish soldiers were nowhere in sight. Someone had thoughtfully left a number of vessels moored to the city side of the waterway. With the townspeople huddling closely around Don John's two representatives, forming a barrier between the queen and her adversaries, Margot and her entourage made a break for the river. "I hastened onto the boat, and my people after me," she recalled. "M. de Barlemont and the agent Du Bois, calling out to me from the bank, told me I was doing very wrong and acting directly contrary to the King's intention." But the two men were helpless in the throng of townspeople, and the soldiers, unaware of her escape, were still waiting on the opposite side of the town, by the road to Namur. "In spite of all their remonstrances we crossed the river with all possible expedition, and, during the two or three crossings which were necessary to convey over the litter and horses, the citizens, to give me more time to escape, were debating with Barlemont and Du Bois concerning a number of grievances and complaints, telling them... that Don John had broken the peace and falsified his engagements with the States; and... that if the troop made its appearance before their walls again, they would fire upon it with their artillery," noted the queen of Navarre. "I had by this means sufficient time to reach a secure distance, and was, by the help of God and the assistance of my guide, out of all apprehensions of danger from Barlemont and his troop."

Not quite. Don John had not secured his reputation as the most able commander in Europe by conceding so easily. Discovering his prey to have slipped from his grasp, and correctly anticipating that she and her party would attempt to make for the safety of a particular castle belonging to one of the comte de Lalain's vassals, he sent a further three hundred men to entrap her. Marguerite managed to arrive at her destination only minutes ahead of the pursuing Spanish soldiers. The drawbridge was lowered, and she and her party were ushered inside the castle's strong walls just as the enemy force loomed on the horizon.

But she had no sooner escaped the Spanish than "I had intelligence sent me that a party of the Huguenot troops had a design to attack me on the frontiers of Flanders," she related with dismay. To circumvent this latest ambush, she decided on a desperate predawn flight. She called for her coaches, but her steward once again opposed her plan and attempted to prevent her departure. Strongly suspecting that he was in league with the Protestants, she thwarted capture by impetuously mounting her horse and, leaving her beautiful carriage behind, riding as fast as she could through the darkness of early morning, accompanied by only a handful of loyal retainers. The deception worked, and she was safely across the border of France before midday.

Never before had she been so close to fear; never had she such need of all of her talents; never had she felt so alive. To return directly to the royal court and the stifling dominion of her brother the king—particularly after Henri's connivance with Don John—was anathema. She went instead to her fortified château at La Fère. Soon after she arrived she was joined by François, who had also found the atmosphere in Paris, where Catherine and Henri had lately returned, unbearable. For two months brother and sister remained together. "I consider it amongst the greatest felicities I ever enjoyed," Marguerite would later write. François reciprocated this sentiment. "Oh Queen! How happy I am with you!" he told her. "Your society is a paradise wherein I enjoy every delight, and I seem to have lately escaped from hell, with all its furies and tortures!"

The excessively rhapsodic language employed to describe their joy in being together at La Fère has led many to suggest—as usual—that

Margot's relationship with François was incestuous, just as her former attachment to her older brother Charles IX had been assumed to be carnal. But of this again there is no evidence. The siblings' affection was rooted in their political and emotional needs, not in sex. They shared a common enemy in Henri III and realized that each had a much greater chance of surviving their older brother's reign if they stood together against him. They might even manage to exert a measure of control over their lives that would not be possible if they faced him individually. More than this, as the youngest and least loved of Catherine's children, they naturally turned to each other for support. Their happiness was based as much on being free from the restrictions and indignities suffered at court as it was in the pleasure they took in each other's company. Henri and Catherine might have the privilege and power, but Margot and François were a team.

And as a team they used these two months—"which appeared to us only as so many days"—as a political summit to formulate their plans. For despite her ignominious retreat, Marguerite's espionage mission to Flanders had in fact been a success. By personally interceding on François's behalf, she had won her brother the regional support he needed to pursue his northern ambitions. The promised meeting with Monsieur de Montigny, the comte de Lalain's brother, came to pass, and there was also a letter from the steadfast Monsieur d'Ainsi reiterating his fealty and pledging the fortress at Cambrai to the queen of Navarre's younger brother. Don John's ferocity and her near escapes had in no way dampened Marguerite's spirits; if anything, her brush with danger had legitimized her participation in the venture and made her a far more active partner. Using her diplomatic skills and his martial abilities and rank as heir to the throne of France, they had won the Peace of Monsieur. Why not try again, but this time reach higher?

To wrest Flanders from Spanish rule was not treason against Henri III but a valid outlet for François's—and French—aspirations in the Netherlands. "M. de Montigny delivered his brother's declaration and engagement to give up the counties of Hainault and

Artois, which included a number of fine cities," Marguerite recalled. "These offers made and accepted, my brother dismissed [the Flemish officials] with presents of gold medals, bearing his and my effigies, and every assurance of his future favor; and they returned to prepare everything for his coming." Having her picture engraved on the emblems as well as François's was very unusual. This was clearly meant to be a joint venture.*

And so it was decided. François would return to court, but only to acquaint Henri and Catherine with his plans and ask for their help in raising the necessary men and supplies as a prelude to his leading an army into Flanders. As he would also require Huguenot assistance—or at least their neutrality—Margot would accompany him to court and again formally request permission to join Henry in Navarre. During the long weeks of summer, while she had been away taking the cure at Spa, Henri III had run out of funds with which to pursue his vendetta against the Huguenots and had been forced to sue for peace, so he no longer had a legitimate reason to keep his sister from her husband. Once back in Navarre, she could resurrect the old triumvirate of herself, Henry, and François. They had proved a potent combination in the past; who knows what they could accomplish in the future? At the very least, this would aid François's efforts in Flanders. Once her younger brother established his sovereignty to the north while her husband held his realm in the south—well, let Henri III try to harm her then.

Of course, it's easy to arrange the future—to adopt ambitious plans involving the participation of many different, often opposing factions—while sequestered in the dreamlike atmosphere of a secluded country estate. Reality can be somewhat more challenging.

---

* It is quite possible that the medallions were intended to prepare the way for François's naming Marguerite as regent should something happen to Henri III and should he, as next in line, ascend to the throne of France. The Netherlands were used to female rule—Charles V, father of Philip II, had appointed his sister Maria, queen of Hungary, to the position in 1531, and she had governed for twenty-four years before resigning in Philip II's favor and being replaced by first the duke of Alva and then Don John. Maria was another of the great queens of the sixteenth century.

15

Royal Rivalries

Above all a prince must endeavor in every action to obtain fame for being great and excellent.

—Niccolò Machiavelli, *The Prince*

AFTER THE TWO MONTHS WITH her brother had passed, with her objectives firmly in mind, Marguerite departed La Fère for the royal court. François had preceded her by a few days, but she soon caught up with him, and together they arrived in Saint-Denis on November 12, 1577. In a show of respect, Henri and Catherine had arranged for the entire court to ride out to welcome the king's younger siblings. "I was received very graciously, and most sumptuously entertained," Margot remembered. "I was made to recount the particulars of my triumphant journey to Liège, and perilous return. The magnificent entertainments I had received excited their admiration, and they rejoiced at my narrow escapes." It was obvious that Henri and Catherine had debated how best to handle this pair of royal truants and had decided to flatter and humor them, at least until they could determine exactly what Marguerite and François had been up to all this time.

They didn't have long to wait. On her very first evening back, after the grand ball in her honor had ended and everyone was on the way home to Paris, Marguerite sought out her mother and Henri and again requested permission to join her husband in Navarre.

Given that the kingdom was officially at peace they could have no objection, she argued, and to her pleasant surprise, "both of them approved of my request and commended my resolution." Pressing her advantage, the queen of Navarre then reminded her mother that she had promised to bestow upon her the dowry that had never been paid, and again "she [Catherine] recollected it well, and the King thought it very reasonable, and promised that it should be done," Margot concluded.

But it wasn't done. Marguerite had intended to stay in Paris for only two weeks and start her journey south to Navarre at the beginning of December. She petitioned repeatedly for her dowry and a means of transportation, but to her frustration found the king and queen mother unceasingly evasive. "Instead of dispatch, I experienced only delay; and thus it continued for five or six months in negotiation," she complained. François had no better luck with his Netherlands project, which Henri III had also pretended to approve. "My brother met with the like treatment, though he was continually urging the necessity for his setting out for Flanders," Margot observed. It did not take the siblings long to realize that they were being deliberately misled and that Catherine and Henri had no intention of letting either of them leave the court.

To have arrived in Paris with such high expectations only to find themselves reduced once more to the role of virtual prisoners was infuriating. Worse, both of them found the atmosphere surrounding Henri III, which was simultaneously cloying and dangerous, repugnant. In their absence, the king's favorites had grown even more powerful. François's position was especially onerous, as he was openly held in contempt by Henri III's *mignons,* to whom the king gave so much latitude that "these licentious young courtiers thought they might do whatever they pleased," Marguerite reported. The duke of Anjou's household, also comprised of combative young noblemen at the peak of their testosterone levels, naturally seethed at every slight. Bussy in particular had trouble containing his temper. "Bussy had a degree of courage which knew not how to give way to anyone," Margot reasoned fondly. In consequence, "some new dispute betwixt them [the *mignons*] and Bussy was constantly starting." This was something of an understatement. On January 10, 1578, after enduring two months of heckling and numerous clashes, Bussy stormed into the *mignons'* quarters at the head of a band of three hundred like-minded toughs and, drawing his formidable blade, dared his antagonists "to fight it out to the death." Only a last-minute intercession by Henri III, forbidding the acceptance of this challenge, stopped the battle from taking place. Even so, a few of the king's attendants, led by Quélus, Henri's longtime favorite, broke into Bussy's apartments late one evening and killed one of his closest friends, an offense the brilliant swordsman did not forget.

Matters came to a head a month later. As was his wont, by way of a reward for services rendered, Henri III had arranged for another member of his inner circle, a *mignon* named Saint-Luc, to marry an heiress — an extremely reluctant heiress, it was true, but that was hardly of primary importance to either the king or the courtier. The wedding was planned for the second week in February and promised to be a raucous, drunken affair at which the bejeweled and elaborately coiffed *mignons* would swagger around at their dandified best, lording it over the other guests. François prudently elected not to attend and urged Marguerite to join him in abstaining from the festivities, a request she had no difficulty granting.

Then Catherine stepped in. Alarmed that Henri might interpret his younger siblings' absence as an insult, she hastily arranged to cover up at least part of this potential indiscretion by pleading a prior engagement for herself, Marguerite, and François. It was a Monday, and the three went out for the day together to the château of Saint-Maur, one of the queen mother's favorite residences, just outside Paris. They stayed to dine, but it was still early when they returned from their excursion. The wedding party was in full swing, and Catherine, again fearing repercussions from an imagined slight to Henri, "well lectured my brother, and made him consent to appear

at the ball, in order not to displease the King," Margot reported.★
So he went.

It was a huge mistake. The moment he entered the room the
mignons went after him, not with swords but with insults. Secure in
the knowledge of their own physical superiority, they taunted François about his clothes, his pockmarks, his misshapen features, and
"other allusions to the meanness of his figure and the smallness of his
stature," Marguerite affirmed. It was the worst kind of bullying, especially inappropriate given the victim's rank as a member of the royal
family and heir to the throne. The duke of Anjou was well aware of
his blemished countenance and had been tormented by his looks since
childhood. What had been painful as a boy was downright intolerable
as a young man in his early twenties. He was the ugly swain in a court
that worshipped male beauty, and every quip landed with the precision of an executioner's ax. He turned pale and fled the room; he
sought out Catherine, and by the time he found her he was in tears.
He informed his mother of his humiliation at the hands of the *mignons*
and the impossibility of his staying at court. He didn't care what anyone said, he told her; he was leaving Paris to go hunting. Catherine,
perhaps feeling a trifle guilty, agreed that he should get away for a bit
and sent word to the king that his younger brother would embark the
next morning on the chase, "as it would put a stop to the disputes
which had arisen betwixt him and the young men, Maugiron, Saint-
Luc, Quélus, and the rest," said Margot, naming the worst of the
offending *mignons*. Her recollection of these events was confirmed by
the envoy from Florence. "The quarrels of Bussy are bound to lead to
a new row between the king and Monsieur, his brother," the ambassador wrote. "The latter is...resolved to withdraw from court...
together with all of his followers."

★ It is clear from this incident that Catherine was no longer in control of the court,
as she had been during the reign of Charles IX. She still managed the day-to-day
administration of the government, but she had to show Henri III all the documentation and obtain his signature. The *mignons* in particular were entirely outside her
authority. Marguerite mentioned that her mother "was greatly uneasy on account of
the behavior of these young men," but she was powerless to do anything about them.

At first Henri, also somewhat penitent, approved his brother's decision. But that was before he referred the matter to his *mignons,* who sensed a chance to rid themselves of their highborn rival once and for all. "The King, however, staying in his closet... with his council of five or six young men, they suggested suspicions in his mind respecting my brother's departure from Court," Marguerite clarified. "In short, they worked upon his fears and apprehensions so greatly, that he took one of the most rash and inconsiderate steps that was ever decided upon in our time; which was to put my brother and all of his principal servants under arrest."

To officially arrest a member of the royal family was no small affair; the action implied treason of the highest order. Catherine, who had gone to bed believing all was well and that François would be leaving in the morning with royal permission, was astonished to be woken in the middle of the night by an enraged Henri accompanied by the captain of the royal guard and a number of soldiers. The king did everything but accuse his mother of complicity in a plot against his life. "How could you, Madame, think of asking me to let my brother go hence?" Henri spat. "Do you not perceive how dangerous his going will prove to my kingdom? Depend upon it, that this hunting is merely a pretense to cover some treacherous design. I am going to put him and his people under arrest, and have his papers examined. I am sure we shall make some great discoveries." So saying, he left with his band of armed guards to personally confront his brother. Fifty-eight-year-old Catherine was obliged to heave herself out of bed and run after him in her dressing gown down the cold corridors to ensure that he did not do irreparable harm to her youngest son.

From there, events spun out of control in a manner not unlike a droll stage play or the comic burlesques for which France is so well known. A startled and much confused François was subsequently awakened in the middle of the night by his brother's banging furiously on his door. Having no idea what was the matter, he sat up in bed and ordered his chamberlain to let the king in. The next thing he knew the room was filled with armed men and Henri was standing over him, bellowing, "I will show you what it is to plot against your sovereign!" The guards were ordered to remove any papers or boxes that might provide evidence while the king searched his brother's bed for incriminating communiqués. A well-thumbed piece of parchment caught his attention. "The King endeavored to force it from him," Margot reported. François "refused to part with it, and earnestly entreated the King would not insist upon seeing it. This only excited the King's anxiety the more to have it in his possession, as he now supposed it to be the key to the whole plot, and the very document which would at once bring conviction home to him. At length, the King having got it into his hands, he opened it in the presence of the Queen my mother and they were both… confounded when they read the contents." It was a love letter from Madame de Sauve.

Despite the absence of any indication of intrigue, Henri had gone too far to back down. He knew he already looked ridiculous, but he decided to bluff his way through rather than concede an error in judgment. When François demanded to know the charges against him, the king regally refused to answer and instead commanded the captain of the guard and his archers to remain in the room and guard the prisoner. Then he went back to bed.

Anxious and afraid, François considered his position. There was no approaching his mother, who had been in the room and accepted the king's decision. Henri had already announced that François's entourage was also under arrest, so there would be no help from that quarter. That left Marguerite.

He began tentatively by questioning the captain of the guard. François "feared some fatal event might succeed these violent proceedings, and he was under the greatest concern on my account, supposing me to be under like arrest," Margot attested. The captain replied that, on the contrary, the queen of Navarre had not been detained. Upon further reflection, this did not seem quite fair to François. After all, what was the good of being a member of a team if he was the only one to bear the burden of adversity? Accordingly, he begged the captain to go get his sister to keep him company, "as I know she loves me so entirely that she would rather be confined with me than have her liberty whilst I was in confinement." So the captain went and woke up Marguerite and had her escorted through the Louvre like a common criminal in the presence of all the courtiers—by this time half the castle was awake—to share her brother's imprisonment. "Though I have received many particular favors since from him [François], this has always held the foremost place in my grateful remembrance," she commented drily.

She was thoroughly frightened by the time she arrived, having, like François himself, no inkling of what had occurred to set the king off in this way. By this time the guard originally assigned to watch over the duke of Anjou had been relieved and replaced by new men, including an older captain who had known Marguerite since childhood. Seeing her distress, he approached her out of hearing of the other soldiers to reassure her. "There is not a good Frenchman living who does not bleed at his heart to see what we see," whispered the captain. "I expect to have the guard of the Prince your brother, wherever he shall chance to be confined; and depend upon it, at the hazard of my life, I will restore him to his liberty."

From this and her younger brother's violent protestations of innocence, the queen of Navarre inferred that in fact nothing of significance had occurred during the previous evening and that the dramatic arrest of François represented just another of Henri's attempts at harassment. Briskly, she took over. "I observed to my brother that we ought not to remain there without knowing for what reason we were detained, as if we were in the Inquisition; and that to treat us in such a manner was to consider us as persons of no account," she reasoned logically. "I then begged M. de l'Oste [the older captain] to entreat the King, in our name...to send someone to acquaint us with the crime for which we were kept in confinement." The guardsman did as he was told, and eventually one of the *mignons* appeared. "With a great deal of gravity, he informed us that he came from the King to inquire what it was we wished to communicate to his Majesty," reported Marguerite. "We answered that we wished to speak to someone near the King's person, in order to our being informed what we were kept in confinement for, as we were unable to assign any reason for it ourselves. He answered, with great solemnity, that we ought not to ask of God or the King reasons for what they did; as all their actions emanated from wisdom and justice." At this, François laughed outright, but his sister, who did not appreciate having been awakened on a cold night in February, dragged out of bed, and humiliated once again in front of the court over what she now understood was a completely specious accusation, "could scarcely refrain from talking to this messenger as he deserved."

Of course she was right. In the cold light of day even Henri understood that he could not keep his brother under arrest without cause and was forced to remove the guard. Rather than apologizing, though, he sent his mother to smooth over any lingering unpleasantness resulting from the events of the previous evening. Catherine took the rather disingenuous approach of blaming François for the episode. "The Queen my mother, coming to his apartment, told him he ought to return thanks to God for his deliverance, for that there had been a moment when even she herself despaired of saving his life; that since he must now have discovered that the King's temper of mind was such that he took the alarm at the very imagination of danger, and that, when once he was resolved upon a measure, no advice that she or any other could give would prevent him from putting it into execution, she would recommend it to him to submit himself to the King's pleasure in everything, in order to prevent the like in future," Marguerite reported.

With the queen mother, as ever, insisting on the outward appearance of harmony, a meeting was held later that day in Catherine's rooms attended by all the highest-ranking members of the court. In yet another scene straight out of a French farce, François was formally required to repledge his allegiance to the king; the king munificently replied that he never had any doubt of his brother's innocence, and the two exchanged the kiss of peace, which was Catherine's favorite form of reconciliation. Bussy and Quélus were also present, and upon being commanded by Henri to take the example of the two royal brothers and leave off all feuding in the future, Bussy, demonstrating the insouciant wit for which he was known, neatly skewered the hypocrisy of the entire episode. "Sire, if it is your pleasure that we kiss and are friends again, I am ready to obey your command," he replied smoothly, then wrapped his arms theatrically around Quélus and kissed him thoroughly, as though he were a woman, much to the amusement of the onlookers.

If this had been a stage play, the curtain would then have dropped, the audience would have applauded enthusiastically, and everybody would have gone out to dinner. But this was not a performance that either Marguerite or François wished to repeat. Henri's midnight arrest of his brother, and Catherine's inability to stop him and subsequent condoning of the king's behavior, had removed the mask of indulgence the pair had worn since the siblings' arrival and made manifest to the queen of Navarre and the duke of Anjou the danger they had placed themselves in by returning to court. In the cold hours before dawn, under the stern gaze of the royal archers, they had huddled together in François's room and laid their plans.

THEY BOTH KNEW THEY had to move quickly. They were still being watched, but it was critical for at least François to get away so that he could raise an army and honor his commitment to his Flemish partisans. As usual, this meant that Marguerite would stay behind and face the danger—and the punishment—for her younger brother's conduct. But the alternative was to remain a hostage to Henri's *mignons* and his moods, and this had recently been proved to be just as perilous.

The problem was how to organize her brother's escape. She couldn't just have him throw on a big cloak and slink away in a borrowed carriage this time; Henri was prepared for that artifice and had increased security at all the portals. It took a few days, but the queen of Navarre eventually formulated a possible exit strategy. "When we consulted upon the means of its accomplishment, we could find no other than his descending from my window, which was on the second story and opened to the ditch, for the gates were so closely watched that it was impossible to pass them, the face of everyone going out of the Louvre being curiously examined," Margot explained. "He begged of me, therefore, to procure for him a rope of sufficient strength and long enough for the purpose. This I set about immediately, for, having the sacking of a bed that wanted mending, I sent it out of the palace by a lad whom I could trust, with orders to bring it back repaired, and to wrap up the proper length of rope inside."

With Catherine and Henri's spies everywhere, the success of the rope-out-the-window method was obviously predicated on the ability of the participants to feign equanimity and go about their business as though nothing out of the ordinary was being contemplated. Alas, François made a terrible conspirator. On the evening of February 14, 1578, just a few days after the fiasco at Saint-Luc's wedding, "when all was prepared...at supper time, I went to the Queen my mother, who supped alone in her own apartment, it being a fast-day and the King eating no supper. My brother...anxious to extricate himself from danger and regain his liberty, came to me as I was rising from table, and whispered to me to make haste and come to him in my own apartment," Margot remembered. "M. de Matignon...whether he had some knowledge of his design from someone who could not keep a secret, or only guessed at it, observed to the Queen my mother as she left the room (which I overheard, being near her, and circumspectly watching every word and motion, as may well be imagined, situated as I was betwixt fear and hope, and involved in perplexity) that my brother had undoubtedly an intention of withdrawing himself, and would not be there the next day; adding that he was assured of it, and she might take her measures accordingly."* So their machinations were known and had been betrayed to Catherine. The queen of Navarre could not disguise her dismay. "I observed that she [Catherine] was much disconcerted by this observation, and I had my fears lest we should be discovered," she admitted.

Her anxiety deepened when, a few moments later, her mother turned and confronted her. "You know," Catherine warned, "I have pledged myself to the King that your brother shall not depart hence, and Matignon has declared that he knows very well he will not be here tomorrow."

Her mother's accusation put Marguerite in an extremely awkward position. She couldn't very well tell the truth and give François away, as then she would be guilty of "proving unfaithful to my brother, and thereby bringing his life into jeopardy." But nor did she wish to engage in the act of telling an outright lie, as this was behavior she "would have died rather than be guilty of."

Her solution was to feign ignorance and try to distract her mother by casting blame and substituting a half-truth for candor. "You cannot, Madame, but be sensible the M. de Matignon is not one of my brother's friends," Marguerite began severely, "and that he is, besides, a busy, meddling kind of man, who is sorry to find a reconciliation has taken place with us." Then she proceeded to choose her words very carefully. "As to my brother, I will answer for him with my life in case he goes hence, of which, if he had any design, I should, as I am well assured, not be ignorant, he never having yet concealed anything he meant to do from me." So saying, she offered her life for her brother's. She did not believe it would come to that—"all

---

* Monsieur de Matignon was a strict Catholic and trusted adviser to the queen mother who would be promoted to Marshal of France the following year. He was the father of Marguerite's childhood companion Torigni, whom Margot had been forced by her husband to dismiss from her household three years earlier. It was Torigni who had to be rescued from Henri III's soldiers. This disturbing incident and her near escape had affected neither her father's career path nor his loyalties.

this was said by me with the assurance that, after my brother's escape, they would not dare to do me any injury"—but in case it did, "I had much rather pledge my life than...endanger my brother's." And that is exactly how Catherine construed her daughter's reply. "Remember what you now say," the queen mother interjected curtly, taking the deal. "You will be bound for him on the penalty of your life."

On this happy note, Marguerite bade her mother good night and retired to her own rooms. Committed to the escape plan—although with the stakes raised slightly more than she had originally expected—she shrugged hurriedly out of her court dress and into bed, dismissing her entourage of ladies-in-waiting. Left with only a skeleton crew of handmaids, she awaited her brother. François had been keeping watch and stole in soon afterward, accompanied by two of his most trusted servants, Simier and Cangé.

They wasted no time. "Rising from my bed, we made the cord fast, and having looked out at the window to discover if anyone was in the ditch, with the assistance of three of my women, who slept in my room, and the lad who had brought in the rope, we let down my brother, who laughed and joked upon the occasion without the least apprehension, notwithstanding the height was considerable," Marguerite related, impressed. Not everyone in François's small band of fugitives was as sanguine as their high-spirited young master was about the prospect of vaulting down a tall stone tower in the dead of night, however. "We next lowered Simier into the ditch, who was in such a fright that he had scarcely the strength to hold the rope fast; and lastly descended my brother's *valet de chambre,* Cangé," Marguerite concluded.

Cangé was still in midair when to her great consternation Marguerite perceived a figure suddenly emerge from the ditch and take off in the general direction of the palace guard. "I was almost dead with alarm, supposing that this might be a spy placed there by M. de Matignon, and that my brother would be taken," she declared. In a panic, the chambermaids, believing they were about to be arrested, sought to destroy the evidence and threw the rope into the fire. Unfortunately, it was very stout rope, highly flammable. A great blaze leaped up from the hearth and caused the chimney to catch fire, sending billowing waves of smoke into the air. If they had hired heralds to blow trumpets or exploded fireworks they could not have attracted more attention. The royal guard came running. They pounded "violently at the door, calling for it to be opened," Margot recalled. "I now concluded that my brother was stopped, and that we were both undone."

Again she thought quickly. She could not let the soldiers in without giving the entire scheme away. The rope was only half burned, and they would easily deduce what had occurred. She would have to bluff. "I told my women to go to the door, and speaking softly, as if I was asleep, to ask the men what they wanted," Marguerite instructed. "They did so, and the archers replied that the chimney was on fire, and they came to extinguish it. My women answered it was of no consequence, and they could put it out themselves, begging them not to awake me." This explanation satisfied the guard and "they went away," Margot reported with evident relief.

But she was not so lucky the next time. Two hours later, the captain of the guard himself banged on her door, and this time there was no denying him entrance. An informer from Paris had just arrived with intelligence relating to the duke of Anjou's brazen flight from court. The queen of Navarre was summoned to an immediate predawn audience with a furious Henri III and Catherine, at which it was expected that she would confirm her culpability in this treasonous enterprise and provide the details of her brother's escape.

HAVING NO CHOICE, MARGUERITE arose from bed and began hurriedly to dress. Her chambermaids had been awakened as well. There was no disguising the precariousness of her situation, and her servants were unable to control their emotions. "One of them was indiscreet enough to hold me round the waist, and exclaim aloud, shedding a flood of tears, that she should never see me more," Margot recounted. The captain of the guard was incensed. "Pushing her away, [he] said to me: 'If I were not a person thoroughly devoted to your service, this woman has said enough to bring you into trouble. But,' continued he, 'fear nothing. God be praised, by this time the Prince your brother is out of danger.'"

The captain spoke the truth. After being let down with the rope, François, Simier, and Cangé had all managed to creep outside the Louvre grounds without being noticed and had subsequently made their way to a prearranged meeting with the always resourceful Bussy at the Abbey of Sainte-Geneviève, very near one of the ramparts of the capital. "By consent of the abbot, a hole had been made in the city wall, through which they passed, and horses being provided and in waiting, they mounted, and reached Angers without the least accident," Margot, much comforted by this information, reported.

François's having gained the impregnability of his home base of Angers, which boasted a massive stronghold, was likely the determining factor in saving Marguerite from Henri III's revenge. As the queen of Navarre had correctly anticipated, the king could not risk provoking the duke of Anjou, who had already shown himself capable of leading a successful attack on the throne, by maltreating his beloved sister. "I found him [Henri III] sitting at the foot of the Queen my mother's bed, in such a violent rage that I am inclined to believe I should have felt the effects of it, had he not been restrained by the absence of my brother and my mother's presence," she affirmed. Still, her situation was sufficiently dire to convince Margot that it might be a good idea, just this once, to set aside those pesky scruples she had about lying. "They both told me that I had assured them my brother would not leave the Court, and that I pledged myself for his stay. I replied that it was true that he had deceived me, as he had them," protested the woman who had painstakingly planned the escape, smuggled in the rope, secured the necessary accomplices, and then personally helped to lower François out her window. "However, I was ready still to pledge my life that his departure would not operate to the prejudice of the King's service, and that it would appear he was only gone to his own principality to give orders and forward his expedition to Flanders," she recovered smoothly.

These last words were confirmed the next morning, when Henri III received a long, reassuring letter from his brother, in which François again declared his fidelity to the Crown and explained that he had only left the court for his own safety and to pursue his ambitions in Flanders. "This caused a cessation of complaints, but by no means removed the King's dissatisfaction," Margot reported frankly. Henri dispatched his mother to Angers to try to persuade the duke of Anjou to return to court. This she was not able to do; nor was she able, despite repeated attempts and a series of tempting marriage proposals aimed at distracting her youngest son's attention, to persuade François to abandon his Netherlands campaign. Despite the determined opposition of Catherine and Henri, who feared Spanish reprisals if the French king's younger brother took up arms in Flanders, the duke of Anjou left France, taking his household with him, and by July 12 was at the city of Mons, deep in Flemish territory, with the promise of an army of some three thousand soldiers to follow.

His initiative was applauded by his sister, who in addition to having imposed her political will over that of her formidable mother and older brother reaped several ancillary benefits from François's military campaign. The critical role Marguerite had played in these events was not lost on Henri III, and a crude attempt was made to conciliate her by "complying with my wishes, that by this means he could withdraw me from my attachment to my brother," she observed. That August, she finally received her dowry—not in cash, as the royal treasury could not afford it, but in land and property, "with the power of nomination to all vacant benefices and offices." Henri even subsidized this with the gift of an annual payment "over and above the customary pension to the daughters of

France, he gave another out of his privy purse," Marguerite noted with satisfaction.

But nothing bespoke her triumph more than the king's at last conceding to her request to be reunited with her husband. In this Henri III was influenced by more than his younger brother's defiance. After François's flight from court, the king's *mignons,* deprived of their favorite target, had turned their attention to goading a new rival: the duke of Guise. An altercation broke out between Quélus and Balzac d'Entragues, a senior member of the duke of Guise's household, very similar to what had occurred previously with Bussy, only this time a duel took place. The duke's men, no strangers to warfare, proved to be exceptionally deadly in hand-to-hand combat. Three of Henri's *mignons* were killed outright, and Quélus himself, being apparently far more proficient with insults than with blades, was stabbed nineteen times and died slowly and painfully over the course of the following few months. Henri was inconsolable at the loss of his favorites. The king "covered their dead bodies with kisses, clipped their blond locks and had them taken for safekeeping, and removed Quélus's earrings, which he himself had given him, putting them on with his own hand," revealed a Parisian chronicler.

To assuage his anger and grief, Henri III turned on Quélus's assailant and demanded that Balzac d'Entragues be arrested and condemned for murder. But the duke of Guise defended his retainer and refused to hand him over to the royal guard. "M. d'Entragues did only what any gentleman ought to have done; if anyone attempts to interfere with him, my sword, which has a sharp edge, shall settle the question," he responded coolly. With this all Henri's old enmity toward his childhood schoolmate, which he had suppressed since the Saint Bartholomew's Day Massacre when he had needed the duke of Guise's help, came rushing back with a vengeance. He would never forget this insult to his beloved Quélus. Afraid to confront his adversary directly—for the valiant duke of Guise was extremely popular in Paris, far more than the king himself—Henri instead attempted to incite him to violence (which could then be used as an excuse for arrest) by spreading rumors about his wife's infidelity. Disgusted but unbowed, the duke of Guise refused to take the bait and instead, like François, simply removed himself and his family and supporters from court.

Having succeeded in alienating the leaders of both the Catholic and the Politique factions in France, it occurred to Henri III that it would behoove him to placate the Huguenots. As usual, he assigned the task of reconciliation to his mother. To further demonstrate his goodwill to his brother-in-law, who by default had been elevated to a higher position of favor with the king than either his younger brother or the duke of Guise, Henri III found that he was, after all, able to overcome his reservations about reuniting his sister with her husband.

And so, after more than six years of marriage, Margot was finally permitted to leave the court to take her place in Navarre. It had taken a little longer and been slightly more complicated than she had expected, but she had accomplished every one of the goals she had set out for herself and her brother at La Fère, no mean achievement. Still, although she had worked hard for this and must have savored her victory, she could not have faced the journey south without some trepidation. It had been nineteen months since she had last seen the husband who had so callously abandoned her to imprisonment and the king's wrath. Much had changed in the interim, it was true. But had he?

16

Queen of Navarre

*Well-ordered states and wise princes have studied diligently
not to drive the nobles to desperation, and to satisfy the
populace and keep it contented, for this is one of the most
important matters that a prince has to deal with.*

—Niccolò Machiavelli, *The Prince*

HENRY OF NAVARRE HAD ONE reason and one reason only for wanting his wife back. His small kingdom needed a line of succession,
which meant that he needed to start a family. In the absence of
divorce or annulment, which the pragmatic king of Navarre had
ruled out as potentially jeopardizing his own standing as next in line
to the throne of France after François (not to mention that divorcing
a royal princess might easily lead to war), Marguerite was the only
woman in Christendom who could provide him with a legitimate
son and heir.

Margot's motives for reestablishing relations with her recalcitrant
husband, however, were far more ambitious. Although she was as
anxious as Henry to produce a scion to Navarre—her position
would be far more secure if she gave birth to a son who might one
day rule France—Marguerite also craved the affection, respect, and
responsibility that were the assumed by-products of a nuptial union
with a sovereign prince. Not for her, the proud daughter of a king
of France, the sort of marriage her lower-born Italian mother had

endured, publicly set aside in favor of a beautiful mistress. Marguerite's rank was superior to Henry's, and she expected to be esteemed accordingly or, at the very least, treated as an equal.

Still, she could not have helped but have misgivings. She had been to Gascony only once, as a child on the Grand Tour, and did not remember much about it except that it had been very hot and then the rain had come down in torrents and ruined her mother's party. As her husband's birthplace and childhood home as well as a Huguenot stronghold, however, Gascony gave Henry every advantage over her. If he wanted to make her life with him unpleasant, he undoubtedly could. She needed his goodwill, and she set out determined to obtain it.

Catherine, who accompanied Marguerite on the journey south in order to treat with Henry, sabotaged her daughter's efforts right from the beginning by bringing along twenty members of the Flying Squadron handpicked for beauty. Madame de Sauve's time seems to have passed; the reigning sirens were now an exotic temptress of Latin ancestry named Dayelle and an equally glamorous Frenchwoman, La Verne. Although at twenty-five Marguerite was still a highly attractive woman in her own right, she understood that she would have to compete for Henry's attention. "For my husband had been greatly smitten with Dayelle, and M. de Thurène [one of Henry's principal officials] was in love with La Vergne," she noted glumly, which of course was the reason Catherine, angling for every advantage in her negotiations, insisted upon bringing the women along in the first place.

The two queens, mother and daughter, attended by Catherine's piquant flock of dazzling ladies-in-waiting, in addition to the usual servants, clergymen, physicians, kitchen staff, ambassadors, and royal counselors, left Paris in August 1578. For Catherine this was a reprise, albeit on a smaller scale, of the Grand Tour, and she sought to replicate the opulence of her former journey. A special tax had to be levied to bear the cost of the expedition, with its carts of gowns and jewels, household supplies, and elaborate props for ceremonial entries into the various towns and cities along the route.*

Marguerite, with so much at stake and so many fascinating rivals with whom to contend, threw herself into the business of standing out and seems for the most part to have succeeded. "I remember (for I was there) that when the queen mother took this queen, her daughter, to the King of Navarre, her husband, she passed through Cognac and made some stay," recounted the courtier Brantôme. "While they were there, came various grand and honorable ladies of the region to see them and do them reverence, who were all amazed at the beauty of the princess, and could not surfeit themselves in praising her to her mother...Wherefore she begged her daughter to array herself most gorgeously in the fine and superb apparel that she wore at Court for great and magnificent pomps and festivals, in order to give pleasure to these worthy dames." Marguerite obligingly put on her court dress, "a gown of silver tissue and dove-color...[with] hanging sleeves, a rich head-dress with a white veil, neither too large nor yet too small." Her appearance drew approbation, even from her mother—"My daughter, you look well," Catherine remarked. When Marguerite then worried aloud that she had better wear all her clothes now, as they were sure to be out of fashion the next time she returned to court, her mother stopped her. "'What do you mean by that, my daughter? Is it not you yourself who invent and produce these fashions of dress? Wherever you go the Court will take them from you, not you from the Court.' Which was true," Brantôme continued, "for after she returned she was always in advance of the Court, so well did she know how to invent in her dainty mind all sorts of charming things."

But despite these triumphs, the closer they came to their appointed rendezvous with Henry in La Réole, near Bordeaux, the more

---

* It is this procession, and Marguerite's later court in Navarre, that Shakespeare lampooned in his comedy *Love's Labour's Lost,* although she was not the target of the satire. English Protestants were disappointed by Henry's compromises with French Catholics. *Love's Labour's Lost* skewers the king of Navarre by depicting him as passionately infatuated with his own wife, an inside joke greatly appreciated in England.

anxiety Marguerite demonstrated about the impression she would make upon her husband. "For three days she has kept herself shut up with three women in attendance; she spends her time in the bath, white as a lily, smelling of sweet lotions. One might say it was a sorceress with all her charms," laughed one of the ladies-in-waiting in a letter home to Henri III in Paris.

At least initially, these extensive preparations seemed to have been rewarded. Henry made every effort to gratify his wife and mother-in-law. Knowing the women's fondness for spectacle, he had arranged for an imposing entourage of some six hundred of his highest-born noblemen, arrayed in their most splendid finery, to accompany him to their first meeting. At the sight of his wife, he heaped compliments on her, and professed himself overcome by joy at their reunion. He even made a point of sleeping with her that night. "I received every mark of honor and attention from the King that I could expect or desire," Marguerite affirmed. For her part, the queen of Navarre demonstrated her worth to her husband almost immediately by deftly intervening in an argument that broke out between Catherine and Henry over the queen mother's strident insistence that her son-in-law accept the authority of a Catholic governor appointed by the Crown.

But this overt display of affection was mere pretense—on both sides. Henry was far more interested in Catherine's Flying Squadron, particularly the enchanting young Mademoiselle Dayelle, than he was in his wife. And no number of sweet-scented baths could disguise from Marguerite the stink of garlic and sweat that formed her husband's natural perfume, nor could she fail to register his short stature and less-than-courtly manners.

Their problems went far beyond mere physical attraction (or lack thereof), however. The part of France to which the queen of Navarre and her mother had traveled was so deeply divided by religious controversy and the suspicion and mistrust engendered by the Saint Bartholomew's Day Massacre that almost every town had declared itself either wholly Catholic or Protestant, with the result that no member of the opposing sect was allowed entrance without specific permission. So, for example, Henry, being of the reformed religion, could not stay with Marguerite in Agen, a Catholic city that formed part of her dowry, and Catherine could not travel farther into Protestant territory than La Réole, "which was held by the Huguenots as a cautionary town; and the country not being sufficiently quieted, she was permitted to go no further," Margot explained.

Even when they found a town willing to accommodate both faiths, the acute political instability of the surrounding countryside frequently disrupted their attempts to promote harmony. In November Catherine hosted a ball at Auch for the king and queen of Navarre and their guests. Henry and a large number of Protestant gentlemen attended, many of them officials in his government. This festive occasion began on a very high note. Marguerite, who loved to dance, welcomed her new subjects with a grace and charm that pleased her husband greatly. The members of Henry's entourage, used to the austerity of their religion, were dazzled by the parade of beauties—one after another—representing the Parisian court. The allure of sermons and scriptures, previously so potent, eroded precipitously in the presence of so much richly dressed loveliness. "We found the Queen and all her maids of honor," remembered the vicomte de Turenne, a senior member of Henry's retinue. "The King of Navarre and the said Queen greeted each other and showed themselves more ready for understanding than on the other occasions when they had met. The violins came up. We all began to dance."

But this was southern France in the second half of the sixteenth century, and love was not allowed to conquer politics, even for one night. In the middle of the affair, just when everyone was having such a good time, a messenger came and whispered in Henry's ear that there had been an uprising at La Réole and that the Protestant governor had changed sides. The king of Navarre, instantly assuming a Catholic plot (in fact it was a party of disgruntled citizens upset with what they considered to be abuses of power), motioned to the vicomte de Turenne, his top lieutenant, and a number of other gentlemen. Moments later they had disappeared from the dance floor and were galloping through the night to a nearby Catholic fortress, which they took by surprise in retaliation. This rather ruined the ball for the queen of Navarre and her remaining guests. Even Henry seems to have felt a bit penitent about spoiling his wife's attempt at promoting concord through revelry. He made a point of rearranging his schedule so that he could return to Auch a few days later to offer his apologies to Marguerite in person and restore conjugal relations with her.

The couple was obliged to spend Christmas and most of January apart—Marguerite and her mother retreated to a Catholic municipality to celebrate the holiday—but beginning in February they spent six weeks together in Henry's capital city of Nérac, where peace deliberations between Catherine and representatives of the Huguenot faction were held. In Nérac, despite the presence of dozens of disapproving Protestant delegates, the collective merrymaking and giddy flirtations between the queen mother's Flying Squadron and the king of Navarre's Huguenot entourage, which had originated at the ball in Auch, were resumed in earnest. There were round-the-clock fetes; dancing commenced even before the midday meal; the city was full of music and lovers. Even the glummest of Henry's men "took a mistress like the others," reported a Huguenot chronicler. The king of Navarre rarely let Mademoiselle Dayelle out of his sight, and the vicomte of Turenne was stricken with love for La Verne. In fact the gentlemen of Navarre were so completely absorbed by the new, exciting activity of making love to agreeable royal courtesans that the queen mother's initial strategy of using the women to distract and inform on the men backfired, and she began to regret that she had brought them in the first place. "It was the intention of the Queen my mother to make but a short stay; but so many accidents arose from disputes betwixt the Huguenots and Catholics, that she was under the necessity of stopping there for eighteen months," Margot observed. "As this was very much against her inclination, she was sometimes inclined to think there was a design to keep her, in order to have the company of her maids of honor."

Despite her husband's obvious dalliance with her mother's demoiselle, it was religion and not infidelity that precipitated the first irrevocable crack in Marguerite and Henry's carefully constructed mask of amiability. The peace conference having finally wound down in a desultory fashion in April 1579, with very little progress being made (except that the Protestants had wrung some additional concessions from the Crown), Catherine left the queen of Navarre with her husband and continued her peace tour into Languedoc alone. Soon after, Henry was called to the Navarrese region of Béarn, so the court removed to the town of Pau, about sixty miles south of Nérac, at the beginning of May.

Pau, a rural seat, boasted an altogether different sort of ethos than any of the towns or hamlets Marguerite had yet encountered. Unrefined, provincial Nérac appeared positively cosmopolitan when compared to Pau. Worse, Pau was uncompromisingly Huguenot. It was only because Margot was Henry's queen that she was permitted entrance into the hamlet at all, and then "the Catholic religion not being tolerated, I was only allowed to have mass celebrated in a chapel of about three or four feet in length, and so narrow that it could scarcely hold seven or eight persons," she recalled. She had brought along her own priest, as was her right, and this information had leaked out into the countryside. As a preventive measure, to protect the general population from backsliding into orthodoxy, the drawbridge to the castle in which she was staying, and in which her tiny closet of a chapel was located, was raised as soon as she entered. But some enterprising residents "having been, for some years, deprived of the benefit of following their own mode of worship... on Whitsunday, found means to get into the castle before the bridge was drawn up, and were present at the celebration of mass, not being discovered until it was nearly over."

The fury of her Huguenot hosts at the handful of Catholic inhabitants who had dared to defy the town's religious strictures was profound, and they hurried to Henry's secretary, Jacques du Pin, whom Marguerite referred to scornfully as Le Pin, to inform on their neighbors. Pin, who was every bit as fanatical a Protestant as the rest of Pau, and who strongly disapproved of his overlord's wife being allowed to remain Catholic instead of being forced to convert to the reformed religion, "ordered the guard to arrest these poor people, who were severely beaten in my presence, and afterwards locked up in prison, whence they were not released without paying a considerable fine. This indignity gave me great offence, as I never expected anything of the kind," Marguerite recalled, still anguished by the memory decades later.

Inflamed with grief and anger—these were *her* subjects, and despite her emphatic, increasingly authoritative commands to desist she had been unable to save them from violence at the hands of her husband's guard—she flew to Henry, whom she found in conference with Pin. "I complained of it to the King my husband, begging him to give orders for the release of these poor Catholics, who did not deserve to be punished for coming to my chapel to hear mass, a celebration of which they had been so long deprived," Marguerite continued, still impassioned. She had not hesitated to do what she could for him at the time of the Saint Bartholomew's Day Massacre, even going down on her knees to save the lives of two of his Huguenot noblemen. Surely her husband could return the favor. However, before Henry could answer, "Le Pin, with the greatest disrespect to his master, took upon him to reply, without waiting to hear what the King had to say. He told me that I ought not to trouble the King my husband about such matters; that what had been done was very right and proper; that those people had justly merited the treatment they met with, and all I could say would go for nothing, for it must be so; and that I ought to rest satisfied with being permitted to have mass said to me and my servants." Never in her life had an official dared to address Margot, a member of the royal family, with anything other than the deepest deference. "This insolent speech from a person of his inferior condition incensed me greatly, and I entreated the King my husband, if I had the least share in his good graces, to do me justice, and avenge the insult offered me by this low man."

Henry was in a bind. There was no question that Pin had overstepped the boundaries of his position by addressing his sovereign's royal consort as though she were the local fishmonger's wife. On the other hand, Pin was a loyal servant who in general handled his duties well, if a little overenthusiastically, and the Catholic interlopers had clearly broken the laws of Pau. Uncertain of what to do, Henry wavered, first telling his wife that he would fire his secretary, then allowing his secretary to talk him out of it. Marguerite had to threaten to leave him before he sulkily agreed to dismiss Pin. "The King, however, continued to behave to me with great coolness," she acknowledged. To punish her, Henry began a highly public affair with another woman (Dayelle having departed earlier with Catherine), who flaunted her position and influence over the king of Navarre and did her best to humiliate Margot.

It wasn't until they left Pau—that "little Geneva," as Marguerite bitterly referred to the town—some two months later that they managed to patch up their marriage. As had happened once before, illness played a critical role in reconciling the king of Navarre to his wife. On the way back to Nérac, Henry came down with a nasty fever, and Marguerite again put aside her wounded feelings to assiduously restore her husband to health. "He took notice of my extraordinary tenderness, and spoke of it to several persons, and particularly to my cousin...who, acting the part of an affectionate relation, restored me to his favor, insomuch that I never stood so highly in it before," Margot related. "This happiness I had the good fortune to enjoy during the four or five years that I remained with him in Gascony."

Marital harmony being so unexpectedly and fortuitously restored, the royal couple returned to Nérac in August of 1579 to set up housekeeping and establish their court. These would be among the happiest years of Marguerite's life. Although Henry was not faithful—he had replaced his Pau amour with a member of his wife's entourage, a girl named Fosseuse, barely fifteen years old—the pair exercised discretion, which allowed Marguerite to maintain her dignity.* "The King was very assiduous with Fosseuse, who, being dependent on me, kept herself within the strict bounds of honor and virtue," Margot explained.

Possessed of her husband's good opinion, removed from the threats and demands of her family, Marguerite was at last free to express herself by organizing her surroundings in a manner compatible with her upbringing and aesthetic. The citizens of Nérac, used to the dreary Calvinism practiced by Henry's mother, Jeanne d'Albret, were delighted to find themselves suddenly treated to a cornucopia of new sights and sounds. The queen of Navarre adored music and dancing, and the sweet songs of lutes and violins could be heard emanating from the grand balls and concerts she arranged in the evenings. Her thirty-three ladies-in-waiting might not have been quite as heavenly as those comprising her mother's Flying Squadron, but in their trendsetting Parisian silks and brilliant jewels, they more than satisfied the local appetite for glamour. Nor was the theater neglected; roving players found a home in Nérac, some from as far away as Italy.

As she had in Paris, Marguerite befriended poets and sought to replicate the diverse cultural milieu of the Green Salon. Her official court poet, the seigneur du Bartas, expressed his appreciation for her patronage with these lines: "Great Henry's daughter, another Henry's queen / Whose beauty's equal never has been seen / Judith thy poet calls thee,—harken, though he raise / Naught worth men's hearing save thy wondrous praise." She invited scholars, both Catholic and Protestant, to Nérac to promote the city as a center of learning; a Huguenot courtier who attended one of these lectures reported that an eminent doctor of science "showed how the wind

---

* "No sooner [had] he lost sight of her than he forgot her," Margot commented drily of her rival from Pau.

blew." Marguerite was able to observe with justifiable pride, "Our Court was so brilliant that we had no cause to regret our absence from the Court of France."

Her cultural stewardship was undoubtedly admirable, but it was for the king and queen of Navarre's tolerance of religious differences that their court at Nérac was most to be commended. Almost alone in France—in western Europe—a Protestant king and a Catholic queen lived without violence. "This difference of religion, however, caused no dispute among us; the King my husband and the Princess his sister heard a sermon, whilst I and my servants heard mass," explained Marguerite. "I had a chapel in the park for the purpose, and, as soon as the service of both religions was over, we joined company in a beautiful garden, ornamented with long walks shaded with laurel and cypress trees. Sometimes we took a walk in the park on the banks of the river, bordered by an avenue of trees three thousand yards in length. The rest of the day was passed in innocent amusements; and in the afternoon, or at night, we commonly had a ball."

Ironically, the promise of Marguerite's marriage before the blood and horror of the massacre—the wedding of Catholic and Huguenot—was fulfilled in this brief moment in Nérac. True, the religious tolerance did not extend beyond the court into the general populace, but by their example she and Henry proved that it *could* be done and therefore *might* be done on a larger scale, given time. But time was exactly what they did not have. Marguerite's lyric description of dappled green paths and lush gardens inevitably evokes images of her court at Nérac as a sort of Eden. And the story of Eden always ends in exile.

PART III

～

The Rival Queens

17

The Lovers' War

*Whoever is the cause of another becoming powerful, is
ruined himself; for that power is produced by him either
through craft or force; and both of these are suspected by the
one that has become powerful.*

—Niccolò Machiavelli, *The Prince*

WHILE MARGUERITE WAS BUSY RESUSCITATING her relationship with
her husband and assembling her court in Nérac, her brother François,
as per the siblings' original plan, was laboring to deliver Flanders
from the tyranny of Spain as a prelude to establishing his own rule.
This enterprise, unfortunately, was not destined to yield the brilliant
success for which its architects had hoped. On the contrary, in a
century famous for bungled opportunities and mismanaged engagements, the duke of Anjou had the distinction of running one of the
briefest and most inept military campaigns of the day. His funds ran
out almost before he got there; his unpaid soldiers, angry and hun-
gry, ransacked the towns they had been hired to protect, raping and
murdering the inhabitants; filth and disease, the inevitable by-products
of war, spread dangerously in their wake, killing thousands. When
Don John himself fell victim to the typhoid epidemic plaguing the
army camps and died in the fall of 1578 at the age of thirty-one,
François prudently decided that it might be best to suspend his

activities in the north until such time as hygienic conditions improved. By January 1579, he was back in France.

Attributing this slight setback to a deplorable lack of funds and international support, the duke of Anjou turned once again to his mother and older brother. Anxious to keep him away from his old allies, the Huguenots and the Politiques, Henri III sent François the money necessary to appear at court. The impoverished duke of Anjou arrived in Paris on March 16, 1579, and found himself once again in the enviable position of being bribed to maintain cordial relations with the Crown. He received one hundred thousand *livres* outright, and the tempting title of lieutenant-general was once again hinted at as a potential reward for services rendered in the not-too-distant future. The marriage negotiations with Elizabeth I were also revived at this time, as a cover for securing English funds and soldiers for a second attempt at Flanders. "The king," reported a Venetian official who was in Paris and observed the warm reconciliation between Henri III and François firsthand, "has such a strong desire to satisfy his brother and completely win him over, with the tranquility of the kingdom depending on it, that he will soon concede this and everything else besides."

Having patched up his relationship with the king, François promptly fell out with Bussy. The abysmal showing in the Netherlands had put everyone in the duke of Anjou's suite a little on edge, and to relieve his feelings, the veteran swashbuckler had argued with another gentleman in service to François. Much to his lord's displeasure, the squabble had escalated to a duel in which Bussy had killed his opponent, running him through with his sword. As it was obviously going to make it more difficult to recruit men for another crack at Flanders if Bussy insisted on using them first as fencing partners, François had rebuked his former favorite. The jocose Bussy, in turn, was reported to have insulted his master by jesting about his unattractive demeanor, always a particular sore spot with

François.* In retaliation, the duke of Anjou betrayed his longtime friend to Henri III by sharing a letter in which Bussy had bragged of a recent conquest with the wife of an official in charge of the hunt, quipping that "he had at length completely lured the grand-huntsman's hind into his net." The king had helpfully passed along this information to the injured husband, who had stood over his wife with his dagger and threatened to cut her throat if she did not cooperate in helping to trap her lover by penning a note to him arranging a romantic interview.

Bussy received the lady's enticing missive on August 19, 1579, and set off to avail himself of the favors it promised that very evening. Alas for the gallant chevalier, when he arrived at the tête-à-tête he found not the comely doe he had so carelessly joked about but her buck of an irate husband accompanied by a band of gentlemen, all with their rapiers drawn for blood. Never one to run from a fight, Bussy leaped instantly into combat and slew many of his attackers. From here, as befit so celebrated a warrior, the chroniclers offer differing versions of the contest. In one, Bussy's ferocity caused his remaining opponents to draw back and, taking advantage of the pause in the action, he attempted to escape by leaping out of a nearby window to the safety of the street below. He would have made it, too, if his jacket had not gotten caught on a particularly inconvenient latch jutting out from the wall. In another, the beleaguered nobleman's blade fractured, but heedless of the danger, Bussy simply tossed it away and swung furniture at his assailants. But no matter the number and disparity of the stories, the outcome was always the same: Louis de Clermont d'Amboise, seigneur de Bussy, the most daring and controversial knight of his age, died that night of multiple stab wounds.

---

* Reputedly, in response to François's warning that he would be ostracized for his behavior, Bussy replied: "I might be more shunned—for everybody would totally avoid me, if my personal appearance was as ill-conditioned as your own."

The news of the great swordsman's assassination reached Marguerite just as she was settling into her new life with Henry in Nérac. Although she never referred to the event, she must have grieved deeply at the loss. This was the second of Margot's lovers to have died a violent, premature death. It was rumored that to compensate she took Henry's first lieutenant, the vicomte de Turenne, into her bed. It is impossible to confirm this gossip with any degree of assurance; certainly both she and Turenne, when accused of intimacy, vehemently denied the charge. But Margot's own romantic temperament and the conspicuously amorous nature of her court lent so much credibility to the story that it didn't matter whether it was true or not; it was believed. "She told her husband that a knight without a love affair was one without a soul. He caressed her servants and she caressed his," asserted a Huguenot member of Henry's court.

This bit of malicious innuendo linking the queen of Navarre with one of her husband's senior officials passed irresistibly from Nérac to Paris, where it was destined to have far more serious consequences for Marguerite than the usual unpleasant hearsay. For no sooner had Catherine returned from her highly touted extended diplomatic excursion than the trumped-up peace she had brokered in the south of France fell apart completely, a situation that Margot, to Henri III's intense annoyance, had predicted in a series of increasingly urgent letters to the royal court. "The King my husband and Maréchal de Biron, who was the King's [Henri III's] lieutenant in Guienne, had a difference, which was aggravated by the Huguenots," Marguerite recalled. "This breach became in a short time so wide that all my efforts to close it were useless...I saw, with great concern, that affairs were likely soon to come to an open rupture; and I had no power to prevent it," she concluded in frustration. Margot's letters advising her older brother to replace Biron with a less belligerent official and the rumor of her scandalous behavior with the vicomte de Turenne arrived in Paris at about the same time. Henri III, believing his sister to be deliberately working against his interests with her husband, saw an opportunity to separate the king of

Navarre from his wife. He sent a letter by special messenger informing Henry of Marguerite's infidelity, just as he had previously passed
along the news of Bussy's affair to the deceived husband, hoping for
similar results.

But Henry, who was far more concerned about the Maréchal de
Biron's behavior than his wife's, failed to take the bait. Instead of
turning on Marguerite, he showed both her and Turenne the letter,
and accepted their protestations of innocence, good-naturedly
remarking that he was used to this sort of stunt from the king of
France. Since along with this unkind note, Henri III had also sent
word that he refused to replace Biron, it is not surprising that open
war broke out soon afterward. Hoping to take their opponents by
surprise, the vicomte de Turenne, as Henry's first lieutenant and best
warrior, immediately left Nérac and took to the field, besieging a
Catholic city. This intelligence making its way north, one of Henri
III's *mignons* spitefully interpreted it as Margot's revenge for the
king's having revealed her illicit affair to her husband. The courtier
drolly dubbed this renewal of hostilities between Huguenots and
Catholics "The Lovers' War," a play on the reputation of the court
of Nérac. As it was far pleasanter to blame his sister for the failure
of his policies than to take responsibility for the conflict himself,
Henri III was easily persuaded of the truth of this explanation and
seethed against Marguerite.

But nothing could have been further from the reality of the situation. As Margot herself emphatically observed, no one had more to
lose by a renewal of hostilities between Catholic and Huguenot than
she. "This was what I feared; I was become a sharer in the King my
husband's fortune, and was now to be in opposition to the King my
brother and the religion I had been bred up in," she despaired. "I
gave my opinion upon this war to the King my husband and his
Council, and strove to dissuade them from engaging in it. I represented to them the hazards of carrying on a war when they were to
be opposed against so able a general as the Maréchal de Biron, who
would not spare them, as other generals had done, he being their

private enemy. I begged them to consider that, if the King brought his whole force against them, with intention to exterminate their religion, it would not be in their power to oppose or prevent it... this war was of such a nature that I could not, in conscience, wish success to either side; for if the Huguenots got the upper hand, the religion which I cherished as much as my life was lost, and if the Catholics prevailed, the King my husband was undone."

Beyond all this, a return of civil war greatly jeopardized François's ambitions in Flanders, as the duke of Anjou could not rationally expect to recruit a new army to invade the Netherlands if all the soldiers in France were already busy fighting each other. Marguerite's hopes were still tied desperately to those of her younger brother; she needed the idea of the northern realm as a possible refuge even more than he did. For this reason there was no voice in the south of France more consistently, more forcefully committed to peace than the queen of Navarre's.

And unfortunately for her husband and the Huguenots he led, her assessment of the Maréchal de Biron's military abilities was only too accurate. Although Henry managed to take a Catholic stronghold early in May 1580, this would represent his sole conquest. By contrast, over the course of the summer and early fall, his opponent succeeded in capturing nearly thirty fortresses or towns claimed by the Protestants. In September, Biron even fired on Nérac. Only a heavy rainstorm and Marguerite's presence (the marshal had agreed, because she was a Catholic and a member of the royal family, not to attack a city in which she was staying) averted a complete disaster for Henry.

In the end it was the prince of Condé who saved the Huguenots from outright defeat. Frustrated by the direction the war was taking, he challenged the king of Navarre for leadership of the party and succeeded in convincing Elizabeth I to provide funds to help raise an army of German soldiers with which to invade France. The possibility of foreign intervention alarmed Henri III and Catherine, and they decided to try to isolate the prince of Condé and split the Huguenot faction by executing a peace treaty with Henry. Since he was at that point on good terms with his younger brother, the king asked François, who had already offered his services in the matter, if he would handle the negotiations. The duke of Anjou arrived in Cognac in October to meet with Henry and Marguerite.

That her younger brother had been chosen for this assignment could not have been more gratifying to Margot. There they were— she, Henry, and François, the three of them working together just as she had hoped and planned. And between them they settled in seven months what Catherine had been unable to accomplish in the more than a year and a half she had spent alternately bribing, scolding, and threatening the numerous local officials she had interviewed on her recent grand tour. "The peace my brother made...was so judiciously framed that it gave equal satisfaction to the King and the Catholics, and to the King my husband and the Huguenots, and obtained him the affections of both parties," Margot observed. Although she gave all the credit to François, Marguerite was clearly instrumental in these negotiations, as by her advice Biron, the source of much of the trouble, was redeployed to her brother's service. "He [François]...acquired from it the assistance of that able general, Maréchal de Biron, who undertook the command of the army destined to raise the siege of Cambrai," the queen of Navarre continued. "The King my husband was equally gratified in the Marshal's removal from Gascony and having Maréchal de Matignon in his place." If Henri III and Catherine had listened to Marguerite and removed the too-aggressive Biron in the first place, hostilities might have been avoided altogether.*

It might be expected that Henri III was pleased with so fortunate and speedy a result, but this was not the case. "My brother returned to France accompanied by the Maréchal de Biron. By his negotiation of a peace he had acquired to himself great credit with both parties, and secured a powerful force for the purpose of raising the

---

* The prince of Condé and his German soldiers were also redirected northward and were a great help to François in his Flanders campaign.

siege of Cambrai. But honors and success are followed by envy," Marguerite warned. "The King beheld this accession of glory to his brother with great dissatisfaction. He had been for seven months, while my brother and I were together in Gascony, brooding over his malice, and produced the strangest invention that can be imagined. He pretended to believe (what the King my husband can easily prove to be false) that I instigated him to go to war that I might procure for my brother credit of making peace!"

This is hindsight, of course. She could not have known the depth of the king's animosity from so great a distance. Unfortunately for the queen of Navarre, events would unfold in so inopportune a fashion that all too soon she would acquire firsthand experience of it.

MARGUERITE DID NOT HAVE long to bask in the successful conclusion of the Lovers' War. The blessings of peace were superseded almost immediately by a new and potentially even more dangerous development. For soon after the negotiations terminated, pretty little Fosseuse, Margot's young lady-in-waiting, discovered herself to be pregnant with Henry's child.

In the nearly three years since she had joined her husband in his southern kingdom, Margot had done her best to produce an heir to the throne of Navarre. At first, knowing her mother's history—an initial barrenness followed by sustained fecundity—Marguerite probably did not worry too much about her own inability to become pregnant. But as the months and then years crept by and she still failed to conceive, it is obvious from her behavior that she became increasingly anxious. She even condescended to make a pilgrimage deep in Huguenot territory to sample the waters of a particular spring known for fertility. One of Catherine's servants, sent to observe the peace negotiations and spy on the participants, reported in a letter of June 1, 1581, that "the Queen your daughter went to the baths close to Pau, which she indicated she did because of her great desire to satisfy the King her husband and bring him the happiness of children."

Fosseuse's pregnancy not only emphasized the hollowness of

Marguerite's efforts in the most humiliating manner possible, it also represented a distinct threat to her position. Henry had conceived a child with another woman; therefore the problem lay with his wife's reproductive ability rather than his. Margot understood very well that her husband would have no use for her if he believed her to be barren. Worse, he was besotted with Fosseuse, and his adoration encouraged the young lady's hopes of becoming Henry's lawful wife. "She altered her conduct towards me entirely from what it was before," Marguerite observed. "She now shunned my presence as much as she had been accustomed to seek it, and whereas before she strove to do me every good office with the King my husband, she now endeavored to make all the mischief she was able betwixt us." This included keeping Henry away from his wife's bed, a contrivance that effectively destroyed the queen of Navarre's chances of redeeming her situation by becoming pregnant herself. "For his part, he avoided me; he grew cold and indifferent, and since Fosseuse ceased to conduct herself with discretion, the happy moments that we experienced during the four or five years we were together in Gascony were no more," Margot concluded bitterly.

Nine months is a long time. The pleasantly diverting milieu formerly established at Nérac deteriorated sharply. Fosseuse, seeking to get away from the prying eyes of the court, "persuaded the King my husband to make a journey to the waters...in Béarn," Marguerite reported. The queen of Navarre declined to attend her husband and his sweetheart on this happy excursion, but she could not ignore the problem. "I had every day news...informing me how matters went," Margot remembered. "Fosseuse...expressed her expectations of marrying the King herself, in case she should be delivered of a son, when I was to be divorced."

An impossible situation, especially for a proud princess of France, and Marguerite strove to contain the damage. Upon Henry and Fosseuse's return from Béarn, she took her rival aside and offered a compromise notable for its reasonableness. "The pregnancy of Fosseuse was now no longer a secret. The whole Court talked of it and not only the Court but all the country. I was willing to prevent the scandal from spreading, and accordingly resolved to talk to her on the subject... 'Though you have for some time estranged yourself from me,'" said the queen of Navarre, "'yet the regard I once had for you, and the esteem which I still entertain for those honorable persons to whose family you belong, do not admit of my neglecting to afford you all the assistance in my power in your present unhappy situation... Tell me the truth, and I will act towards you as a mother. You know that a contagious disorder has broken out in the place, and, under pretence of avoiding it, I will go to Mas-d'Agenois, which is a house belonging to the King my husband, in a very retired situation. I will take you with me, and such other persons as you shall name. Whilst we are there, the King will take the diversion of hunting in some other part of the country, and I shall not stir thence before your delivery. By this means we shall put a stop to the scandalous reports which are now current, and which concern you more than myself.'"

But Fosseuse did not wish to be separated from Henry or removed from court. She was still quite young—only seventeen—and did not perhaps fully appreciate the precariousness of her position. Although she was by this time six months pregnant, she must have felt that she was successfully hiding her condition under her court dress, and, like many teenagers before her, she tried to bluff her way out of her predicament. "Far from showing any contrition, or returning thanks for my kindness, she replied, with the utmost arrogance, that she would prove all those to be liars who had reported such things of her; that, for my part, I had ceased for a long time to show her any marks of regard, and she saw that I was determined upon her ruin," Marguerite remembered. "These words she delivered in as loud a tone as mine had been mildly expressed; and, leaving me abruptly, she flew in a rage to the King my husband, to relate to him what I had said to her. He was very angry upon the occasion, and declared he would make them all liars who had laid such things to her charge. From that moment until the hour of her delivery, which was a few months after, he never spoke to me."

Henry's experience of childbirth being as limited as Fosseuse's, it's possible that he actually believed that the whole affair would be over quickly and quietly with no great inconvenience to either himself or his loved one. If so, he was soon to be educated. Fosseuse slept in a large room with Marguerite's other maids of honor. Her contractions started at dawn, while she and the other women were still in bed. Sharp, searing, sustained pain that builds to a crescendo then slowly recedes only to repeat itself every five minutes or so turned out to be much more frightening and difficult to hide in close quarters than Fosseuse had anticipated. In her wretchedness, she called for the court physician and implored him to rouse the king of Navarre and notify him of her pitiful condition. Although Henry and Marguerite were no longer sharing the same bed, they were sleeping in the same room, so when the doctor entered, he woke up the queen of Navarre as well as the king.

"The physician delivered the message as he was directed, which greatly embarrassed my husband," Marguerite observed drolly. "What to do he did not know. On the one hand, he was fearful of a discovery; on the other, he foresaw that, without proper assistance, there was danger of losing one he so much loved. In this dilemma, he resolved to apply to me, confess all, and implore my aid and advice... Having come to this resolution, he withdrew my curtains, and spoke to me thus: 'My dear, I have concealed a matter from you which I now confess. I beg you to forgive me, and to think no more about what I have said to you on the subject. Will you oblige me so far as to rise and go to Fosseuse, who is taken very ill? I am well assured that, in her present situation, you will forget everything and resent nothing. You know how dearly I love her, and I hope you will comply with my request.'"

Henry was indeed fortunate in his wife. She didn't have to do it. But Marguerite had probably already suspected that it would come to this, and she saw a chance to remind her husband of her worth and perhaps save the marriage. "I answered that I had too great a respect for him to be offended at anything he should do, and that I would go to her immediately, and do as much for her as if she were a child of my own," she replied with a generosity that few women would have been able to summon under similar circumstances. Still struggling to contain the scandal as effectively as possible, the queen of Navarre at once took command of the situation by dismissing her husband. "I advised him, in the meantime, to go out and hunt, by which means he would draw away all his people, and prevent tattling," she instructed briskly. Henry, only too glad to have an excuse to absent himself from what he was just beginning to recognize might devolve into a taxing enterprise, agreed with alacrity.

And so Margot hauled herself out of bed in the frigid darkness of the very early hours of a winter morning, dressed quickly, and went to her husband's mistress. The first order of business was obviously to get the girl away from the other maids of honor. The queen of Navarre pretended to her women that Fosseuse was ill with a contagious disease and needed to be quarantined so she could have her moved to a remote part of the castle where her cries would not be heard. Fosseuse was in labor the whole day, and Margot and her doctor, along with some domestics, remained by her side hour after hour, soothing her. At last the baby came. "It pleased God that she should bring forth a daughter, since dead," Marguerite observed.

As soon as she could after delivery, having satisfied herself that Fosseuse was out of danger, Marguerite had the teenager returned to her quarters on the pretext that her illness had passed. "Notwithstanding these precautions, it was not possible to prevent the story from circulating through the palace," Margot admitted. Still, the queen of Navarre felt that she had done the best she could to protect both the mother and her reputation. It had been a difficult delivery, but Fosseuse was at least alive, so Henry should be pleased. Exhausted from the demands of so trying a day, Marguerite retired early, shrugged out of her heavy court dress, and collapsed into bed.

But her ordeal was not yet over. Fosseuse, who had expected to end the day triumphantly, universally admired as the proud mother of a healthy young prince, found herself instead the object of scurrilous gossip and scandal. Feeling her disgrace for the first time, she urgently sought protection. "When the King my husband returned from hunting he paid her [Fosseuse] a visit, according to custom," Marguerite continued. "She begged that I might come and see her, as was usual with me when any one of my maids of honor was taken ill. By this means she expected to put a stop to stories to her prejudice. The King my husband came from her into my bedchamber, and found me in bed, as I was fatigued and required rest, after having been called up so early. He begged me to get up and pay her a visit."

This was too much. Marguerite, who desperately wanted to be a mother but could not have children of her own, had just spent the whole day bringing her husband's illegitimate daughter into the world. She was tired and already in bed; she did not want to get up and struggle into her many layers of finery in order to pay a meaningless courtesy call to inquire into the health of a young woman whose physical condition, as both of them knew only too well, had been her sole preoccupation for the previous twelve hours or so. Marguerite had put aside her own humiliation, her own overwhelming desire for love and affection, in order to aid a young woman in need, but the crisis had passed and she was not going to participate in Henry's demeaning charade one moment longer. "I told him I went according to his desire before, when she stood in need of assistance, but now she wanted no help; that to visit her at this time would be only exposing her more, and cause myself to be pointed at by all the world," Marguerite lashed out. The wound was clearly as fresh when she wrote these words decades later in her memoirs as it had been on the evening it occurred. For his part, Henry reacted churlishly. He'd had a perfectly good day's hunting ruined by his girlfriend's complaints and the news that he did not have a son after all. Margot should have had him hang around all day as a witness; he might have behaved a little more charitably. "He seemed to be greatly displeased at which I said, which vexed me the more as I thought I did not deserve such treatment after what I had done at his request in the morning; she likewise contributed all in her power to aggravate matters betwixt him and me," Marguerite contended.

Although the king and queen of Navarre would remain husband and wife for nearly two decades longer, their marriage was effectively over from this point on. Marguerite did not expect Henry to love her or to be faithful to her, but she did demand, not unreasonably, that he treat her with the honor and respect due her as a wife and member of royalty. To have her altruistic behavior toward his mistress thrown back in her face in so insulting a manner represented an unjustified and ultimately unpardonable lapse of etiquette. For the first time since she had come to Nérac, Marguerite was deeply unhappy.

She must indeed have found her situation intolerable, for she came to a decision that would have been unthinkable at any time prior to this unfortunate episode. For years, ever since she had returned to Paris from her Grand Tour, Catherine had been trying to coax Henry and Marguerite back to court. There were several reasons for this, but the primary one was that both Henri III and the queen mother had come to believe, particularly after the Lovers' War, that it was a mistake to leave the king and queen of Navarre in the south of France, where their actions could not be controlled. Together, Margot and Henry made entirely too strong and influential a couple; it was felt that they were operating independently of the Crown's authority. Catherine, ever confident of her own abilities to persuade, was moreover convinced that she could return Henry to Catholicism if only she could get him back to court, and she was hoping to use her daughter to lure him north for this purpose. Henri III, too, wished the king of Navarre back in Paris to separate him from his Huguenot followers in southern France, but he had his own dark reasons for wanting his sister to return as well.

There were always messengers and letters going back and forth from Nérac to Paris, and news of Fosseuse's illegitimate pregnancy inevitably made its way to the royal court. Shrewdly judging that this might be a good time to renew her request for a visit, Catherine sent her daughter not only a heartfelt letter in which she expressed her strong desire to see her again after so long an absence but also the money necessary to underwrite the sojourn. "The King and the Queen both wrote to me," Marguerite reported. "I received three letters, in quick succession; and that I might have no pretence for staying, I had the sum of fifteen hundred crowns paid me to defray the expenses of my journey. The Queen my mother wrote that she would give me meeting in Saintonge, and that, if the King my husband would accompany me so far, she would treat with him there, and give him every satisfaction with respect to the King. But the King and she were desirous to have him at their Court, as he had been before with my brother." Catherine and Henri had learned from their recent successful accommodation with François that even a small amount of ready money could be a powerful incentive to return to court. "The length of time I had been absent in Gascony, and the unkind usage I received on account of Fosseuse, contributed to induce me to listen to the proposal made me," Margot admitted.

The money turned out to be a trap that Marguerite could not resist. She saw only escape: escape from a provincial court that no longer suited her; escape from a husband who doted on a troublesome, absurdly puffed-up handmaiden; escape from the dour, unpleasant Huguenots, with their everlasting sermons and complaints. Her brother François was in England, where there were rumors that he was to be wed to Elizabeth I. He had recovered from his initial defeat; his army had relieved the siege of Cambrai and taken the fortress and the immediate surroundings; he was about to be named duke of Brabant, a province some 150 miles to the northeast, which included the city of Brussels, an important position. She wanted to help him, and she could do that much better from Paris than from Nérac.

It wasn't that she had forgotten what Henri III and his court were like — far from it. But she desperately needed a change, and this was the only avenue open to her. "I had too long experience of what was to be expected at their Court to hope much from all the fine promises that were made to me," she noted, referring to her mother and Henri III. "I had resolved, however, to avail myself of the opportunity of an absence of a few months, thinking it might prove the means of setting matters to rights. Besides which," the queen of Navarre continued, "I thought that, as I should take Fosseuse with me, it was possible that the King's passion for her might cool when she was no longer in his sight, or he might attach himself to some other that was less inclined to do me mischief."

She nonetheless dutifully tried to get Henry to come with her, but he would only escort her part of the way—the king of Navarre knew better than to put himself within range of the talons of the royal court. Also, he was not nearly as unhappy as his wife. In fact, the only thing that really upset him about her leaving was that she was taking his mistress with her. "It was with some difficulty that the King my husband would consent to a removal, so unwilling was he to leave his Fosseuse," Marguerite observed drily. "He paid more attention to me, in hopes that I should refuse to set out on this journey to France; but as I had given my word in my letters to the King and the Queen my mother that I would go, and as I had even received money for the purpose, I could not do otherwise."

Because she could pay her own way, Henry was unable to stop her, and she left Nérac at the end of January 1582, to make the slow journey north to the capital. Margot had always loved Paris. She craved the chic ambience of its exclusive salons; she wanted to throw off her old clothes and buy all new luxurious frocks, hear the latest music, read the fashionable poets, lead the dancing at extravagant costume fetes, and in so doing forget what had passed at Nérac. It was this that drove her forward—her desire to once again shine at court, to see her old friends and renew her place in haute society. For this she was willing to risk subjecting herself to her older brother's whims and temper. She told herself that it could not be worse than what she had endured from her husband and his mistress.

And she had one other compelling motive for abandoning her husband's southern domains to take her chances at the royal court of France.

She was in love.

18

A Royal Scandal

Whoever becomes the ruler of a free city and does not destroy it, can expect to be destroyed by it.

—Niccolò Machiavelli, *The Prince*

His name was Jacques de Harlay, seigneur de Champvallon. Like Bussy before him, he was in service to her brother François. Margot had probably been introduced to him as early as the summit at La Fère, but Bussy had still been alive then, and it wasn't until the duke of Anjou and his suite appeared in Gascony in the fall of 1580 to mediate in the aftermath of the Lovers' War that the flirtation intensified. Champvallon's date of birth is unknown, but he seems to have been about Marguerite's age, or perhaps even a little younger, as he was unmarried when he met her and held the position of *grand écuyer,* or chief squire, in François's household.

It's easy to see the source of the attraction. The seigneur de Champvallon was universally acknowledged to be one of the finest specimens of masculinity in France. Certainly Marguerite thought so. She nicknamed him Narcissus, and in the nineteen surviving love letters she wrote to him over a period of several years, the word *beautiful* is ubiquitous. "I kiss a million times those beautiful eyes, that beautiful hair, my dear and sweet fetters; I kiss a million times that beautiful mouth," she penned. Her lover was a "beautiful angel, a beautiful miracle of nature," she continued adoringly in another.

The queen of Navarre's infatuation with her younger brother's servant had been remarked upon during the final months of François's stay in Gascony; the same Huguenot courtier who had accused her of improper relations with the vicomte de Turenne asserted that she had been caught conspicuously dallying with Champvallon one day while her husband was away from the castle. While this particular report may have been overstated or even spurious—the courtier was openly antagonistic to Marguerite and would later write a scathing satire of the queen of Navarre and her court—there is no doubt at all that Margot fell wholly, passionately, almost absurdly in love with this man.★

Champvallon had of course departed Gascony with François and the rest of the duke of Anjou's entourage in April of 1581, leaving Margot alone to deal with the public humiliation imposed on her by Fosseuse's pregnancy. Small wonder, then, that the queen of Navarre clung to the memory of her affair with this highly desirable chevalier as proof that she, too, was immoderately loved. By the time she left Nérac for Paris she was nearly twenty-nine years old, a tricky age for any woman. She had been physically rejected by her husband in favor of a younger paramour—actually a series of younger paramours—and longed to feel that she was still the ravishing beauty she had been a decade earlier. The affair with Champvallon fulfilled that need.

The object of her affections was aware that he aspired above his rank by pursuing her and had been humbly grateful for her favors. Champvallon was a far less complicated person than his royal mistress. To him love was an exceedingly pleasant way to while away what might otherwise have been the somewhat tedious hours spent

---

★ Of all her correspondence it would be these letters that survived. They are one of the reasons Margot's prominent role as a political figure in France has been overlooked or discounted by historians. They are the sort of letters that everyone writes at one time or another, usually late at night after too much wine. They make her look ridiculous, and this has been her enduring image. But the affair with Champvallon represents only one small episode in a long life of wielding considerable influence and should be weighted as historical evidence accordingly.

at a provincial court. The queen of Navarre made for an appropriately impressive conquest, and, as these things go, Champvallon seems to have been genuinely smitten with her in the beginning.

But Margot's definition of love was far more comprehensive than simple physical attraction. She wanted to lose herself completely—intellectually and spiritually as well as sensually—in intimacy. With so large an emotional void to fill, she sought a love that was purer, deeper, and more profound than any that had come before. She demanded nothing less than a melding of two bodies, two minds, two souls into one. Champvallon did not perhaps fully appreciate her philosophy on this subject when he began the affair.

AT THE COMMENCEMENT OF her journey northward, however, it was her husband's behavior, not her lover's, that occupied Marguerite. She understood that Catherine and Henri III wanted both the queen *and* king of Navarre to appear at court and that it was her job to get Henry there. That was another reason she took Fosseuse with her; she figured Henry was much more likely to tag along if his mistress were included on the sojourn, and she was right. She got him as far as La Mothe Saint Héray, a small village about halfway between La Rochelle and Poitiers, where Catherine had arranged to meet them at the end of March 1582. The prince of Condé and a large party of Huguenots were present as well, and the company spent three days haggling over the usual Protestant grievances against the Crown. Catherine tried to conciliate Henry in an effort to coax him on to Paris, but the king of Navarre, having experience of his mother-in-law's promises, chose not to take the bait. He surprised everyone by suddenly decamping for the safety of his own territory of Béarn, even though he had promised Marguerite that he would escort her at least as far as Fontainebleau, where Henri III had traveled to receive his sister and brother-in-law. His abrupt departure compromised Margot's position with the king of France before she had even set foot at the royal court. "I beg you very humbly, think what credit they [Catherine and Henri] can place in any of my words which concern you, for they can only believe either that I am very ill informed or that I wish to deceive them," she wrote to her husband. "This is not the way to give me means to help your affairs, a thing which will prejudice you more than myself."

Despite her misgivings, to Marguerite's great relief, neither her mother nor her older brother appeared to hold her failure to deliver Henry against her; if anything, they showed her an uncommon degree of respect and sympathy. This was part of an overall strategy on the part of the Crown to try to control François, who despite sustained opposition from his mother and older brother was still committed to intervening militarily in Flanders. Henri and Catherine were well aware that the queen of Navarre exerted considerable influence over her younger brother, and they were determined to transfer Margot's primary allegiance away from him and toward the king. As they had with François, this encouragement took the form of outright bribery. Knowing her daughter to be hopelessly in debt—Margot had inherited the family love of splendor and continually outspent her resources, a state of affairs that had caused a bitter, long-running squabble with the poor courtier assigned to manage her household accounts—Catherine bestowed upon the queen of Navarre the lucrative duchy of Valois, which had formerly comprised a significant portion of the queen mother's own estate. For his part, Henri III went through the motions of receiving his sister with honor and affection, although the ambassador from England, observing the family reunion at Fontainebleau, did report back to London that the king's attachment to his sister seemed a little forced. Notwithstanding this prescient piece of candor, the court then moved on to the capital, arriving on May 28. There, flush with the proceeds of her new duchy, Marguerite immediately purchased a grand house and settled down to renew her life in Paris.

For all the outward appearance of harmony, however, Margot was acutely aware that she was going to need all her diplomatic skills to navigate a path through the many hostile and often conflicting interests at court. The immediate problem was to reconcile her position as queen of Navarre — for despite Henry's treatment of her, she still wished to maintain the illusion of a successful marriage — with her family's desire for her husband to appear at court. Her early letters to Henry reflect her struggle to be true to both sides. She writes in the manner of a helpmeet, forwarding news and her own discerning observations of the atmosphere surrounding Henri III. The king "professed much in fine language," she reported circumspectly. "Very different is the truth to what we were told of Monsieur de Maine [younger brother of the duke of Guise]. He has grown so strangely fat that he is deformed. Monsieur de Guise is very thin and aged. They are little followed, and often give parties for tennis, games of ball, and pall-mall to draw the nobility to them, but those who go twice may be sure of a reprimand [from Henri III's *mignons*, still very much in power], which is proof enough of a jealousy between them and the Dukes." From this she segued effortlessly to her role as conciliator between husband and family. "If you were here you would be the man on whom both sides depend," she cajoled. "You would gain the servants you have lost, owing to the length of these troubles, and would acquire more of them in a week than you would all your life time in Gascony...I beg you very humbly to receive this as from the person who loves you most, and who most desires your good fortune, as indeed I trust experience will teach you," she concluded with obvious sincerity.

But no matter how hard she tried to demonstrate her goodwill or be of genuine service to her husband, something always got in the way of their reconciliation, and her stay in Paris was no exception. The story of Henry's long-running affair with Fosseuse, culminating in the birth of a child, was exactly the sort of naughty tittle-tattle Henri III's *mignons* loved best. The gossip had preceded Marguerite to court, where even though the baby had died the mere fact of the infant's brief existence was enough to violate Catherine's strict rules of propriety. The queen mother, vexed that her daughter would continue to allow someone who had engaged in such publicly scandalous behavior to remain part of her entourage, took it upon herself to exile Fosseuse from court and send her back to her family in disgrace. Marguerite, again seeking to appease both sides, acquiesced to her mother's wishes but, cognizant of her husband's intransigence when it came to Fosseuse, sought to lessen the blow by arranging for the girl to wed an important nobleman and so rescue her reputation, an act that under the circumstances represented a kindness of no little magnitude.

Not that it mattered to Henry, who was so furious when he found out that he immediately dispatched a messenger bearing an irate letter to his wife berating her for dismissing his girlfriend and demanding that Fosseuse be reinstated. But Marguerite was no longer in Nérac, where her husband made the rules. "You say that there will be nothing for me to be ashamed of in pleasing you," she wrote back sharply in reply, clearly striving, despite her anger and humiliation, for a tone of rationality. "I believe it also, judging you to be so reasonable that you will not command me to do anything which may be unworthy of a person of my quality; nor which affects my honor, in which you have too much interest. And, if you demand that I shall keep near my person a girl whom you, in the opinion of every one, have made a mother, you will find that that would be to put me to shame, both by reason of the insult to which you subject me, and on account of the reputation that I should thereby acquire. You write me that, in order to close the mouths of the King, the Queens, and those who speak to me about it, I should tell them that you love her, and that, for this reason, I love her too," she continued. "This reason would be a good one, if I were speaking of one of your servants, whether male or female, but of your mistress!... I have suffered what, I will not say a princess, but a simple demoiselle does not suffer, having succoured her [Fosseuse], concealed her fault, and always kept her near my person. If you do not call that being desirous of pleasing you, I know not what you can expect," she finished in exasperation.

Margot would undoubtedly have preferred to keep her husband's stinging reprimand to herself, but the messenger bearing Henry's letter was indiscreet, and within days the whole court knew of the quarrel between the king and queen of Navarre over the dismissal of Fosseuse. Catherine, in particular, was outraged. The problems caused by philandering husbands was a topic dear to her heart, and she was only too eager to dispense advice to her son-in-law. She dashed off her own scathing letter to Henry, interfering in Margot's favor, one of the very few times she took her daughter's side on any issue. "My Son," she wrote. "I was never so astonished as to hear the language which Frontenac has repeated to many people as the message which he had carried, by your commandment, to your wife. It is something which I would not have believed if, when I asked him, he had not told me himself that it was true...You are not the first young husband who hasn't been very wise in affairs of this sort, but I am sure that you are the first and the only one who, after such a thing had happened, could use such language to his wife...She is the sister of your King, who helps you more than you think...That's not the way to treat women of such a house as hers; to scold them publicly at the wish of a common courtesan—for all the world, not only all France, knows about the child she has borne—and to send her such a message by a little gentleman showing his impudence by accepting such a commandment from his master!" Catherine sputtered. "I advised her to do it and on the spot I sent away that pretty little animal...I am sending you the Sieur de Curton, who will tell you the rest of what I have to say to you."

The effect of his mother-in-law's scolding missive on the erring husband was somewhat less than efficacious. The breach between Henry and Marguerite, already wide, became insurmountable. In recognition of this, Margot's helpful letters to her husband dwindled. She seems to have given up. Instead she turned her attention to her brother François's affairs—and to Champvallon.

IN THE YEAR SINCE he had left Gascony, François's prospects for advancement had shown considerable promise. His Flemish campaign had been helped enormously by the actions of Philip II, who, upon the death of the old ruler of Portugal, had claimed the kingdom for his own over the objections of several other candidates, including Catherine. To reinforce his somewhat shaky pretensions to the newly vacated throne, Philip had sent the indomitable duke of Alva at the head of a large army to occupy Lisbon. This strategy had gone a long way toward resolving the question of succession definitively in his favor.

But it had also given the rest of Europe pause. Was it the best policy, many wondered, to simply sit back and let Philip II take whatever he desired? Nobody wanted to go to war with powerful Spain, but the sudden, unilateral annexation of Portugal did make it seem as though the Spanish king was getting a trifle greedy. Moreover, if the other European powers were to fight back, the Netherlands was the obvious choice of battleground. Philip had had to pull many of his men out of the region in order to have enough soldiers to invade Lisbon, leaving the Spanish occupation in the north at its lowest level in years. And there was François, already in position and clamoring to make the attempt. It was a question of being in the right place at the right time.

But military campaigns require money, men, and supplies— mostly money—and François was perpetually in debt. In August of 1581 he had raised another army and taken Cambrai from the Spanish, but because of a lack of specie had been unable to follow up on the victory. As a result he spent more of his time as a fund-raiser than as a general. He spent three months in England at the end of 1581 ostensibly wooing Elizabeth I when actually his goal was to shore up his finances. Elizabeth played along, pretending to consider a marriage alliance, a ruse that fooled no one. "The primary object of his visit is to ask for money," the Spanish ambassador reported bluntly, "and the queen is inclined to give it to him."

She did give it to him surreptitiously, as did Henri III and even Catherine (although, fearing Spanish retaliation, officially the king and queen mother remained opposed to the duke of Anjou's Flemish campaign). But although the overall sums were often substantial, the money was dispensed fitfully, in dribs and drabs. There was never enough to launch a full-scale attack.

The covert payments were sufficiently encouraging, however, to win François the support of the Netherlanders themselves. In February 1582, just after Marguerite had left Nérac and was on her way to Paris, her brother was installed with great ceremony as the duke of Brabant. François, dressed in the traditional vestments of ruby velvet trimmed in ermine, rode through Antwerp on a magnificent white horse, pledging his life and "whatever it pleased the king his lord and brother and the queen of England to lend him" in order "to protect them [the citizens of the Netherlands] and to restore their ancient liberties." In turn, the various states in the region, including Brabant, Holland, and Flanders, pledged to provide their new duke with an annual stipend amounting to some two million *livres,* which should have been more than adequate to support his military effort.

Unfortunately, by May 1582, when Marguerite arrived in Paris, the Netherlanders had only advanced some thirty-two thousand *livres,* which was a far cry from two million. François, unable to pay his soldiers and faced with massive defections as a result, was forced to appeal once again to his older brother for funds. Henri III was not pleased to be continually dunned for money but felt he had no choice other than to subsidize the new duke of Brabant, at least on some minimal level. As the Venetian ambassador observed, the king of France, "not wanting to drive his brother to complete despair... will aid him with a good sum, which together with the first grant, amounts to 100,000 *écus* [approximately three hundred thousand *livres*]. And with that plus the 100,000 the States [the Netherlands] are obliged to pay him every month and whatever aid he receives from the queen of England, it is hoped that he can make some headway in Flanders."

Marguerite was naturally thrilled with François's investment as duke of Brabant; this was what she had wanted all along. But it also meant an extended absence from her lover, Champvallon, who formed part of her brother's suite and remained with him in Antwerp. It is clear from her letters that Margot pined for him. "Let it never be said that marriages are made in heaven; the gods do not commit so great an injustice... But, my radiant sun, let us scatter the clouds of these unhappy obstacles which separate our bodies, but which can never separate our souls—united in an eternal destiny and bound with a deathless bond," she wrote with somewhat alarming intensity to the absent Champvallon. It therefore came as a rude surprise to discover that during their separation, while she had been consumed with preparing for an ecstatic reunion, her devoted swain had gotten himself engaged to the pretty sister of the duke of Bouillon, quite an advantageous match.

Her disappointment was cruel. Coming so soon after the disintegration of her own marriage, Champvallon's betrayal unnerved her, accentuating her fears that love and her own beauty were slipping away from her. "There is no longer justice in Heaven nor fidelity on earth," she burst out at him by letter. "O God! What must my soul bear? What more remains, O merciless Heaven, to overwhelm me with such sorrow?" Her previous experience of scandal and humiliation were only too evident in her next words. "Triumph, triumph over my too ardent love!" she despaired. "Boast of having deceived me; laugh and mock at it with her... When you receive this letter, the last, I beg you to return it to me," she concluded bitterly, "since I do not desire that at this fine interview, to which you are going this evening [Champvallon evidently intended to call on his fiancée's family], it serves for a topic of conversation to the father and the daughter."

Her unhappiness was profound and affected her judgment. She sought to lose herself in a round of forced gaiety—late-night parties, dancing, music. Brantôme noted that she was openly critical of the royal court and made many enemies, including two of the most powerful of Henri III's *mignons*.

NOT MUCH HAD CHANGED at the royal court in the four years Margot had been away. The *mignons* were still prominent, although due to the fatalities of many of Henri's former favorites, violence was no longer encouraged. Instead, those who fell afoul of the close circle of counselors surrounding the king were attacked with gossip and slander. To fill the emotional void created by the loss of Quélus, Henri III had particularly attached himself to two new *mignons,* the duke of Épernon and the duke of Joyeuse. These young men, whom he called his sons (the duke of Joyeuse was barely twenty), had been singled out for truly astonishing gifts of wealth and position. Although neither came from a particularly ancient or distinguished family, the king had nonetheless made them peers of France, outranking nearly every other member of the aristocracy. This had naturally caused a great deal of discontent and jealousy among the more established elite. Specifically, a deadly enmity had arisen between the duke of Épernon and the duke of Guise over the preferment shown to the king's favorite; this was the reason the Guises' tennis parties were not well attended.

As for the duke of Joyeuse, Henri III was so taken with this retainer that he arranged to make him his brother-in-law by marrying him to his wife's sister. Margot was present at this wedding, which was held in Paris in October 1582. A chronicler composed a detailed account of the festivities, rumored by a foreign envoy to the court to have cost the royal treasury "two million in gold." Henri and his protégé wore matching outfits "so covered with embroidery, pearls and other precious stones that their value could not be estimated, and at every one of the seventeen feasts which followed the marriage, all the lords and ladies came in costumes of which the larger part were of cloth of gold or of silver; enriched with laces, gimp and embroideries in gold and silver and with precious stones and pearls in great number and great value," the courtier reported. "Everybody was amazed at so great luxury and such an enormous and superfluous expense which was made by the King and by the others of his court by his express commandment, in a time which was...very hard and severe for the people, eaten and gnawed to the bone, in the country, by the soldiers and, in the cities, by new taxes," he concluded darkly.

While Henri III caroused in splendor at the duke of Joyeuse's lavish wedding, his brother François was struggling to hold together what remained of his army in the absence of the money promised by the combined states of the Netherlands. A knight attached to his suite detailed the plight of the French forces that autumn and early winter. "All those poor soldiers left in the fields are without any food or supplies. It is so bad that they come into Antwerp in groups of a hundred, thirty, forty, fifty, completely naked on occasion. Every morning on his way to Mass His Highness [François] gives each of them an *écu*. Nevertheless, more than three hundred have died in the fields from hunger and cold," the officer deplored. Desperate, François sent messenger after messenger to Henri begging for funds. "Everything is falling apart in ruin," he wrote in October. "It would be better to promise me only a little money and keep your word than to promise so much and not send anything at all." In November came another pleading missive. "I find that my expenses amount to some 200,000 *livres* per month, which I cannot meet without the aid of the king," François reiterated. "I beg him...to assist me as he promised to do." Then, in December, knowing his sister was at court and hoping she could do something to promote his cause, he sent Champvallon to Paris.

Although newly married, Champvallon understood that it behooved him to placate his master's sister, and he soon succeeded in reviving the romance. Marguerite was happy to have him back, so happy, in fact, that she forgot to be discreet. The details of their affair were evidently so public that it was reported that the queen of Navarre entertained her lover "in a bed lighted by many tapers, lying between two sheets of black taffeta, and surrounded by other luxuries." Two members of Margot's household, Madame de Duras and Mademoiselle de Béthune, acted as liaisons for the intrigue, passing notes back and forth and arranging meetings.

The queen of Navarre understood the risk she was taking—she had ample evidence of the gleefully malevolent attitude at court toward those caught in acts of sexual imprudence. Only the year before, her close friend Henriette de Clèves, duchess of Nevers (rumored to have enshrined the severed head of her lover, Coconnas, as Marguerite had that of La Môle), had been induced by one of the king's *mignons* to engage in a compromising correspondence. Although the flirtation does not seem to have progressed beyond the letter-writing stage, the very existence of the love notes was enough to condemn their author, as the king's favorite well knew. To curry favor with his master, he handed over the lady's epistles. Henri III had waited until the entire court was present at yet another magnificent fete in order to confront the duchess. Summoning her to his side, he read each of her letters aloud to the great amusement of those in the crowd within earshot. No saber ever dealt a blow as deadly as the one poor Henriette received that memorable evening. The duchess of Nevers fled the ball in disgrace and the next day resigned her position as lady-in-waiting to the queen of France.*

But Marguerite was happy for the first time in years and too much in love to stop "so rapturous a game," as she called it. Probably in the back of her mind was the thought that she and Champvallon could always flee to the Netherlands and that François, who as the duke of Brabant was obviously coming up in the world, would protect her. But as she and the rest of the court were soon to discover,

---

* It has never been established what grievance Henri III held against the duchess of Nevers that caused him to engineer her downfall. It is interesting to note, however, that this incident occurred at the time of the Lovers' War, for which the king blamed his sister. It is just possible that, being unable to punish Margot herself, Henri III avenged himself on her friend instead.

the duke of Brabant was in no position to protect anyone, not even himself.

THROUGHOUT THE FRIGID MONTHS of November and December 1582 and into January of 1583, François sat in the fields outside Antwerp and watched in mounting frustration as the army he had cobbled together was gradually decimated, with some three thousand men dying from hunger, cold, lack of supplies, and disease. His poignant pleas to the various states and cities of the Netherlands to honor their financial commitment to him were ignored; Henri III had similarly suspended further clandestine payments to his younger brother, pleading the poverty of the royal treasury; and even Elizabeth I, who could usually be counted upon to send something along, declined to advance additional monies. It was a difficult situation for any commander to navigate, but the course of action François adopted in order to solve his problems was, it must be admitted, particularly unwise. Specifically, he decided to get the money he felt was owed him by sacking Antwerp, one of the cities he had sworn to protect. This was akin to trying to win a duel by suddenly whirling around and stabbing your own second.

Unfortunately for François, his plan was not only ill-advised, it was also leaked to the town's magistrates. By the time he and his starving soldiers burst through the gates of the municipality at noon on January 17, 1583, the citizens of Antwerp were ready for him. Instead of helpless civilians, the French force faced a mob of angry burghers armed for battle. Caught in the narrow streets, overwhelmingly outnumbered, François's troops were slaughtered where they stood. Those who tried to get away were stopped at the gates, where their corpses fell "one on top of the other, [so] that no one could possibly pass through," as a French officer remembered. A thousand died, and several hundred more were captured; François himself only narrowly escaped a similar fate by abandoning his men and fleeing the city.

The news of this fiasco reached Paris two days later and shocked the court. François's humiliation reflected shamefully on France and, by extension, the Crown. To have the cream of French knighthood, led by the king's own brother, indulge in so villainous an act, only to then find themselves routed by a bunch of Dutch shopkeepers! A furious Henri III disavowed his sibling completely. "My said brother...has gone to Flanders against my advice and counsel, as you well know, and neither I nor the queen mother ever had any knowledge or inkling of that deed in Antwerp, which I swear before God," he dashed off to his envoy in England in February. The king was not alone in his anger. "I have never seen this court more full of trouble, envy and hard feeling and the chief nobles more aroused than they are for that which has happened in Flanders: I mean the bad luck of the brother of the King," wrote one of Catherine's most senior ladies-in-waiting to a member of the Guise family. "The Queen Mother is so afflicted over it that all her servants are in the greatest trouble... There are so many malcontents that the number is infinite," she warned.

This defeat marked a turning point not only in François's career but in Marguerite's as well. The queen of Navarre's unwavering commitment to her younger brother and her strong advocacy of his Netherlands campaign made her a partner in his dishonor. Overnight, her position at court became much more precarious.

In spite of this, she remained in secret communication with François, encouraging him to regroup his forces in order to make another attempt. By so doing she acted expressly against both her mother's and the king's wishes. Again, she understood the danger of opposing the Crown, but as with Champvallon she had too much of herself invested in the Netherlands project to give it up. Her alliance with François was the source of her political power. He was her only bargaining chip, her safeguard against the vagaries of both her husband's and the king's court. He must succeed.

It was this, her surreptitious urging on of François, that marked her undoing. Henri III, suspecting that she was attempting to persuade his younger brother to flout his authority, had her watched closely. The court understood what was happening and turned against her. It was only a matter of time before the salacious details of her affair with Champvallon were used as an excuse to persecute her. In June she became ill, which gave Henri III the excuse he needed to begin the process of ridding himself of his sister's presence. "The Queen of Navarre is pregnant—or suffering from dropsy," the ambassador from Tuscany reported in a letter to his superiors.* Henri demanded that she dismiss Madame de Duras and Mademoiselle de Béthune, whom he suspected not only of encouraging his sister's extramarital affair but also of smuggling her letters to François. Marguerite refused but, cognizant of the deterioration in her circumstances, strove to protect her lover by urging him to flee the city. "Please God that on me alone this storm may expend itself," she wrote fervently to Champvallon. "But to place you in danger—! Ah no, my life: there is no suffering so cruel to which I would not prefer to submit. How better can I show this than by depriving myself of you. Go. Go."

It was Catherine who confirmed the king's suspicions. The queen mother had gone north to meet her youngest son to try to convince him to surrender his ambitions in the Netherlands. They met in Chaulnes, near Amiens, on July 11. François was ill with a troubling cough, and after a few days with his mother she broke him down and he agreed to follow her advice. But she no sooner left than he changed his mind, a reversal attributed by Catherine to the queen of Navarre's influence. Marguerite, her mother reported to Henri III, had sent a messenger to François "to turn him away from his promises and make him take up some new evil intent," by which she meant that Margot had persuaded him not to give up after all but to recruit a new army and try again in Flanders.

That was all the king needed to hear. Taking advantage of Catherine's absence (for although the queen mother had supplied

---

* Whatever the nature of her illness, it was not a pregnancy. With all her love affairs, Marguerite never bore a child.

her son with proof of his sister's sedition, it is unlikely she would have agreed with his manner of dealing with the problem), he attacked.

On the evening of August 8, 1583, the king threw another of his grand fetes. The queen of France being out of town visiting relatives, Henri III asked Marguerite to stand as hostess in her place. Margot never referred to this episode, but it seems likely from her subsequent actions that she had no inkling of her brother's true intentions. She may even have taken the request as a sign that the king's attitude toward her was thawing. In any event, she accepted his invitation and at the appointed time appeared at the Louvre magnificently gowned, as befit her status as a queen and member of the royal family. After the customary banquet, she assumed her seat on the raised throne at the head of the company. The musicians raised their instruments; the dancers took their places; the ball commenced.

Soon afterward, Henri III, accompanied by a number of his *mignons,* including Margot's particular nemesis, the duke of Épernon, made his way to her side. Addressing his sister in a voice loud enough to be heard above the strains of the music, without the least note of warning, he launched into a tirade, accusing Marguerite of wanton promiscuity and of descending to the worst forms of lewdness. He listed her lovers one by one, beginning with Champvallon, with whom he accused her of having a child. He then went on to Bussy, La Môle, and numerous others, "naming so precisely dates and places that he seemed to have been a witness of the incidents of which he spoke," reported a shocked diplomat from Austria who happened to be present at the dance. Marguerite, stunned by the ambush, sat helpless with mortification as her brother continued his pitiless tongue-lashing to the general entertainment of her enemies before finally pronouncing a sentence of immediate banishment so as to "deliver the Court from her contagious presence."

She fled the room, and the next morning, masked and accompanied by a few members of her household, including Madame de

Duras and Mademoiselle de Béthune, she left Paris by closed coach. But her trials were only beginning. No sooner had she departed the city, a chronicler reported, than her party was intercepted by some sixty members of the king's guard charged with detaining her maids of honor for questioning. The soldiers treated the occupants of the carriage with stinging contempt, roughly pulling off the ladies' masks in an effort to identify the women. "Miserable wretch, do you dare to lift your hand against the sister of your king?" Marguerite demanded, outraged. "I am acting on his orders," the captain returned coolly. Both Madame de Duras and Mademoiselle de Béthune were arrested over their mistress's protests; only after their removal from the coach was she allowed to continue her journey. The queen of Navarre had made it no more than a mile down the road when she spotted Henri III's distinctive coach coming toward her. Seeking the king's clemency, Margot leaned out her window in an attempt to hail her brother, but Henri refused to acknowledge her presence, staring past her with brutal indifference.

If she had not known it before, she knew then that Paris was lost to her and that her only hope of recovering her reputation was to return to Gascony to try to patch up her marriage. But she dreaded approaching her husband. By the rules of sixteenth-century France, she was now officially labeled a fallen woman. The news of her disgrace and banishment was no doubt already speeding gleefully ahead of her. Henry would be within his rights to repudiate her. She could not bear to arrive in Nérac only to be cruelly dressed down and summarily banished, as she had been from the royal court. The humiliation would be too great.

She could not go back, and she feared to go forward. There was nothing to do but wait to see how Henry would react.

19

The Queen's Revolt

*It is necessary for a prince to possess the friendship of the
people; otherwise he has no resource in times of adversity.*

—Niccolò Machiavelli, *The Prince*

MARGUERITE WAS CORRECT: WORD OF her abasement reached Nérac
in a matter of days, and, just as she had feared, Henry instantly recognized that she had given him the means to renounce her. The
temptation to do so must have been very strong. He hadn't wanted
her back even before the scandal.

But the king of Navarre also knew an advantageous bargaining
position when he saw it. The king of France had been so unwise as
to insult Henry's wife and throw her out of Paris? Henry could use
this incident to wrest concessions from the Crown. Accordingly, he
sternly forbade Marguerite to return to Nérac and instead sent a
Huguenot emissary to the royal court to express his outrage over his
wife's treatment (and so begin negotiations). "It is an affront which
no princess of her rank has ever before received," observed the
envoy, who later recorded this discussion in his memoirs. "It is
impossible to conceal it...all Europe is discussing it. The King of
Navarre has reason to fear that the Queen his wife has committed
some very criminal act, since you yourself, Sire, whose kindness is
so well known, have been able to treat thus your own sister. Of
what then is she guilty to be so cruelly humiliated?...If she has

deserved the affront, he [Henry] demands justice from you against her, as the master of the house, the father of the family. But," said the ambassador (cleverly leaving the door open for a counteroffer), "if she is the victim of false reports, he begs you to punish openly those who have calumniated her." In a further demonstration of just how upset he was over this infamous insult to his wife's reputation, Henry rode out and captured the valuable Catholic stronghold of Mont-de-Marsan, just north of Pau, as a means of soothing his injured feelings.

The king of Navarre's immediate warlike response to his wife's humiliation revealed to Henri III the considerable political drawbacks associated with his outburst. The king could not afford to marshal an army in order to quell a new round of hostilities in the south. Recognizing the need to placate his brother-in-law, he temporized. The haggling went on for months, during which time Marguerite, ostracized and demeaned, was powerless to influence her fate. Lacking money or support, she was forced to appeal to her husband for shelter. Henry, who was clearly enjoying having the moral upper hand for a change, ordered her from one temporary residence to another. He kept her in a state of suspense, deliberately blowing hot and cold, sometimes treating her with sneering contempt and on other occasions writing to assure her that "were it not for the meddlers who have troubled our affairs, we should have the pleasure of being together at this hour."

Utterly wretched and fearing that the scandal would be used as an excuse for either her husband or her brother to rid themselves of her entirely, Marguerite appealed to her mother to send a trusted servant to at least confirm that the rumors that she was with child, or had ever delivered a child, were entirely erroneous. "Madame, [I] implore you very humbly to be unwilling to permit that the pretext of my death be used at the expense of my reputation...that it may please you that I have some lady of quality and worthy of trust, who may be able, while I am alive, to bear witness to the condition in which I am [i.e., not pregnant], and who, after my death, may be present, when my body is opened, in order that she may be able, through the knowledge of this last injustice, to make every one aware of the wrong which has been done," she concluded bitterly in a letter to Catherine.

When confronted later, Henri III claimed that in banishing his sister he had acted upon the queen mother's counsel, and Catherine did not contradict him. But clearly the manner in which he had accomplished the punishment had left the Crown open to censure, not to mention the possibility of renewed hostilities with the king of Navarre. Catherine now moved swiftly to limit the damages to the royal family. She began by convincing Henri III to set free Marguerite's two ladies-in-waiting, Madame de Duras and Mademoiselle de Béthune. She sent one of her most accomplished officials, Pomponne de Bellièvre, formerly president of the Parlement of Paris, to Henry to negotiate for Marguerite's return to Nérac. "I beg you do not abandon the matter of my daughter, nor return before you have, if possible, put her once more on good terms with her husband; because, if you return before this is done, I am very much afraid that we shall fall again into our earlier history, to the ruin of this poor kingdom and the too great infamy of all our family," she instructed her emissary. At his mother's prodding, Henri III backed away from his original position. "Kings are often liable to be deceived by false reports," he wrote loftily in a letter delivered by Bellièvre to his brother-in-law. "Calumny has not always respected the conduct and morals of even the most virtuous princesses—as, for example, the Queen your mother. You cannot be ignorant of all the evil that was said of her." Henry was reported to have laughed outright at this helpful parallel. "His Majesty does me too much honor," he told the queen mother's envoy. "First he calls my wife a whore then he tells me that I'm the son of one!"

It took a full eight months, but Bellièvre eventually hammered out a deal that allowed both men (if not Marguerite) to save face. This was accomplished by laying the full blame for the incident on the entirely expendable Madame de Duras and Mademoiselle de

Béthune, for whose deplorable behavior and deceptions Margot was forced to apologize abjectly to her brother the king. For his part, Henry got to keep Mont-de-Marsan and several other important towns in Gascony as recompense for the injury done to his reputation through the contemptible actions of his wife's servants. Even then, however, the king of Navarre, who already had another girlfriend and had no desire to be burdened again with his queen, had to be more or less forced to take Margot back by his advisers, one of whom wrote to him that his "love-affairs, which are carried on so openly, and to which you devote so much time, are no longer seasonable. It is time, Sire, for you to make love to all of Christendom, and especially to France."

And so, on April 13, 1584, a month before her thirty-first birthday, Marguerite and the exceedingly reluctant Henry were finally reunited in Gascony. It was immediately clear to even the most casual observer that their reconciliation was in name only. The couple spent several hours pacing back and forth in sharp conversation; Henry was evidently laying down the law. "The King and Queen arrived about four o'clock, and were alone together, walking in the gallery of the Castle of Nérac until evening," reported a Huguenot diplomat attached to the prince of Condé, who was present at the king of Navarre's court that day. "When they were at table (it was very late, and the candles were lighted), I saw this Princess weeping incessantly, and never did I see a countenance more washed with tears nor redder from weeping. And much did I pity her, seeing her there seated by the King her husband, who was carrying on I know not what vain talk with his gentlemen, without speaking a word to this Princess, neither he nor any other."

Over the course of the ensuing weeks, her husband's plan for their marriage was made plain to Marguerite. As had been the case with her mother before her, she was to hold the title of queen but not to inhabit the office. That position was reserved for Henry's new mistress, Diane d'Andoins, countess of Guiche.* It was Diane who held sway over Henry, who counseled him and influenced his policy; she who held first place in his kingdom; she who was allowed to move freely through Gascony with him. The king and queen of Navarre, Marguerite was informed by her husband, were from this point on to live separate lives: he with Diane, whom he had installed in Pau; Margot in Nérac—or wherever Henry and Diane were not.

There were many levels of irony to this situation, but the principal incongruity was how unlike Diane was to any of Henry's previous infatuations and how similar in fact she was in breeding, culture, and temperament to *his own wife*. Diane was no seasoned coquette like Madame de Sauve or impressionable young girl like Fosseuse. She was only five years younger than Marguerite and came from an extremely honorable aristocratic family—not as prestigious as Margot's, of course, but still very old and respected. She, too, was a mature woman interested in politics who advised Henry on strategy. Diane even had classical literary pretensions, answering to the name of Corisande, a character in a popular chivalric tale. And she, too, wished to be queen of Navarre.

Marguerite, with no place else to go, had little choice but to accept her situation. And then a mere two months after she arrived, just when she thought she could not be more tormented, came word that the duke of Anjou and Brabant, heir to the throne of France, had died.

FRANÇOIS WAS PRONOUNCED DEAD of tuberculosis on June 10, 1584, at the age of twenty-nine. He was the second of Catherine's children to succumb to the disease. Latent since childhood, his symptoms had become acute over the previous six months. Margot had known he was ill, but it was possible that she was not warned of the seriousness

---

* An astonishing coincidence that both Marguerite's and her mother's marital bêtes noires should be named Diane.

of his condition; as late as May, Catherine, relying on the opinion of her doctors, believed he would recover.

The queen of Navarre's grief was intense. With the death of her younger brother she had lost her one ally and protector, her only hope of recovering some semblance of her former stature and dignity. While he was still alive she could yet exhort herself to exercise patience, believing that everything would change once he inherited the throne. Now even this slender possibility had vanished. She could not attend the funeral, held in Paris, but shrouded her rooms in Nérac in black silk and retreated into mourning.

The confusion and sorrow Marguerite experienced at the loss of her younger brother was echoed by the rest of the kingdom. For with François's demise came the shocked recognition that, both legally and by tradition, the new heir to the throne was none other than the Huguenot Henry of Navarre, first prince of the blood.

To have a Protestant as the next in line to inherit the crown of France (for it was clear by this time that Henri III would have no children) was unthinkable to the Catholic faction, which still represented an overwhelming majority of the population. Anticipating this, Henri III dispatched his closest adviser, the duke of Épernon, to Nérac to try to persuade the king of Navarre to reject the reformed religion and return to orthodoxy. Margot, who held Épernon responsible for her humiliation at court, was livid at her older brother's choice of messenger. The queen of Navarre at first refused to receive the ambassador, but Henry, who desired above all to be publicly named as heir to the throne and could not afford to have his wife insult the king's envoy, intervened with quiet but ominous authority.

"I see very clearly that I can neither flee from nor avoid the misfortune of this visit," she wrote despondently to Bellièvre, who still served as intermediary between Nérac and the royal court. "It is not the first mortification nor will it be the last that will come to me from that quarter, but since my life has been reduced to the condition of slavery, I will yield to a force and power I cannot resist." Still, even in her unhappiness and resignation, there were glimmers of her old spirit, an indication that she was not yet entirely beaten down. "The day on which he [Épernon] arrives, and so long as he remains, I shall dress myself in garments which I shall never wear again: those of dissimulation and hypocrisy," she concluded crisply. Henry might have spared her this latest indignity, since he had no intention of converting. "A man's religion could not be put on and off like his shirt," he informed Épernon.

Even if Henry had agreed to return to Catholicism it is not certain that the majority of the kingdom would have accepted the sincerity of the gesture. But the king of Navarre's refusal to recant made it easy for his enemies and touched off a succession crisis. The duke of Guise, representing the Catholic League, was pushed into open rebellion. On December 31, 1584, in the company of his family and a large number of supporters, he signed the Treaty of Joinville, an alliance with Spain whereby Philip II agreed to provide him with a whopping six hundred thousand crowns annually to fight the Huguenots and keep Henry off the throne. With the money, the duke raised an army and began to seize towns and cities. By February he controlled almost all of northeast France. On March 31, 1585, he went even further and published the Declaration of Péronne, a stinging indictment of Henri III's government, with particular emphasis on the king's wasteful extravagance, his unreasonable promotion of his favorites, and his leniency toward the Huguenots. The duke of Guise used this proclamation to urge his fellow Catholics to rise up against the scourge of Protestantism. By March, the kingdom was once again consumed in a civil war.

And this time, Marguerite, too, joined the fray.

AFTER THE FRACAS OVER the duke of Épernon's visit, Margot's relationship with her husband and his mistress had continued to deteriorate. Three in a marriage is never a particularly genial situation, but by the winter of 1584 the queen of Navarre had begun to suspect Diane of more than the usual petty jealousy and vindictiveness.

François's death and Henry's subsequent rise to next in line for the French throne, however contested, had significantly increased her husband's value in the world. The Protestants were rallying around him. In December, Elizabeth I and a number of Swiss and German lords had signed a pact pledging to uphold Henry's rights to the throne. And although he did not make an official announcement, Henri III, who hated the duke of Guise, had indicated that he was strongly considering naming the king of Navarre as his legitimate heir. If Henry did succeed in overcoming the odds and ascending to the throne, his wife would ascend along with him. To become queen of France was no small incentive, and there is evidence that Diane did indeed harbor ambitions to secure this title for herself.

The problem was that the options for disposing of the existing queen of Navarre were limited. The customary route of acquiring an annulment, for example, was out, as the pope, also concerned that a Huguenot might ascend to the throne of France, had already condemned Henry as a heretic. Petitioners who had been excommunicated were unlikely to be granted the favor of an annulment. There was always the possibility that natural causes might carry Marguerite away, but she was only thirty-one and, in Diane's opinion, depressingly healthy and strong. That left murder. It is clear that Margot understood this and that an attempt was made on her life. She reported in a letter that one of her ladies had "fallen very ill" — by which she meant she had been poisoned — after partaking of a broth intended for herself. There were also rumors at court that she was to be abducted, and then simply disappear, and "many other designs of a like nature," she noted grimly.

If Henry did not actually condone his wife's assassination, he was certainly doing all he could to harass her. In February he infuriated her by intercepting letters she had written to her mother, arresting her messenger, and claiming that she had betrayed confidential information to the royal court (which would have been a neat trick, as she had seen her husband only once since the duke of Épernon's visit the previous August). In March, believing himself to have been the target of a potential poisoning, he openly debated bringing Margot to trial and, if she were found guilty, condemning her to execution, a course of action so patently ridiculous that he was eventually talked out of it by his own counselors. "A villain has endeavored to poison the King of Navarre; but either because the poison was not sufficiently virulent, or because the prince's constitution was too strong, the venom did not take effect," observed a Huguenot envoy from Austria on March 6, 1585. "The wretch [poisoner] attempted to kill himself with a pistol," he added.

It did not take long for Marguerite to come to the conclusion that her chances of surviving her husband's and his mistress's animosity diminished the longer she remained within their power. But where to go and whom to trust? François was dead, and Henri III was her sworn enemy. She knew her mother, fearful of further scandal, would never tolerate her leaving her husband, even if remaining in Nérac meant putting her life in jeopardy. Catherine made no secret of her dislike for her daughter or the fact that she believed Margot had brought on her own marital problems. "I beg you, before you leave, to lay before her all the things which... ought to be considered and done by persons of her rank," the queen mother had instructed Bellièvre while he was still on assignment in Nérac. "For not only our life but also the company which we have around us has a great deal to do with our honor or dishonor and especially for princesses who are young and who think they are beautiful," she continued scornfully. "Perhaps she'll say to you as she's always said, that I have all sorts of people around me and that I kept company with all sorts of people when I was young... I beg you to say to her that she mustn't do any more as she had done and make much of those to whom he [Henry] makes love, because he will think that she is very glad that he loves somebody else in order that she may be able to do the same. Don't let her cite me as having done the same thing, because, if I made good cheer to Madame de Valentinois [Diane de Poitiers], that was the King and besides I always made it quite plain to him that it was to my very great regret." No, Marguerite could not look to her mother for help.

But she was still a queen and a princess of France, possessed of rank, courage, and influence, and these qualities were not to be underestimated. Having been pushed to the limit and believing with complete justification that her life was in danger, she resolved upon a desperate plan. Toward the middle of March she petitioned her husband to allow her to spend Easter in the Catholic town of Agen, a municipality she knew well, as it formed part of her dowry. Henry, only too happy to be rid of her for a few weeks, agreed. The queen of Navarre left the court and arrived at her destination on March 19, 1585. To avert suspicion, she traveled very quietly, with only a few of her ladies and gentlemen for company, although by evening the rest of her household had followed her and was installed behind the city's strong walls. The townspeople welcomed her warmly. Marguerite had visited many times before and was known for her piety and generosity. They were happy to have her there.

It was only later, as more and more courtiers and servants arrived, followed by an influx of knights and soldiers, that the outline of the queen's design became clear. Unbeknownst to Henry, Marguerite had reached out through her network of spies and begun a secret correspondence with the duke of Guise. The queen of Navarre had joined the Catholic League.

THE DUKE OF GUISE was Marguerite's obvious choice of ally. Not because he and she had once been romantically involved but because they shared a common enemy in the duke of Épernon. If anything, the duke of Guise loathed the king's favorite even more than Margot did, and not just because he had kept attendance down at his tennis parties. For years the duke of Guise had watched with growing frustration as Henri III dispensed honor after honor, title after title, property after property on the upstart Épernon—all the wealth and privileges that the duke of Guise was convinced were due him by right of rank, service, and ability. The duke had started his rebellion to rid the kingdom as much of Épernon as of the Huguenots.

Soon after her arrival in Agen, Marguerite sent a secret messenger volunteering her active support for the Catholic League in the critical region of Gascony, and the alliance was struck. In return, the duke of Guise promised to advance the queen of Navarre fifty thousand crowns and sent a letter to Philip II asking him to forward the money "in order that she whom we have established as an obstacle to her husband, may not be abandoned by her people."

On the strength of this commitment Margot launched into action. She used the month of April to discreetly gather her forces. In a gesture of defiance to both her husband and Henri III, she reinstated Madame de Duras and Mademoiselle de Béthune as her ladies-in-waiting. Madame de Duras's husband was appointed commander of the queen of Navarre's troops. As word of her alliance with the league leaked out, Catholic noblemen, some sent by the duke of Guise but the majority from the surrounding area, poured into Agen. She told the magistrates at a formal meeting of the local council that she required the soldiers as bodyguards, "having reason to mistrust the King of Navarre and several of his religion." No one doubted this explanation. Agen was a Catholic town; the citizenry feared and hated Henry and his Huguenots as much as his wife did. That Henry and Diane were complicit in plots against Margot was confirmed at this time by Bellièvre, who wrote to Catherine on April 18 that "I have not failed to speak...of the wrong that the King of Navarre is committing in preferring the friendship of the countess [Diane] to that of his wife, who has been constrained to return to Agen, to protect herself from the countess, who is plotting against her life."

But by May it was clear that Marguerite intended to use the regiment she was assembling at Agen not simply for defensive purposes but to take control of the area and expand league operations in Gascony. To this end, the duke of Guise sent her François de Lignerac, seigneur de Pleaux, an experienced governor and high-ranking member of the Catholic faction in central France. With Lignerac came a suite of cavalry, including a red-haired young captain named Jean d'Aubiac, who was reported to have exclaimed upon meeting the queen of Navarre, "What a woman! If I could go to bed with her they could hang me an hour afterward." Aubiac was exactly the sort of daring, cocksure swain to whom Marguerite had been attracted in the past, and his undisguised admiration must have made a welcome change from her husband's callous rejection.

Marguerite's rebellion had been aimed at her husband, but by allying with the duke of Guise she was also defying the authority of her brother the king, who had condemned the actions of the Catholic League as treason against the Crown. An incensed Henri III dispatched a commander of the royal army, the Maréchal de Matignon, to Gascony to wrest Agen away from his sister. When Catherine, who had been sent to negotiate a truce with the duke of Guise (whose territorial conquests by then included large segments of Normandy and Poitou in addition to Champagne, Burgundy, and Picardy), discovered that her daughter had left her husband and was at the center of league activities in Gascony, she burst out bitterly in a letter to Bellièvre that "she had been so troubled that she had really thought she was about to die, for she had never been so overwhelmed by any affliction that had come to her...I see that God has left me this creature [Marguerite] for punishment of my sins through the affliction which she gives me every day. She is my curse in this world." Never mind that it was Catherine and Henri III, as much as the king of Navarre and his mistress, who had left Margot with little choice but to rebel or face assassination.

An even greater transgression on Marguerite's part, in the opinion of her husband, mother, and brother, however, was that her side in the war was winning. By summer, sixty-six-year-old Catherine, faced with the league's overwhelming military success and fearing that her son would lose his throne completely if the conflict were not brought to an immediate halt, abruptly conceded to the duke of Guise's demands. The peace treaty, signed at Nemours on July 7, represented a complete repudiation of previous royal policy. It revoked the Edict of Toleration and made Protestantism illegal in France. By this agreement, Henry's claim to the French crown was denied and Henri III was forced to declare war on the king of Navarre and all his Huguenot supporters. The Catholic League and its adherents were allowed to keep all the territory they had conquered. The terms were so favorable that even the duke of Guise (who had many years of experience negotiating with Catherine and was under no illusion as to the value of her word) understood that the king and queen mother were simply buying time. "We are well advertised from all sides that their intention is to deceive us and we well believe it," he noted. Nonetheless, the treaty represented a significant political victory for the league, as evidenced by Henry's outraged reaction. "I hear now that our Majesties have arranged a peace with the authors of the League on the condition that...a good part of your subjects should be banished...and the conspirators armed with the force and authority of the King against them and against me, who hold such rank in this realm," he shot back indignantly.

Marguerite was not a signatory to this agreement, and as a sovereign in her own right she evidently did not feel herself bound by its terms, particularly as she was well aware that her husband would never countenance a pact so prejudicial to his interests. She had lived with Henry long enough to have become familiar with his military strategy, and in July she paid him the very great compliment of emulating his methods. Specifically, she launched a series of lightning raids on the neighboring towns, all of them Huguenot and recognizing Henry as their liege lord, and by these means succeeded in surprising and capturing the nearby stronghold of Tonneins.

Alas, she could imitate Henry's battle plans but not his experience or ferocity.* The king of Navarre was a *much* better commander than Madame de Duras's husband, and after a dozen years of waging guerrilla war against the Catholics in Gascony, seizing small towns

---

* Catherine once described Henry in this way to a foreign diplomat: "Nobody in the world leads a more strenuous life than he does. He never has a fixed time for sleeping or eating; he lies down to sleep with his clothes on. He sleeps on the ground. He eats at any time. I brought him up with my sons and he gave me more trouble than all the rest of the boys put together."

and fortresses like Tonneins was as easy for Henry as spearing a rabbit on a hunt. He struck back instantly, slaughtering the small battalion of troops his wife had left behind to hold the city and laying siege to Agen itself.

Marguerite, pressed, appealed once again to the duke of Guise. The promised financing from Spain had yet to arrive, and she was in urgent need of it. The duke reiterated to Philip II the need to support the queen of Navarre's campaign against her husband, but the king of Spain failed to deliver, evidently believing that he had already contributed sufficiently to the Catholic cause in France. Margot, daily expecting to receive funds that never materialized, was left to deal with an increasingly threatening situation on her own.

As her younger brother François had discovered before her, it is very difficult to wage war without an adequate supply of money. The queen of Navarre's unpaid soldiers, penned up in Agen, became unruly and began to frighten the citizenry. It was August, and the weather was stifling hot and humid; worse, plague, the inevitable companion of war, had descended on the city, further demoralizing the inhabitants. To meet expenses, Margot was forced to levy additional taxes on the local population, never a popular move. But the denouement came when, acting on the advice of Madame de Duras's husband and the other cavalry officers, Marguerite mandated that fifty of the town's finest homes, set on coveted high ground, be demolished in order to erect a new, more secure royal fortress on the spot.

The townspeople, particularly the fifty formerly affluent families evicted from their residences, who then had to stand by and watch while their possessions were tossed into the street and their houses destroyed, could hardly believe that this was the same queen of Navarre whom they had welcomed into the city less than six months before. That queen of Navarre had been generous and obliging; this one was grasping and imperious. Marguerite had probably not meant to be callous; the action was portrayed to her as a wartime measure necessary for her protection. It simply didn't occur to her that she was ruining other people's lives, particularly as she had offered to pay for the appropriated property once the expected funds from Spain arrived. But by that time no one believed her, and anyway no sum could compensate for the loss of the venerable ancestral dwellings.

If the Huguenot king of Navarre had been their only alternative, it is likely that the inhabitants of Agen, overwhelmingly Catholic, would never have betrayed their queen. But it was well known that Henri III had sent the Maréchal de Matignon to retake the city from his sister in the name of the Crown. An appeal to this commander meant that orthodoxy would be preserved in Agen. Accordingly, a deputation from the town escaped Marguerite's guard under cover of darkness. They found Matignon and the royal army, explained the problem, and offered to revolt if he would help them. Matignon, who had been hesitant to openly attack the city—despite Henri III's commands, Marguerite was still the king's sister, and it was never an intelligent career move to launch an assault on a member of the royal family—was only too happy to have a surrogate force take the blame. A satisfactory strategy was immediately devised. The town deputies, still operating undercover, slipped surreptitiously back into Agen bearing a declaration from Matignon officially sanctioning the revolt and promising to support the effort with one of his own regiments provided that the townspeople "treat the Queen of Navarre, her ladies, and maids-of-honor with the honor, respect and very humble service which was their due." This was Matignon's insurance policy against any future recriminations by Marguerite herself or any other member of the royal family. Alliances changed so precipitously in the Valois family, one could never have too much protection, the general reasoned.

The sad truth was that the citizen militia hurriedly conscripted by the town magistrates was much better organized and more disciplined than Marguerite's professional recruits. Taking advantage of the soldiers' late nights and even later mornings, the rebellion began at daybreak, when most of the guard was still in bed. The townspeople, well armed, overcame the troops stationed at one of the gates to the city and unlocked the doors. This was the signal for Matignon and his regiment, who had been lurking just outside the town, to burst through and begin the fight. Taken by surprise, the queen of Navarre's small force was overcome before noon.

It was the morning of September 25, 1585. Marguerite heard the fighting but probably did not know the degree of danger until François de Lignerac, the intermediary sent by the duke of Guise, appeared outside her quarters accompanied by the red-haired cavalry officer Jean d'Aubiac and an additional forty or fifty mounted guards. According to both Brantôme and Aubiac's brother, who afterward wrote a letter describing these events, Lignerac brusquely informed the queen of the town's revolt and advised her to flee with him immediately or face capture by the French king's forces. Not wishing to put herself once again at her brother's mercy, and with no time even to call for her own horse, Marguerite immediately swung herself into the saddle behind Lignerac. Madame de Duras, who probably feared Henri III even more than Margot did, performed the same maneuver behind another gentleman, and the party galloped off.

They had just enough of a head start to get safely out of Agen. Once in the open, they turned north, toward Lignerac's territory in central France, with Matignon and his men in full pursuit.

20

Prisoner of War

Fortresses may or may not be useful according to the times;
if they do good in one way, they do harm in another.
                    —Niccolò Machiavelli, *The Prince*

FOR FIVE DAYS MARGUERITE AND her escort raced on, seeking the
safety of the fortress of Carlat, where Lignerac's brother, le seigneur
de Marcé, commander of a small regiment of soldiers, was stationed,
charged with holding the citadel for the Catholic League. Carlat was
in the mountainous region of Auvergne, where it was difficult to
ride but easy to hide. Somewhere along the way, Matignon, who
feared leaving the region around Agen unprotected against Henry's
forces, gave up the chase. But the queen of Navarre and her companions, unaware of their pursuer's withdrawal, did not slacken their
pace and successfully achieved their destination on September 30.
Margot must have been exhausted; she had traveled more than a
hundred miles through rough terrain since her precipitate flight
from Agen.

As the most secure compound in the area, Carlat represented her
obvious choice of refuge. Even better, Marguerite owned the castle
outright. It was one of the properties Henri III, faced with the problem of providing for his sister's dowry, had bestowed upon her some
years earlier in lieu of cash. Centuries old, situated at the crest of a
steep cliff, ringed by a massive wall, and guarded by high stone

towers, the enclosure formed part of a great estate, boasting its own small church in addition to an immense formal château and other equally impressive outlying buildings. Accessible only by a single rocky pathway, Carlat was as close to unassailable as it was possible to get.

Unfortunately it was also unlivable, as its owner soon discovered. Grand residences required large sums and regular upkeep, not to mention protection from looters, and no one had actually resided in Carlat for many years. The once opulent palace had fallen into considerable disrepair. Margot arrived to find her new quarters picked clean of all their former luxury, right down to the holes in the windows where the panes of glass had been removed.

Again her royal status saved her, or at least mitigated her suffering. The citizens of Agen, anxious to honor their commitment to Matignon, treated her ladies-in-waiting and the rest of her household staff with considerable solicitude. Those who served the queen of Navarre but had been left behind in her escape were allowed to pack up and follow their mistress, but in a much more decorous and comfortable fashion. In addition, all her belongings, including her couch, bedding, and gowns—even her carriages and jewelry—were carefully wrapped and transported to Carlat. It took more than two months, until the beginning of December 1585, but eventually Marguerite was reunited with her retainers and was even able to sleep once again in her own bed.

But her situation remained extremely precarious. She had spent all her money in anticipation of the promised fifty thousand crowns from Spain and so lacked the financial resources necessary even to support her household. Her secretary, who apparently did not enjoy living in a ruined castle in a remote mountainous region in the middle of winter, attempted to improve his circumstances by trying to extort money from her. When she refused to pay, he lashed out at her in a very rude fashion and was consequently discharged from her service. In retaliation, he went straight to Paris with some of the confidential letters he had been entrusted with prior to his dismissal.

These were missives from Marguerite to the duke of Guise confirming her participation in the Catholic League. The secretary put them directly into the hands of the king.

Both Catherine and Henri III had already known that Margot had joined the Catholic League—she had made no secret of it—but now they had irrefutable proof. Not that this was any longer a crime. By conceding to the terms of the peace treaty signed at Nemours the previous summer, the king was now technically on exactly the same side of the succession conflict as his sister and the duke of Guise. Of course, in reality, Henri III despised and feared the popular duke and was only waiting for a chance to avenge himself on his supposed ally. But so far the duke, an exceptional general, had proved far too formidable for Henri III to confront directly. When on February 15, 1586, soon after Marguerite's secretary had betrayed her, the duke of Guise entered Paris at the head of a large procession, the citizenry thronged the pavement to catch a glimpse of the celebrated warrior. "Very few or no courtiers rode in front of us, but a great host of the nobility that I guess there to have been five or six hundred," recounted the cardinal of Guise, who accompanied his brother on this excursion. "We did not see the king that day, and on our way to the Hôtel de Guise along the few streets one has to travel I have never seen such acclamation by the people, for all the houses and streets were crammed with men."

The duke of Guise might have been too intimidating to oppose publicly, but Margot was a different story. When the queen of Navarre fell seriously ill in her drafty, ramshackle castle that February and March, both Henri III and Catherine openly hoped for her death and were disappointed to hear of her recovery in May. Catherine in particular had a reason for wishing her daughter harm. The king of Navarre had put together a substantial army and was threatening to employ an additional twenty thousand German and Swiss mercenaries, financed by Elizabeth I. The queen mother, desperate to stop this invasion, had determined to solve the succession problem and so end the conflict by coaxing her son-in-law back to orthodoxy. Catherine planned to pull this off by bribing Henry with a brand-new, very attractive bride on the condition that he break his ties with the Huguenots and formally renounce the reformed religion. Obviously this happy marital project could not be consummated while Marguerite still lived. If the queen of Navarre didn't see fit to die of her own accord from illness, both Catherine and Henri III believed that she should be hurried along to the grave. "If I were to repeat all that is being said, Sire," hinted the Tuscan ambassador ominously in an official report home, "it would indeed be *materia tragica*." The Crown's attitude toward Margot and the plots against her life were so public that even the duke of Guise was aware of them. Catherine and Henri III had "tragic designs [for Marguerite]," he informed an envoy from Spain with whom he was in regular contact, "the details of which would make the hair of your head stand up."

The queen of Navarre was aware of her family's animosity and consequently feared capture by the king's forces above all else. True, the stronghold of Carlat could withstand a frontal assault, but her experience at Agen had taught her to fear betrayal from within. And, as had recently been made manifest by her secretary, she had no money with which to purchase the loyalty of her servants, while it was clear that Henri III would reward handsomely those who undertook to deliver his sister into his hands. This made her even more vulnerable to treachery. Soon after receiving her letters to the duke of Guise, the king had sent his sister a sinister message commanding her to leave Carlat or face "the most rigorous punishment."

The strain imposed by external forces was exacerbated by the solitary nature of her confinement. Marooned under desolate conditions, frightened at the prospect of eventual retribution by the king, the inhabitants of the fortress of Carlat, in their collective search for a way out of a rapidly deteriorating situation, appear to have turned on one another. Although no detailed account of the turmoil has survived, subsequent events would indicate that a power struggle took place among the various military officers for control of the castle—and, by extension, the queen. The first cracks appeared that summer, culminating in a murder that took place in Marguerite's presence. "I hear it said that the Queen Mother has lately been lamenting with Silvio that Monsieur de Lignerac had stabbed to death the son of an apothecary in the bedchamber of the Princess of Béarn [Marguerite]," the Spanish ambassador observed in a letter to Philip II on July 19, 1586. "So close to her bed was it that she was all stained with blood, and they say that this was done through jealousy, which makes the matter worse," he recounted with obvious relish, the implication being that Margot was sleeping with one or perhaps both the participants.

This slur on her daughter's reputation was Catherine's work. Anyone with any knowledge of the queen of Navarre's somewhat exalted views of love, and of her own rank, would view with great suspicion the notion that she had suddenly decided to become intimate with the boy who delivered her potions.* Nor, it would soon be made clear, was she at all enamored of Lignerac. But the episode occurred at exactly the time that the queen mother was promoting her scheme to convert Henry by tempting him with a new wife. To broadcast that Marguerite had brazenly descended into utter depravity lowered her value to both her husband and the Catholic League and so served Catherine's purposes very well.

By fall the gloom at Carlat had deepened to despair. In September, Lignerac's brother, who had been the senior authority representing the Catholic League, died suddenly from undisclosed causes. His death created an opening at the top level of command for which both Lignerac and the young red-haired cavalry officer Jean d'Aubiac

---

* Impossible to know what happened with any certainty but it seems far more likely that she suspected Lignerac was untrustworthy (as indeed he proved to be) and was using the apothecary's son, whom she had met when she was ill, as a spy or to smuggle messages out of the castle. Either that or the boy was delivering medicines and simply found himself in the wrong place at the wrong time. Margot never had more than one lover at a time throughout her life, and this position, as events later developed, was clearly held by Aubiac.

competed. At almost the same time, Mary Stuart was condemned for treason and sentenced to be executed by Elizabeth I. This blow sent ripples of outrage throughout the league in France, which had been a strong supporter of the Scottish queen's right to the English throne. If Marguerite had believed that her rank protected her from a similar fate, Elizabeth's action quickly disabused her of the notion. And the English queen was a model of tolerance next to Henri III.

Then came the news that the royal army, led by the king's second-favorite *mignon,* the duke of Joyeuse, another of Marguerite's particular enemies, had descended upon the region around Auvergne, where Carlat was situated. The implication was clear. Henri III intended to use crushing force to capture—or kill—his sister.

THE ARRIVAL OF JOYEUSE and his soldiers precipitated a crisis among the queen of Navarre's company. Unhappy with Lignerac's leadership and questioning the older man's loyalty to his mistress, Jean d'Aubiac, who had apparently succeeded in his quest to win Marguerite's affections, challenged his superior for command of the fortress—and lost. According to a Huguenot commander serving the king of Navarre who later recounted these events, after his victory over his rival Lignerac brusquely informed Marguerite that "d'Aubiac must leap the rock [die]." To save her lover, Margot was forced to hand over all her remaining jewelry to the commander. But even so, she only succeeded in having the prisoner's sentence commuted from execution to banishment. Weighing her situation carefully, the queen of Navarre then took a calculated risk and, despite the alarming proximity of the royal troops, joined Aubiac in fleeing the fortress. "She would rather go away and change her abode than abide here without him," the Huguenot commander sneered, intimating that infatuation had overwhelmed her judgment. It may have been simple passion that prompted Margot—she did throw herself body and soul into her love affairs—but in this instance, self-preservation might also have played a crucial role in her decision to leave. After all that had happened, to remain alone and unprotected with the greedy Lignerac, who had already demonstrated a certain degree of murderous vindictiveness in the incident with the apothecary's son, could easily have appeared the more perilous alternative. Additionally, Margot seems to have feared (with good reason, as it later turned out) that Lignerac intended to betray her by opening the castle to Henri III's forces. The Tuscan ambassador reported in a letter home that it was "certain that the King was the cause of the flight of the Queen of Navarre."

Accordingly, Marguerite and Aubiac, along with a small number of trusted retainers, decamped by horseback on October 14, 1586. Their object was to reach the castle of Ibois, which lay north of Issoire, where Joyeuse's army was quartered. As Ibois belonged to Catherine, Marguerite may have had the idea of throwing herself on the queen mother's mercy, hoping to persuade her to use her influence to blunt the king's wrath. Inexplicably, the hostile Lignerac, far from trying to stop the queen of Navarre from leaving Carlat, instead helpfully arranged to have a nobleman of his acquaintance, the seigneur de Châteauneuf, meet her party halfway to guide her safely to her destination.

For three days Marguerite rode through the countryside, trying to reach Ibois. When Châteauneuf failed to rendezvous with the queen's party as planned, she and Aubiac were forced to find their own way to the castle. It was a rough passage. With Henri III's knights and foot soldiers stationed at all the main municipalities and thoroughfares, Margot could not take the risk of revealing her whereabouts by taking shelter in a town. She and her retainers traveled mostly under cover of darkness, an imperative that made the journey even more treacherous. Compelled to cross the Allier River in the dead of night, she nearly drowned.

Finally, in the predawn hours of October 17, she and her weary party located the haven they sought. But no sooner had the queen of Navarre achieved the presumed safety of Ibois than an intimidating regiment of royal cavalry galloped up to the walls of the château and loudly commanded that the doors to the villa be opened so they could search the premises. Châteauneuf, it seemed, was an informer. Acting on his intelligence, Joyeuse had sent a large company under the direction of the marquis de Canillac to apprehend the king's sister.

Resistance was futile—Ibois had neither the armaments nor the fortifications of Carlat—but Marguerite nonetheless did her best to forestall, or at least delay, their entry. She knew Canillac; he was the son of her childhood governess, Madame de Curton, who had taught Margot to love Catholicism and had replaced her book of hours those many years ago when her brother Henri had teased her by throwing it into the fire. While the queen negotiated, she searched desperately for a way to conceal Aubiac. Familiarity with Henri III's methods indicated that her lover was in as much trouble as she was. She could bear the pain of her own punishment but not his. Margot must have done a good job of keeping the king's soldiers at bay, because she had time to have Aubiac's telltale red hair shaved off and to find a secret compartment in the chimney for him to hide in. But all her precautions turned out to be useless. Châteauneuf's information had obviously been very precise. Canillac knew all about Marguerite's lover and found him easily as soon as he and his men entered the castle, which they did later that day.

Having identified Aubiac, Canillac had him dragged from his hiding place and sent to a nearby prison. Then he turned to Marguerite, who was tearfully pleading for her chevalier's life, and pronounced her under arrest in the name of the king.

THE RIGHTEOUS SATISFACTION BOTH Henri III and Catherine experienced upon being informed by urgent messenger that the marquis de Canillac had succeeded in apprehending the queen of Navarre is evident from the tone of the instructions that the king dashed off in response. "Tell Canillac not to budge until we have made the necessary arrangements," Henri wrote in his own hand to one of his ministers. "Let him convey her to the Château of Usson. Let, from this hour, her estates and pensions be sequestrated, in order to reimburse the marquis for his charge of her. As for her women and male attendants, let the marquis dismiss them instantly, and let him give her some honest demoiselle and waiting-woman, until the Queen my good mother orders him to procure such women as she shall think suitable. But, above all, let him take good care of her. It is my intention to refer to her in the letters patent, only as 'my sister' and not as 'dear and well-beloved.' The Queen my mother enjoins upon me to cause d'Aubiac to be hanged, and that the execution takes place in the presence of this wretched woman, in the court of the Château of Usson. Arrange for this to be properly carried out. Give orders that all her rings be sent to me, and with a full inventory, and that they be brought to me as soon as possible," he added.

Canillac received these instructions on November 8, but before he had a chance to act on them, a second royal missive arrived. Henri III had evidently had time to reflect and decided he had been too lenient. "The more I examine the matter, the more I feel and recognize the ignominy that this wretched woman brings upon us," proclaimed the king. "The best that God can do for her and for us, is to take her away...As for this Aubiac, although he merits death, both in the eyes of God and men, it would be well for some judges to conduct his trial, in order that we may have always before us what will serve to repress her [Marguerite's] audacity, for she will always be too proud and malignant. Decide what ought to be done, for death, we are all resolved, must follow. Tell the marquis not to budge until I have furnished him with Swiss and other troops."

The king's orders were carried out with dispatch. Marguerite was conveyed under heavy guard to the massive fortress of Usson, outside Issoire, on November 13. Several days later a hasty tribunal was organized, and Aubiac was declared guilty of an unspecified crime (no record of the trial has survived) and sentenced to death. Although he was of sufficient rank to merit beheading, he was instead hanged as a common criminal. Margot, who was en route to her new prison, was at least spared the sight of his execution. This was an act of kindness on Canillac's part, especially as Aubiac's punishment was reported to be exceptionally gruesome. Apparently it took the vital young man so long to die that his hangman got bored and flung him still breathing into his grave.

The forbidding château of Usson, where Marguerite, surrounded by her Swiss Guard, was held prisoner, had been employed for centuries by a series of French monarchs as the equivalent of a state penal institution. It was considered to be absolutely secure, a vast emptiness into which criminals and traitors were deposited and never heard from again. The queen of Navarre was utterly desolate, "treated like the poorest and most abandoned of creatures," lamented the envoy from Tuscany with rare compassion. In a surviving letter to her mother and brother, Margot "threw herself at their feet and begged them to have pity on a long misery." To Catherine, "who had brought her into this world and wished to take her out of it," Margot wrote in anguish that she hoped to find the courage "to kill herself before she would fall into the hands of her enemies and face degrading ruin."

Prolonging her agony was her brother's decision not to render a final verdict on her transgressions until Twelfth Night—January 7, 1587. Marguerite well understood that, precedent having been so recently set by Elizabeth I's condemnation of Mary, Queen of Scots, Henri III would find it far easier to hand down a sentence of death in her own case.

The two-month delay in Marguerite's judgment—from early November of 1586, when Henri III had first been informed of his sister's capture, to January 7, 1587—was not arbitrary. Catherine was scheduled to meet with the king of Navarre on December 13, 1586, at a villa outside Cognac. With her came her granddaughter Christine of Lorraine, daughter of Margot's gentle sister Claude.★ Christine was intended as an inducement to Henry to agree to disband his Huguenot army and return to Catholicism. If he did so,

---

★ Claude had died more than a decade earlier, in 1575, at the start of Henri III's reign. By the time of this peace summit with the king of Navarre, Marguerite and Henri III were Catherine's only surviving children.

Catherine and Henri III would see to it that Marguerite was disposed of so he could marry the young, unsullied Christine in her place. It was a typical Catherine solution: in Christine she had found a marital candidate who would link Henry to both the royal family and the Guises, and this, in her mind, would be sufficient to end the succession conflict.

Although Henry had at one point also considered murdering his wife, to his very great credit he rejected the queen mother's proposals definitively. This may have been because he had absolutely no intention of abandoning the Huguenot cause and returning to Catholicism and so wasn't the least bit tempted by Catherine's rather heavy-handed attempts to persuade him. Or it could have been that hearing the queen mother blithely discuss peace terms that involved executing her daughter led him to reflect that if she could behave this way toward Marguerite, her own flesh and blood, she would certainly have no qualms about doing the same to him one day. Whatever Henry's reasoning, the duke of Retz, who was present at these negotiations, testified that the king of Navarre made a point of declaring that he "would never consent to such an execrable misdeed."

And so, in a bit of fascinatingly improbable historical symmetry, Henry unknowingly repaid the debt he had owed his wife since the time of the Saint Bartholomew's Day Massacre, when she had saved his life by refusing the divorce dangled so temptingly by Catherine. For by rejecting the queen mother's overtures he delivered Marguerite from what would almost certainly have been a death sentence. Instead, on January 7, 1587, Henri III issued a decree condemning his sister to life imprisonment.

He was almost immediately sorry. A mere six weeks later came the news that the queen of Navarre had turned the tables on her brother completely and taken the formidable château of Usson in the name of the Catholic League.

BRANTÔME ALWAYS MAINTAINED THAT Marguerite's comeliness was the determining factor in the marquis de Canillac's decision to transfer his allegiance from the king to the duke of Guise, and indeed this was the prevailing opinion at the time of her coup. "The Marquis de Canillac carried her off, and brought her to Usson," her old friend enthused. "But, soon afterwards, this lord of a very illustrious house saw himself the captive of his prisoner. He thought to triumph over her, and the mere sight of her ivory arms triumphed over him, and henceforth he lived only by the favor of the victorious eyes of his beautiful captive." Certainly her breeding and good looks worked in her favor, but Canillac had other sentiments to consider as well. There was, for example, the general contempt the inhabitants of France, and particularly the citizens of Paris, had for their king. Henri III's popularity was so low that during the Christmas season the queen mother's spies had uncovered a plot by a local chapter of the Catholic League to occupy the Louvre and murder the king and all his council. A frightened Catherine had warned her son "not to go about any more alone and to have good care taken about what he ate." The duke of Guise's prospects, on the other hand, had never looked more hopeful. It was clear that, if he so chose, the duke could take over the government at any time.

As Madame de Curton's son, Canillac was a devout Catholic, Marguerite knew. It was only a matter of convincing him where his true interests and advantage lay. It helped that Henri III had not had the foresight to forward some immediate monetary reward to the marquis. Margot, on the other hand, made sure to sign a document that read, "in consideration of the very signal and very acceptable services which she has received and hopes to receive from Jean de Beaufort, Marquis de Canillac, [Marguerite] gives, cedes, and transfer[s] to him and his all the rights that she may possess over the county of Auvergne and other estates and lordships in the said county of Auvergne…also the sum of 40,000 écus, payable as soon as it will be possible to discharge it…and the first vacant benefices in our estates up to the annual value of 30,000 livres."

Whatever Canillac's deciding motivation, this was a clear triumph for the queen of Navarre. Overnight, her jailer became her protector. The formidable Swiss Guard was summarily expelled and a line of communication opened to the Catholic League's headquarters. By February 14 the duke of Guise was able to send a letter announcing the triumph to his contact in Spain. "I do not intend to fail to advise you that the negotiations begun by me with the Marquis de Canillac have happily succeeded, and I have persuaded him to cast in his lot with our party, and, by this means, assure the person of the Queen of Navarre, who is now in full security," he wrote. "And I rejoice at this, as much on her account as for the acquisition that it has brought us, of a very great number of places and châteaux, which renders the Auvergne country perfectly assured to us...You can understand how this matter has affected the King of France, seeing that the Marquis has dismissed the garrison which his Majesty had placed there, which is the first proof of his good faith that I demanded of him." To further ensure the surrounding area and his ally's security, Guise sent a company of soldiers to Canillac to help guard the queen.

Mary Stuart was put to death on February 8. Her gruesome beheading—it took three strokes to decapitate her, and the executioner missed her neck entirely on the first blow, hitting the back of her head instead, so that she was conscious and in obvious fear and pain before he could raise the ax a second time—sparked outrage in France and Spain and precipitated a crisis.

But Marguerite, who had come within a scratch of the king's pen of replicating this terrible fate, had instead managed to manipulate her circumstances and find a way out of her dilemma. By the spring of 1587, the queen of Navarre was no longer a helpless prisoner in a cell, vulnerable to the perpetual intrigues of brother, mother, or husband, but mistress of perhaps the mightiest fortress in France. So invulnerable was her new abode that "the sun alone could enter by force," admitted a chronicler of the period.

21

Three Funerals and a Mass

How laudable it is for a prince to keep good faith and live with integrity, and not with astuteness, everyone knows. Still the experience of our times shows those princes to have done great things who have had little regard for good faith, and have been able by astuteness to confuse men's brains.

—Niccolò Machiavelli, *The Prince*

CATHERINE AND HENRI III COULD hardly credit the news of Canillac's defection. "The marquis swore and promised to set the queen of Navarre at liberty!" an astonished queen mother informed her son by letter. But there was nothing either of them could do to enforce the king's will. Marguerite's deliverance was simply another reflection of the growing impotence of the Crown.

Moved to action, Henri III decided to try to take momentum away from the duke of Guise and win over some of his adherents by promoting himself rather than the duke as the ultimate defender of Catholicism. That summer the king announced that he would personally oversee the war against the Huguenots. He divided up the royal army and sent Joyeuse with one division into Poitou to confront Henry, then cleverly assigned the duke of Guise to lead another regiment east to intercept the German and Swiss troops who had been recruited to come to the Huguenots' aid. In this way the king sought to forestall the invasion, which he and Catherine greatly feared, while putting the man he most hated in danger.

Henri III made a great show of his desire to rid the kingdom of Huguenots, but after the queen mother's repeated negotiations with the king of Navarre his motives were considered suspect. A nuncio sent by the pope to the court of France summed up the general mood of the citizenry in a report back to Rome. "The hate of the people for the government is great and the King, in spite of his power, is poor and his prodigality makes him poorer. He shows remarkable piety and at the same time detests the Holy League. He is about to make war on the heretics and is jealous of the success of the Catholics. He wants the defeat of the heretics and is also afraid to have them defeated. He fears the defeat of the Catholics and desires it...He does not believe in himself but all his trust is in d'Epernon...Guise is adored by the people but hated by the King, while the King loves d'Epernon, whom the people hate," the nuncio concluded.

The results of the Crown's renewed campaign against heresy were not promising. Henry's army trounced Joyeuse's at a battle on October 20, giving the Huguenots a much-needed boost in morale. The duke of Guise had more success against the Germans and Swiss, but Henri III, fearful that an all-out victory would only add to his nemesis's prestige, sent Épernon to bribe the mercenaries to leave the kingdom before the duke had an opportunity to strike the decisive blow. Deprived of his quarry, an outraged duke of Guise wrote to his Spanish contact "of the strange favors and overt connivance that Epernon shows to the enemy." Insult was added to injury when the king, touting his favorite's achievement as a triumph for peace, rewarded Épernon by making him governor of Normandy and Admiral of France (a position formerly held by Joyeuse, who had, unfortunately, died in combat), two immensely prestigious and lucrative titles, both of which the duke of Guise believed should have gone to him.

It was an inopportune moment to vex the head of the Catholic

League. For some time Philip II had been building a fleet of warships, known as the Spanish Armada, for the purpose of invading England and overthrowing Elizabeth I. Work on the last of the galleons was completed in the spring of 1588, and the ships were set to sail from Spain in early May. While Philip II was confident that he would prevail, he did, however, prefer that Henri III, whom he considered less than vigilant when it came to opposing Protestantism, not be tempted to intervene on Elizabeth's behalf. Accordingly he asked his ally the duke of Guise if he couldn't arrange a small diversion to keep the king of France occupied while the Spanish Armada exterminated the English navy.

The duke of Guise was only too happy to comply. Under his direction the Catholic League made plans to assassinate the duke of Épernon, occupy the Louvre, and take the king captive. Henri III was alerted to the plan and to forestall the coup sent Épernon to Normandy and sternly forbade the duke of Guise to enter Paris. The duke saw fit to disobey the royal command and rode into the capital on May 9, 1588. Thousands of Parisians once again lined the streets to catch a glimpse of their hero. "Long live Guise! Liberator of France, pillar of the Church, exterminator of heretics!" they cried. To prevent her son's violent overthrow, a panicked Catherine pretended that she had invited the duke. Having no choice, Henri III accepted her deception and met with his adversary. The king used this interview to try to persuade Guise to forswear his animosity toward Épernon out of loyalty to the Crown. "He who loves the master should love the dog," the king noted reprovingly. "Provided that he does not bite," returned the duke.

Unsatisfied with this response, Henri III decided to reassert his authority a few days later by bringing four thousand soldiers of the royal guard into the capital on May 12 to intimidate the league. This turned out to be a big mistake. Instead of backing down, the citizenry leaped into action. They erected blockades in the streets to trap the members of the guard and then shot at them with harquebusiers from the windows and balconies above. By noon there were dead soldiers everywhere. The next day Henri III was forced to flee the city, leaving the duke of Guise in control of Paris. The uprising, immediately dubbed the Day of the Barricades, made it "certain that the King of France will have his hands so tied before the Armada sails that it will be impossible for him even in words, still less by deeds, to help the Queen of England," rejoiced the Spanish ambassador in a letter to Philip II.

The king having cravenly escaped without his aged mother, it fell, as always, to Catherine to try to salvage the situation by negotiating with the Catholic League. Fearful that the armada, which by summer was poised for battle, would be turned against the French Crown after the defeat of the English, she strongly advised her son to accede to the duke of Guise's demands. Accordingly, on July 15, Henri III signed a new edict demoting Épernon and instead showering new honors upon the duke, including the coveted title of lieutenant-general. The Guise family was also granted a number of major cities in France, including Orléans, Boulogne, and Angers. This capitulation by the Crown "put almost absolute authority in the hands of the Duke of Guise," observed the ambassador from Venice.

Two weeks later, on July 28, 1588, to Philip II's great chagrin, the nimble English navy obliterated the bulky Spanish Armada, a twist of fate that saved the Crown of France as much as it did that of Elizabeth I.

SOON AFTER THE DEFEAT of the armada, Henri III had a falling-out with his mother. The Catholics having suffered a setback and consequently weakened, he blamed her for his submission to the league's demands. He accused Catherine of favoring the duke of Guise and plotting his advancement at court. Her descent from power was swift. In September Henri III abruptly replaced his most senior counselors, all of them Catherine's close confidantes, with new officers who were instructed to ignore the queen mother. Catherine was no longer to be involved in the day-to-day operations of his government. Worse, he stopped confiding in her or asking her advice. The envoy from Venice, who was at court during the shake-up, noted the queen mother's misery. "Seeing a thing of such importance done without her knowing anything about it, she is entirely beside herself," he reported.

The court was at Blois, where the king intended to remain until after Christmas. At the beginning of December, sixty-nine-year-old Catherine, already plagued by obesity and gout, came down with a bad cold and fever and was confined to her bed. Being ill and removed from the circles of power for some months, she was consequently unaware of the fact that her son and three of his innermost circle had secretly decided on December 20 to emulate her strategy at the time of the Saint Bartholomew's Day Massacre and deliver the kingdom from its enemies by assassinating the duke of Guise.

Clandestine plots being what they were at Henri's court, the duke of Guise was warned the very next day by no less than three reputable sources—the papal nuncio, his mother, and his mistress (the ever-communal Madame de Sauve, still in the game)—that the king intended to have him killed. But the duke refused to take the threat seriously. "He would not dare," Guise snorted. On the morning of December 23, 1588, as he made his way to the royal chambers, having been summoned to an urgent meeting with the king, all sorts of people stopped him in the hallway to caution him to turn back, that he was about to meet his death, but he belittled them. "Fool," he said under his breath of one of these retainers.

So he walked into the royal anteroom, ordered his breakfast—prunes—and then, as the door to the inner sanctum swung open, took his leave of those of Henri's counselors assembled near the fire and entered the king's bedchamber. Once inside, he found himself confronted not by his sovereign, who was nowhere in sight, but by members of the king's guard. As this was somewhat strange, he turned back toward the door that had been shut behind him, at which point he was pinioned by three of the officers. With cries of "Traitor! You will die for it!" they repeatedly thrust their daggers into his chest and throat despite his desperate pleas for mercy.

Bleeding copiously, the thirty-nine-year-old duke of Guise, savior of Paris and the Catholic League, managed momentarily to push himself away from his assailants and stagger across the room before collapsing onto the floor. He expired a few minutes later at the foot of the king's great bed.

Catherine, whose sickroom was located directly beneath her son's bedchamber, heard the scuffle overhead and inquired anxiously as to the cause of the commotion. Eventually her son came down into his mother's bedroom to enlighten her. According to her doctor, who was present at this edifying interview, Henri III addressed his mother as follows: "Good day, Madame, I beg you to forgive me. Mr. de Guise is dead. I have had him killed, having got ahead of him in what he planned to do to me. I could not bear his insolence any longer...knowing and proving every hour that he was sapping and mining...my rule, my life, and my realm, I made up my mind to do this deed...God has inspired and aided me to do it, whom I am now going solemnly to thank in church at the sacrifice of the mass," the king added piously. "I wish to be the King and no longer prisoner and a slave as I have been from the 13th of May until this hour in which I begin again to be the King and the Master," he concluded with grim resolve. Then he left.

If the doctor feared that this disturbing news would deal a death-blow to his patient, he did not know the queen mother. Catherine fretted, but she also rallied. Her son needed her. By New Year's Day her fever had broken. "In spite of the great trouble of her mind and her inability to see any way of meeting the dangers of the hour, the Queen Mother is convalescent and in eight days we hope she can return to her ordinary way of living," the royal physician was able to record in his medical journal.

No, it was not the fact of the murder itself but her commitment to her adored Henri III and her belief in her own abilities to smooth over even the most difficult situations that condemned her. Hearing that his mother had improved, the king asked if she wouldn't mind visiting her old friend the aged cardinal of Bourbon, whom Henri

III had, unfortunately, been forced to place under house arrest for collaborating with the Guises, to see if she couldn't reason with him. Anxious to begin the inevitable process of conciliation that she understood would be necessary if the Crown were to withstand the violent repercussions of the king's action, she immediately dragged herself out of bed and, over her doctor's strenuous objections, had herself dressed and carried in a chair over to the cardinal's drafty apartments.

Having been removed from events and therefore not in possession of all the details of her son's behavior in the wake of the assassination, the queen mother did not perhaps fully appreciate the magnitude of the job she had ahead of her. The cardinal of Bourbon, who was old and weak, had been treated very badly by Henri III. As a cousin of the king of Navarre, the cardinal had stood to inherit the realm if Henry remained a Huguenot and his claim to the throne were negated. After the murder of the duke of Guise, the king had had the cardinal arrested and dragged into the royal bedchamber to view the corpse of his former ally. "Fool! Knave! Puppet! Do you recognize that?" Henri III had growled at the quaking prelate. "But for your age, old imbecile, I would treat you the same... What! You aspired to become the second person in my kingdom!... I will make you so little, that the least in my realm shall be greater than you!"

The cardinal was consequently in no mood for conciliation. Even worse, despite Catherine's vehement denials of having participated in the crime, the churchman refused to believe her. (That's the trouble with setting a precedent like that of Saint Bartholomew's Day. One little massacre and you're tainted for life.) "Oh madame, madame!" he decried during his audience with Catherine, "this is your doing! This is your device! Oh, madame, it is you who have slain us all!" Still very weak and unwell, and highly indignant at being accused of a crime that (for once) she had not committed, Catherine broke down. "O God, this is too much! Take me away; I have no strength left!" the queen mother moaned in reply. Catherine was hurriedly removed to her own rooms, where she took again to her bed.

The next day, attended by the king and queen and her grand-daughter Christine of Lorraine (daughter of Claude), Catherine made her will. Although unable to leave her couch, she nonetheless summoned what was left of her strength and demonstrated a con-siderable degree of concentration. She was extremely generous to her granddaughter and other extended family members, leaving them jewels and property. The queen mother was also careful to make appropriate bequests as a reward to her many loyal servants. She was equally scrupulous in her punishment of those deemed unworthy of her largesse. As a final act of revenge, she made a point of disinheriting Marguerite, her only surviving daughter, completely.

By January 3 her fever had returned, and that evening it spiked. She was sinking fast. The next day she was able to confess and received the last rites.

Finally, on January 5, 1589, Catherine de' Medici, queen of France in her own right, the mother of three kings and two queens and the woman who had effectively ruled the realm for three decades, died at about one in the afternoon in the arms of her son. An autopsy conducted that evening revealed that the venerable queen mother of France had succumbed to pleurisy. It seems likely that she would have survived her illness had she not insisted upon getting out of bed prematurely in the height of winter in order to deal with her son's fiasco. Her physician certainly believed this to be the case. Based on the results of the autopsy, the "condition of health in her bodily organs, if the grace of God had kept her from [the disease], would have given her many years of life," he noted gravely in his journal.

MARGUERITE COULD NOT HAVE attended her mother's funeral even if she had managed to obtain an official safe conduct to do so (which, given her brother's overt hostility toward her, was unlikely). The assassination of the duke of Guise had thrown the kingdom once again into turmoil. Like the cardinal of Bourbon, the distraught inhabitants of Paris were convinced that Catherine had been behind the murder of their beloved duke. Rather than mourn the queen mother, they publicly threatened to disrupt her funeral procession and sling her corpse into the Seine if the king attempted to bury her at the Abbey of Saint-Denis, as was her due.* Henri III was forced instead to inter Catherine in the decidedly less illustrious provincial church of Saint-Sauveur. Immediately upon her death, the magnificent furnishings that had adorned the queen mother's rooms in Paris were seized by her many creditors and sold at auction as recompense for the massive indebtedness incurred by the Crown's extravagance.

Henri III also felt the wrath of the Catholic League. The king's image was defaced; he was vilified by priests and municipal officials alike, and enraged mobs attacked the gilded sepulchers that he had erected to honor his favorite murdered *mignons*. The masters at the University of Paris issued a learned treatise effectively deposing Henri on the grounds of immorality and absolving the inhabitants of the realm from their collective vows of loyalty. The pope excommunicated him.

On January 30, 1589, a memorial service was held in honor of the slain duke of Guise in Paris. In direct contrast to the queen mother's relatively low-key requiem, held in out-of-the-way Blois, the Mass commemorating the assassination victim was held in the vast, awe-inspiring Cathedral of Notre-Dame, which was filled with weeping, somberly clad mourners. All the churches of Paris were similarly draped with black cloth, a special fast was decreed, and the next day a procession of barefoot penitents paraded through the streets of the city. By February, the last remaining Guise brother, the duke of Mayenne, was in control of Paris, and the Catholic League held the majority of the realm, including Rouen, Orléans, Lyon, Toulouse, and nearly all of northern and eastern France.†

Henri III was left with no choice but to approach his brother-in-law

---

* The Abbey of Saint-Denis, completed in the thirteenth century, was the official burial site for kings of France and their families.

† Henri III had also arrested and executed a third brother, the cardinal of Guise, soon after the murder of Guise himself.

the king of Navarre for aid. "Five months ago I was condemned as a heretic unworthy to succeed to the crown and now I am its principal supporter," Henry crowed in a letter to his mistress Diane. By April the two kings had formally agreed to join forces and had raised a not insignificant army to combat the operations of the Catholic League, whose militias were commanded by the duke of Mayenne. There were still some royal companies, jealous of the Guises' authority, that had remained loyal to Henri III, and the duke of Épernon, recalled to his master's service, brought still more troops with him. To these were added Henry's twelve hundred cavalry and four thousand Huguenot foot soldiers and marksmen, supplemented by the usual German and Swiss mercenaries.

Henry, who had been fighting and leading his men for years, was in his element, and his ferocious participation proved invaluable to the king. The duke of Mayenne, on the other hand, lacked both his dead brother's military skills and his commanding presence. Beginning in May, Henri III saw his prospects brighten considerably as town after town, city after city that had been pledged to the Catholic League was retaken in the name of the Crown. By July, Paris itself was surrounded and under siege.

Then, on July 31, 1589, an obscure Jacobin monk appeared at the royal camp, located at Saint-Cloud, about six miles west of Paris, insisting that he had a secret communication for the king from high-ranking supporters within the capital. He implied that these citizen patriots were in a position to open the gates of the city to their sovereign. With him he had letters of recommendation (obtained under false pretenses, as it turned out) from two royalists who had been captured and were being held in the Bastille. He arrived too late in the evening to obtain the desired audience with the king—Henri III had already retired for the night—but the next morning, August 1, he was admitted into the royal presence. When the king inquired into his business, his visitor pulled out a letter and handed it to him. As Henri was attempting to read it, the monk suddenly darted forward and, flashing a stout blade that had been concealed beneath his robe, stabbed the king full in the stomach. The assailant was immediately set upon and killed by the royal guard, but the damage had been done. Although at first the king's surgeons believed their patient would recover, it was soon clear that the wound was mortal. A chronicler recorded that, having been informed that it might be expedient for him to receive the last rites after all, Henri III took the time to call the king of Navarre to his bedside in order to formally recognize him as his legitimate heir. "May my crown flourish on your head, and may your reign be prosperous as that of Charlemagne our puissant ancestor!" the king was reputed to have exclaimed weakly. "I have commanded all the great officers of the crown to take the oath of allegiance to you."

The next day, in the dim, dark hours before dawn, less than two weeks after his thirty-eighth birthday, Henri III, mercurial monarch of France and Poland, followed his mother and the duke of Guise to the grave. Having failed to provide a male heir, by right of succession the throne fell to the first prince of the blood, Henry of Navarre. And in France, when a king ascended to a throne, his wife ascended with him.

Which meant that, legally, Marguerite de Valois was the new queen of France.

OF COURSE JUST BECAUSE Henry had a lawful right to the throne, and Henri III had recognized the king of Navarre as his legitimate successor, didn't necessarily mean that the rest of the kingdom concurred with this arrangement. Quite the opposite. By long-standing convention stretching back to the reign of Charlemagne, French sovereigns were supposed to be emphatically Catholic, and the vast majority of the population was in favor of maintaining this conservative tradition. Even many of the Crown's "great officers" who had fought side by side with Henry over the course of the previous few months and taken the vow of loyalty to him at the dying king's request reneged as soon as they discovered that the king of Navarre had no intention of abjuring Protestantism.

Despite Henry's somewhat vague promise to consider seeking Catholic instruction at some unspecified date in the future and his far more forceful and tempting assurances that those who remained constant to him would be rewarded with high state appointments and great wealth—which would be theirs just as soon as he finished conquering the kingdom—he lost fully half his army within a week of Henri III's assassination. For their part, the Catholic League refused even to consider the prospect of an unrepentant heretic on the throne and instead immediately recognized Henry's relation the old cardinal of Bourbon, still under house arrest in Blois, as the new king of France. In fact, extrapolating from known population figures and the proportion of Catholics to Protestants in France at the time of Henri III's death, it has been conjectured that five out of six French subjects were adamantly opposed to the idea of a Huguenot as ruler of the realm.

Having five-sixths of the population against you is not a helpful ratio. With so many of his captains and soldiers defecting, Henry was forced to lift the siege of Paris. He and his modest army spent the next three years fighting to assert his claim to the throne. Although Elizabeth I provided badly needed money and troops and he won some significant military victories—mostly in Normandy— Paris and the Catholic League held out strongly against him. Even worse, Philip II sent Spanish soldiers to supplement Mayenne's forces. By the early spring of 1593, even Henry had to admit that he was no closer to ascending to the throne of France than he had been while Henri III was still alive.

Then the Spanish ambassador arrived in Paris with a seductive proposition for the members of the Catholic League. The elderly cardinal of Bourbon having passed away in 1590, Philip II proposed to marry his daughter Isabella, child of the French princess Elizabeth de Valois, to an appropriate Frenchman (presumably a member of the Guise family), then have her crowned queen of France.★

★ Elizabeth, it will be remembered, was Catherine de' Medici's eldest daughter (Marguerite's sister), who had been married as a teenager to the much older Philip II. Elizabeth died in childbirth twenty-five years earlier, in 1568.

Although this violated the Salic law, which forbade the French throne to pass to a candidate through the female line of succession, the Spanish ambassador silkily suggested that, in these difficult and dangerous times, this small technicality might be overlooked.

The envoy's proposal, which the Catholic League seemed poised to accept, represented a far more serious threat to Henry's prospects than if Philip II had sent a second armada to France just to eliminate him. One of Henri III's former courtiers, who did not wish to see his once great kingdom fall under the subjugation of the hated Spanish, sat down with the king of Navarre in May and read him the riot act. Henry's window of opportunity was closing fast, the counselor informed him brusquely. The kingdom was about to proclaim a new sovereign, and it wasn't going to be Henry. To realize his birthright, the king of Navarre must make up his mind to publicly convert to Catholicism, and he must do so immediately. Otherwise he might just as well pick up his precious Huguenots and go home for the duration. Personally, the counselor remarked, he couldn't see why Henry wouldn't want to be "king of all France, gaining more in an hour at Mass than you have in twenty victories and twenty years of perilous labors," but of course that was up to him.

The heavy weight of religious conviction and the touching loyalty of his Huguenot followers, thousands of whom had died for him in battle, vied with ambition in Henry's breast. Ambition won handily.

On May 17, less than a week after this conversation took place, Henry let it be known through a spokesman that he had been "in secret a Catholic" all this time and now felt the need to officially convert. He invited representatives of the Church to meet him in Saint-Denis in July with the object of instructing him in the ways of Catholicism in preparation for his return to orthodoxy. In honor of this joyful occasion, Henry invited all Paris to witness his rehabilitation.

And so, on the morning of July 25, 1593, a great procession composed of some one hundred priests and clerics, and nearly a thousand knights, courtiers, and aristocrats, solemnly escorted the king of

Navarre through the streets of Saint-Denis. Their destination was the sacred abbey where the crypts of all French sovereigns and their spouses (with the recent exception of Catherine de' Medici) were interred. Once arrived at the church, Henry read a prepared statement acknowledging the ascendancy of the Catholic religion and the pope on earth and asking for forgiveness and to be received once again into the community of the faithful. Then he confessed, received absolution, and very publicly participated in the ritual observance of Mass.

When he emerged from the abbey, the crowd roared its approval. Although his official coronation would not take place until February 27, 1594, in that moment Henry became sovereign of France.

Eight months after his return to Catholicism at Saint-Denis, on March 22, 1594, King Henry IV made his triumphant entry into Paris. As his first official act, he made sure to attend Mass at Notre-Dame. Philip II's ambassador, attended by a large contingent of Spanish soldiers, was still in the city, having fought Henry's candidacy to the bitter end. Gracious in victory, the new king not only granted the ambassador and his military companions a safe conduct out of the capital, he acknowledged their departure with a highly respectful tribute. "What a great king!" the Spanish ambassador was overheard to exclaim under his breath as he paraded past his benefactor's quarters. "My respects to your master, but don't come back!" Henry hollered from his window.

With his acceptance by the Catholic inhabitants of Paris, for whom he had wisely issued a general amnesty forgiving their participation in the wars opposing his right to the throne, Henry knew he had gotten what he wanted at last. He was indisputably king of France.

Now all he had to do was deal with his queen.

22

The Return of the Queen

In as much as the legitimate prince has less cause and less necessity to give offence, it is only natural that he should be more loved; and, if no extraordinary vices make him hated, it is only reasonable for his subjects to be naturally attached to him.

—Niccolò Machiavelli, *The Prince*

THROUGH ALL THE YEARS OF assassination and civil war preceding Henry's conversion, Marguerite had by choice remained resolutely sequestered in the secure stronghold of Usson. Despite her isolation, she was not completely untouched. The succession conflict raged in the south of France as it did in the north, and in March 1590, Henry's forces routed those of the Catholic League in a battle at Cros-Rolland, a small town just north of Issoire, so close to her château that she could probably smell the smoke from the artillery. Most of the region of Auvergne subsequently fell to her husband's partisans as well, the exception being her fortress, which was too arduous to assail. Unable to take the castle in a frontal offensive, her enemies instead conspired to strike from within. In January 1591, an attempt was made on her life. An official account of the event by local authorities reported that the captain of her own guard tried "to kill the Queen of Navarre by pistol-shot in her very chamber." The gun did go off, but luckily the assassin narrowly—very narrowly—

missed the mark. Margot survived unharmed, protected by the underframing of her voluminous hoop skirts, where the iron ball had lodged, the sixteenth-century version of a bulletproof vest.

Even without the attempted murder, these were extremely difficult years for Marguerite. She was rendered so impoverished by her mother's disinheritance and her husband's antipathy that she was forced to beg Elizabeth of Austria, Charles IX's widow, for money with which to purchase food and other basic necessities. But her kindhearted former sister-in-law died in 1592, leaving Margot deprived of her benefactor and so insolvent that she had to divest herself of nearly every portable asset, right down to the silverware, in order to maintain her skeletal household.

And then Henry decided to convert.

Among the myriad issues raised by this unexpected resolution came the question of what to do about Marguerite. If by his action Henry became king, as was expected, he was going to need a queen who could give him a son and heir. This ruled out his current wife (even if he had wanted her, which he most definitely did not). Margot had recently turned forty. If she hadn't successfully conceived already, it was unlikely that she would do so in the future.

And anyway Henry already had a candidate for future queen of France—his latest mistress, Gabrielle d'Estrées. Nearly twenty years younger than the king of Navarre, Gabrielle had summarily replaced Diane, with whom Henry (no doubt to Marguerite's great satisfaction) was no longer even on speaking terms. But in order to wed Gabrielle, Henry was going to have to rid himself of Margot, and the easiest way to do this was to have the marriage annulled. Accordingly, in April of 1593, he put one of his closest counselors, Philippe Du Plessis-Mornay, in charge of this delicate negotiation. Philippe dispatched a trusted envoy to the château of Usson bearing the king of Navarre's "good favor and protection" and the outline of a lucrative deal: if the queen would give her consent to and active participation in her husband's quest for an annulment, Henry was prepared to offer her an outright cash settlement of 250,000 *écus*, a yearly income of twelve thousand *écus,* and a house of her choice anywhere but Paris.

Marguerite knew an opportunity when she saw it. Although she would no doubt have liked to be queen of France, she recognized that the chances of this happening were very slim and that if she held out for that honor Henry might turn on her. She had had enough experience with death threats to be grateful that his first approach had been friendly. Accordingly she responded enthusiastically to the emissary's overture. She wrote immediately to Du Plessis-Mornay, praising "the kindly disposition of the King my husband [and] the honor which it has pleased him to do me in assuring me of his favor, the possession in the world which I hold most dear." She even went to the lengths of cultivating Philippe himself in the hopes of encouraging the dialogue. "If you will oblige me by assisting in the carrying through of what has thus begun so well, on which depends all the repose and security of my life, you will place me under an immortal obligation, and I shall be very desirous of showing myself, by every means, your most affectionate and faithful friend," she cajoled. She was rewarded immediately with a note from Henry himself, expressing "my extreme contentment at the resolution which you have taken to bring our affairs to a satisfactory conclusion" and not neglecting to assure her of his intention to send a first installment "for the payment of your debts and pension as quickly as can be desired."

But divorce proceedings—or, rather, petitions for an annulment, for the king of France was seeking separation on the grounds that he and his wife had married within the prohibited bounds of consanguinity without first obtaining the necessary papal dispensation and that additionally Margot had been forced into the union against her will by her family—were notoriously long, drawn-out affairs, and Henry and Marguerite's proved no exception. It took the pope until September of 1595 just to lift the ban of excommunication against the king and readmit him as a member of the Catholic Church in good standing. By that time Henry's mistress Gabrielle, although married to another man for appearance's sake, had already given Henry an illegitimate son. This led to further complications, as it was unclear what the status of the boy would be if the king later married Gabrielle and had other, legitimate children by her. The proceedings dragged on.

But by her swift concurrence with his request, Marguerite had bought herself her husband's goodwill, and this produced immediate monetary relief and an improvement in her living conditions. She began once again in a small way to indulge her taste for culture, although she replaced the gaiety and grand balls of her youth with a far more tranquil atmosphere devoted to piety and introspection. She still heard music daily, but her vocalists came from the choir of the local cathedral. "Now that the world has abandoned her she has found help in God alone, whom she serves every day most devoutly," observed her old friend Brantôme, who came to visit her at Usson in 1593. "Never does she miss a celebration of the Mass," he added. Again in a small, regional way, she undertook the patronage of poets and writers. Many of these came from nearby Lyon, where much of the literary community was consumed with a new aesthetic that attempted to synthesize religion and passion—the doctrine of ideal love, possibly inspired by proximity to the queen. That several books on the subject of ideal love were dedicated to "Madame Marguerite of France, Queen of Navarre," attests at the very least to Margot's sympathetic interest and support for the authors.

. Marguerite had not given herself over entirely to religious devotion. While at Usson she reputedly began a relationship with her choirmaster, with whom she was close for many years; in 1595, she raised him to the nobility and later made him a high official in her household. One of her other visitors, the Huguenot scholar Joseph Juste Scaliger, sniffed that while in retirement Margot "has as many men as she wishes, and she selects them herself"—this was probably an allusion to the choirmaster, as no other name is coupled with hers during this period.

But it was to her love of reading that Marguerite gave herself mostly during the long years of solitude at the château of Usson. Her library consisted of some three hundred volumes, including works by poets, scholars, and novelists such as Dante, Petrarch, Boccaccio, Ronsard, and du Bellay as well as many demanding works of history and science. "She is very anxious to obtain all the fine new books that are being composed, those of holy subjects as well as those of the humanities," reported Brantôme, "and when she begins to read a book, long though it may be, she will not stop until she comes to the end, and often she forgets food and sleep thereby." It was during this period, too, that she found her own literary voice and began work on her memoirs. She structured the story of her life in a number of letters to Brantôme, who was then similarly engaged in writing a series of biographies of celebrated women, including one of Marguerite herself. "I have been induced to undertake writing my Memoirs the more from five or six observations which I have had occasion to make in your work, as you appear to have been misinformed respecting certain particulars," Margot explained in her correspondence. "These Memoirs might merit the honorable name of history from the truths contained in them, as I shall prefer truth to embellishment... They are the labors of my evenings, and will come to you an unformed mass, to receive its shape from your hands... Mine is a history most assuredly worthy to come from a man of honor, one who is a true Frenchman, born of illustrious parents, brought up in the Court of the Kings my father and brothers, allied in blood and friendship to the most virtuous and accomplished women of our times, of which society I have had the good fortune to be the bond of union," she wrote.

It was well that she had this project to occupy her, for by the beginning of 1599 she and Henry still had not obtained the desired annulment. This had far more to do with the question of who Henry's future wife would be than the behavior of his present one. Gabrielle, the king's mistress, while not a Huguenot herself, was very close friends with Henry's sister, Catherine, one of the staunchest Protestants in France, and the pope worried that if the king married his lover she might encourage him to relapse into heresy. Consequently he refused to authorize the necessary inquiry into the matter that was a prerequisite to annulment.

In April of 1599, however, Gabrielle herself settled the question to Rome's satisfaction by unexpectedly dying in childbirth, thus paving the way for papal approval. Accordingly, on September 24, the pontiff ordered the various parties involved in the petition to be examined by representatives of the Church as a final step before annulment. Although the inquiry was to be held at the Louvre in Paris, Marguerite received permission to give her testimony privately at Usson, fearing that she might break down in front of an audience. "Never did I consent willingly to this marriage," her signed statement read. "I was forced into it by King Charles IX and the Queen my mother. I besought them with copious tears but the King threatened me that, if I did not consent, I should be the most unhappy woman in the realm. Although I had never been able to entertain any affection for the King of Navarre, and said and repeated that it was my desire to wed another prince, I was compelled to obey. To my profound regret, conjugal affection did not exist between us during the seven months which preceded my husband's flight in 1575. Although we occupied the same couch, we never spoke to one another."* Additionally, two members of Catherine de' Medici's household, including her chambermaid, testified on Marguerite's behalf, reporting her many tears of refusal prior to the wedding and her mother's subsequent threats "to make her the most wretched lady in the kingdom" if she did not go through with the marriage.

Margot's affidavit was convincing. On November 10, 1599, the pope declared the union of Henry of Navarre to Marguerite de

---

* A Huguenot chronicler openly antagonistic to Margot reported that upon reading this testimony, Henry teared up and cried, "Ah! The wretched woman! She knows well that I have always loved and honored her, and that she cared nothing for me, and that her bad behavior has for a long time been the cause of our separation." It is very difficult to picture Henry responding with an emotion (other than sarcasm) to anything Marguerite said or did at this point. All one can say about this recitation is that if this was indeed the way the king of Navarre felt about the queen during their marriage, he certainly hid it well.

Valois to be null and void. On December 17, this decision was publicly confirmed by the Parlement of Paris, which authorized "both His Most Christian Majesty and Her Serene Highness the Queen to contract other alliances." The very next day, a grateful Henry wrote to his former wife: "My Sister—The persons delegated by our very holy father to decide upon the nullity of our marriage, having at length pronounced their decision to our common desire and satisfaction, I did not wish to defer longer...to inform you of it on my part, and to renew the assurances of my affection for you...I desire you also to believe that I do not intend to cherish and love you the less, on account of what has taken place, than I did heretofore," Henry continued, apparently without irony. "But, on the contrary, that I intend to exercise more solicitude than ever in regard to everything which concerns you, and to make you recognize, on all occasions, that I do not intend to be henceforth your brother merely in name, but also in deed...Further, I am very satisfied with the frankness and candor of your prudence, and I trust that God will bless the rest of our days, by a fraternal friendship accompanied by a public felicity, which will render them very happy."

And this time he meant what he said, for less than two weeks later, on December 29, 1599, by letters patent, Marguerite was granted the honorary title of queen as well as duchess of Valois, and her entire dowry returned to her along with the rest of Henry's settlement. She was forty-six years old and wealthy in her own right. And with wealth came independence.

But more important, against all the odds, she had survived the murderous brutality of her family and her times. She was free of a marriage that she had never wanted, that had been arranged under false pretenses, and that should never have taken place. In this she embodied France itself.

ALTHOUGH AS PART OF her compensation Henry had offered his former wife her choice of a number of stately homes in which to reside (the château of Usson was too important a stronghold to remain in her possession indefinitely), Marguerite at first elected to stay where she was. At least initially, this was likely because after so many death threats and scares the queen wished to ensure that political conditions remained stable and the king's attitude toward her benign before venturing out of the safety of her fortress. But there was also the difficulty that Henry, worried about the effect she might have on the capital—she was, after all, the last surviving member of her family and could easily have allowed herself to be used as a figurehead by those who sought to oppose his rule—had denied her Paris. And it was clearly to Paris that Margot wished most to return.

So she took her time and planned her strategy well, paving the way for her eventual departure. From her vantage point in the south of France she kept a close watch on both regional affairs and matters of state. When in October 1600, Henry chose Marie de' Medici as his new wife—not out of respect for Catherine but because he owed the bride's father, Francesco de' Medici, Grand Duke of Tuscany, who had helped support his war effort, a whopping 1,174,000 *écus* and this was the only means Henry could find to pay back the debt—Marguerite immediately wrote to Marie, proffering her congratulations as well as her "good will dedicated to serving and honoring" her and graciously signing the note "your very humble and obedient servant, sister, and subject."* When soon thereafter Marie became pregnant, Margot resolutely put aside what were surely feelings of regret to celebrate the event. "The happy news that the Queen is with child will be received nowhere with more joy than by me," she wrote bravely to Henry in a letter of March 17, 1601.

---

* By contrast, Henry's latest mistress referred to Marie as "that fat banker's daughter," a sneer eerily reflective of the sort of prejudice Catherine de' Medici had faced seventy years earlier, when she first came to France as a young bride. And Henry, who did not love Marie and had not wanted to marry her, treated his Italian wife exactly as Henri II had treated Catherine—he used Marie for breeding but otherwise openly humiliated her by flaunting his many mistresses, whom he insisted live in the Louvre with the royal couple. Some things never change.

Having taken pains to place herself on an affectionate footing with her former husband and his new family, Marguerite then sought to further reassure Henry of her good intentions by proving her absolute loyalty to the Crown. This she managed to do by providing the king with information concerning a clandestine revolt against his government formulated by her nephew Charles de Valois, count of Auvergne, who lived nearby. (Charles de Valois was Charles IX's illegitimate son by Marie Touchet, his Protestant mistress.) Margot wrote to Henry that she knew that the conspirators coveted the stronghold of Usson but that she was determined not to let it fall into their hands. "The chief care that I have in preserving this place is that when I quit it I may make a gift thereof to Your Majesty, to whom I had dedicated it," she apprised him. "This ill-advised boy [Charles de Valois] holds many places in this country, houses which he usurped from the late Queen my mother. But with the aid of God, your Majesty may be assured that he will never set foot here."

Finally, in 1605, she felt sure enough of herself and her position to make an attempt (despite Henry's stated restriction) to return to Paris. The previous year Marguerite had started a lawsuit against Charles de Valois, who had been the beneficiary of her mother's largess when Catherine had seen fit to disinherit her, and Margot used the necessity of following up on this legal action as her excuse for wishing to visit the capital. She wrote to Henry in March, asking for formal permission to travel to the château of Madrid, in the Bois de Boulogne, six miles west of the center of Paris. She was not dissuaded when she received no reply but packed up anyway and left the citadel—"my ark of refuge," Marguerite called it—the first week in July. She had not been outside the immediate vicinity in nearly nineteen years— not since she had first arrived at the château as a prisoner in November 1586. As a final gesture of goodwill, to forestall against any possible objection from Henry to her returning to Paris, she formally left the mighty castle to the Crown. "From your Majesty I received it, and to your Majesty I return it," she said simply.

As her entourage wound its way northward, she met one of

Henry's ministers on the road near Orléans. He tried to get the queen to change her destination, even offering her the exquisite castle of Chenonceaux, which had been Henri II's adoring gift to Diane de Poitiers before Catherine had jealously snatched it back after his death, but Marguerite was not to be deterred. She had evidently expected something like this, because she had come armed with a further peace offering: she had information, she advised the minister, regarding a new conspiracy against the king. The official did not believe her—her intelligence "contained as much falseness as truth," he snorted to Henry—but he passed it along anyway. To his great surprise it was discovered to be accurate.

This last expedient proved decisive. Although clearly it was not Henry's first choice that his former wife take up residence so near to his government, she had made such a show of devotion that he could not reasonably find an excuse to turn her away. Accordingly, he made the best of it. When Marguerite finally arrived at the Bois de Boulogne on August 2, 1605, she found the seigneur de Champvallon, the only one of her previous lovers to survive, and the eleven-year-old duke of Vendôme, Henry's cherished eldest son by the deceased Gabrielle, waiting for her—the equivalent of a welcome home gift from the king.

So BEGAN THE MOST peaceful and congenial years of Marguerite's life. The day after her arrival she wrote to Henry to thank him for his thoughtfulness in sending his son to greet her. "It is easy to see that he is of royal birth, since he is as beautiful in person as he is in advance of his age in intelligence," she pronounced. "I was never more enchanted than whilst admiring this marvel of childhood, so full of wisdom and serious conversation." Such affectionate flattery could obviously not go unrewarded. A few days after receiving her letter, the king himself appeared at her door for an official visit.

If Henry was apprehensive about meeting Marguerite after the passage of so much time, she quickly put him at his ease. She knew, at fifty-two, that she was not the striking beauty she once was. As so often happens with age, she had put on weight, and her complexion was no longer creamy. "If I ever were possessed of the graces you have assigned to me, trouble and vexation render them no longer visible, and have even effaced them from my own recollection," she sighed in a letter to Brantôme. "So that I view myself in your Memoirs, and say, with old Madame de Rendan, who, not having consulted her glass since her husband's death, on seeing her own face in the mirror of another lady, exclaimed, 'Who is this?'" Once svelte, Margot's fuller figure in later life was considerably amplified by the curious, old-fashioned metal plates she insisted on wearing tucked beneath the yards of material that comprised her sweeping skirts, an oddity in the capital. "There were many doors through which she could not pass," sniggered one of Henry's courtiers, who couldn't understand why the queen clung to a look so outmoded— but then again, he had never been shot at point-blank range and survived.

Perhaps it was precisely the absence of any flicker of physical attraction between Henry and Margot—or, rather, the relief of no longer needing to pretend to try to create a sexual spark—that freed them from a repetition of their past mistakes and allowed them to approach each other with a civility that by degrees broadened into genuine warmth. As soon as it became clear that there were going to be no more scenes or recriminations, Henry relaxed. He stayed chatting for three hours on that first visit and even kidded her, as he took his leave, that she should think about not spending so much money and keeping more reasonable hours, to which she lightly replied that, alas, these traits ran in her family and she was far too old to change them now.

When the king finally departed, it was with a promise to introduce her to the not-quite-four-year-old dauphin, Louis, his eldest son by Marie de' Medici. True to his word, he sent the child in a carriage the next day; Marguerite spotted the royal insignia and went out to greet him. Louis had evidently been drilled in the etiquette demanded by the occasion, for he stopped short in front of her, lifted his hat solemnly, and piped up, "Vous soyez la bien venue, maman ma fille!" (You are very welcome, mama my girl!) His princely duty accomplished, he ran to give her a hug. Charmed, Margot returned his affection and praised his effort, pronouncing admiringly, "How handsome you are! You have certainly the royal air of commanding," and the next day sent him an exquisite diamond-and-emerald figurine of a boy with a sword sitting on a dolphin, not neglecting to include a jeweled hair ornament for his younger sister, two-year-old Elizabeth.

Her success was complete when, on August 28, less than a month after her arrival, she was received in state at the Louvre by the king and queen of France. Marie de' Medici, jealous of her position, at first refused to move forward to greet her husband's first wife until she was publicly reprimanded by Henry, who informed his current spouse that Marguerite was the last of the ruling family of Valois and was therefore entitled to every courtesy by virtue of her rank and blood.

After this Margot was accepted as a member in good standing of the royal dynasty, a sort of favorite family aunt. Henry called her My Sister, and, despite the initial awkwardness, she and Marie de' Medici became good friends. With no children of her own, Marguerite gravitated toward the royal offspring. A chronicler related that he once witnessed the king, the dauphin, and the former queen of Navarre in the bedroom of Marie de' Medici, Henry and his son sitting on the couch with Marguerite on her knees in front of them, all three of them playing with a little dog.

So friendly did Margot become with her ex-husband and his family that a mere five months after her arrival, her château in the Bois de Boulogne was deemed too remote for the comfortable exchange of the many social visits between the two households. Accordingly, in December she moved into the center of Paris, to the magnificent Hôtel de Sens, the former residence of an archbishop, less than half a mile from the Louvre. She was forced to vacate this address only a few months later, however, when on April 5, 1606, one of her attendants was murdered just outside her front door as he was in the act of helping his mistress down from her coach.

The victim had been a particular protégé of Marguerite's; although he had been born into the laboring class (his father was a carpenter), she had ennobled him and brought him with her to Paris from the château of Usson. He was young and good-looking, and for this reason it was assumed that he was the queen's lover and that the slaying had been a crime of passion, but as the murderer's family had been implicated in the recent conspiracies against the Crown, the more likely motive was revenge for having passed along damaging information. Marguerite, both frightened and incensed, dashed off a letter to Henry. "Monseigneur," she wrote, "an assassination has just been committed, at the door of my hotel, before my eyes, opposite my coach, by a son of Vermont, who has shot with a pistol one of my gentlemen named Saint-Julien. I beg your Majesty very humbly to order justice to be done...If this crime is not punished, no one will be able to live in security." It is a measure of just how far Margot had advanced in his opinion that the king had the gunman immediately apprehended, tried, and sentenced to be hanged the following day outside the Hôtel de Sens so that his ex-wife could watch from her window.

But this morbid incident represented an anomaly; on the whole Marguerite enjoyed her time in Paris immensely. The following month, on May 30, 1606, she won a great victory when the lawsuit she had originated challenging her mother's decision to disinherit her in favor of Charles de Valois was decided in her favor. The verdict, based on her parents' wedding contract, which very strictly decreed that royal estates could be handed down only to the couple's legitimate offspring, reversed Catherine's deathbed instructions. Margot, as the sole surviving member of her family, inherited all her mother's property. Among other projects, the queen used her newfound wealth to begin work on a splendid villa located directly across from the Louvre. The building was completed in 1608, at which point Marguerite took up residence.★ So she and Henry, who as king and queen of Navarre had spent as little time as possible in proximity to one another, were now affectionate next-door neighbors.

Once established in her new palace, at the age of fifty-five, Margot fell easily into the role of grande dame. As Henry had never been particularly fond of dressing up, and his wife had limited experience of French customs, Marguerite added some much-needed glamour to the capital. Possessed, finally, of a queenly income (which she managed nonetheless to outspend at an alarming rate), she was able at last to indulge her love of music, culture, and fashion in as opulent a manner as she liked. A young English aristocrat, later ambassador to France, left a description of one of her entertainments: "I also betook myself to the Court of Queen Margaret in the palace which bears her name," he reported. "There I witnessed many ballets and masquerades, during which the queen did me the favor to place me near her chair, not without arousing the astonishment and envy of several of those who were wont to enjoy that honor."

An eminent Parisian attorney who also attended some of Margot's parties remarked on what an able hostess she was and on the quality of the philosophical debates, in which she often took part, at her salons. "After these distinguished gentlemen finished their discourses, there would follow music of violins and singing, and finally the lutes. All played with a marvelous art, bringing pleasure to the royal mistress and as much to her guests, who felt greatly honored to be of the company," he recalled. When the new king of Spain, Philip III (Philip II having died in 1598), sent ambassadors to Paris to try to promote better relations, it was Queen Margot who organized the ball in their honor. The meal was both "magnificent and sumptuous...which they say cost her four thousand crowns," the

---

★ The École Nationale Supérieure des Beaux Arts is now located where Marguerite's beautiful mansion once stood.

impressed envoy reported back to Madrid. "Among the strange con-
fections were three silver dishes whereon were displayed a pome-
granate tree, an orange tree, and a lemon tree, so cunningly made
that not one person present but thought them natural."

Marguerite was no less extravagant in her donations to charity
than she was in her secular life. She dispensed hundreds of thousands
of *livres* annually to the holy orders, to hospitals, and to the indigent.
She heard Mass three times a day, and the poor knew to gather on
her doorstep, as she always distributed alms on her return from
church. Similarly, she took the occasion of handing out a hundred
gold coins and an equal number of loaves of bread on every holiday,
including her birthday. In 1608 she built a chapel and two years later
began work on a church. For these acts of kindness she was beloved
in Paris.

But it was her political altruism that represented her true contribution to the kingdom. By her background and family allegiance
she could easily have sowed dissent and made it far more difficult
for Henry to rule. Instead she became his helpmeet. Her support, as
the last surviving member of the Valois dynasty, was of inestimable
advantage to the king in healing the realm of the wounds of the
religious wars, and Henry recognized this. He who had shunned her
advice while they were married now frequently ambled over to her
court to consult her on matters of state. There was no greater evidence of Marguerite's graciousness than her participation at the
coronation of Marie de' Medici, held at Saint-Denis on May 13,
1610. Informed that Henry's seven-year-old daughter, Elizabeth,
would take precedence over her in the procession and that she could
not wear a fleur-de-lis mantle similar to Marie's, she nonetheless
attended the enthronement of her replacement with good grace
(although she did insist on wearing a crown and an immense cloak
of purple velvet, symbol of royalty).

The value of this symbolic gesture of goodwill was immediately
apparent when, the next day, May 14, a Catholic fanatic leaped out
of the crowd and accosted Henry's carriage as it attempted to nego-

tiate a busy city street. Clinging to the coach door, dagger in hand, the zealot stabbed the king three times in the neck and chest through the open window. "It's nothing," said Henry, veteran of countless battles, just before he lost consciousness, the blood pouring from his severed aorta. Minutes later, he was dead.

MARGOT WAS AT A party celebrating her fifty-seventh birthday when she received the news of the king's assassination. She left immediately and went straight to the Louvre to be with Marie and the children. She made an effort in the days following the tragedy to be of assistance to the widowed queen of France. Marguerite's was one of the few dinner invitations Marie accepted on her rare sojourns out of the Louvre. Margot also made a point of publicly honoring her ex-husband and seemed genuinely grieved at his loss, not just for the kingdom but privately as well. "Queen Marguerite caused a beautiful service to be sung at the Augustines, for the repose of the soul of the deceased King, whose affectionate wife she had been for twenty-two years, and who voluntarily agreed, with the dispensation of the Pope, to the dissolution of the marriage, chiefly because the Lord had not blessed her with happy offspring, which was greatly desired by good Frenchmen," admitted a Huguenot chronicler who had not always been so charitable in his descriptions of the former queen of Navarre.★

The Parlement of Paris acted swiftly in the wake of the stabbing, confirming the dauphin as the rightful heir to the throne and according Marie de' Medici the regency of France until her son came of age. At the coronation ceremony, held at Rheims that October, Marguerite stood sponsor, along with the prince of Condé, at the confirmation of the nine-year-old king, Louis XIII. Marie

---

★ Marguerite always believed the assassination to be the work of her old enemy the duke of Épernon. The evidence for this came from one of Margot's former servants who claimed to have proof of a connection between the murderer and the duke. But the servant was subsequently confined to a lunatic asylum, and it is generally accepted today that Henry's killer operated on his own.

also appointed Margot as godmother to her second son, Gaston, born in 1608.

As regent, Marie de' Medici actively pursued an alliance with Spain. She arranged to wed Louis XIII to Philip III's daughter Anne of Austria and to marry her daughter Elizabeth to Philip's eldest son. When, two years into her regency, a group of noblemen used these nuptial alliances as a pretext to revolt, Marguerite, who knew all the parties well, attempted to mediate, urging the leaders of the group to abandon the rebellion and return to obedience. She further allied herself publicly with the regency by hosting a lavish engagement party for Elizabeth on August 26, 1612.

It was again in the Crown's interests that she attended the opening of the Estates-General in December 1614. A dispute had arisen over the levying of a new tax, and Marguerite helped to work out a compromise solution. But it was a very cold winter, and she caught a chill. Over the next three months, the chill gave way to fever, and she became seriously ill. On March 26, 1615, she was told the end was near and heard last rites. Louis XIII sent his own physician to attend the queen, but the surgeon was unable to help her. Sometime between eleven and midnight the following evening, Marguerite de Valois, once queen of Navarre and princess of France, succumbed to infection at the age of sixty-one.

"On March 27, there died in Paris Queen Marguerite, the sole survivor of the race of Valois; a princess full of kindness and good intentions for the welfare and repose of the State, and who was her only enemy," the count of Pontchartrain, minister of state under Marie de' Medici, reported. "She was deeply regretted," he added sadly.

Epilogue

IN CONTRAST TO THEIR HOSTILITY toward her mother, the citizens of Paris grieved openly over Marguerite's passing. The queen's body was placed on public display, and throngs of visitors came to view her remains and pay their respects. "There is a crowd as great as at any ballet," observed an eyewitness. The entire royal family went into mourning, and when, as had happened with Catherine, Margot's creditors descended upon her château demanding payment, Marie de' Medici undertook to settle the deceased queen's debts. This was only fitting, as in a last act of generosity Marguerite had left her entire estate, with the exception of a few small bequests, to Henry and Marie's son, the thirteen-year-old king of France, Louis XIII. Margot was buried at Saint-Denis, in the abbey where her father, Henri II, and her four brothers were interred. Catherine's remains had also been quietly moved from Blois to the same sanctuary in 1610 after Henry's assassination, so the family that had been so bitterly divided in life was finally reunited in death.

Over the centuries, Catherine de' Medici's reputation has slowly recovered from the disapprobation with which she was generally regarded in Europe at the time of her demise. There is even a movement afoot to rehabilitate the queen mother as a skilled chief executive who negotiated the turbulent era in which she lived as well as could possibly be expected. At the very least, Catherine is today universally considered to have been an able disciple of Machiavelli, expertly playing off various factions to her own and her family's advantage. The evidence for this is usually based on Machiavelli's well-known assertion that "a prudent ruler ought not to keep faith when by so doing it would be against his interest, and when the reasons which made him bind himself no longer exist," and that to be successful a prince must be able "to be a great feigner and dissembler."

Certainly Catherine de' Medici was a noted feigner and enthusiastic dissembler, but unfortunately these traits alone do not satisfy Machiavelli's criteria for leadership. A careful reading of *The Prince* reveals that honor and what Machiavelli called virtù—ability, strength of character, and vision—were as necessary to the state as the pragmatic deceit he recommended; also, he stressed many times how vital it was that a ruler take great pains to avoid being despised. Catherine prevaricated so consistently and artlessly that she soon lost all credibility, a situation that only created more problems for the kingdom. She almost never planned ahead but reacted moment by moment to varying stimuli. This meant that the Crown rarely anticipated events and so was frequently caught by surprise. In addition, Catherine's fear of losing her position forced her to make increasingly unsustainable compromises. Finally, her authorship of the atrocities committed at the time of her daughter's wedding absolutely excludes her from being elevated to the rank of elite, or indeed tolerable, leadership. Even today, after more than four centuries and a revolution, the wound from the Saint Bartholomew's Day Massacre lingers in France—run a finger down that scar and the country still shivers.

The standing of Marguerite de Valois, on the other hand, has suffered from the reverse treatment. Respected and admired at the time of her death, over the centuries Catherine's youngest daughter has come to be regarded as a sensual dilettante who put her own romantic inclinations ahead of her duty to the kingdom. Today she is remembered—if she is known at all—as the sympathetic but ultimately tragic heroine of Alexandre Dumas's classic novel *La Reine Margot.*

But even Dumas's portrayal, favorable though it may be, fails to give Marguerite's intelligence and courage their due. It has become commonplace to suggest that a historical figure anticipated modern attitudes, but in Margot's case this happens to be true. Here, hundreds of years before the advent of the feminist movement, was a strong, spirited, resolute individual unafraid to confront sexual mores. It is for this reason more than any other that her reputation has been systemically denigrated. Her desire to love and be loved—her willingness to engage in a series of passionate affairs—has overshadowed every other aspect of her life. This is especially ironic considering the licentious nature of her surroundings. By any measure the carnality attributed to her brothers and her husband dwarfs the queen of Navarre's sensual experiences. And although Catherine de' Medici cannot be accused personally of wanton behavior, she clearly encouraged it in others in order to gain political advantage. Alone among her family, Margot refused to use sex as a weapon and searched only for love.

But the queen of Navarre was so much more than the sum of her affairs. Acutely aware of the vulnerability of the position forced upon her by her marriage, Marguerite nonetheless steadfastly refused to accept victimhood and instead strove throughout her life to carve out a measure of independence and influence for herself. To an astounding degree, considering the variety and potency of the forces ranged against her, she succeeded. The political ascension of her brother François may be traced directly to his sister's participation in and sponsorship of his interests. Although painted as a scapegoat for the kingdom's woes by her family, Marguerite in fact consistently counseled peace between Catholics and Huguenots and presided over one of the very few courts in Europe where, at least briefly, religious tolerance was officially sanctioned. She only took up arms as a last resort when compelled to do so in her own self-defense. And she was invaluable to Henry IV, both as a political symbol and an advocate, in helping to secure his rule and that of his successors after the death of her brother Henri III.

But for her inability to conceive a child, Marguerite might well have gone down in history, as Henry IV did, as one of the great French rulers. Instead she is simply Queen Margot, who saved her husband — and, by extension, the kingdom. "I have no ambition and I have no need of it," she once wrote, "being who and what I am."

Acknowledgments

It is not an overstatement to say that this book would not have been possible without Alan Samson, my editor and publisher at Weidenfeld & Nicolson. Mine was a work that needed a knight of rare courage and vision and from the beginning Alan brilliantly and steadfastly protected and championed the book. He is proof that publishing's best days are not behind it. The same is true of my two wonderful agents, Michael Carlisle and Peter Robinson, and of Asya Muchnick, my editor at Little, Brown, whose enthusiasm and care for *The Rival Queens* was inspiring. I owe you all a great debt— thank you.

Similarly, I am so very grateful for the help and encouragement I received from Jeannette Seaver, who took the time to read the book in manuscript and then so generously recommended it to others. A big thank you also to Christopher Mason for his kind promotion of my work.

As I have done with two of my previous books, I relied for help with some of the original translations on my dear friends Marie-Paule de Valdivia and Christine Lamarche-Arène, two charming Frenchwomen who were never too busy to puzzle out a phrase or help me find a source in Paris. *Merci beaucoup!* I must also thank Jamie Nathan, Ayelet Rubin, and Zmira Reuveni at the National Library of Israel for their kind assistance in securing permission rights for the 1575 map of La Rochelle and to Joo Lee of the Leemage agency for the beautiful color images of Catherine, Marguerite, and the other members of the royal court.

Lastly, to my husband, Larry, and my daughter, Lee, who put up with far too many conversations about people who have been dead for five hundred years, and without whose love and support I would be lost, thank you for your patience, advice, and understanding! None of this would be worth it without you.

Notes

Epigraphs

vii   "Dear native land!"': *Memoirs of Marguerite de Valois,* xix. This is an English translation of the poem based on the Latin version published posthumously in 1686.

vii   "The lady left alone": Lemesurier, *Nostradamus, Bibliomancer,* 200.

Introduction

4   "the greatest beauty": Bourdeïlle and Saint-Beuve, *Illustrious Dames of the Court of the Valois Kings,* 156.

4   "On my return": Ibid.

4   "never was seen the like": Ibid., 161.

4   "The beauty of that queen": Ibid., 154.

5   "If he should ever": Chamberlin, *Marguerite of Navarre,* 63.

6   "I blazed in diamonds": *Memoirs of Marguerite de Valois,* 55.

Chapter 1. "The Queen, My Mother"

11   "Fortune is the ruler": Machiavelli, *The Prince,* 105.

12   "I was then about four": *Memoirs of Marguerite de Valois,* 31.

13   "The King said, 'Why so?'": Ibid.

13   Her mother, a French countess...with the same ailment: The rumor attributing Catherine's mother's death to her father's syphilis came from their contemporary, the maréchal de Florange, who wrote about it in his memoirs. See Knecht, *Catherine de' Medici,* 8.

13   "She comes bearing the calamities": Sichel, *Catherine de' Medici and the French Reformation,* 29.

14   "so gentle and pleasant": Frieda, *Catherine de Medici,* 26.

14   "very obedient": Héritier, *Catherine de' Medici,* 35.

14   "I have never seen anyone": Roeder, *Catherine de' Medici and the Lost Revolution,* 31.

15   "This man is the scourge of God": Ibid., 34.

16   "The girl has come to my court": ("J'as reçu la fille toute nue"): Roeder, *Catherine de' Medici and the Lost Revolution,* 41.

17   "I am a king again!": Hackett, *Francis the First,* 324.

18n   "short and thin; her features": Héritier, *Catherine de' Medici,* 27.

18n   "She is a beautiful woman": Sichel, *Catherine de' Medici and the French Reformation,* 24.

19   A Welshman who saw him: For further descriptions of François I by his contemporaries, see Knecht, *Renaissance Warrior and Patron,* 105.

19   His appetites...Caesar: For this anecdote, see Princess Michael of Kent, *The Serpent and the Moon,* 15.

20   "battle of giants": Knecht, *Renaissance Warrior and Patron,* 77.

20   "my daughter": Princess Michael of Kent, *The Serpent and the Moon,* 163.

23   *"beaucoup":* Cabanès, *Le Cabinet Secret de L'Histoire,* 36.

23   "a beautiful, fair woman": Princess Michael of Kent, *The Serpent and the Moon,* 202.

23   "never used her so well": Ibid.

24   *la levrette:* Ibid., 201.

25   "address her as Madame": Ibid., 240.

25   Even the pope...pearl necklace: Héritier, *Catherine de Medici,* 49.

26   "the right of control": Ibid., 51.

26   "His Majesty...eight hours with her": Roeder, *Catherine de' Medici and the Lost Revolution,* 67.

26   "When the King has told her": Ibid.

27   "wise and prudent governesses": Princess Michael of Kent, *The Serpent and the Moon,* 257.

27   "my allies": Ibid., 224.

27   "Monsieur de Humyères...and recommend you to him": *Lettres de Catherine de Médicis.* The full French text of the letter, dated December 21, 1546, can be found at: http://www.archive.org/stream/lettres decatheri01cathuoft/lettresdecatheri01cathuoft_djvu.txt. I am indebted to Marie-Paule de Valdivia for the translation that appears in the text.

> Monsieur de Humyères, j'ay recue la lectre que m'avez escripte, el m'avez faict bien grand plaisir m'avoir mandé des nouvelles de mes enflans. Je suys bien ayse de quoy madame de Humyères est arrivée là pour le soulaigement qu'elle vous fera au gouvernement de mes dils enflans. Monsieur et moy ne les vous recommandons poinct, pour l'asseurance qu'avons du soing que vous et Madame de Humyères prenez à leurtraictement. Je vous prye, Monsieur de Humyères, continuer à me faire souvent sçavoir de leurs nouvelles, car plus grand plaisir ne sçauriez faire à Monsieur et à moy, qui sera l'endroict où je prieray le Créateur, Monsieur de Humyères, après m'esire recommandée à vous, qu'il vous doinct ce que désirez.
>
> Escript à Compiengne, le xxi c jour de décembre M V e\LVI. La byen vostre, Caterine.

28   "God will give a royal line": Sichel, *Catherine de' Medici and the French Reformation*, 38–39.

28   "I feel for you in your trouble": Roelker, *Queen of Navarre*, 72.

29   "disguised as bourgeois ladies": Ibid., 181–82.

29   "I cannot refrain from thanking you": Princess Michael of Kent, *The Serpent and the Moon*, 244.

30   "not fit to call themselves our servants": Héritier, *Catherine de Medici*, 67.

30   "the daughter of merchants" ("Cette fille de marchands"): Roeder, *Catherine de' Medici and the Lost Revolution*, 81.

Chapter 2. The King Is Dead, Long Live the King

31   "However strong your armies": Machiavelli, *The Prince*, 10.

32   "She is still so troubled": Roeder, *Catherine de' Medici and the Lost Revolution*, 169.

32   "Up to this hour": Ibid., 162.

33   "this being the good pleasure": Sichel, *Catherine de' Medici and the French Reformation*, 101.

34   "the house of Guise ruleth": Knecht, *Catherine de' Medici*, 61.

35   Tiger of France: Roelker, *Queen of Navarre*, 148.

35   "Raked up from the gold": Sichel, *Catherine de' Medici and the French Reformation*, 104.

35   "A bold thief hides himself": Ibid.

35   "The court": Whitehead, *Gaspard de Coligny*, 78.

35   "One is continually burning": Ibid., 75.

35   At this stage, Michele Suriano, ambassador from Venice, reported that there were about four hundred thousand Huguenots in the kingdom out of a total of sixteen million subjects at the time of Francis's ascension. See Héritier, *Catherine de' Medici*, 104–5.

36   "Now is the time to spend money": Ibid., 111.

37   "are in such feare": Whitehead, *Gaspard de Coligny*, 82.

37   "The Duke himself set out": Castelnau, *Memoirs of the Reigns of Francis II and Charles IX of France*, 37.

38   "I know nothing about disputations": Sichel, *Catherine de' Medici and the French Reformation*, 110.

38   In what would evolve: According to recent scholarship, Coligny wrote a letter to Catherine after the conspiracy of Amboise advising her that the Crown would be continually under attack if the Guises were not replaced and advocating that she take on the responsibility for the government of France herself. See Shimizu, *Conflict of Loyalties*, 38–39.

39   "Till that is arranged": Sichel, *Catherine de' Medici and the French Reformation*, 111.

40   "would give his life": Ibid.

43   "If they see that affairs": Roeder, *Catherine de' Medici and the Lost Revolution*, 222.

44   "If he refuses to obey": Ibid.

44   "You cannot arrive": Ibid., 223.

45   "is the most cowardly" Roelker, *Queen of Navarre,* 148.

45   "I have [come] back this morning": Sichel, *Catherine de' Medici and the French Reformation,* 113.

46   "The Queen was blyeth of the death": Whitehead, *Gaspard de Coligny,* 90.

48   "She thought of herself": Roeder, *Catherine de' Medici and the Lost Revolution,* 236.

49   "No man has ever attacked": Sichel, *Catherine de' Medici and the French Reformation,* 114.

49   "We are lost": Carroll, *Martyrs and Murderers,* 126.

Chapter 3. The Queen and the Colloquy

50   "It must be considered": Machiavelli, *The Prince,* 25.

51   "Our Queen, then Dowager of France": Fraser, *Mary Queen of Scots,* 119.

51   "Adieu France!": Ibid., 131. The exact quotation is "Adieu France! Adieu France! Adieu donc, ma chère France...Je pense ne vous revoir jamais plus."

51n   "You are not to lose": Waldman, *Biography of a Family,* 51. See also Van Dyke, *Catherine de Médicis,* 1:208.

52   "If the winds are favorable": Ibid., 135.

52   "Since it has pleased God": Roeder, *Catherine de' Medici and the Lost Revolution,* 239.

52   "he is not very strong" Héritier, *Catherine de' Medici,* 266.

53   "swollen and deformed": Frieda, *Catherine de Medici,* 177.

53   "one of the ugliest": Ibid.

54   "so strictly brought up": *Memoirs of Marguerite de Valois,* 42.

55   negated her claim: "Everything done...in the matter of the government should be revoked because done by persons who had no power to act," was the ruling of the Estates General. This was a deliberate revocation of the powers assumed by the queen mother. See Van Dyke, *Catherine de Médicis,* 1:198.

56   "too heavy": Ibid., 210.

56   "In twenty cities": Ibid., 203.

56   "I want to tell you plainly": Ibid., 200–201.

57   "What would you do": Roeder, *Catherine de' Medici and the Lost Revolution,* 280.

57   "The whole Court was infected": *Memoirs of Marguerite de Valois,* 31–32.

57   "My brother added threats": Ibid., 32–33.

58   "I do not believe": Van Dyke, *Catherine de Médicis,* 1:217.

59   "You will find that I am not as black": Carroll, *Martyrs and Murderers,* 150.

59   "We say that His body": Ibid., 151.

59   "Blasphemy! Blasphemy!" (in Latin, "Blasphemavit!"): Ibid.

61 "If they ask you what it is": Van Dyke, *Catherine de Médicis,* 1:224.

62 "I hear that the Queen means": Roeder, *Catherine de' Medici and the Lost Revolution,* 296.

62 "I do not think": Ibid.

62 "You will be carried off at midnight": Ibid.

65 "My talk is of nothing": Van Dyke, *Catherine de Médicis,* 1:224.

65 Go do something about it!: For an in-depth examination of the duke of Guise's mother's influence and her role in precipitating the massacre at Vassy, see Carroll, *Martyrs and Murderers,* 5–12.

66 "Kill! Kill! By God's death": Ibid., 18.

Chapter 4. A Short War...

67 "A prince should therefore have": Machiavelli, *The Prince,* 63.

67 "All the Chief Citizens went out": Castelnau, *Memoirs,* 138.

68 "save the children": Van Dyke, *Catherine de Médicis,* 1:242–43.

68 "Burn this instantly!": Ibid.

68 "could no more fight Guise": Ibid., 245–46.

70 "I have been anxious": Ibid., 251–52.

70 "It would be impossible": Whitehead, *Gaspard de Coligny,* 117.

71 shipped back to Italy: For more on the Catholic plan to force Catherine out of France, see Whitehead, *Gaspard de Coligny,* 118, and Van Dyke, *Catherine de Médicis,* 1:265.

71n "one of the triumvirate": Bourdeïlle and Saint-Beuve, *Illustrious Dames at the Court of the Valois Kings,* 61.

72 "In that case we shall have to": Carroll, *Martyrs and Murderers,* 165.

72 "Now, friends, the day is ours!": Whitehead, *Gaspard de Coligny,* 143.

72 "Courage, my friends": Ibid.

74 "this death is the greatest good": Carroll, *Martyrs and Murderers,* 170.

74n "He had spoken lightly": Macdowall, *Henry of Guise and Other Portraits,* 19.

75 She had a long memory. The queen mother told Condé of her relief at the duke of Guise's death: "by the forces he had about the King and her, she was no less a prisoner than Condé had been," see Van Dyke, *Catherine de Médicis,* 1:278. "To this hour, she [Catherine] is persuaded that M. de Guise wanted to take possession of the kingdom," letter from Chantonnay, the Spanish ambassador, in Macdowall, *Henry of Guise and Other Portraits,* 18. To a diplomat from Savoy she was overheard to say, "Such are the works of God; those who sought to destroy me are dead." Héritier, *Catherine de Medici,* 223.

75 pile of human excrement: Translated from the memoirs of Brantôme, the cardinal found "a great stinking shit on the seat of his ceremonial chair." See Carroll, *Martyrs and Murderers,* 173.

76 "I have often heard your grandfather": Van Dyke, *Catherine de Médicis,* 1:292.

Chapter 5. . . . *And a Long Trip*

77 "One who wishes to obtain": Machiavelli, *The Prince,* 68.

77 eight thousand horses: See Héritier, *Catherine de Medici,* 238.

78 a hair-raising fifty million *écus:* Ibid., 231.

79 "they perceived a large Inchanted Tower": Castelnau, *Memoirs,* 272.

79 "dispel the Magick": Ibid.

81 "You'll see . . . she'll convert you all": Roelker, *Queen of Navarre,* 161.

81 "It is not an unalloyed": Ibid., 343.

82 "He shows himself very firm": Ibid., 399.

82 "Write me to relieve my anxiety": Ibid., 203.

83 "more princes than Salon": Hogue, *Nostradamus,* 282.

83 "I have only come": Ibid., 284.

84 "Get out fast": Lemesurier, *Nostradamus, Bibliomancer,* 12.

86 "Near Geneva terror will be great": Nostradamus, *Almanach pour l'an 1565,* at http://www.crystalinks.com/nostradamusalmanacs.html.

86n "[I composed] in dark and cryptic sentences": Hogue, *Nostradamus,* 167.

87 "As a fine reward": Ibid., 192.

87 Moreover, Diane de Poitiers: Nostradamus himself contradicts the idea that he was sent on to Blois. In a letter to Jean Morel he very clearly states that just before he left Paris he was visited by "a very becoming great lady" who wanted to have his methods examined by officials from the Justice department. A government investigation being the last thing he wanted, Nostradamus told her not to bother— he was leaving for Provence in the morning! Nostradamus scholar Ian Wilson believes this "great lady" was Diane de Poitiers, and I agree with him. See Wilson, *Nostradamus: The Man Behind the Prophesies,* 95–96.

88 "There is another prediction": Ibid., 254–55.

88 According to Nostradamus's son: For more on his son's recollections see Hogue, *Nostradamus,* 282–93.

88 "Your Majesty should know": Ibid., 200.

89 "promises a fine future": Ibid., 293.

89 "Tomorrow there leaves secretly": Ibid., 292.

89n "The first objection you have urged": Sichel, *The Later Years of Catherine de' Medici,* 8.

89n "I should be very glad": Ibid., 8.

90 "Ere I forget": Lemesurier, *Nostradamus, Bibliomancer,* 16.

90 "thought by the King": Van Dyke, *Catherine de Médicis,* 1:313.

90 "the King undertakes": Ibid., 311.

91 "the Queen Mother . . . greatly desires": Roelker, *Queen of Navarre,* 230.

91 "the most beautiful words in the world": Van Dyke, *Catherine de Médicis,* 1:315.

91 even though Margot was already engaged: This alliance had been publicly confirmed four years earlier, while Antoine was still alive, at a dinner in August of 1561. See Roelker, *Queen of Navarre*, 162.

93 "here their Majesties": *Memoirs of Marguerite de Valois*, 35.

93 "shepherdesses dressed in cloth of gold": Ibid.

93 "a large troop of musicians": Ibid.

93 "when, lo! Fortune no longer favoring": Ibid., 36.

94 "So your husband suspects me?": Roeder, *Catherine de' Medici and the Lost Revolution*, 364.

94 "What makes you suppose, Madame": Ibid.

94 "My dear daughter, you have become": Ibid.

94 "extremely cold about religion": Van Dyke, *Catherine de Médicis*, 1:323.

95 "I perceived that they kept him": Roeder, *Catherine de' Medici and the Lost Revolution*, 365.

95 "At St. Jean de Luz the tears": Van Dyke, *Catherine de Médicis*, 1:324.

95 "If the agreement which the Duke": Ibid.

96 to borrow even more from Italian bankers and raise taxes: The prince of Condé publicly championed a lowering of taxes and referred to the greed of the Italian banking community. See Knecht, *Catherine de' Medici*, 115. Catherine also defaulted on five hundred thousand *écus* due England under the terms of an earlier treaty at this time. See Héritier, *Catherine de' Medici*, 256.

96 "I know that many in France": Bourdeïlle and Saint-Beuve, *Illustrious Dames at the Court of the Valois Kings*, 72.

Chapter 6. The Flying Squadron

99 "Experience shows that there have been": Machiavelli, *The Prince*, 80.

100 "Never did a woman who loved": Frieda, *Catherine de Medici*, 83.

100 "Usually her Court was filled": Bourdeïlle and Saint-Beuve, *Illustrious Dames at the Court of the Valois Kings*, 79–80.

101 "Although I knew it was bad": Roelker, *Queen of Navarre*, 373.

102 "She is beautiful, discreet, and graceful": Ibid.

102 seated beside him at an official banquet: At the end of August 1561, when Antoine de Bourbon was still alive, the engagement between Marguerite and Henry, first entered into while Henri II was still alive, was tacitly reconfirmed in this way. See Roelker, *Queen of Navarre*, 162.

104 "very much surprised": Ibid., 242.

104 "she was all the angrier": Ibid.

105 all sixteen thousand of them: See Parker, *The Army of Flanders*, 28.

106 "Her majesty knows that no one is better": Roeder, *Catherine de' Medici and the Lost Revolution*, 393.

106 confessed himself a "tyrant": Carroll, *Martyrs and Murderers*, 188.

106 "by love or by force": Ibid.

107 "to keep up her Interest" Castelnau, *Memoirs*, 309.

107 "the reason why the King's subjects": Van Dyke, *Catherine de Médicis*, 1:380.

108 "I freely confess never to have seen": Whitehead, *Gaspard de Coligny*, 184.

108 "promise a long time ago": Van Dyke, *Catherine de Médicis*, 1:360.

109 "brought about by the greed": Ibid., 361.

109 they were all "vermin!": Ibid., 375.

110 "Young as I am, Madame": Héritier, *Catherine de' Medici*, 268.

110n "Henry's stereotypical lifestyle": Crompton, *Homosexuality and Civilization*, 331.

112 "really wanting what she said she didn't want": Van Dyke, *Catherine de Médicis*, 1:376.

113 "The stag is in the net": Ibid., 387.

114 "For Christ and country!": Whitehead, *Gaspard de Coligny*, 206.

114 "I leave to your own imagination": *Memoirs of Marguerite de Valois*, 38.

115 "It is...impossible for me": Ibid., 39.

115 "Dear sister, the nearness of blood": Ibid., 40.

115 "You know the high situation in which": Ibid., 40–41.

116 "was entirely a new kind of language": Ibid., 42.

116 "I shall sacrifice all the pleasures": Ibid., 43.

116 "Be the first with her": Ibid., 41.

116 "Your brother has been relating": Ibid., 44.

117 "I felt a satisfaction and a joy": Ibid.

Chapter 7. Fall from Grace

118 "A prince is...esteemed when": Machiavelli, *The Prince*, 95.

118 "She did me the honor": *Memoirs of Marguerite de Valois*, 44.

118 "I spoke of my brother's affairs": Ibid.

119 "Upon our arrival": Ibid., 46.

119 "She asked him why he made that observation": Ibid., 46–47.

119 "He began by observing": Ibid., 47.

120 "I did not omit to say everything": Ibid., 48.

120 "ordered me never to speak": Ibid.

121 "Sir, after doing what you have done": Macdowall, *Henry of Guise*, 25.

124 "My brother's words had made": *Memoirs of Marguerite de Valois*, 48.

124 "She flew into a passion": Ibid., 48–49.

124 "He came and sat at the foot": Ibid., 49.

125 "came daily to see me": Ibid., 50–51.

126 "There is nothing talked of publicly": Macdowall, *Henry of Guise*, 28.

126 "The ladies at court are real stirrers": Carroll, *Martyrs and Murderers*, 189.

126 "did not dare to reproach him": *Memoirs of Marguerite de Valois*, 51.

126 "of use to have children": Mariéjol, *A Daughter of the Medicis*, 15.

127 "I tell you clearly what I think": Van Dyke, *Catherine de Médicis*, 2:11–12.

127 "The King of Spain was using": *Memoirs of Marguerite de Valois*, 51–52.

128   "To engage in battle with these people": Wood, *The King's Army*, 125.
129   "eight or ten good leagues": Whitehead, *Gaspard de Coligny*, 227.
130   "We defeat them again and again": Roelker, *Queen of Navarre*, 339.
131   "I no longer have need": Carroll, *Martyrs and Murderers*, 189.
131   "Not a single person": *Memoirs of Marguerite de Valois*, 52.
131   "forward this match": Ibid., 51.
131   "Every day some new matter": Ibid.
131   "I resolved to write to my sister": Ibid., 52.
132   "She readily saw through it": Ibid.
132   marry a "negress": Carroll, *Martyrs and Murderers*, 190.

Chapter 8. The Marriage Trap

133   "One ought never to allow a disorder": Machiavelli, *The Prince*, 16.
134   "will not show himself": Van Dyke, *Catherine de Médicis*, 2:57.
134   "To be plain": Whitehead, *Gaspard de Coligny*, 245. The exact quote is:
      "To be playne, the only thinge that I feare in this matche is the
      consyderatyon of the delycasye of her majestyes eye and of the harde
      favor of the gentleman besides his dysfygurying with the smaule pockes:
      which yf she shoolde see with her eye, I mysdowbt mych yt woolde
      withdrawe her leekying to proceade."
137   "the King, my son": Roelker, *Queen of Navarre*, 346.
138   "Better to die by a bold stroke": Whitehead, *Gaspard de Coligny*, 237.
139   "His chief attendant, the Count de Retz": Van Dyke, *Catherine de
      Médicis*, 2:61.
139   "My mother loves him so much": Frieda, *Catherine de Medici*, 226.
139   "is to be found": Whitehead, *Gaspard de Coligny*, 238.
139   call the admiral *mon père*: Roeder, *Catherine de' Medici and the Lost
      Revolution*, 429.
140   "We are too old": Ibid., 431.
140   "I cannot imagine why": Roelker, *Queen of Navarre*, 355.
140   "is a resolution I have taken": Ibid., 358.
141   "Upon the success of the Navarre marriage": Shimizu, *Conflict of
      Loyalties*, 160.
141   "A marriage was projected": *Memoirs of Marguerite de Valois*, 53–54.
141   "he would be damned unless": Van Dyke, *Catherine de Médicis*, 2:56.
142   "It is perfectly well understood": Whitehead, *Gaspard de Coligny*, 240.
142   "the Admiral told him very politely": Ibid., 239.
142   "The war would maintain his authority": Shimizu, *Conflict of Loyalties*, 174.
142   "In Paris there are a growing number": Carroll, *Martyrs and Murderers*,
      200.
143   "if the king ordered": Ibid., 201.
143   "Madame has paid me great honor": Roelker, *Queen of Navarre*, 368.
144   "I am being obliged to negotiate": Ibid., 372.

144   "My son, since writing this letter": Ibid., 374.

144   "the Queen of Navarre wishes": Ibid., 363.

145   "Two days ago *Navarra*... Madame has pretended to be indisposed":
       Ibid., 377–78.

146   "Every enticement will be offered": Ibid., 381.

147   "The Queen of Navarre lies": Ibid., 388.

147   "Whilst the Queen of Navarre": *Memoirs of Marguerite de Valois*, 54–55.

148   "You must decide whether to obey me": Diefendorf, *The Saint
       Bartholomew's Day Massacre*, 79–80.

149   "After all the pains": Sichel, *The Later Years of Catherine de' Medici*, 139.

149   "His Majesty refuses to adventure": Ibid., 148.

Chapter 9. Queen Margot

151   "It cannot be called a virtue": Machiavelli, *The Prince*, 37.

151   "The Comte de Retz and I": Roelker, *Queen of Navarre*, 355.

152   "had the graces of a courtier": Ibid., 402.

152   "crude beyond the pale": Ibid., 385.

152   "Henry needed much affection": Ibid., 407.

153   "be able to get the king": Sutherland, *The Massacre of St Bartholomew and
       the European Conflict*, 275.

153   "to make her the most": Mariéjol, *A Daughter of the Medicis*, 206.

154   "So great was the magnificence": Hotman, *A true and plaine report of the
       furious outrages of Fraunce*, 36.

155   "a garden, filled with greens": Mariéjol, *A Daughter of the Medicis*, 35.

156   "So great is the familiarity": Hotman, *A true and plaine report of the furious
       outrages of Fraunce*, 37.

159   "If he had simply walked": Diefendorf, *The Saint Bartholomew's Day
       Massacre*, 88.

159   "The shot came from the window": Whitehead, *Gaspard de Coligny*, 259.

159   " 'Sdeath! Shall I never have": White, *The Massacre of St. Bartholomew*, 391.

159   "His face turned pale": Ibid., 391. The Venetian ambassador's name is
       Giovanni Michiel, and his exact words were: "Si facesse pallido e restasse
       smarrito oltro modo e senza dir parola si ritirasse."

159   "Everyone supposed it had been done": Diefendorf, *The Saint
       Bartholomew's Day Massacre*, 88.

160   "You bear the wound": White, *The Massacre of St. Bartholomew*, 395.

161   "went to the King in his closet": *Memoirs of Marguerite de Valois*, 58–59.

162   "the Admiral must be ever": *Memoirs of Marguerite de Valois*, 59.

162   "concluded with observing": Ibid., 59–60; the italics are mine.

162n   "As for the harquebus shot": Diefendorf, *The Saint Bartholomew's Day
       Massacre*, 92.

163   "she had vowed to avenge": Ibid., 59.

163   "which rendered him deserving": Ibid., 58.

163 "The King had so great a regard": Ibid., 57.

165 "Kill them! Kill them all!": Héritier, *Catherine de Medici*, 323.

165 "I was perfectly ignorant": *Memoirs of Marguerite de Valois*, 62.

165 "The Huguenots were suspicious of me": Ibid.

166 "They called in the duke of Guise": Diefendorf, *The Saint Bartholomew's Day Massacre*, 94.

166 "I placed myself on a coffer": *Memoirs of Marguerite de Valois*, 62.

167 "more dead than alive": Ibid., 63.

167 "As soon as I reached my own closet": Ibid.

167 "For my part I was unable": Ibid.

167 "as soon as day broke": Ibid., 64.

168 "Are you not the Admiral?" White, *The Massacre of St. Bartholomew*, 418.

168 "Well done, my men": Ibid., 419.

168 "Kill, kill!": Ibid., 427.

169 "cruelly butchering those they encountered": Goulart, *Mémoires de l'estat de France sous Charles IX*, 295.

169 "Carts filled with the dead bodies": Ibid.

169 "But then…the king gave the order": Diefendorf, *The Saint Bartholomew's Day Massacre*, 95.

169 "As soon as I beheld it was broad day": *Memoirs of Marguerite de Valois*, 64–66.

171 "God knows if I will ever see you": Pitts, *Henri IV of France*, 63.

172 "in birth and rank": Diefendorf, *The Saint Bartholomew's Day Massacre*, 90.

172 The queen mother made a point of rising: See Knecht, *Catherine de' Medici*, 163, and Van Dyke, *Catherine de Médici*, 2:119.

172 "As I write, they are killing them all": Roeder, *Catherine de' Medici and the Lost Revolution*, 463.

173 "She has grown ten years younger!": Sichel, *Catherine de' Medici and the French Reformation*, 6.

174 "Five or six days afterwards": *Memoirs of Marguerite de Valois*, 66.

175 "'Madame, since you have put the question'": Ibid.

Chapter 10. Queen of Paris

176 "Whoever thinks that in high personages": Machiavelli, *The Prince*, 34.

177 "On All Hallows' Eve": Williams, *Queen Margot*, 113.

178 "many a time I have heard": Mariéjol, *A Daughter of the Medicis*, 48.

180 the Muses or the Nymphs: Viennot, *Marguerite de Valois*, 78.

180 "unique pearl and everlasting flower": Ibid., 80. The exact quote is: "Perle unique du monde et sa fleur immortelle."

180 "The king spends much": Roelker, *Queen of Navarre*, 375.

181n There seems to have been: As recounted in Petitot, *Collection Complète des Mémoires relatifs a L'Histoire de France* 45:82.

184 "I salute you as the mother": Van Dyke, *Catherine de Médicis*, 2:135.

185 "For my part, the most becoming": Bourdeïlle and Saint-Beuve, *Illustrious Dames at the Court of the Valois Kings,* 159.

186 "She seemed to them so beautiful": Ibid., 154.

186 "a second Minerva, goddess of eloquence": Ibid., 164.

186 "that divine woman": Freer, *Henry III,* 1:236.

187 "For some months before he quitted": *Memoirs of Marguerite de Valois,* 67.

187 "Go! Go! You will not stay long": Sichel, *The Later Years of Catherine de' Medici,* 215.

188 "The Huguenots, on the death of the Admiral": *Memoirs of Marguerite de Valois,* 67.

190 "M. de Miossans, a Catholic gentleman": Ibid., 68.

190 "I went immediately to the King": Ibid.

190 "I begged they might be excused": Ibid., 68–69.

190 "All this while my brother Alençon": Ibid., 69.

191 "Madame, you are the cause of all!": Freer, *Henry III, King of France and Poland,* 1:244. The exact phrase is "Madame, vous êtes cause de tout!"

192 "The excitement was very great": Mariéjol, *A Daughter of the Medicis,* 59.

193 "We set off": *Memoirs of Marguerite de Valois,* 70.

193 "daily growing worse": Ibid., 69.

193 "They could at least have waited": Roeder, *Catherine de' Medici and the Lost Revolution,* 511.

193 "I was suffered to pass": *Memoirs of Marguerite de Valois,* 71.

194 "God! May I die": Van Dyke, *Catherine de Médicis,* 2:159–60.

194 "My husband, having no counselor": *Memoirs of Marguerite de Valois,* 70.

194n In fact, the image: Petitot, *Collection Complète des Mémoires,* 45:84.

195 "to them both, a very humble": Mariéjol, *A Daughter of the Medicis,* 62.

195 "With God's help I accomplished": *Memoirs of Marguerite de Valois,* 70.

195 "You see, my lords": Mariéjol, *A Daughter of the Medicis,* 62.

195 "May God and the Blessed Virgin": Petitot, *Collection Complète des Mémoires,* 45:84. In French: "Dieu ait merci de mo name, et la benoiste Vierge! Recommandez-moi bien aux bonnes graces de la reine de Navarre et des dames!"

195 But the memoirs of the duke of Nevers: *Les Memoires de Monsieur Le Duc de Nevers,* 1:75.

196 "begged that I should take": Van Dyke, *Catherine de Médicis,* 2:165.

196 "my mother": Ibid.

196 "the only stay and support": *Memoirs of Marguerite de Valois,* 71.

196 "He begged me that I should send": Van Dyke, *Catherine de Médicis,* 2:165.

196 "You know how much I love you": Ibid.

Chapter 11. Of Mignons and Mistresses

197 "[A prince] is rendered despicable by being thought changeable": Machiavelli, *The Prince,* 79.

198 "He has been imbued by him": Crompton, *Homosexuality and Civilization*, 331.

200 "Amidst the embraces and compliments": *Memoirs of Marguerite de Valois*, 75.

200 "I have forbidden any subject of my lord": Freer, *Henry III, King of France and Poland*, 1:369.

200 "Mademoiselle de Montigny": *Memoirs of Marguerite de Valois*, 76–78.

201 "Upon this occasion": Ibid., 78.

202 "I do not give the least": Ibid., 78–79.

202 "She would not hear a word": Ibid., 80.

202 "She had discovered…matters were set to rights again": Ibid., 82–83.

203 "The bad administration of money": Roeder, *Catherine de' Medici and the Lost Revolution*, 531–32.

204 "The most important and chief point": Wood, *The King's Army*, 281. For further data on the disastrous state of the kingdom's finances, see Wood, 295–300.

205 "The king is a young man": Freer, *Henry III, King of France and Poland*, 1:389.

205 "white pumps, high slippers": Wintroub, "Words, Deeds, and a Womanly King," 392.

206 "For four whole days": Van Dyke, *Catherine de Médicis*, 2:178.

206 "The king made jousts": Crawford, "Love, Sodomy, and Scandal," 527.

206 "wear their hair long": Ibid., 524.

206 "The King arrived…with his troop": Ibid., 528.

207 "this strong desire of the Queen Mother": Van Dyke, *Catherine de Médicis*, 2:176–77.

208 "After staying some time at Lyons": *Memoirs of Marguerite de Valois*, 84.

209 "This occasioned such jealousy": Ibid., 84–85.

209 "I now turned my mind to an endeavor": Ibid., 85–86.

210 "that puissant Hercules": Freer, *Henry III, King of France and Poland*, 2:11.

210 "start by being the master": Pitts, *Henry IV of France*, 74.

210 "I would rather that you reigned": Freer, *Henry III, King of France and Poland*, 2:35–36.

211 "slept, ate and played": Pitts, *Henry IV of France*, 73.

211 "persuaded the King my husband": *Memoirs of Marguerite de Valois*, 85.

212 "now entered more fully": Ibid., 86.

212 "my brother likewise": Ibid.

Chapter 12. The Great Escape

213 "The character of people varies": Machiavelli, *The Prince*, 26.

213 "without equal in our time": Williams, *Queen Margot*, 164. The exact quote in French is "le nonpair de son temps."

213 "an invincible courage": Ibid.

213   "received with all the favor": *Memoirs of Marguerite de Valois,* 86.

214   "an acquisition which": Ibid., 87.

214   "had no peer for courage": Mariéjol, *A Daughter of the Medicis,* 72.

214n   "it is only with difficulty": Frieda, *Catherine de Medici,* 318.

214   "It is much discoursed": Crawford, *Love, Sodomy and Scandal,* 519.

215   delayed for hours: See Baillon, *Histoire de Louise de Lorraine,* 50–51.

215   "The quarrel between the King of Navarre": Holt, *The Duke of Anjou and the Politique Struggle During the Wars of Religion,* 49.

215   "The court is the strangest place": Van Dyke, *Catherine de Médicis,* 2:189.

216   "At Paris my brother was joined by Bussy": *Memoirs of Marguerite de Valois,* 86–87.

216   "The King...mentioned it to the Queen": Ibid., 87–88.

217   "They knew that he was always": Ibid., 89.

217   "Bussy is assassinated!": Ibid., 90.

218   "The next day Bussy showed himself": Ibid., 91.

218   "The Queen my mother": Ibid., 92.

218n   "commanded a regiment of guards": Ibid., 89.

219   "One night my husband": Ibid., 93.

219   "From this time he treated me": Ibid.

220   "Henri, by the grace of his mother": Potter, "Kingship in the Wars of Religion," 489. The entire quote is "Henri, par la grâce de sa mère incertain roi de France et de Pologne imaginaire, concierge du Louvre, marguilier de Saint-Germain l'Auxerrois et de toutes les églises de Paris, gendre de Colas, godronneur des collets de sa femme et friseur de ses cheveux, visiteur des étuves, gardien des Quatre Mendiants, père conscript des Blancs-Battus et protecteur des Caputiers."

221   "The King...told my husband": *Memoirs of Marguerite de Valois,* 94.

221   "I was so greatly offended": Ibid., 95.

221   "A few days after this": Ibid.

222   "It was concerted betwixt them": Ibid., 97.

222   "The King and the Queen my mother": Ibid., 98.

223   "There was now a general alarm": Ibid.

223   "They observed that": Ibid., 99.

223   "The major part of the nobility of the realm": Holt, *The Duke of Anjou and the Politique Struggle During the Wars of Religion,* 51.

224   "I was in tears the whole night": *Memoirs of Marguerite de Valois,* 99.

224   "Meanwhile my husband": Ibid.

225   "He prevailed on the King": Ibid., 102.

225   "Accordingly, they proceeded to the house": Ibid., 104.

226   "to enrich only a very few persons": Holt, *The Duke of Anjou and the Politique Struggle During the Wars of Religion,* 53.

227   Guast was discovered murdered: See *Mémoires-Journaux de Pierre de L'Estoile,* 1:92–93.

228   "when he was killed": Williams, *Queen Margot*, 181.

229   "he regretted only two things": Chamberlin, *Marguerite of Navarre*, 155.

229   "He quite forgot his promise": *Memoirs of Marguerite de Valois*, 100.

229   "The King, supposing that I": Ibid., 101.

229   "My child, you are giving yourself": Ibid., 105–6.

Chapter 13. A Royal Hostage

231   "Men commit injuries": Machiavelli, *The Prince*, 34.

231   "I remained a close prisoner": *Memoirs of Marguerite de Valois*, 107.

232   "Some few days after": Ibid., 108–9.

232   "Meanwhile, the King my husband": Ibid., 107–8.

232   "I received this letter during": Ibid., 108.

233   "I had found a secret pleasure": Ibid., 112–13.

234   "of his firm resolution": Ibid., 110.

234   "acquainted the King with my brother's": Ibid.

234   "the King…on a sudden": Ibid., 111.

234   "expressed her hopes": Ibid.

234   "raised by the Huguenots": Ibid., 113.

235   "a free, public, and general": Holt, *The Duke of Anjou and the Politique Struggle During the Wars of Religion*, 66.

235   "With respect to these": *Memoirs of Marguerite de Valois*, 114.

235   the Peace of Monsieur: Ibid., 66.

235n   "in order to hate the Huguenots": Holt, *The Duke of Anjou and the Politique Struggle During the Wars of Religion*, 81.

236   "My mother, however, opposed it": *Memoirs of Marguerite de Valois*, 114.

236   "The peace being thus concluded": Ibid., 114–15.

236   "The Queen my mother expressed herself": Ibid., 115.

237   "When I still insisted upon going": Ibid., 115.

237   "There is much heartburning": Holt, *The Duke of Anjou and the Politique Struggle During the Wars of Religion*, 68.

238   "A league was formed": *Memoirs of Marguerite de Valois*, 118–19.

238   "had made the peace": *The Duke of Anjou and the Politique Struggle During the Wars of Religion*, 69.

238   "After some time, M. de Duras arrived": *Memoirs of Marguerite de Valois*, 118.

239   "The King received him very graciously": Ibid., 117–18.

239   "The King turned his thoughts": Ibid.

240   "The King called my brother": Ibid., 119.

241   "I went directly to the closet": Ibid., 121–22.

242   "I found them all of the opinion": Ibid., 122.

242   "He stated that he was": Ibid., 123–24.

243   "My brother acquiesced": Ibid., 124.

243   "She was as good as her word": Ibid., 126.

244   "ordered a courier": Ibid., 127.

Chapter 14. Queen of Spies

245 "A prince need trouble little": Machiavelli, *The Prince,* 81.

245 "I travelled in a litter": *Memoirs of Marguerite de Valois,* 129.

246 "excited great curiosity": Ibid.

246 "a polite and well-accomplished man": Ibid., 131.

246 "I employed all the talents": Ibid., 131.

247 "took every opportunity of discoursing": Ibid., 132.

247 "Although he had hitherto": Ibid., 133–34.

247 "On our arrival at Mons": Ibid., 134.

248 "the Countess and I were on so familiar": Ibid., 135.

248 "We entertain the utmost dislike": Ibid., 136–37.

248 "to which he has an ancient claim": In the late fourteenth century and for most of the fifteenth, Flanders was ruled by the duke of Burgundy (younger brother of Charles V, king of France) and his descendants. For more on this, see my earlier book *The Maid and the Queen: The Secret History of Joan of Arc.*

249 "I told her that the King of France...who do him favors": *Memoirs of Marguerite de Valois,* 137–38.

249 "He explained to me": Ibid., 140.

250 "considerable value": Ibid., 141.

251 "After an exchange of compliments": Ibid., 142.

251 "Namur appeared with particular advantage": Ibid., 143.

251 "The house in which I was lodged": Ibid.

251 "seemed more proper for a great king": Ibid.

252 "Don John having sent": Ibid., 144.

252 "In short, Don Juan": Ibid., 144.

252 "and there took a most polite": Ibid., 145.

253 "I was every morning": Ibid., 155.

253 "he had found it entirely changed": Ibid., 157.

254 "the King had repented": Ibid., 158.

254 "I found I was in great danger": Ibid., 157.

254 "as he was acquainted": Ibid., 159.

254 "Mondoucet did not return": Ibid.

254 "who most certainly acted towards me": Ibid.

255 "I suspected a plan": Ibid.

255 "They paid no respect": Ibid., 160–61.

255 "In the morning we were suffered": Ibid., 161.

256 "In consequence...it was a day": Ibid.

256 "They bawled out to us from within": Ibid., 161–62.

256 "At length I got him into my lodgings": Ibid., 162.

256 "At length, after much bawling": Ibid., 163.

257 "The principal person amongst them": Ibid., 163.

257 "Thus had they concerted a double plot": Ibid., 164.

258 "Accordingly, I assembled as many": Ibid., 165.

258 "resolved to act according to my counsel": Ibid.

258 "Hereupon, the citizens flew": Ibid.

259 "escorted by two or three": Ibid., 166.

259 "I hastened onto the boat": Ibid.

259 "In spite of all their remonstrances": Ibid.

260 "I had intelligence": Ibid., 169.

260 "I consider it amongst": Ibid., 170.

260 "Oh Queen! How happy I am": Ibid.

261 "which appeared to us": Ibid., 171.

261 "M. de Montigny delivered": Ibid., 171–72.

Chapter 15. Royal Rivalries

263 "Above all a prince must endeavor": Machiavelli, *The Prince*, 95.

263 "I was received very graciously" *Memoirs of Marguerite de Valois*, 172.

264 "both of them approved": Ibid., 173.

264 "she recollected it well": Ibid.

264 "Instead of dispatch": Ibid.

264 "My brother met with": Ibid., 173–74.

264 "these licentious young courtiers": Ibid., 175.

264 "Bussy had a degree of courage": Ibid.

265 "some new dispute betwixt them": Ibid.

265 "to fight it out to the death": Holt, *The Duke of Anjou and the Politique Struggle During the Wars of Religion*, 96.

265 "well lectured my brother": *Memoirs of Marguerite de Valois*, 177.

266 "other allusions to the meanness": Ibid.

266 "as it would put a stop": Ibid., 178.

266 "The quarrels of Bussy are bound": Holt, *The Duke of Anjou and the Politique Struggle During the Wars of Religion*, 96.

266n "was greatly uneasy on account": Ibid., 176.

267 "The King, however, staying": *Memoirs of Marguerite de Valois*, 178.

267 "How could you, Madame": Ibid., 178–79.

267 Catherine was obliged to heave herself: See *Memoires-Journaux de Pierre de L'Estoile*, 1:230–35. Marguerite's version of events is supported by this account.

268 "I will show you what it is": *Memoirs of Marguerite de Valois*, 179.

268 "The King endeavored to force it": Ibid., 180.

268 "feared some fatal event": Ibid., 180–81.

269 "as I know she loves me": Ibid., 181.

269 "Though I have received": Ibid.

269 "There is not a good Frenchman": Ibid., 186.

269 "I observed to my brother": Ibid., 186–87.

269 "With a great deal of gravity": Ibid., 187.

270   "could scarcely refrain from talking": Ibid.
270   "The Queen my mother": Ibid.
271   "Sire, if it is your pleasure": Ibid., 191.
272   "When we consulted": Ibid, 195.
272   "when all was prepared": Ibid., 195–96.
273   "I observed that she was much": Ibid., 196.
273   "You know I have pledged myself": Ibid., 197.
273   "proving unfaithful to my brother": Ibid.
273   "would have died rather than be": Ibid.
273   "You cannot, Madame, but be": Ibid., 197–98.
273   "all this was said by me": Ibid., 198.
274   "I had much rather pledge my life": Ibid.
274   "Remember what you now say": Ibid.
274   "Rising from my bed": Ibid.
274   "We next lowered Simier": Ibid.
274   "I was almost dead with alarm": Ibid., 199.
275   "violently at the door": Ibid., 199–200.
275   "I told my women": Ibid., 200.
275   "they went away": Ibid.
275   "One of them was indiscreet": Ibid., 200–201.
276   "Pushing her away": Ibid., 201.
276   "By consent of the abbot": Ibid., 199.
276   "I found him sitting": Ibid., 201.
276   "They both told me": Ibid.
277   "However, I was ready still": Ibid.
277   "This caused a cessation": Ibid., 202.
277   "complying with my wishes": Ibid., 203.
277   "with the power of nomination": Ibid.
277   "over and above the customary": Ibid.
278   "covered their dead bodies": Crawford, "Love, Sodomy, and Scandal," 532.
278   "M. d'Entragues did only": Macdowall, *Henry of Guise,* 90.

Chapter 16. Queen of Navarre

280   "Well-ordered states and wise princes": Machiavelli, *The Prince,* 81.
281   "For my husband had been greatly": *Memoirs of Marguerite de Valois,* 205.
282   "I remember (for I was there)": Bourdeïlle and Saint-Beuve, *Illustrious Dames at the Court of the Valois Kings,* 158–59.
283   "For three days she has": Mariéjol, *A Daughter of the Medicis,* 107.
283   "I received every mark of honor": *Memoirs of Marguerite de Valois,* 205.
284   "which was held by the Huguenots": Ibid.
284   "We found the Queen and all her maids": Mariéjol, *A Daughter of the Medicis,* 109.
285   "took a mistress like the others": Williams, *Queen Margot,* 254.

285   "It was the intention of the Queen my mother": *Memoirs of Marguerite de Valois*, 205.

286   "the Catholic religion not being tolerated": Ibid., 206.

286   "having been, for some years": Ibid., 206–7.

287   "ordered the guard to arrest": Ibid., 207.

287   "I complained of it": Ibid.

287   "Le Pin, with the greatest disrespect": Ibid.

287   "This insolent speech": Ibid., 208.

288   "The King, however, continued": Ibid., 209.

288   "little Geneva": Ibid.

288   "He took notice of my": Ibid., 210.

289   "The King was very assiduous with Fosseuse": Ibid., 211.

289   "Great Henry's daughter": Mariéjol, *A Daughter of the Medicis*, 120.

289   "showed how the wind blew": Ibid., 121.

289n "No sooner [had] he lost sight of her": Ibid., 209.

290   "Our Court was so brilliant": *Memoirs of Marguerite de Valois*, 210.

290   "This difference of religion": Ibid., 211.

Chapter 17. The Lovers' War

293   "Whoever is the cause of another": Machiavelli, *The Prince*, 16.

294   "The king has such a strong desire": Holt, *The Duke of Anjou and the Politique Struggle During the Wars of Religion*, 116.

295   that "[I] had at length": Ibid., 239.

295n "I might be more shunned": Freer, *Henry III, King of France and Poland*, 2:231.

296   "She told her husband": Chamberlin, *Marguerite of Navarre*, 209.

296   "The King my husband": *Memoirs of Marguerite de Valois*, 211–12.

297   "This was what I feared": Ibid., 212–14.

299   "The peace my brother made": Ibid., 221.

299   "He [François]...acquired from it": Ibid., 221.

299   "The King my husband was equally": Ibid., 221–22.

299   "My brother returned to France": Ibid., 222.

300   "the Queen your daughter went": Merki, *La Reine Margot et la Fin des Valois*, 248.

301   "She altered her conduct towards me": *Memoirs of Marguerite de Valois*, 224.

301   "For his part, he avoided me": Ibid.

301   "persuaded the King my husband": Ibid.

301   "I had every day news": Ibid., 225.

301   "The pregnancy of Fosseuse was now": Ibid., 226–27.

302   "Far from showing any contrition": Ibid., 227–28.

303   "The physician delivered the message": Ibid., 228–29.

303   "I answered that I had": Ibid., 229.

304   "I advised him": Ibid.

304 "It pleased God" Ibid.

304 "Notwithstanding these precautions": Ibid.

305 "When the King my husband": Ibid.

305 "I told him I went according": Ibid., 230.

305 "He seemed to be greatly displeased": Ibid.

307 "The King and the Queen both wrote": Ibid., 231.

307 "The length of time I had been": Ibid.

307 "I had too long experience of": Ibid., 231–32.

308 "It was with some difficulty": Ibid., 232.

Chapter 18. A Royal Scandal

309 "Whoever becomes the ruler of a free city": Machiavelli, *The Prince,* 22.

309 nicknamed him Narcissus: Chamberlin, *Marguerite of Navarre,* 227.

309 "I kiss a million times": Williams, *Queen Margot,* 271.

309 "beautiful angel, a beautiful miracle": Viennot, *Marguerite de Valois,* 194.

311 "I beg you very humbly, think what credit": Mariéjol, *A Daughter of the Medicis,* 135.

313 "professed much in fine language": Ibid., 137.

313 "If you were here you would be": Chamberlin, *Marguerite of Navarre,* 224.

313 "I beg you very humbly to receive this": Mariéjol, *A Daughter of the Medicis,* 137–38.

314 "You say that there will be": Williams, *Queen Margot,* 285–86.

315 "My Son, I was never so astonished": Van Dyke, *Catherine de Médicis,* 2:290–91.

316 "The primary object of his visit": Holt, *The Duke of Anjou and the Politique Struggle During the Wars of Religion,* 158.

317 "whatever it pleased the king": Ibid., 168.

317 "not wanting to drive his brother": Ibid., 173.

318 "Let it never be said": Mariéjol, *A Daughter of the Medicis,* 144.

318 "There is no longer justice": Ibid., 140.

318 "Triumph, triumph over my too": Williams, *Queen Margot,* 288.

318 Brantôme noted that she: Viennot, *Marguerite de Valois,* 192–93.

319 "two million in gold": Van Dyke, *Catherine de Médicis,* 2:279.

319 "so covered with embroidery": Ibid.

320 "All those poor soldiers": Holt, *The Duke of Anjou and the Politique Struggle During the Wars of Religion,* 179.

320 "Everything is falling apart": Ibid.

320 "I find that my expenses": Ibid., 180.

320 "in a bed lighted by": Mariéjol, *A Daughter of the Medicis,* 143.

321 "so rapturous a game": Mariéjol, *A Daughter of the Medicis,* 144.

322 "one on top of the other": Holt, *The Duke of Anjou and the Politique Struggle During the Wars of Religion,* 183.

323 "My said brother...has gone": Ibid., 188.

323 "I have never seen this court": Van Dyke, *Catherine de Médicis,* 2:304.

324 "The Queen of Navarre is pregnant": Chamberlin, *Marguerite of Navarre*, 229.

324 "Please God that on me alone": Ibid., 230.

324 "to turn him away from his promises": Mariéjol, *A Daughter of the Medicis*, 147.

325 "naming so precisely": Williams, *Queen Margot*, 293.

325 "deliver the Court from her": Ibid.

326 "Miserable wretch, do you dare": Chamberlin, *Marguerite of Navarre*, 232–33.

Chapter 19. The Queen's Revolt

327 "It is necessary for a prince": Machiavelli, *The Prince*, 43.

327 "It is an affront which no princess": Williams, *Queen Margot*, 297–98.

328 "were it not for the meddlers": Ibid., 302.

328 "Madame, [I] implore you": Ibid., 299–300.

329 "I beg you do not abandon": Van Dyke, *Catherine de Médicis*, 2:293.

329 "Kings are often liable": Chamberlin, *Marguerite of Navarre*, 237.

330 "love-affairs, which are carried on": Williams, *Queen Margot*, 303.

331 answering to the name of Corisande: The name comes from the fourteenth-century work *Amadis de Gaule*. Corisande was a romantic heroine in the story.

332 "I see very clearly": Mariéjol, *A Daughter of the Medicis*, 159.

333 "The day on which he [Épernon] arrives": Williams, *Queen Margot*, 308–9.

333 "A man's religion could not be": Ibid., 309.

334 "fallen very ill": Mariéjol, *A Daughter of the Medicis*, 163.

334 "many other designs": Ibid.

335 "A villain has endeavored": Williams, *Queen Margot*, 313n.

335 "I beg you, before you leave": Van Dyke, *Catherine de Médicis*, 2:294–95.

337 "in order that she whom we have": Williams, *Queen Margot*, 320.

337 "having reason to mistrust the King": Mariéjol, *A Daughter of the Medicis*, 164.

337 "I have not failed to speak": Williams, *Queen Margot*, 315.

338 "What a woman!": Chamberlin, *Marguerite of Navarre*, 248.

338 "she had been so troubled": Van Dyke, *Catherine de Médicis*, 2:327.

339 "We are well advertised": Carroll, *Martyrs and Murderers*, 261.

339 "I hear now that our Majesties": Van Dyke, *Catherine de Médicis*, 2:326.

339n "Nobody in the world": Ibid., 327.

341 "treat the Queen of Navarre": Chamberlin, *Marguerite of Navarre*, 253.

342 According to both Brantôme and Aubiac's brother: For Brantôme's version of this story, see Brantôme, *Oeuvres Complètes*, 8:69–71. For the letter written by Aubiac's brother, see Viennot, *Marguerite de Valois*, 220.

Chapter 20. Prisoner of War

343 "Fortresses may or may not be useful": Machiavelli, *The Prince*, 92.

345 "Very few or no courtiers": Carroll, *Martyrs and Murderers*, 262.

346 "If I were to repeat": Mariéjol, *A Daughter of the Medicis*, 183.

346 "tragic designs": Ibid.

346   "the most rigorous punishment": Williams, *Queen Margot*, 329.

347   "I hear it said": Mariéjol, *A Daughter of the Medicis*, 177.

348   "d'Aubiac must leap the rock": Ibid., 179.

348   "She would rather go away": Ibid.

349   "certain that the King was the cause": Ibid.

350   "Tell Canillac not to budge": Williams, *Queen Margot*, 331.

351   "The more I examine the matter": Ibid., 331–32.

352   "treated like the poorest": Ibid., 333.

352   "threw herself at their feet": Van Dyke, *Catherine de Médicis*, 2:340.

352   "who had brought her into": Ibid.

353   "would never consent to such": Mariéjol, *A Daughter of the Medicis*, 183.

354   "The Marquis de Canillac": Williams, *Queen Margot*, 333.

354   "not to go about any more": Van Dyke, *Catherine de Médicis*, 2:339.

354   "in consideration of the very signal": Williams, *Queen Margot*, 335–36.

355   "I do not intend to fail": Ibid., 334–35.

355   "the sun alone could enter": Chamberlin, *Marguerite of Navarre*, 264.

Chapter 21. Three Funerals and a Mass

356   "How laudable it is for a prince": Machiavelli, *The Prince*, 81.

356   "The marquis swore": Viennot, *Marguerite de Valois*, 233.

357   "The hate of the people": Van Dyke, *Catherine de Médicis*, 2:346.

357   "of the strange favors": Carrol, *Martyrs and Murderers*, 271.

358   "Long live Guise!": Ibid., 274.

358   "He who loves the master": Ibid.

359   "certain that the King of France": Van Dyke, *Catherine de Médicis*, 2:366.

359   "put almost absolute authority": Ibid., 375.

360   "Seeing a thing of such importance": Ibid., 380.

360   "He would not dare": Carroll, *Martyrs and Murderers*, 290.

360   "Fool," he said: Ibid., 291.

360   "Traitor! You will die for it!": Ibid.

361   "Good day, Madame, I beg": Van Dyke, *Catherine de Médicis*, 2:394–95.

361   "In spite of the great trouble": Ibid., 396.

362   "Fool! Knave! Puppet!" Freer, *Henry III, King of France and Poland*, 3:76.

362   "Oh madame, madame!": Ibid., 85.

362   "O God, this is too much!": Ibid.

363   "condition of health in her": Van Dyke, *Catherine de Médicis*, 2:397.

365   "Five months ago I was condemned": Pitts, *Henri IV of France*, 141.

366   "May my crown flourish": Freer, *Henry III, King of France and Poland*, 3:109.

368   "king of all France": Pitts, *Henri IV of France*, 169.

368   "in secret a Catholic": Ibid., 170.

369   "What a great king!": Ibid., 182.

369   "My respects to your master": Ibid.

Chapter 22. The Return of the Queen

370 "In as much as the legitimate prince": Machiavelli, *The Prince*, 8.

370 "to kill the Queen of Navarre": Mariéjol, *A Daughter of the Medicis*, 193.

371 "good favor and protection": Ibid., 200.

372 "the kindly disposition of the King": Williams, *Queen Margot*, 347.

372 "my extreme contentment...as can be desired": Merki, *La Reine Margot et la Fin de Valois*, 391. Original quote: "ce m'a été un extreme contentement de la resolution que vous avez prise d'apporter au bien de nos affairs...touchant votre pesion et au payment de vos dettes, je vous ferai bailer telles et si sûres expéditions et assignations que le saurez desirer." For all Marguerite's correspondence to Henry concerning the divorce, see Marguerite de Valois, *Mémoires et Lettres*, 300–43.

373 "Now that the world has abandoned": Mariéjol, *A Daughter of the Medicis*, 216.

373 "Never does she miss": Ibid.

373 "Madame Marguerite of France": Ibid., 224.

373 "has as many men as she wishes": Ibid., 217.

374 "She is very anxious": Ibid., 218.

374 "I have been induced to undertake": *Memoirs of Marguerite de Valois*, 29–30.

375 "Never did I consent willingly": Chamberlin, *Marguerite of Navarre*, 270–71.

375 "to make her the most wretched": Mariéjol, *A Daughter of the Medicis*, 206.

375n "Ah! The wretched woman!": Williams, *Queen Margot*, 359.

376 "both His Most Christian Majesty": Ibid.

376 "My Sister—The persons": Williams, *Queen Margot*, 359–60.

377 "good will dedicated": Mariéjol, *A Daughter of the Medicis*, 209.

377 "The happy news": Ibid.

377n "that fat banker's daughter": Ibid.

378 "The chief care that I have": Ibid., 210.

378 "my ark of refuge": Chamberlin, *Marguerite of Navarre*, 274.

378 "From your Majesty I received": Mariéjol, *A Daughter of the Medicis*, 228.

379 "contained as much falseness": Williams, *Queen Margot*, 367.

379 "It is easy to see": Ibid., 368–69.

380 "If I ever were possessed": *Memoirs of Marguerite de Valois*, 27–28.

380 "There were many doors": Mariéjol, *A Daughter of the Medicis*, 244.

380 even kidded her: For this anecdote, as related by L'Estoile, see Merki, *La Reine Margot et la Fin de Valois*, 413. Original quote: "disait qu'à son arrivée le roi l'avait requise de deux choses, l'une que pour mieux pourvoir à sa santé elle ne fît plus, comme elle avait coutume, la nuit dujour et le jour de la nuit; l'autre, qu'elle restreignît ses libéralités et devînt un peu ménagère de son bien. Du premier, elle promit au roi d'y apporter ce qu'elle pourrait pour contenter Sa Majesté, encore qu'il lui

fût fort malaisé, pour la longue habitude et nourriture qu'elle en avait prise; mais qu'au regard de l'autre il lui était du tout impossible, ne pouvant jamais vivre autrement et tenant cette libéralité de sa race."

381 "Vous soyez la bien venue": Williams, *Queen Margot,* 370.

381 "How handsome you are!": Ibid.

381 A chronicler related: For the story of Marguerite playing with the dog, see Merki, *La Reine Margot et la Fin de Valois,* 414.

382 "Monseigneur, an assassination": Ibid., 374.

383 "I also betook myself": Mariéjol, *A Daughter of the Medicis,* 236.

383 "After these distinguished gentlemen": Ibid., 236–37.

383 "magnificent and sumptuous": Ibid., 240.

385 "It's nothing": Pitts, *Henri IV of France,* 329.

385 "Queen Marguerite caused a beautiful": Williams, *Queen Margot,* 382–83.

386 "On March 27": Ibid., 385.

Epilogue

387 "There is a crowd as great": Mariéjol, *A Daughter of the Medicis,* 246–47.

388 "a prudent ruler ought not": Machiavelli, *The Prince,* 75.

388 "a great feigner and dissembler": Ibid., 76.

390 "I have no ambition": Mariéjol, *A Daughter of the Medicis,* 247.

Selected Bibliography

Aubigné, Theodore-Agrippa de. *His Life to His Children.* Translated by John
Nothnagle. Lincoln, NE, and London: University of Nebraska Press,
1989.

Baillon, Charles, Comte de. *Histoire de Louise de Lorraine, Reine de France,
1553–1601.* Paris: Chez Léon Techener, 1884.

Beeching, Jack. *The Galleys at Lepanto.* New York: Charles Scribner's Sons, 1982.

Bourbon, Antoine de, and Jeanne d'Albret. *Lettres D'Antoine de Bourbon et De
Jehanne D'Albret.* Paris: Librairie Renouard, 1877. Full text at: http://
archive.org/stream/lettresdantoined00antouoft#page/n5/mode/2up.

Bourdeïlle, Pierre de, and C. A. Saint-Beuve. *Illustrious Dames of the Court of the
Valois Kings.* Translated by Katharine Prescott Wormeley. New York:
Lamb Publishing Co., 1912.

Brantôme, Pierre de Bourdeïlle, seigneur de. *Oeuvres Complète, publiées D'après
les Manuscrits avec variantes et fragments inédits pour la Société de l'histoire de
France par Ludovic Lalanne.* Vol. 8, *Des Dames.* Paris: Chez Mme. Ve. Jules
Renouard, 1875.

Brézol, Georges. *Henri III et Ses Mignons.* Paris: Les Éditions des Bibliophiles,
n.d. [191–?].

Brion, Marcel. *The Medici: A Great Florentine Family.* Translated by Giles and
Heather Cremonesi. New York: Crown Publishers, Inc., 1969.

Cabanès, Augustin. *Le Cabinet Secret de l'Histoire.* Paris: Albin Michel, 1905.

Cameron, Keith. *Henri III, A Maligned or Malignant King? Aspects of the Satirical
Iconography of Henri de Valois.* Exeter: University of Exeter Press, 1978.

Carroll, Stuart. *Martyrs and Murderers: The Guise Family and the Making of Europe.*
Oxford: Oxford University Press, 2009.

Castelnau, Michel de. *Memoirs of the Reigns of Francis II and Charles IX of
France... Done into English by a Gentleman.* Facsimile of the 1724 British
Library edition. Farmington Hills, MI: Gale ECCO, 2005.

Catherine de' Medici. *Lettres de Catherine des Médicis.* Ed. Gustave Baguenault de
Puchesse. 5 vols. Paris: Imprimerie Nationale, 1880.

———. *Lettres de Catherine des Médicis.* Ed. Hector de la Ferrière. 5 vols. Paris:
Imprimerie Nationale, 1880.

Chamberlin, E. R. *Marguerite of Navarre.* New York: Dial Press, 1974.

Crawford, Katharine. "Catherine de Médicis and the Performance of Political Motherhood." *The Sixteenth Century Journal* 31, no. 3 (Autumn 2000), 643–73.

———. "Love, Sodomy, and Scandal: Controlling the Sexual Reputation of Henry III," *Journal of the History of Sexuality* 12, no. 4 (October 2003), 513–42.

Crompton, Louis. *Homosexuality and Civilization.* Cambridge, MA: Belknap Press of Harvard University Press, 2003.

Diefendorf, Barbara B. *The Saint Bartholomew's Day Massacre: A Brief History with Documents.* Bedford Series in History and Culture. Boston: Bedford/St. Martin's, 2009.

Diggs, Sir Dudly, ed. *The Compleat Ambassador, or, Two Treaties of the Intended Marriage of Qu. Elizabeth of Glorious Memory Comprised in Letters of Negotiation of Sir Francis Walsingham, Her Resident in France (1655).* London: Tho: Newcomb, 1655.

Farge, James K. *Orthodoxy and Reform in Early Reformation France: The Faculty of Theology of Paris, 1500–1543.* Leiden: E. J. Brill, 1985.

Fraser, Antonia. *Mary Queen of Scots.* New York: Delta Trade Paperbacks, 1993.

Freer, Martha Walker. *Henry III, King of France and Poland: His Court and Times.* 3 vols. New York: Dodd, Mead and Company, 1888.

Frieda, Leonie. *Catherine de Medici: Renaissance Queen of France.* New York: HarperPerennial, 2006.

Goulart, Simon. *Mémoires de l'estat de France sous Charles IX,* 2nd ed. Vol. 1. Geneva: Henry Wolf, 1578.

Graham, Victor E., and W. McAllister Johnson. *The Royal Tour of France by Charles IX and Catherine de' Medici: Festivals and Entries, 1564–6.* Toronto: University of Toronto Press, 1979.

Greengrass, Mark. *France in the Age of Henri IV: The Struggle for Stability.* London and New York: Longman, 1984.

Hackett, Francis. *Francis the First: First Gentleman of France.* New York: Literary Guild, 1934.

Héritier, Jean. *Catherine de' Medici.* Translated by Charlotte Haldane. New York: St. Martin's Press, 1963.

Hibbert, Christopher. *The House of Medici: Its Rise and Fall.* New York: William Morrow & Company, Inc., 1975.

Hogue, John. *Nostradamus: A Life and Myth.* London: Element Books, Ltd., 2003.

Holt, Mack P. *The Duke of Anjou and the Politique Struggle During the Wars of Religion.* Cambridge Studies in Early Modern History. Cambridge: Cambridge University Press, 1986.

Hotman, François. *A true and plaine report of the furious outrages of Fraunce, & the horrible and shameful slaughter of Chastillion the admirall, and diuers other noble and excellent men, and of the wicked and straunge murder of godlie persons, committed in many cities of Fraunce, without any respect of sorte, kinde, age, or degree.* London: Henry Bynneman, 1573.

Joubert, André. *Un Mignon de la Cour de Henri III: Louis de Clermont, Sieur de Bussy d'Amboise, Gouverneur d'Anjou.* Paris: Librairie E. Lechevalier, 1885.

Knecht, R. J. *Catherine de' Medici*. London and New York: Longman, 1999.

————. *Renaissance Warrior and Patron: The Reign of Francis I*. Cambridge: Cambridge University Press, 1994.

Lemesurier, Peter. *Nostradamus, Bibliomancer: The Man, the Myth, the Truth*. Pompton Plains, NJ: Career Press, Inc., 2010.

Lesort, André, ed. *Lettres de Catherine de Médicis*. Vol. 2. Paris: Imprimerie National, 1880.

L'Estoile, Pierre de. *Mémoires-Journaux*. Vol. 1. *Journal de Henri III, 1574–1580*. Ed. G. Brunet, A. Champollion, E. Halphen, P. Lacroix, C. Read, and T. de Larroque. Paris: Librairie des Bibliophiles, 1875.

Macdowall, H. C. *Henry of Guise and Other Portraits*. London: Macmillan and Co., Ltd., 1898.

Machiavelli, Niccolò. *The Prince*. Translated by Luigi Ricci. London: Grant Richards, 1903.

Manetsch, Scott M. *Theodore Beza and the Quest for Peace in France, 1572–1598*. Leiden, Boston, and Köln: Brill, 2000.

Marguerite de Valois. *Mémoires et Lettres, Nouvelle Édition, Revue sur les manuscrits des Bibliothèques du Roi et de L'Arsenal et Publiée par M. F. Guessard*. Paris: Chez Jules Renouard et Cie., 1842.

————. *Memoirs of Marguerite de Valois, Queen of Navarre, Written by Herself*. Paris and Boston: Grolier Society, 1900.

Mariéjol. Jean H. *A Daughter of the Medicis: The Romantic Story of Margaret of Valois*. Translated by John Peile. New York: Harper & Brothers, 1929.

Merki, Charles. *La Reine Margot et la Fin des Valois (1553–1615)*. Paris: Plon-Nourrit et Cie., 1905.

Her Royal Highness Princess Michael of Kent. *The Serpent and the Moon: Two Rivals for the Love of a Renaissance King*. New York: Touchstone, 2004.

Monluc, Blaise de. *The Habsburg-Valois Wars and the French Wars of Religion*. Ed. Ian Roy. London: Longman, 1971.

Nevers (Louis de Gonzague, duc de). *Les Mémoires de Monsieur le Duc de Nevers, Prince de Mantoue, Pair de France Gouvenor et Lieutenant General pour Les Rois Charles IX Henry III et Henry IV en Diverses Provinces de ce Royaume*. 2 vols. Paris: Chez Thomas Jolly (vol. 1) and Chez Louis Billaine (vol. 2), 1665.

Parker, Geoffrey. *The Army of Flanders and the Spanish Road, 1567–1659: The Logistics of Spanish Victory and Defeat in the Low Countries' Wars*. 2nd ed. Cambridge Studies in Early Modern History. Cambridge: Cambridge University Press, 2004.

Parker, T. H. L. *John Calvin: A Biography*. Philadelphia: Westminster Press, 1975.

Petitot, Claude Bernard. *Collection Complète des Mémoires relatifs a L'Histoire de France par M. Petitot*. Vol. 45, *Memoires pour Servir a L'Histoire de France et Journal de Henri III de Henri IV par Pierre de L'Estoile*. Paris: Focault, 1825.

Pitts, Vincent J. *Henri IV of France: His Reign and Age*. Baltimore: The Johns Hopkins University Press, 2009.

Potter, David. "Kingship in the Wars of Religion: The Reputation of Henri III of France." *European History Quarterly* 25 (1995): 485–528.

Robbins, Kevin C. *City on the Ocean Sea: La Rochelle, 1530–1650: Urban Society, Religion, and Politics on the French Atlantic Frontier.* Leiden, New York, and Köln: Brill, 1997.

Roeder, Ralph. *Catherine de' Medici and the Lost Revolution.* New York: Viking Press, 1937.

Roelker, Nancy Lyman. *Queen of Navarre: Jeanne d'Albret, 1528–1572.* Cambridge, MA: Belknap Press of Harvard University Press, 1968.

Shimizu, Junko. *Conflict of Loyalties: Politics and Religion in the Career of Gaspard de Coligny, Admiral of France, 1519–1572.* Vol. 114 of Travaux D'Humanisme et Renaissance. Geneva: Librairie Droz, 1970.

Sichel, Edith. *Catherine de' Medici and the French Reformation.* Reprinted from the 1905 edition. Honolulu: University Press of the Pacific, 2004.

———. *The Later Years of Catherine de' Medici.* London: Archibald Constable & Co., Ltd., 1908.

Smoley, Richard. *The Essential Nostradamus.* New York: Jeremy P. Tarcher/Penguin, 2006.

Sully, Maximilien de Béthune, duke of. *The Memoirs of the Duke of Sully, Prime-Minister to Henry the Great.* Translated by Charlotte Lennox. 5 vols. Philadelphia: Edward Earle, 1817.

Sutherland, N. M. *The French Secretaries of State in the Age of Catherine de Medici.* Westport, CT: Greenwood Press, 1976.

———. *The Massacre of St Bartholomew and the European Conflict 1559–1572.* New York: Harper & Row, 1973.

Van Dyke, Paul. *Catherine de Médicis.* Vols. 1 and 2. New York: Charles Scribner's Sons, 1922.

Viennot, Eliane. *Marguerite de Valois: "La reine Margot."* Paris: Perrin, 2005.

Waldman, Milton. *Biography of a Family: Catherine de Medici and Her Children.* Boston: Houghton Mifflin Company, 1936.

White, Henry. *The Massacre of St. Bartholomew: Preceded by a History of the Religious Wars in the Reign of Charles IX.* London: John Murray, 1868.

Whitehead, A. W. *Gaspard de Coligny: Admiral of France.* London: Methuen & Co., 1904.

Williams, H. Noel. *Henri II: His Court and Times.* New York: Charles Scribner's Sons, 1910.

———. *Queen Margot: Wife of Henry of Navarre.* New York: Charles Scribner's Sons, 1907.

Wilson, Ian. *Nostradamus: The Man Behind the Prophecies.* New York: St. Martin's Press, 2002.

Wintroub, Michael. "Words, Deeds, and a Womanly King," *French Historical Studies* 28, no. 3 (Summer 2005), 387–413.

Wood, James B. *The King's Army: Warfare, Soldiers, and Society during the Wars of Religion in France, 1562–1576.* Cambridge: Cambridge University Press, 1996.

Illustration Credits

Map of La Rochelle (p. 137): *Rochella Munitissimum Galliae Opp.* Digital Source: Braun and Hogenberg, *Civitates Orbis Terrarum II* [First Latin edition of volume II], 1575, Eran Leor Cartographic Collection, National Library of Israel.

Insert p. 1 (top): *Portraits en pied d'Henri II et de Catherine de Médicis, roi et reine de France.* Peinture anonyme Française, 16ème siècle. Musée du Château Anet. © Josse/Leemage.

Insert p. 1 (bottom): *Portrait suppose de Diane de Poitiers, maitresse de Henri II dans son bain.* Peinture de François Clouet, 1560-1570. National Gallery of Art, Washington. © Luisa Ricciarini/Leemage.

Insert p. 2 (top): *Portrait de François Ier, roi de France.* Peinture de Jean Clouet, c. 1530. Musée de Louvre, Paris. © Josse/Leemage.

Insert p. 2 (middle): *Portrait d'Antoine de Bourbon, roi de Navarre, père du roi Henri IV.* Peinture de l'Ecole Française du 16ème siècle. Musée du Château de Versailles. © Josse/Leemage.

Insert p. 2 (bottom): *de Jeanne d'Albret, reine de Navarre.* Peinture de François Clouet, 1570. Musée Condé, Chantilly. © Josse/Leemage.

Insert p. 3 (top): *Vue du massacre des Protestants de Wassy (Vassy) perprete le 01/03/1562 par les gens de François Ier de Lorraine 2ème duc de Guise et marquant le dèbut des guerres de religion.* Gravure Collection particulière. © Josse/Leemage.

Insert p. 3 (middle): *Portrait en pied de François de Lorraine, duc de Guise.* Peinture de Peter Pourbus (1523-1584). Musée des Beaux Arts, Nancy. © Josse/Leemage.

Insert p. 3 (bottom): *Portrait de l'admiral Gaspard de Coligny.* Peinture anonyme, 16ème siècle. Musée du Protestantisme, Paris. © Josse/Leemage.

Insert p. 4 (top): *Portrait de Catherine de Médicis, reine de France.* Peinture d'après François Clouet, 16ème siècle. Musée Condé, Chantilly. © Josse/Leemage.

Insert p. 4 (middle): *Portrait de François II, roi de France.* Peinture d'après François Clouet, vers 1553. Musée Condé, Chantilly. © Josse/Leemage.

Insert p. 4 (bottom): *Portrait en pied de Charles IX, roi de France.* Peinture de François Clouet, 16ème siècle. Musée Carnavalet, Paris. © Josse/Leemage.

Illustration Credits

Insert p. 5 (top): *Portrait de Marguerite de Valois, 1561.* Peinture de François Clouet. Museu Nacional de Soares dos Reis, Porto. © Lylho/Leemage.

Insert p. 5 (middle): *Portrait du roi de France Henri III avec une boule d'oreille.* Peinture anonyme, 16ème siècle. Musée Granet, Aix en Provence. © Jean Bernard/ Leemage.

Insert p. 5 (bottom): *Portrait de François Hercule de France, duc d'Alençon.* Peinture de l'atelier de François Clouet, 16ème siècle. Musée du Louvre, Paris. © Josse/Leemage.

Insert p. 6 (top): *Portrait de Marguerite de Valois ou la reine Margot.* Peinture d'après François Clouet, 16ème siècle. Musée Condé, Chantilly. © Josse/Leemage.

Insert p. 6 (middle): *Portrait d'Henri IV, roi de France.* Peinture de l'Ecole Française, 16ème siècle. Musée du Château de Pau. © Josse/Leemage.

Insert p. 6 (bottom): *Portrait d'Henri Ier de Lorraine, duc de Guise dit le Balafre.* Peinture de François Quesnel, 16ème siècle. Musée Carnavalet, Paris. © Josse/Leemage.

Insert p. 7 (top): *Gabrielle d'Estrées, maîtresse du roi Henri IV et sa soeur la duchesse de Villars.* Peinture de l'Ecole de Fontainebleau, 1575–1600. Musée du Louvre, Paris. © Josse/Leemage.

Insert p. 7 (bottom): *Bal à la cour du roi Henri III et de la reine Catherine de Médicis dit Bal du duc d'Alençon.* (Les souverains sont representes a gauche dont le reine Margot.) Peinture de l'Ecole Française de la deuxième motié du 16ème siècle. Musée du Louvre, Paris. © Josse/Leemage.

Insert p. 8: *Le roi Henri III sur son lit de mort, assassiné par le moine Jacques Clément le 1/08/1589, donné pourvoir à Henri de Navarre (futur Henri IV).* Détail d'une tapisserie. Musée National de la Renaissance, Ecouen. © Josse/Leemage.

Index

About the Author

NANCY GOLDSTONE's previous books include *The Maid and the Queen: The Secret History of Joan of Arc; Four Queens: The Provençal Sisters Who Ruled Europe;* and *The Lady Queen: The Notorious Reign of Joanna I, Queen of Naples, Jerusalem, and Sicily.* She has also coauthored five books with her husband, Lawrence Goldstone. She lives in Sagaponack, New York.